D1389577

The GDR Remembered

Studies in German Literature, Linguistics, and Culture

The GDR Remembered

Representations of the
East German State since 1989

Edited by
Nick Hodgin and Caroline Pearce

 CAMDEN HOUSE
Rochester, New York

First published 2011
by Camden House

Camden House is an imprint of Boydell & Brewer Inc.
668 Mt. Hope Avenue, Rochester, NY 14620, USA
www.camden-house.com
and of Boydell & Brewer Limited
PO Box 9, Woodbridge, Suffolk IP12 3DF, UK
www.boydellandbrewer.com

ISBN-13: 978-1-57113-434-9
ISBN-10: 1-57113-434-4

Library of Congress Cataloging-in-Publication Data

The GDR remembered: representations of the East German state since
1989 / edited by Nick Hodgin and Caroline Pearce.
    p. cm. — (Studies in German literature, linguistics, and culture)
Includes bibliographical references and index.
ISBN-13: 978-1-57113-434-9 (hardcover : alk. paper)
ISBN-10: 1-57113-434-4 (hardcover : alk. paper)
    1. Germany (East) — In popular culture. 2. Germany (East) —
In literature. 3. Germany (East) — In motion pictures. 4. Germany
(East) — Historiography. 5. Collective memory — Germany. 6. Popular
culture — Germany. I. Hodgin, Nick. II. Pearce, Caroline. III. Title.
IV. Series.

DD281.6.G37 2011
943'.1087—dc22

2011015940

This publication is printed on acid-free paper.
Printed and bound in Great Britain by
CPI Antony Rowe, Chippenham and Eastbourne

Contents

Illustrations

Acknowledgments

WE ARE MOST GRATEFUL to Professor Margaret Littler and other members of the editorial board of *German Life and Letters* who kindly awarded funds toward publication of this volume. We would like to thank our colleagues at Sheffield, especially Professor Michael Perraudin and Professor Henk de Berg, and at Manchester for their support and encouragement. The contributors to this volume deserve our thanks for both their diligence and their patience with editorial requests. We are grateful, too, to the two anonymous readers, whose reports were both thoughtful and constructive. We are also indebted to Jim Walker at Camden House, who provided invaluable editorial support and sound advice throughout the project, and whose forbearance we especially appreciated. Mary Fahnestock-Thomas and Jane Best provided invaluable editorial assistance during the final stages of the project. Finally, we would like to thank Lucy and Simon for their patience and understanding.

Nick Hodgin and Caroline Pearce
Sheffield, February 2011

Introduction

Nick Hodgin and Caroline Pearce

Twenty years after the "peaceful revolution" in the German Democratic Republic (GDR) iconic images of the fall of the Berlin Wall and the joyous crowds crossing the border from East to West were once again transmitted around the world. Thousands congregated at the "Festival of Freedom" ("Fest der Freiheit") at the Brandenburg Gate on the night of 9 November 2009. State dignitaries from the former Eastern and Western blocs joined representatives from unified Germany in commemorating the victory of freedom and civic courage over dictatorship and repression and in highlighting the importance of the collapse of Communism for European unification and the global political order. The event was as much about media spectacle as it was about solemn speeches, concluding with the toppling of a line of giant dominos placed along part of the former border between East and West Berlin. The Festival of Freedom crowned a year of commemorative events, conferences, exhibitions, documentaries, and publications marking the fall of the Berlin Wall. These continued into 2010, the twentieth anniversary of the Unification Treaty.

The narrative presented by the official commemorations focused on the victory of democracy over Communism and on values inherent in the Federal Republic of Germany (FRG) since 1949. The government adopted the slogan "Freiheit, Einheit, Demokratie," and the Interior Ministry's website on the commemorations is titled "20 Jahre Einheit 2009–10: 60 Jahre Bundesrepublik." Kornelia Lobmeier argues that media coverage of the events has tended to focus on the fall of the Berlin Wall, with the events of autumn 1989 elsewhere in the GDR somewhat sidelined.[1] She suggests a number of reasons for the surprising lack of public focus on the "peaceful revolution." On a practical level this has something to do with the familiarity of footage of Berlin on 9 November 1989; images of the demonstrations in smaller towns in the GDR are less readily available and perhaps make less of an impact. Moreover, from a western German perspective it was not until the fall of the wall that change in the GDR became a tangible reality. A further reason may be a divergence between official and private remembrance. From an eastern German perspective, the commemoration of the "peaceful revolution" may evoke bittersweet memories: the joy of freedom but also the aware-ness that only a minority of the population took part, and also a sense of disappointment that the hopes of the time have not since come to fruition. What is clear is that the positive narrative of unification pre-sented to the world on 9 November 2009 is but one of a range of inter-pretations and recollections and does not reveal the full complexity of the impact that unification has had on both eastern and western Germans.

When discussing the fall of the Berlin Wall and the subsequent col-lapse of Communism in the GDR and across much of the former Eastern Bloc, historians and other commentators are apt to talk of the initial euphoria and how quickly this gave way to disappointment and bitter-ness as eastern Germans realized that the system in which the large majority had placed their faith when casting their ballots in 1990 did not immediately provide them with the material comforts and benefits long associated with the FRG's *Wirtschaftswunder*.[2] Before 1989 the West Germans had reached some uniformity in their attitude to the "other" Germans who lived beyond the wall. This attitude involved certain stereotypes and vague assumptions about the GDR but did not preclude a level of mostly passive sympathy. The GDR was codified by a series of negative features that stemmed from the view of the East as a totalitarian regime. The focus, therefore, was on political and social restrictions including an array of human rights abuses and brutal physical repression, the most infamous example of which — the suppressed uprisings in June 1953 — prompted the West Berlin authorities to rename the Charlottenburger Chaussee the "Strasse des 17. Juni" the following month.

It was ironic that those aspects of East German society that had ear-lier aroused sympathy were later to be incorporated into a complex net of suspicion that was cast over the population of the new *Bundesländer*. Previously viewed as victims, they were now variously upbraided as potential Stasi informers, inefficient workers, or a society of meek indi-viduals whose failure actively to challenge their state could be interpreted as passive support. It was ironic, too, that the FRG's prosperity, long envied by those in the GDR and long cherished by West Germans as one of the constituent features of their postwar identity, was seemingly threatened by the addition of some sixteen million compatriots to the population of the Federal Republic and by the long-term financial obliga-tions required of the latter to prop up the feeble economy of the new *Länder*.

Against this background some journalists reporting from the twenti-eth anniversary of German unification in 2009 noted that Europe's big-gest party was in fact a rather muted affair.[3] It was not just the impossibility of being able to replicate the spontaneity or invoke the genuine and profound emotion that ending forty years of division had originally prompted. Where free beer had been impulsively offered by West German bars twenty years ago and bottles of champagne uncorked as East Germans crossed the border, such spontaneous generosity was no longer seen as an option, not least perhaps because of the financial straits in which Germany (and much of Europe) now found itself. It was less an occasion for repeating the elated celebrations of 1989–90 than a time for sober reflection. Germany's financial problems may be inextricably linked to wider global developments, but they are often understood locally. The crowds that gathered to celebrate on the streets of the German capital in 2009 were not the first to assemble in large numbers since 1989. The introduction in 2005 of controversial but much-needed economic reforms (the so-called Hartz IV package) saw considerable numbers of eastern Germans take to the streets to protest against a policy that would be most dramatically felt in the new *Länder*. Prompted by these demonstrations, *Der Spiegel* offered a largely unsympathetic and pessimistic survey of the situation in the east in a special issue under the provocative title "Jammertal Ost."[4]

Der Spiegel's designation invokes one of the pejoratives aimed at eastern Germans and often heard in postunification rhetoric, the "Jammerossi." Both it and its antonym, the "Besserwessi," held much currency in the 1990s. Both are imperfect stereotypes that have proved remarkably durable, so much so that Wolf Biermann's early observation of the two communities — "Der Westen powert und boomt und jauchzt / Der Osten jammert und humpelt" (1991) — still encapsulates present-day prejudices.[5] Given some of the predictions made at the time of unification (of which Kohl's vision of "blühende Landschaften" was to become the most satirized), commentators were reluctant to say when exactly the differences between the two populations would dissipate; many estimated that it would take a generation before Willy Brandt's optimistic assessment — "Nun wächst zusammen, was zusammengehört" — would really take effect. Surveys demonstrate continuing divisions in attitudes between those in the eastern and western regions, even among those with no direct experience of the Cold War's geopolitical arrangement. The apparent need to bridge a continued gap in knowledge and understanding was demonstrated by the government's "Deutschland-Tour" in summer 2010, a touring exhibition on the GDR shown in fifty German towns and cities. Finance Minister Wolfgang Schäuble opened the tour with the optimistic call for Germans to stop regarding each other as "Ossis" or "Wessis,"[6] but the misunderstandings between the two regions have not dissipated. Indeed, the potential is there for these to increase as direct memories fade or are distorted by the media. In 2010 an eastern German woman whose application for a job in Stuttgart was returned with the comment "Ossi" tried to sue the company for discrimination based on her ethnic background. Though the courts eventually ruled against the plaintiff, finding that eastern Germans do not comprise a separate ethnic group, the case attracted considerable attention and highlighted continuing tensions between eastern and western Germans.[7]

That both those who did experience unification and young eastern Germans born after 1989 should identify positive aspects of life in the GDR has proved to be as shocking to some as has the related revelation that, according to a study conducted in 2008, young Germans from both east and west wrongly identify Brandt as an SED politician or believe the Allies or the FRG to have been the architects of the Berlin Wall.[8] Such historical confusion and ignorance constitute an issue to which schools in Germany are expected to respond and to redress. Surveys regularly confirm that education on the GDR period in both the former East and the former West Germany is lacking (due in part to the emphasis on teaching about the National Socialist past). However, pedagogical approaches in schools are not the only factor in shaping attitudes to the former East German state. In eastern German families the parents' nostalgia for the GDR may fog any clear understanding of what the GDR was, while western parents may still be influenced by the characterization of the GDR as "totalitarian" that held sway in the FRG before unification.

Themes and Focus of This Book

In the years since unification a wide variety of interpretations and representations of the East German state have emerged, some underlining the repressive nature of the GDR and others pointing wistfully to a lost sense of community. Remembrance of the GDR consists of multiple narratives and concerns much more than the demise of East Germany, hence it is just as important to consider recollections of the development, structure, and everyday life of the GDR as it is to portray reactions to its collapse. There is an ongoing debate about explanations and documentation of the East German state in which private and collective memory, history, and nostalgia collide. This book sets out to consider some of the ways in which the GDR has come to be remembered in the years since its dissolution. The contributors to this volume analyze a range of factors influencing the formation of memory, for example the different perspectives of eastern and western Germans, the contrast and conflict between individual and collective narratives, and the extent to which past historical events and ideology, future expectations, and generational change influence recollections of the GDR. These themes are examined by reference to three kinds of cultural formations: literature and film, museums and memorials, and generational and societal narratives.

Part 1: Remembering the GDR in Literature and Film

Interest in the GDR mushroomed as soon as the state ceased to exist. It was not just a matter of professional historical scrutiny but also of personal inquiry: the state's archives offered both professional historians and other interested individuals the opportunity to investigate and inspect records and documents that exposed both the GDR's inner workings and the people who had been part of its machinery. Looking back at the GDR was also a melancholic enterprise; nostalgic retrospection and the sometimes sorrowful realization that the GDR past was indeed a foreign (and now defunct) country proved to be as significant a feature as was the energetic historical analysis. Poets and intellectuals were among the first to mourn the GDR. In the opening chapter here, Laura Bradley examines representations of GDR theater in post-*Wende* literature and film, asking how they intervene in memory debates about the GDR. She focuses on Andreas Dresen's *Stilles Land* (Silent Country, 1992), a film considered of only minor significance on its release but since acknowledged as one of the key films of the immediate postunification period and one that regularly features in retrospectives, especially recent cultural programs looking back at the end of the GDR. Dresen's film, set in the eastern German provinces, offers a de-dramatized account of the GDR's demise; its protagonist, an ambitious young theater director, is more concerned with staging a play than he is with the real-life drama taking place. Dresen's muted portrayal offers a counternarrative to the popular account of the state's collapse.

Prevailing attitudes toward the GDR are challenged in varying degrees in two further texts examined by Bradley. Emine Sevgi Özdamar's novel *Seltsame Sterne starren zur Erde* (Strange Stars Gaze toward Earth, 2003) thematizes nostalgia through its Turkish-German narrator's desire to recapture the lost world of Brecht and Weigel, but it also challenges nostalgia for the East German state by allowing other theater practitioners to question the narrator's rose-tinted view of it. A more concerted critique of nostalgia is evident in Barbara Honigmann's epistolary novel *Alles, alles Liebe!* (With All My Love, 2000). Honigmann, a German-Jewish writer, is particularly skeptical of the GDR's self-declared anti-Fascism. Her experiences of the East German state evince those negative and uncomfortable aspects often ignored in other postunification texts — here especially anti-Semitism — and emphasize the tendency toward forming cliques and the endless compromises that East Germans were forced to make.

In the following essay Anna O'Driscoll identifies melancholy as a sentiment that has increasingly come to the fore in the postunification period. She examines the melancholy that underpins postunification texts by three prominent eastern German writers, Christoph Hein's *Frau Paula Trousseau*

(2007), Monika Maron's two novels *Endmoränen* (Terminal Moraines, 2002) and *Ach Glück* (Oh Happiness, 2007), and Christa Wolf's diary publication *Ein Tag im Jahr* (One Day a Year, 1960–2000, 2003), together with details of contemporary historical events. These texts, which feature middle-aged female protagonists, present a discouraging view of life in unified Germany (but resist any rosy view of the GDR) and are characterized by boredom, hopelessness, a sense of personal redundancy and impotence, and a palpable melancholy and despair, though O'Driscoll emphasizes that this disillusionment is not unique to life since 1989 but stems also from disappointments already felt during the GDR.

The GDR may not have provided the inspiration for as many novels as has the Third Reich, but numerous authors have engaged with East German history since 1989. In his essay Stuart Parkes examines the view of the GDR in postunification literature but from the perspective of non-eastern German writers and three different generations. He looks first at Martin Walser's *Die Verteidigung der Kindheit* (The Defense of Childhood, 1991), which reflects Walser's increasing interest in and often controversial ideas about all-German issues. Unlike the slew of nostalgic texts published in recent years, the three texts Parkes discusses — including the first serious appraisal of Jan Böttcher's well-received novel *Nachglühen* (Afterglow, 2008) and Jacques-Pierre Amette's prize-winning Cold War thriller *La Maîtresse de Brecht* (Brecht's Mistress, 2003), a fictional account of the playwright's last years — present a mostly negative portrayal of the GDR. Parkes assesses what they might have in common and to what extent they provide more than a clichéd picture of the East German state.

The legacy of the GDR has taken on a defined role in popular culture, with audiences flocking to films claiming to depict it "as it was." Original East German films are regularly screened (primarily by networks in eastern Germany), and film scholars have enthusiastically attended to the back catalogue of the Deutsche Film-Aktiengesellschaft (DEFA) and rescued from anonymity films that were shelved (that is, withdrawn from exhibition) by the Party. One version of the GDR that resonated strongly with audiences in Germany and abroad was the award-winning Stasi drama *Das Leben der Anderen* (*The Lives of Others*, Florian Henckel von Donnersmarck, 2007). In his chapter, Nick Hodgin considers the film's national and international reception, as well as its endorsement in Germany by those who regard it as an educationally useful — even necessary — GDR narrative, and questions, among other things, the claims of authenticity by both its director and its champions. He discusses Donnersmarck's film in the context of postunification debates and offers a chronology of Stasi films, few of which have had anything like the impact on post-GDR discourse that has *Das Leben der Anderen*, which public figures such as the former prime minister of Bavaria Edmund Stoiber praised for exposing the "wahre[s] Gesicht der DDR-Diktatur."[9]

Part 2: Remembering the GDR through Memorials and Museums

In 2000 Rita Süssmuth, CDU politician and then president of the Bundestag, said of eastern Germans, "Wir im Westen wussten zu wenig von ihrer Vergangenheit, ihren Empfindungen, ihren Beziehungen zu uns. Wir waren tatsächlich nicht vorbereitet auf die Wiedervereinigung und waren in vieler Hinsicht Unwissende."[10] That the relationship between east and west was asymmetrical was a fact that had been recognized even before unification. Monika Zimmermann, a West German correspondent in East Berlin, noted in June 1989: "Denn ebenso wie die Westdeutschen den zweiten deutschen Staat gelegentlich aus dem Auge und damit aus dem Bewußtsein verlieren, haben sich die Menschen in der DDR trotz hermetischer Abriegelung und verordneter Informationssperre über Jahrzehnte nicht davon abhalten lassen, gerade das zu tun, was eigentlich verhindert werden sollte. Sie haben das Interesse am anderen Teil Deutschlands bewahrt."[11]

The situation has since changed; every aspect of the GDR has been scrutinized. Across the country (but mainly in eastern Germany) visitors can pore over material goods from the former GDR, from matchboxes to shopping bags, cleaning products, and clothing, and the proliferation of museums enables a forensic examination of the minutiae of GDR life. The interest in preserving material traces of the GDR corresponds to a general tendency to establish what Pierre Nora terms "lieux de mémoire" (realms of memory) to try and hold on to a past and prevent it from fading from popular consciousness. Nora defines these *lieux de mémoire*, whether museums, memorials, or commemorations, as an attempt to preserve the relics of a past that we might not have experienced, to revive abandoned memories, and to recreate ritual within society, but stresses that these relics can only provide "illusions of eternity."[12]

In her chapter in this volume Silke Arnold-de Simine considers the development of the DDR Museum in Berlin and the Dokumentationszentrum Alltag der DDR (Documentation Center of Everyday Culture in the GDR) in Eisenhüttenstadt as two examples of institutions charting everyday life in East Germany. Interestingly, both museums were proposed by western Germans, suggesting a desire to fill the gaps identified by Süssmuth. Arnold-de Simine discusses these museums in the context of the development of the "memory museum," which, rather than merely documenting history, aims to encourage identification, empathy, and an active response on the part of the visitor. She challenges the perception that museums of everyday life in the GDR are necessarily apolitical and encourage "Ostalgie," but also acknowledges the challenges presented by their approach to history. The lack of narrative explanation in the Eisenhüttenstadt museum may mean that its exhibits are only understood by visitors from eastern Germany, whereas in its attempt to present a hands-on, fun experience of a life that most visitors will not have experienced, the DDR Museum perhaps ventures too far into the realms of "histotainment."

As already mentioned, the Berlin Wall — "never simply a concrete edifice, but actually a panoply of symbols, myths and images . . . a textual and intertextual phenomenon" — is the most prominent image associated with German unification, despite the fact that few traces of it now remain.[13] The eagerness to preserve the former border is relatively recent — there was a rush to demolish it in the wake of unification — but the wall has become one of the main tourist attractions of unified Berlin. Visitors flock to see remaining stretches of wall such as the East Side Gallery, along with the Checkpoint Charlie Museum and the Berlin Wall Memorial at Bernauer Strasse, and there are a multitude of tours offering to reveal the "reality" of divided Berlin. The undoubted fascination with the former border is not always coupled with understanding: visitors may be unsure whether they are viewing the wall from east or west, and of course the concrete structure they see cannot give an accurate impression of the full and menacing extent of the East-West border.

Two chapters here, one by Günter Schlusche and the other by Perrti Ahonen, address the role of the Berlin Wall in commemorating the GDR. The history and current extension of the Berlin Wall Memorial and Documentation Center at Bernauer Strasse (the wall at this location provided one of the most prominent symbols of divided Berlin, with the border running along the middle of the street and cutting across a graveyard) forms the focus of Schlusche's article. An architect and city planner and more recently planning and building coordinator at the Berlin Wall Memorial, he offers some insight into the memorial debates and charts the often contested efforts to preserve the border strip as a site of historical importance, this often involving complex negotiations over land ownership. The memorial at Bernauer Strasse and its planned extension are designed to stress the authenticity and historical significance of the location without aiming to reconstruct the past. Schlusche defines the site's significance as a place of both commemoration and learning and outlines its objectives of presenting both eastern and western perspectives on the site and encouraging visitors to engage actively with the past. He places the development of the Bernauer Strasse memorial in the context of the conceptual changes and evolving public perceptions of the culture of remembrance in postwar Germany and outlines the memorial's further objectives.

Pertti Ahonen provides a more critical assessment in his essay, which explores the public commemoration of the Berlin Wall since unification and how this has reflected broader east-west discourses on the GDR legacy. Significantly, he shows how commemoration of the wall was for a long time dominated by western triumphalism, with eastern perspectives largely ignored or discredited. The commemorative focus was on the victims of Communist oppression, while the GDR's practice of commemorating border guards who had fallen in the line of duty was phased out. Ahonen traces the recent shift toward a more coordinated and multifaceted approach to the commemoration of the wall underpinned by an official memorialization strategy from the Berlin Senate, but he maintains that this is still not politically neutral, with the prime focus still on the wall as a symbol of repression and injustice.

The focus on Berlin has often diverted attention from the equally important development of the memorial landscape in the new *Bundesländer* outside Berlin, which may be influenced more by regional than by national interests and politics. Andreas Wagner, a research associate at the Political Memorials of Mecklenburg-West Pomerania, describes in his essay memorialization in Mecklenburg-West Pomerania since unification. He identifies the need for historical revision after unification as well as the challenges of addressing a multilayered past. This has involved researching former sites of National Socialist repression that were ignored during the GDR, as well as the *Speziallager* (special camps) and judicial facilities from the period of Soviet occupation, which remained taboo under the GDR. In addition there is a broad range of references to the East German past in Mecklenburg-West Pomerania, including former Stasi sites and prisons and remains of the German-German border. There are also memorials marking the fall of the Berlin Wall, though — perhaps for the reasons outlined at the start of this chapter — very few on the "peaceful revolution." Many of the memorialization initiatives since unification in this federal state, as in the new *Länder* overall, have resulted from citizens' initiatives. A public committee of enquiry was established to address the issue, but Wagner indicates the difficulties in reaching a consensus on how they should be represented, especially as this was often bound up with personal confrontation with the recent past.

One of the main challenges to memorialization in postunification Germany has been the issue of how to appropriately remember both the GDR and the National Socialist past. Central to this debate is the issue of whether comparisons between the two are legitimate or serve to erase their respective distinctive features. In her essay Caroline Pearce discusses confrontation with Germany's "double past" at memorial sites in the new *Länder* with authentic links to the Nazi past and the post-1945 (Stalinist and/or East German) regime. She focuses on official strategies for memorialization of the "double past," starting with the government's first memorial site concept (*Gedenkstättenkonzeption*) developed in 1998–99. This sought to formulate a balanced strategy for memorialization that treated both pasts on their own terms. However, in practice the consensus on memorialization prioritized remembrance of the Holocaust in line with the (left-liberal) strategy of *Vergangen-*

heitsbewaltigung established in the West before unification. The essay goes on to discuss the controversies surrounding subsequent memorial site concepts at both the regional and the national level, notably those apparently seeking to blur the Nazi and GDR pasts into one "totalitarianist" narrative. Pearce also addresses how the diverging memories of victims' groups inform and complicate the debate on memorializing the "double past," and she explains how the different elements of the "double past" are unequally weighted as a result of popular perceptions of history.

Part 3: *Ostalgie*, Historiography, and Generational Memory

The final section of this book considers societal, historiographical, and generational approaches to remembering the GDR. Importantly, these revisit the concept of "Ostalgie." No matter how banal its details and features or unserious its stance, *Ostalgie* is a development that both responds to and articulates profoundly important issues about modern Germany. Commentators were initially intrigued and amused by the eastern Germans' nostalgia for the GDR when it first emerged in the early 1990s; the ironic celebration of the past was, it seemed, partly iconoclastic, a belated reckoning with the SED dictatorship. However, it proved to be much more than the inconsequential trend that people first imagined (and perhaps hoped for) and developed a significant economic profile and national and international media presence (in the form of television shows and hit films), all of which fomented debates concerning the politics of memory and contemporary German identity.

Indeed, ostensibly trivial, commonplace features of the GDR past have in some cases been instrumental in regrouping an eastern German community. This may be explained in terms of ease — reviving a favored brand of chocolate is of course far easier than restoring a steelworks — but also in terms of effect. Although both olfactory and gustatory senses are important in stimulating memory, biting into a bar of Rotstern Schokolade is more likely to stimulate positive memories than are the noxious fumes emitted by the former foundries and chemical works. In this sense the significance of *Ostalgie* relates more to its effect on local (that is, eastern German) morale than to its capacity to restore the fortunes of small businesses. *Ostalgie* also functions, as the late Daphne Berdahl observed in her valuable ethnographic research into eastern German life, as a kind of "counter-memory," an "attempt to recuperate, validate, and anchor a collective memory of a shared past."[14]

Occasionally the cause has had no obvious economic purpose, as shown by the furor that erupted when it was announced that the *Ampelmännchen,* the spry pedestrian figure found on eastern traffic lights, was to make way for its western counterpart. Finally rescued from forced retirement, the figure has become so popular that it now features as one of the emblems of modern Berlin (rather than of East Germany, as some have claimed), and there is a booming industry selling related memorabilia. It has been suggested that the campaign to save the figure succeeded ultimately because it was "free of the taint of totalitarianism." Yet symbols of the regime, the flags and badges and military uniforms, have also been commodified, though these are typically pitched at consumers from outside (eastern) Germany.[15] While eastern Germans first connected with their personal histories by focusing on the material past, outsiders' interest in the GDR often centered on explicitly Socialist tokens, mementos of the anti-Fascist ideology that had been the cornerstone of the official state-defined identity but with which the GDR population never convincingly connected. That these remnants of the past are dismissed by eastern Germans appears to be of little consequence to their western collectors, for whom they act as "the preferred emblems of their own imagined GDR."[16]

Citizens of the former GDR state of course have their own "imagined GDR." When considering the sense of loss regarding the GDR, it is generally not the state that is missed but the ideals with which it was problematically associated, as well as some of the basic but important comforts (child care, inexpensive foods, cheap public transport, etc.). Looking to the past in order to see the future is one of the issues on which Peter Thompson reflects in his essay, which uses a Blochian analysis of eastern German consciousness over the decades since unification. Thompson's interpretation of *Ostalgie* posits it as a natural response to eastern Germans' "temporal, psychological, social, geographical, and political dislocation" but sees it also as a "loss of a loss," a contradiction that the journalist Christoph Dieckmann, one of the more thoughtful contributors to postunification discourse, has described in similar terms: "Ostalgie bezeichne das Heimweh nach einer DDR, wie sie gewesen wäre, wenn sie nicht die DDR gewesen wäre."[17]

Thomas Ahbe also examines the development of *Ostalgie* but views it in part as a reaction to slanted media discourses on the East German past. The media has played an important and often contested role in narrating the GDR past and in chronicling developments since 1989. Ahbe suggests that the media's representation of eastern German issues and of GDR history privileges western viewpoints, not least because the media discourse is largely dominated by westerners. The representation of *Ostalgie* within this discourse is also a way of defining a western German identity as a counter to that in the east. Ahbe discusses the "master narratives" established by the two German states after the war and how the residual impact of socialization in both states perpetuates divisions in both the society and the economy of unified Germany.

Ahbe's chapter includes a discussion of postunification surveys of eastern German perspectives on the GDR. An enormous number of such surveys have been conducted since unification — only three years later Robin Ostow suggested that the eastern Germans must be the most interviewed people in the world.[18] On the one hand such surveys serve to fill the gaps in knowledge between eastern and western Germany. How useful or even reliable some surveys are is of course debatable: that eastern Germans are keener on sex *unter freiem Himmel* than are their western cousins is ostensibly a detail of prurient appeal, but even surveys such as this fit into a wider narrative that invariably seeks to underline continuing differences (in attitudes toward gender roles, children's weight, electricity consumption — the list goes on) between east and west.[19] Moreover, as Ahbe notes, these surveys are often analyzed by a west-dominated media.

Ahbe points out that those too young to remember the GDR are quicker to condemn it as an *Unrechtsstaat* (an unjust or criminal state) than those with direct experience of life in the former East Germany. This is an interesting parallel to the confrontation with the National Socialist past in West Germany, which became more vehement as younger generations found out about the crimes of their parents' generation. In her essay here Mary Fulbrook focuses on the important distinction between the memory narratives of different generations of eastern Germans. Rather than being extrapolated from surveys or secondary literature, attitudes toward the GDR are based on the results of more than 270 qualitative and quantitative questionnaires carried out with eastern Germans. These interviews reveal some especially interesting information about the different generations' memories of growing up in the GDR. Most memoirs and autobiographies focusing on the GDR have been written by young authors (born in the late 1960s, or in the 70s or 80s), many of whom offer a retrospectively imagined eastern German state, whether self-consciously or not. However, Fulbrook turns her attention to a different generation, the so-called 1929ers, who, with a few notable exceptions (Christa Wolf, for example), feature much less in post-1989 scholarship and surveys.[20] Fulbrook assesses and compares this generation's different memories and levels of attachment to the GDR with two later generations — those born during the war (dubbed "the Children of the Third Reich") and those born in the first postwar decade — whose experiences of postunification Germany have gone some way to shaping, or indeed changing, their attitudes to the GDR. These attitudes are characterized by a yearning but not, she argues, a nostalgia for that past. Fulbrook concurs with Ahbe in arguing that East German socialization continues to affect the outlook of citizens of the former GDR.

Oral histories and autobiographies are increasingly popular in reconstructing recent history. The accounts of those who experienced the GDR firsthand seek to broaden what may be considered narrow, reductive historical accounts. However, in contrast to the "consecutive account of all that happened in a particular point in the past" that defines what John R. Gillis terms "elite memory," such "memories from below" often make "no effort to fill in all the blanks."[21] Balanced and accurate historiography is thus required to provide the factual context for what may be partial accounts. Since unification, historians from both eastern and western Germany have clashed in their approach to documenting and describing the East German state. Disagreements within the historical profession are of course nothing new — and certainly not in Germany. As Andreas Huyssen has noted, modern German history is "characterized by rupture rather than continuity, instability of representation rather than security of self-understanding."[22] Before unification both East and West Germany manipulated or relativized recent history to bolster their newly established identities and present themselves as the "better state." In the GDR, for example, expedient historical narratives were routinely provided in order to trace a revolutionary spirit that would fortify and legitimize the SED's position. Unification inevitably terminated the practice of shifting blame for the Nazi past between the two states. It also necessitated a reappraisal of both GDR and twentieth-century history, which has not been without conflict.

Stefan Berger's essay examines the development of the historical profession in East and West Germany and in particular the consequences of unification for East German historiography. After the Second World War the historical profession in the GDR was reorganized along SED-conformist Marxist-Leninist lines in contrast to the more conservative orientation of West German historiography. Yet despite differing approaches there was increased dialogue between East and West German historians in the years leading up to the *Wende*. Berger describes how after 1990 western German historians were quick to discredit the output of their colleagues from the east as having little more than propaganda value, and how only a handful of GDR historians were accepted into academia in unified Germany. Berger discusses the impact of the overall loss of a specific East German historiography in Germany, for example the sidelining of Marxist perspectives, which are still represented elsewhere in Western Europe as well as in post-Communist Eastern Europe.

Relevance and Readership

The significance of remembering the GDR goes far beyond the symbolic commemorations marking the twentieth anniversary of unification. Debates on how this past is and should be remembered do not just inform academic writing and historiography but also have a direct impact on the politics and society of contemporary Germany. Politicians may instrumentalize the GDR past to serve current political agendas, and the question of whether the GDR was an *Unrechtsstaat* influences political interpretations of the unified German state. As we have seen, the legacy of this past also has economic consequences: while the trade in *Ostalgie*-related products may be booming, grave economic inequalities still exist between eastern and western Germany, in part as a result of differing patterns of socialization. This legacy also continues to permeate everyday life in the new *Länder*, with many citizens still working through their experiences and memories of the GDR regime and the constant reminders of the past in the present, for example the revelation that many former Stasi members are now employed by the Brandenburg police force.

Memory of the GDR past is thus still very much an "active" one and represented by a range of communities of memory. Yet with the passage of time it is also accompanied by the inevitable shift from communicative to cultural memory. Many young Germans increasingly gain their perspectives on the GDR from sources including books, films, museums, and the media, although the impact of familial memory transmission should not be underestimated. Those who transmit cultural memory have a responsibility to present a non-biased approach, and yet in practice the narratives they present will be selective and favor some aspects over others. This volume provides some insight into the competing narratives and the paradoxes and ambiguities of GDR history that often result in polarizing the focus on repression and on everyday life in the GDR. Indeed, the essays here represent some quite different assessments of the process of remembering the GDR. Finally, it is important to note that the discourse on remembering the GDR continues to be relevant for both eastern and western Germans: attitudes to the GDR in both parts of the country influence the development of national identity.

The GDR Remembered is designed to appeal to general readers as well as students and specialists. Each chapter contains the necessary context to be read as a stand-alone piece and includes a range of useful bibliographical resources for further reading. Taken together, the chapters present an overview of the complex and evolving debate on representations and recollections of the GDR, a debate that will have relevance for many years to come as eastern and western Germans continue to work through their relationship to the GDR regime, and subsequent generations assess its impact on German identity as a whole.

A Note on Terminology

Throughout this book the capitalized terms East and West German and East and West Germany refer to the two states prior to unification and the lower-case forms eastern and western German and eastern and western Germany refer to the two regions after unification.

Notes

[1] See Kornelia Lobmeier, "Das Herbst 1989," paper at the conference "Beratung gegen Rechtsextremismus trifft auf Geschichte," Leipzig, 23 June 2009 (Berlin: Bundesprogramm "kompetent. Fur Demokratie," 2009).

[2] See Hans-Joachim Maaz "Viele Ostdeutsche sind nicht geheilt," interview by Stefan Berg and Michael Sontheimer, *Spiegel Online*, accessed 29 July 2010, http://einestages.spiegel.de/static/authoralbumbackground/4748/_viele_ost-deutsche_sind_nicht_geheilt.html.

[3] See for example Roger Boyes, "Berlin Wall Party Tempered by Shadow of Kristallnacht for Germans," *The Times*, 9 November 2009, http://www.timeson-line.co.uk/tol/news/world/europe/article6908807.ece.

[4] See *Der Spiegel*, 20 September 2004.

[5] The qualities that have been attributed to eastern and western Germans are described in countless books. In *Das Buch der Unterschiede: Warum die Einheit keine ist*, ed. Jana Simon, Frank Rothe, and Wiete Andrasch (Berlin: Aufbau-Verlag, 2000), young Germans give some sense of the ubiquity of these stereo-types. Also see Wolf Biermann, "Dideldumm," in *Vom einen Land und vom Andern: Gedichte zur deutschen Wende*, ed. Karl Otto Conrady (Leipzig: Suhrkamp, 1993), 82–84, here 83.

[6] See "20 Jahre Deutsche Einheit: Deutschland-Tour" (Presse- und Informa-tionsamt der Bundesregierung, 2011), accessed 29 July 2010, http://www.bundesregierung.de/nn_843756/Content/DE/Artikel/2010/07/2010-07-01-start-deutschlandtour.html.

[7] See "Im 'Ossi' nichts Neues," *Sueddeutsche Zeitung* (online), 15 April 2010, http://www.sueddeutsche.de/karriere/doch-kein-volksstamm-im-ossi-nichts-neues-1.10170.

[8] "Schüler haben keine Ahnung von DDR," *Focus*, 25 July 2008, http://www.focus.de/panorama/vermischtes/studie-schueler-haben-keine-ahnung-von-ddr_aid_320236.html.

[9] "Stoiber würdigt 'Das Leben der Anderen,'" *PR-inside.com*, 20 March 2007, http://www.pr-inside.com/de/stoiber-wuerdigt-das-leben-der-anderen-r71069.htm.

[10] Rita Süssmuth, "Zehn Jahre deutsche Einheit: Eine kritische Bilanz," *Aus Politik und Zeitgeschichte* (B 1–2/2000), http://www.bpb.de/publikationen/NN4R8S,0,Zehn_Jahre_deutsche_Einheit%3A.html.

[11] Monika Zimmermann, "Typisch DDR," *Frankfurter Allgemeine Zeitung*, 19 June 1989, cited in *Dagewesen und Aufgeschrieben: Reportagen über eine deutsche Revolution*, ed. Dieter Golombeck and Dietrich Ratzke (Frankfurt am Main:

Institut für Medienentwicklung und Kommunikation GmbH, 1990), 45–47, here 45.

[12] Pierre Nora, *Realms of Memory*, vol. 1, *Conflicts and Divisions*, ed. Lawrence D. Kritzman, transl. Arthur Goldhammer (New York: Columbia UP, 1992), 6–7.

[13] Sunil Manghani, *Image Critique and the Fall of the Berlin Wall* (Bristol: Intellect Books, 2008), 36.

[14] Daphne Berdahl, *On the Social Life of Postsocialism: Memory, Consumption, Germany* (Bloomington: Indiana UP, 2010), 55 and 56 respectively.

[15] See Joe Moran, "History, Memory, and the Everyday," *Rethinking History* 8, no. 1 (2004): 51–68; and Svetlana Boym, *The Future of Nostalgia* (New York: Basic Books, 2001), 196.

[16] Paul Betts, "The Twilight of the Idols: East German Memory and Material Culture," *The Journal of Modern History* 72 (2000): 731–65.

[17] Christoph Dieckmann, "Kindereien," *Die Zeit*, 29 September 2005.

[18] See Robin Ostow, "Restructuring Our Lives: National Unification and German Biographies," *The Oral History Review. Journal of the Oral History Association*, 21, no. 2 (Winter 1993): 1–8.

[19] See "Umfrage: Wie wiedervereint sind wir eigentlich im Bett?" *Berliner Zeitung*, 2 October 2009, http://www.bz-berlin.de/erotik/wie-wiedervereint-sind-wir-im-bett-article601551.html. The article, "Ein erotischer Ost-West-Vergleich zum Tag der Einheit," delights in the ironic inversion of key concepts, thus "Nur Ostdeutsche lieben grenzenlos" and "Eingemauert haben sich die Westdeutschen im Bett."

[20] The following authors have all written one or more well-received texts about life in the GDR: Claudia Rusch (b. 1971), Jakob Hein (b. 1971), Daniel Wiechmann (b. 1974), Robert Ide (b. 1975), Jana Hensel (b. 1976), and Susanne Fritsche (b. 1979). Fritsche, who was ten when the wall fell, was praised for her personal account of GDR history, ostensibly intended for young Germans with little knowledge of the East German state. See Susanne Fritsche, *Die Mauer ist gefallen: Eine kleine Geschichte der DDR* (Munich: Carl Hanser Verlag, 2004).

[21] John R. Gillis, "Memory and Identity: The History of a Relationship," in *Commemorations: The Politics of National Identity*, ed. John R. Gillis (Princeton, NJ: Princeton UP, 1996), 3–24, here 6.

[22] Andreas Huyssen, "The Inevitability of Nation: German Intellectuals after Unification," *October* 61 (Summer 1992): 65–73, here 68.

Part 1: Remembering the GDR in Literature and Film

1: From Berlin to Prenzlau: Representations of GDR Theater in Film and Literature

Laura Bradley

> *Wir treten aus unseren Rollen heraus.*
> *Die Situation in unserem Land zwingt uns dazu.*
> — Knut Lennartz, *Vom Aufbruch zur Wende*[1]

THESE ARE THE OPENING LINES of a resolution that was first read out on 6 October 1989 after a performance at the Staatsschauspiel Dresden and that has since come to epitomize the political role of GDR theater practitioners during the *Wende*. As Loren Kruger argues, the lines functioned both as "exhortation and performative utterance," calling on spectators to join the actors in abandoning the roles prescribed for them by the state.[2] The resolution quickly came to serve as the master script for activity in other ensembles, marking the moment at which GDR theater made the transition from sporadic dissent to opposition. While similar resolutions were drawn up in other workplaces and organizations, theater had the opportunity to go public: to open its doors for discussion, host political meetings, and activate its professional networks. In East Berlin, theater practitioners met in the Deutsches Theater to organize the demonstration that took place on Alexanderplatz on 4 November 1989. In provincial Bautzen, meanwhile, the Deutsch-Sorbisches Volkstheater supplied platforms and sound equipment for public political meetings.[3] By December the Union of Theater Practitioners had already commissioned a volume to document the historic role played by theaters that autumn. The published volume contained resolutions from forty-four GDR theaters together with photographs and newspaper articles.[4] It is only on close reading that the subtle but important political differences among the demands made in these resolutions become apparent.

This public image of a united theater contrasts with the view expressed by the director Christoph Schroth in 1990 in response to a questionnaire about GDR theater. Schroth immediately challenged the premise behind the questionnaire, stating: "Ich kann nicht von *dem* 'DDR-Theater' reden" (*VA*, 62). He explained: "Es gab in der DDR sehr unterschiedliches Theater, viel schlechtes, konventionelles, angepaßtes, braves Theater. . . . Aber es gab auch bestimmte Häuser, die dem Theater in der sozialistischen Gesellschaft eine wesentliche Funktion geben wollten, die Bestehendes nicht bestätigen, sondern kritisch in Frage stellten" (*VA*, 62). Schroth's differentiated portrait of GDR theater now has an artistic corollary in the contrasting filmic and literary representations that have emerged since unification as texts and films about the GDR have proliferated. This chapter focuses on the film *Stilles Land* (1992), directed by Andreas Dresen; the epistolary novel *Alles, alles Liebe!* (2000), by Barbara Honigmann; and the hybrid autobiographical novel *Seltsame Sterne starren zur Erde* (2003), by Emine Sevgi Özdamar.[5] In each case the author limits the narrative perspective to a specific period in the GDR's history: Dresen and his coauthor, Laila Stieler, focus on the *Wende*, and Honigmann and Özdamar set their texts in the 1970s. Even so, their representations of East German theater reflect postunification concerns about how the GDR should be remembered, the value of its artistic achievements, and its political legacies.[6] Dresen, Honigmann, and Özdamar share a preoccupation with experiences that do not feature in dominant postunification narratives about the GDR, and in the case of Honigmann and Özdamar this preoccupation is related to their respective positions as a German Jewish and a Turkish German writer.

The representation of theater in these works is closely informed by the personal and professional experience of their creators. Andreas Dresen is the son of Adolf Dresen, one of the GDR's leading theater directors from the mid-1960s until his emigration in 1977, and of the actress Barbara Bachmann, who subsequently married Schroth. Dresen worked briefly as a sound technician at the Mecklenburgisches Staatstheater in Schwerin, and his film is additionally based on interviews with theater practitioners in Anklam, Parchim, and Rudolstadt, three small theaters that did not attract attention beyond their immediate regions in the late 1980s.[7] Barbara Honigmann worked as a dramaturge in Brandenburg and at two leading theaters in East Berlin, the Deutsches Theater and the Volksbühne, and her father was married to the actress and singer Gisela May. In the late 1970s Özdamar came from Istanbul to work as an actress and director's assistant at the Volksbühne, and in the 1980s she returned to act at the Berliner Ensemble (BE). This personal experience is reflected in the authors' close attention to the day-to-day business of theater, from rehearsals and productions to bureaucracy and conversations in the canteen. This interest in the theatrical process distinguishes their works from *Das Leben der Anderen* (2006), a film written and directed by Florian Henckel von Donnersmarck, who grew up in the West and has no firsthand experience of GDR theater. In Donnersmarck's film theater functions chiefly as an exotic backdrop and as a metaphor for the GDR as a performance and surveillance society. Only two scenes are set in the theater itself and one of these scenes takes place after unification, so this film will not be considered here.[8]

Restaging the Revolution: *Stilles Land* (1992)

Stilles Land focuses on the provincial East German experience of autumn 1989, modulating this experience to take account of the subsequent economic dislocation. By 1992, the privatization and restructuring of the GDR's state-owned industries had taken unemployment in the eastern regions to 1.17 million, and the euphoria of autumn 1989 seemed a distant memory.[9] Theaters were not exempt from the threat of closure as they struggled to cope with falling subsidies and attendance figures. In this context *Stilles Land* was designed to perform a therapeutic function for its intended eastern German audience: it works through recent events using self-irony and a sympathetic distance. In an interview Dresen explained: "Die ganze Zeit — das, was wir erlebt haben — ist eigentlich ziemlich bitter, und ich glaube, da muss man den Mut haben, darüber zu lachen und zu sagen, wir sehen es uns mit einer leichten Ironie und Humor an, das Ganze."[10] While Massimo Locatelli argues that the film "never gives up a paternalistic, caricature-like tone in its representation of the local inhabitants," Dresen's irony is never patronizing.[11] It is directed equally toward the newcomer from East Berlin and the West German outsider, not just his provincial actors. In fact Dresen's insistence on self-irony suggests that he is treating the viewer — like himself — as a later version of the film's characters. Although the film initially attracted only small audiences, it has come to be seen as a key film about the *Wende*.[12]

Although Kristie A. Foell sees melodrama, whether in film or literature, as the genre in which "German unification finds its commensurate expression,"[13] Dresen opts for a low-key approach and relocates the events of autumn 1989 to a provincial theater, thus situating the film in the cultural tradition of provincial refractions of grand revolutionary models as seen in Goethe's *Der Bürgergeneral* and Hacks's *Moritz Tassow*. While the film was shot in Anklam and characters refer to the local river Peene, the town itself is never named. This allows it to stand metonymically for the provinces, rather like Nestroy's "Krähwinkel." But Dresen abandoned the original plan of calling his film "Provinztheater" on the grounds that this title would be derogatory, even disrespectful of those involved in the 1989 protests.[14] Moments of farce are carefully contained, used to resituate events in the everyday rather than to ridicule the characters. The film's actual title is ambivalent and alludes to Wolf Biermann's song "Noch," written in 1968 during the Prague Spring:

Das Land ist still
Wie Grabsteine stehen die Häuser
Still. Das Land ist still. Noch.[15]

The title "Stilles Land" thus evokes the paralysis of the GDR, conveyed in the film through long shots of the empty countryside and town. But through its focus on the historical moment when the paralysis ended, the film also justifies Biermann's faith that the paralysis will be temporary. The postunification perspective of the director and viewer adds another set of resonances absent from Biermann's poem: the film functions in part as an elegy for a tranquility that has now been lost.

Stilles Land refuses to engage in the postunification culture of recrimination epitomized by the 1990 *Literaturstreit* and by the flood of revelations about artists who had collaborated with the Stasi — revelations that led a number of theater practitioners to lose their jobs. While much of the media was intent on dividing artists into perpetrators and victims in the early 1990s, these concerns are absent from the film. Only the Party Secretary and, to a lesser extent, the manager Walz emerge as SED supporters within the theater, and the film depicts theater practitioners as ordinary GDR citizens in a workplace. As the camera's gaze travels across the auditorium in the opening scenes, we see the actors drinking coffee, playing cards, knitting, and sharing holiday photos as they wait for Walz to welcome them back for the new season. The impact of political events is uneven. As Walz delivers his routine speech, the actor Felix tells the director's assistant, Claudia, that five hundred people are crossing the border each day, but she looks up only briefly from her book. Unable to stand this inertia, Horst, an older, politicized actor, calls out: "Sag mal lieber was zu Ungarn. Und zur Prager Botschaft!" But Walz and his Party Secretary insist on keeping up appearances, agreeing not to mention Horst's intervention in their report to the authorities. The opening scenes thus set up an opposition between the advocates of change (Horst and Felix) and stability (Walz and the Party Secretary), with Walz supporting the regime through his desire for a quiet life. He advises the Party Secretary to let sleeping dogs lie, an attitude that governs his managerial approach. A framed quotation from Kleist's *Der zerbrochne Krug* on his office wall reads: "Und finde ich gleich nicht alles, wie es soll, / Ich freue mich, wenn es erträglich ist."[16] The other company members are merely the spectators of this conflict, which at this point is marginal to their personal lives. The actress Uschi's concern is not that the lead actor has left the GDR for Hungary, but that he has done so while owing her twenty marks.

It is hard to identify this theater as a substitute for the GDR media, let alone as a center of resistance. The young director, Kai, embodies a more idealistic view of theater. He is a newcomer from East Berlin and he decides to stage Samuel Beckett's *Warten auf Godot*, a play that had been excluded from the GDR repertoire until 1987, when it was staged at the Staatsschauspiel Dresden. In the film the play contrasts sharply with the company's usual repertoire of fairy tales, pantomimes, and German classics. Kai insists that *Warten auf Godot* is topical and relevant, yet he is initially unable to move beyond clichés to political analysis; he cannot explain the causes of the characters' entrapment. It is only after attending a meeting of the New Forum in the local church that he starts to realize that Vladimir and Estragon must take responsibility for their situation: "Es liegt an den beiden, dass sie einfach nicht von der Stelle kommen. . . . Ausweglosigkeit! Ist Quatsch. Die gibt es nicht. Nur in ihren Köpfen." This recognition leads him to change his production concept, yet he fails to translate his new understanding of Beckett's characters into empathy with his actors. In rehearsals Kai twice mistakes moments of genuine despair and frustration — involving Horst and Felix — for brilliant acting. As Anthony Coulson comments, "in his determination to dramatize the social reality, he only sees the play, not the people who actually perform it."[17] This myopia affects Kai's reading of political and social reality, which he regards as a distraction from the "real" business of theater. He snaps at Claudia: "Ich — ich — ich — habe keine Zeit für irgendwelche Spielereien, Spaziergänge, sinnlose Diskussionen, Katzen. Mann, Mann, Mann, Mann, Mann. Wenn ich daran denke, dass in drei Wochen Premiere ist." Just a couple of frames later we see his impatience with actors who arrive late for rehearsals because they have been trying to follow political events on television. The juxtaposition of these episodes suggests that Kai is guilty of precisely those failings for which he criticized Claudia, namely misplaced priorities.

Dresen's treatment of the theater's protest against conditions in the GDR renounces melodrama in favor of what Seán Allan terms the "heroism of the ordinary."[18] Late at night the actors draw up a resolution expressing their concern at the authorities' refusal to face up to political reality and demanding an open discussion. Yet rather than presenting the composition of the resolution as a utopian moment of solidarity, Dresen writes the subsequent fragmentation of the opposition into the event as Horst and Felix turn on each other. The rebellion's limits become clear when the theater practitioners hand their resolution to Walz, and both he and a reluctant Party Secretary sign it. After a long shot focusing on Kai as he reads out the resolution onstage, the film cuts to a shot of spectators sitting in silence in a half-empty auditorium. While this results in an anticlimax, the prolonged silence simultaneously invokes the risks and uncertainty involved in protest, until the applause does eventually start and spread. Kai's courage is underlined by Walz's failure to act. In an example of Brecht's "Nicht, Sondern Prinzip," Walz takes the resolution to the mailbox and then decides not to send it, but to stow it away in his desk drawer instead.[19] Ever the opportunist, he finally posts the resolution after Egon Krenz, Erich Honecker's successor, has decreed that open discussion is the order of the day. Significantly, Dresen does not denounce Walz's opportunism; he simply presents it as a sign of human weakness, an approach that is entirely in keeping with his renunciation of melodrama.

Throughout the film events in East Berlin remain a distant reality. The main political events occur offstage, mediated at first through competing radio broadcasts from East and West and then through television as the actors try and fail to receive a signal from the West. It is only when the actor Theo goes to Berlin to get a more powerful antenna that the physical dangers of protest become clear: Theo's fear is still palpable as he recounts the sight of water cannon and police batons and tells of his arrest. The arbitrary power of the police is summed up in the comment, "Heute gibt es eine andere Vorstellung, und wir bestimmen, was gespielt wird." His use of the language of theater denotes a symbolic occupation of a space that rightly belongs to Theo and his colleagues. But these events are far removed from the reality in the provinces. While a local demonstration does take place, an overhead shot reveals just how small it is. The local policemen are comic refractions of their Berlin counterparts: when the older one looks at his watch and says "Jetzt geht es los," it transpires that he is actually referring to a soccer match. Meanwhile, his younger colleague is unable to take incriminating photographs of the demonstrators because his camera is broken. On one level this challenges the common perception that the GDR's surveillance system was monolithic, while simultaneously making a point about the poor quality of the GDR's consumer products. However, it also marks a symbolic shift in power: the policeman's camera may have broken, but Theo takes photographs of the theater's actions on the night the wall comes down, indicating that the writers of history have changed. Dresen goes on to show how the story of the "revolution" is transformed as it is processed into memory and aligned with the emerging narrative of the collapse of state power. As Theo retells the story of his arrest in Berlin, the previously all-powerful policeman mutates into a stock comic figure. Theo appropriates the policeman's power and quick-wittedness, claiming to have won a decisive victory in the encounter.

Stilles Land does not look back at the GDR with nostalgia, but it does point forward to the disillusionments that followed its collapse. Thomas, a West German theater practitioner, performs the role of the colonizer by importing Western marketing practices into the theater. Here Dresen's irony targets not only Thomas but also his uncritical reception by the local theater practitioners — showing again that his key interest lies in self-examination rather than in apportioning blame. Comedy arises from the contrast between the tour that Kai received at the start of the film and the one that Thomas receives now: stopping beside the portrait of a deceased actor whom he had previously declared to be an alcoholic, Walz now claims that he was "einer unserer besten." Whereas the company had ostracized Kai and teased him for being an outsider, they hang uncritically on Thomas's every word — as Dresen shows by cutting out his voice as the handheld camera moves around the group of rapt listeners. But the hopes invested in the new glossy posters and placard are symbolically and poignantly shattered when a stone smashes through the glass display case, previously so carefully cleaned by the theater's porter. Neither a new audience nor the promised television crew materializes, and the premiere of *Warten auf Godot* is a flop. The production has failed to keep pace with political reality even though Kai changed his staging concept once more after Krenz's speech. Thomas's departure for Hamburg with Claudia is again symbolic: he has taken one look at this exotic East German theater and left for home, together with Kai's ex-girlfriend.

Theater in the 1970s:
Alles, alles Liebe! and *Seltsame Sterne*

Honigmann and Özdamar take us back to an earlier period of GDR theater in the mid-1970s, before the mass exodus of theater practitioners that followed Wolf Biermann's expatriation in 1976. This was a highly productive and creative period for several leading GDR theaters, such as the Volksbühne under Benno Besson and the Berliner Ensemble under Ruth Berghaus. Yet their cultural experiments were contested: Berghaus was under fire at the Berliner Ensemble, caught between conservatives and radicals, and the performance run of August Strindberg's *Fräulein Julie* — directed by B. K. Tragelehn and Einar Schleef at the BE — was cut short in 1975. These contradictions were encapsulated in the proviso tacked onto Honecker's promise of "keine Tabus" in art and literature, namely that art and literature must still proceed from Socialist principles, and in the fact that Honecker had spearheaded the attack on critical films and theater productions at the infamous Eleventh Plenary of the SED in 1965.[20]

The contradictions in this period are reflected in the contrasts between the representations of 1970s theater by Honigmann and Özdamar. Their texts deal with overlapping periods: Honigmann's epistolary novel *Alles, alles Liebe!* runs from November 1975 to January 1976, while Özdamar's *Seltsame Sterne* starts in November 1975 and ends in January 1978. The theatrical circles depicted in *Alles, alles Liebe!* and *Seltsame Sterne* also overlap, and the texts share thematic preoccupations with the persistence of anti-Semitism and the extent of solidarity in East German theater communities. Both texts engage with *Ostalgie*, the wave of nostalgia for the GDR that emerged in the late 1990s and became the subject of heated debate in the media, but they do so from different perspectives. Honigmann writes against *Ostalgie*, placing the emphasis firmly on repression and anti-Semitism in the GDR. She offers an uncompromising portrait of provincial stagnation in Prenzlau, countering the discourse of East German suffering since unification by focusing on her Jewish protagonist's experiences of exclusion in the GDR itself. While the narrative perspective is limited to 1975–76, the authorial perspective is that of the emigrant: in 1984 Honigmann chose to leave the GDR and settle in Strasbourg. By contrast, Özdamar offers us the perspective of a Turkish protagonist who has chosen to work in the GDR because of its rich theatrical tradition and who initially identifies the GDR with Brecht and Besson. The protagonist moves with relative ease between the two halves of the divided city, comparing them with her native Turkey. In contrast to Dresen's attempt to depict generic experiences in the GDR provinces in *Stilles Land*, both works view the GDR from the perspective of outsiders.

In *Seltsame Sterne* Özdamar searches for a way of remembering the GDR that avoids *Ostalgie* and yet allows for a recuperation of the aspirations and utopian potential of critical GDR theater. She estranges the material by limiting the narrative perspective to her Turkish narrator-protagonist, who is positioned as an outsider close to the center of events. As Moray McGowan comments, this enables Özdamar to use her narrator as a point of view "from which to engage with German narratives, histories and memory cultures with which they are not embroiled or compromised, unlike those positions from which these histories and memories are usually viewed and explored."[21] While Özdamar thematizes nostalgia through the narrator's longing to recapture the lost world of Brecht and Helene Weigel, she contrasts her narrator's rose-tinted view of the GDR with the views of critical left-wing intellectuals and theater practitioners such as Rudolf Bahro and Gabi Gysi. And whereas Honigmann deploys the multiple perspectives of the epistolary novel to confirm stagnation, Özdamar uses multiple views to create dissonances and contradictions for the reader to resolve.

Authenticity and Stylization

Honigmann and Özdamar play with historically verifiable details in their narratives, referring to specific places, theater practitioners, and productions, whereas Dresen presents us with a typical, unnamed provincial theater. Honigmann's use of these details remains circumspect; she leaves names incomplete or disguises them, but only half-heartedly. It is a short step to identify the character Einar as Einar Schleef, Heiner as Heiner Müller, and Thomas as Thomas Brasch. Honigmann has since acknowledged the historical basis of the production of Lorca's *Bernarda*

Albas Haus in *Alles, alles Liebe!*, telling Gabriele Eckart: "eigentlich hat [das Projekt] genauso stattgefunden, wie ich es im Buch beschrieben habe."[22] Similarly, the text refers to productions known to have taken place at the Deutsches Theater, including *Doña Rosita bleibt ledig* (*AAL*, 62). These details allow Honigmann to claim the authority to represent GDR theater authentically, a claim that is reinforced by the biographical information on the inside cover. Yet by twisting and omitting details, Honigmann reminds her readers that she has produced a stylized, fictionalized narrative that does not adhere strictly to the historical record. The protagonist's name, Anna Herzfeld, signals the absence of Lejeune's autobiographical pact, whereby the reader is assured that the author, narrator, and protagonist are one and the same person.[23] Even so, the illustration on the cover of the 2003 edition, painted by the author, depicts a letter addressed to Honigmann. This playfulness indicates that the text combines semi-autobiographical elements and fictional strategies, as if Honigmann is entering into a game of cat and mouse with the reader. This corresponds to her own description of her writing as "etwas wie ein autobiographisches Schreiben zwischen Enthüllen und Verstecken."[24]

While Honigmann's historical referents remain relatively unobtrusive, Özdamar makes far greater play of authenticity and referentiality, including not only full names but also details of the biographies and private lives of members of the GDR's *Prominenz*, including the dramatist Heiner Müller, the director Matthias Langhoff, and the former culture minister Klaus Gysi. The text draws extensively on documentary material relating to Özdamar's own theater work: there are sketches of rehearsals at the Volksbühne, photographs of figurines that Özdamar made for a production of *Der kaukasische Kreidekreis*, and even a research proposal that the director Frank Castorf devised when she was planning to write a PhD dissertation. Yet despite the numerous parallels with Özdamar's own life and despite all the documentary material, the narrator hesitates to identify herself explicitly as Özdamar. The first oblique reference comes as late as page 183 — "Türken-Emi" — and it is only on page 240 that Frank Castorf calls her "Emine."[25]

Seltsame Sterne renounces the constructed wholeness of autobiography in favor of a fragmentary, open structure. The narrative of part 1 is interrupted by literary quotations, newspaper headlines, and one sketch (e.g., *SS*, 9, 14, 83), and the fragmentation becomes still more pronounced in part 2. Here Özdamar opens up the already fragmented form of the diary so that the text becomes a repository for documentary material, graffiti, and dialogue set out as it would be in a play. These diverse forms reflect the narrator's efforts to preserve her experiences, a problem that presents itself most urgently in her theater work. The drawings are fleeting and incomplete, and the phonetic spellings and grammatical errors in the captions indicate the artist's rush to capture the images. The significance of this project lies in the narrator's understanding of drama as a repository for the utopian impulses of the past: "Im Theater stehen die Toten auf. . . . Die Toten wollen weiterleben, um sich in die kommenden Geschichten der Welt einzumischen" (*SS*, 170). As the narrator seeks to rediscover Berlin's past through its theater, she simultaneously tries to capture her experiences at the Volksbühne in her diary and drawings, preserving a time capsule of that world for her unacknowledged postunification readers. These details assume a far greater importance here than in Honigmann's work, and they serve to assert the value and enduring relevance of the GDR's socially committed theater. In *Seltsame Sterne* writing takes on the role of recuperation: Özdamar is writing against the anxiety of erasure at a time when traces of the GDR were being systematically removed from Berlin's cultural and physical landscape.[26]

Theater and Anti-Fascism

Alles, alles Liebe! and *Seltsame Sterne* offer a more critical examination of the GDR than *Stilles Land*. They identify an endemic anti-Semitism in society, challenging the state's insistence that it had made a clean break with the practices of the Third Reich. As such they imply that recent incidences of xenophobia and racist violence in eastern Germany cannot be attributed simply to the economic dislocation experienced during the unification process.[27] Yet this is where the similarity ends, for Honigmann and Özdamar differ in their assessment of anti-Fascism in the GDR. Honigmann's protagonist refers to anti-Fascism as "der erlogene Gründungsmythos dieses Landes" (*AAL*, 127–28), arguing that it has made no substantial inroads on popular attitudes as seen in the views of those working in provincial theater. Theater thus serves as a microcosm of society, and a theater meeting in Prenzlau reveals how anti-Semitism now finds an outlet in state-sanctioned anti-Zionism. Anna reports how news of a UN resolution against Israel rouses her colleagues from their apathy: "Aber komisch, wenn darüber informiert wird, daß die UNO-Vollversammlung beschlossen hat, den Zionismus 'als Form des Rassismus und der rassischen Diskriminierung' zu 'verurteilen', da wachen sie alle auf, denken sowieso, daß Zionismus ein Schimpfwort ist" (*AAL*, 73). Anna's testimony is corroborated by the experiences of her Jewish friend Eva in Meiningen, who is relegated to playing the witch in the pantomime. She tells Anna, "Das Theater ist Schmiere und die Leute sind Schweine, jedenfalls die meisten, Nazis und Antisemiten" (*AAL*, 14). The fact that Eva's chief tormenter is cast in the role of the enlightened Jewish hero in *Nathan der Weise* (*AAL*, 50) symbolizes the way in which anti-Fascism has become a ritualized performance in the GDR; it is a script that the actors have learned by rote, but have not internalized.

Honigmann's cynical view of GDR anti-Fascism contrasts with the view presented in *Seltsame Sterne*, where it emerges as the basic impulse behind the Volksbühne's productions. This anti-Fascism is rooted in lived experience, not official rhetoric. The narrator hears stories about the death marches from Sachsenhausen, learns from the actor Hasso von Lenski about how his mother was imprisoned in Buchenwald, and tells how Matthias Langhoff's father, Wolfgang, was incarcerated in a concentration camp. By recuperating what Simone Barck calls "die vielfältigen Formen eines praktizierten, realen Antifaschismus" in the GDR,[28] Özdamar counters postunification cynicism regarding the hollowness of "prescribed" anti-Fascism. She locates anti-Semitism in the world outside the Volksbühne: her narrator encounters anti-Semitic and racist attitudes in everyday settings in both East and West Berlin. In the East, for example, a man tells the narrator, "Ich bin Deutscher, Preuße, mein Blut ist deutsch, rein"; "bis vor dreißig Jahren waren wir eine arische Rasse, jetzt sind wir gemischt, kaputt" (*SS*, 137). John Pizer ignores comments such as these when he concludes simply, "*Seltsame Sterne* recalls the solidarity and respect for national as well as ethnic alterity in East Berlin."[29] The Volksbühne does not emerge as a microcosm of GDR society, but as an enlightened enclave and a "moralische Anstalt." According to Özdamar's narrator, it has remained true to the ideals and aspirations of the postwar returning exiles, whose work has yet to be completed.

Theater Communities and State Intervention

Özdamar's representation of the Volksbühne offers us a tight-knit community of like-minded artists. The narrator integrates quickly into this community: her difference is welcomed and her acceptance is symbolized when a photograph of her with her Turkish grandmother is included in the program for Besson's production of *Hamlet* (*SS*, 215). This community and its productions support the idea of theater as a creative space, suggesting that the Volksbühne benefited from a cultural thaw under Honecker. According to the narrator, Heiner Müller expressed a guarded optimism about political developments, reportedly saying, "Trotz der alltäglichen Widersprüche könnten die Menschen hier ja seit ungefähr drei Jahren ein bißchen länger schlafen" (*SS*, 149). While restrictions on expression in the media continue, these restrictions are depicted as increasing the power of language and art: "Als Hamlet im Stück sagt, 'Es ist etwas faul im Staate Dänemark', lachten die Zuschauer. Heiner Müller: 'Das Wort hat in Ostberlin eine große Wirkung'. Ein Schauspieler sagte: 'Im Westen kann man alles schreiben und sagen, aber das Wort hat dort keine Wirkung. Zuviel Information, zu viele Zeitungen'" (*SS*, 215). In this way a relatively sanguine view of East German censorship emerges. State intervention is not seen to affect the Volksbühne's work; in fact, the only explicit threats of theater censorship occur in Turkey and in West Berlin, when the narrator stages a play in a Turkish children's home in Kreuzberg (*SS*, 168).

Other characters soon challenge the narrator's view of the GDR as a site of political liberation and professional fulfillment, supplying the political consciousness that she lacks. Gabi Gysi tells her: "Dein Glück ist nicht das Glück der anderen. Du normalisierst die Mauer. Für dich bedeutet hier zu sein eine Erweiterung deiner Möglichkeiten, zu arbeiten und zu leben. Andere aber sehen ihre Möglichkeiten beschränkt" (*SS*, 182). Rudolf Bahro, one of the leading Marxist critics of the SED, warns the narrator against viewing the Volksbühne as representative of the GDR. According to the narrator he argues: "In der DDR haben bürokratische Mechanismen verhindert, daß durch Kritik der Sozialismus in der DDR lebendig erhalten wird. Den Bürokraten sei jemand, der viel Phantasie habe, nicht sympatisch. Am Theater gibt es diese Phantasie, die Bürokratie aber ist faul, der Wunsch nach Erfindungen sei tot" (*SS*, 91). But if theater is an enclave, it is an imperiled one. The narrator reports that her colleagues are nervous before the premiere of Müller's play *Die Bauern* even though the rehearsal has gone well (*SS*, 90). What she fails to realize is that this anxiety almost certainly has a strong political dimension: *Die Bauern* was a revised version of *Die Umsiedlerin*, which had provoked a major scandal at its premiere in 1961 and had not been performed since.[30] While the premiere passes without incident, Bahro's arrest and Biermann's expatriation signal that the cultural thaw — such as it was — is ending, and the narrator hears rumors of tensions between Besson and the Culture Ministry (*SS*, 233). At the end of the novel we sense that the Volksbühne's community is breaking up: Besson leaves for Paris with the narrator, and Langhoff departs for Hamburg.

Although *Alles, alles Liebe!* is set in the period identified in *Seltsame Sterne* as a cultural thaw, it offers a dystopian vision of institutional theater. Where Özdamar uses multiple perspectives to complicate the impression we receive of the GDR and its theater, Honigmann uses them to create a picture of universal institutional stagnation. Theaters function as closed communities, marginalizing anyone who threatens their homogeneity. While Anna's colleagues in Prenzlau are unaware of her Jewish identity, her physical appearance, artistic views, and arrival from Berlin all mark her as different. She is insulted as a "Zigeuner" on her way to the theater and shunned in the canteen (*AAL*, 5, 66). These experiences are of a different order from the difficulties Kai initially encounters in *Stilles Land*, and they are corroborated by Eva's struggles in Meiningen. Anna concludes that theater communities bear no resemblance to the ideals of the plays that they perform; they are workplaces like any other, populated by "sozialistische Theaterbeamte und kaputte Typen" (*AAL*, 135).

The contrast between the representation of GDR theater in *Seltsame Sterne* and *Alles, alles Liebe!* cannot simply be attributed to differences between East Berlin and the provinces. Honigmann refers to some of the same theater practitioners as Özdamar and to the Volksbühne canteen, but she never actually takes the reader inside. This gives the impression that her characters are on the fringes of the established theater world. In other, explicitly autobiographical texts Honigmann has written of her marginalization at the Volksbühne, where she "saß . . . mehr als Statistin zwischen den beiden Komplizen [Heiner Müller and the director Fritz Marquardt] an den langen Nachmittagen des Seufzens, Stöhnens und Schweigens, die Arbeitsgespräche genannt wurden."[31] Her literary and autobiographical reflections on her time at the Deutsches Theater — thinly disguised as the "Berliner Theater" in *Eine Liebe aus nichts* — also end in disappointment (DS, 156).

The question for Anna and her friends is whether they can create their own theater community either within or outside the official system. Sufficient like-minded practitioners do exist, but they are scattered across provincial theaters: Bosch (the director Jürgen Gosch) and Heidemarie are in Schwerin, Eva is in Meiningen, and Anna is in Prenzlau. Eva writes: "Das Schlimmste, Anna, ist, daß wir alle so vereinzelt sind. Ein Einzelner aber vermag am Theater auch nicht das geringste ausrichten. Wir müßten zusammen arbeiten und eine richtige Theatertruppe gründen können, wir und all die anderen von unseren Freunden, die genauso einsam und vereinzelt an den Provinztheatern sitzen" (*AAL*, 15–16). The characters repeatedly attempt to find an institutional base for their work, first in Schwerin, then Prenzlau, then Greifswald; yet the first two attempts fail and we assume that the third probably will, too. The system offers little opportunity for individual initiative, and state interference is emphasized at every turn. *Stella* is dropped in Schwerin — as indeed it was — and Bosch and Heidemarie are described as "verzweifelt" (*AAL*, 86).[32] In Prenzlau Anna has to hand over her production of Philipp Hafner's play *Der Furchtsame* to her rival and is dismissed by the manager (*AAL*, 163–64). This structure of repeated disappointment serves to counter postunification attempts by some former GDR theater practitioners and writers to relativize censorship, either by presenting it as a stimulus to creativity or by comparing it to the "censorship" of the free market.[33]

The only moments of hope in *Alles, alles Liebe!* are located outside institutional theater. Anna and her friends stage rehearsals for a private, unauthorized production of Lorca's play *Bernarda Albas Haus*, which Anna experiences as a form of liberation: "Bei unseren Bernarda-Proben ist es doch auch anders. Weil noch alles offen ist? Weil wir uns das Stück selbst ausgewählt haben? Weil wir so viel darüber gesprochen und gestritten haben? Weil wir nicht von Anfang an Rollen festgelegt haben? Weil wir noch an Spontaneität und Leidenschaft glauben?" (*AAL*, 136). Honigmann stresses, however, that this temporary niche is not a solution: the characters long to enact these principles in their daily work, "nicht nur an den Wochenenden," and all they actually want is to stage a "normal" play in a "normal" manner (*AAL*, 59). Moreover, references to the tensions that arose during their summer retreat suggest that withdrawal may itself result in stagnation. Eva comments, "In der Einsiedelei suchen wir Abgeschiedenheit und Einsamkeit, aber wenn wir ehrlich sind, langweilen wir uns dort auch ein bißchen, trotz der Anhänglichkeit aneinander und all der Kunst, die wir entfalten" (*AAL*, 17). The risk is that the closed world of the niche actually replicates the claustrophobia that the characters are trying to escape. Their efforts to create a private theater community emerge less as an attempt to enact a utopian ideal than as a means of damage limitation or as a survival strategy. This reaches its most drastic formulation when Anna, reflecting on her theater productions, wonders "was wir tun sollten oder müßten, damit wir . . . doch noch einen Platz für uns finden, an dem wir es vielleicht bis zum Ende aushalten und nicht aus dem Fenster springen müssen wie Stefans Mutter" (*AAL*, 34).

Conclusion

Dresen, Honigmann, and Özdamar use their representations of GDR theater to make contrasting claims about lived experience in the GDR and, by implication, its place in the cultural memory of the Berlin Republic. In 1992 Dresen adopted an inclusive, non-confrontational approach toward a target audience that had only just emerged from the GDR and was grappling with the challenges of unification. His film does not diminish the efforts or achievements of those who protested for change, but it does seek to recuperate authentic experience from the media images that flashed around the world in the autumn of 1989. In 2000 and 2003 respectively, Honigmann and Özdamar were engaging with the emergence of *Ostalgie* from positions outside mainstream eastern German discourse, from their respective positions as a German Jewish and a Turkish German writer. Honigmann writes as a victim of the GDR, resisting *Ostalgie* and attempts to recast eastern Germans as victims, in this case as the victims of unification. By contrast, events in *Seltsame Sterne* are mediated explicitly through the perspective of the immigrant and nomad: the protagonist has chosen to come to the GDR because of its theater, experiences it as a liberation compared to the Turkish dictatorship, and travels relatively freely between East and West Berlin. While Honigmann uses the multiple perspectives of the epistolary novel to confirm the experiences of the protagonist and create an impression of ubiquitous stagnation, Özdamar uses the multiple perspectives of her characters to complicate her narrator's idealistic view of the GDR. Her narrative thus testifies to the value and singularity of individual memory and to the importance of a pluralistic memory culture.

The different agendas of Dresen, Honigmann, and Özdamar mean that GDR theater comes to represent different things. *Stilles Land* offers us the *theatrum mundi*: *Godot* parallels the situation of the ensemble members, and the unnamed small town functions as a microcosm of provincial GDR society. For Özdamar's narrator and her colleagues the Volksbühne functions as an island of creativity, representing the aspirations and ideals that led Brecht and Langhoff to settle in the GDR after the Second World War. By these means she seeks to recuperate these ideals for the reunified Germany. Yet Honigmann's protagonist regards the GDR as having nothing in common with the ideals of the returning exiles, and *Alles, alles Liebe!* does not single out any values in the GDR of the 1970s that might be worth preserving. For Honigmann GDR theater is both a microcosm and a restricted enclave: institutional theater is a microcosm of an unhealthy, stagnant society, but private, unauthorized theater offers a means of creating something more authentic. Unlike Özdamar, however, she remains pessimistic about the viability of creative theater, emphasizing that it is compromised, short-lived, and possible only as long as it is tolerated by the state.

Notes

[1] Knut Lennartz, *Vom Aufbruch zur Wende: Theater in der DDR* (Velber: Erhard Friedrich, 1992), 58–59 (hereafter cited in text as *VA*).

[2] Loren Kruger, "Wir treten aus unseren Rollen heraus: Theater Intellectuals and Public Spheres," in *The Power of Intellectuals in Contemporary Germany*, ed. Michael Geyer (Chicago: U of Chicago P, 2001), 183–211, here 183.

[3] Michael Lorenz, "Das Deutsch-Sorbische Volkstheater als Keimzelle und Sprachrohr der Wende in Bautzen und Umgebung" (2005), Stadtarchiv Bautzen, Abgabe Michael Lorenz.

[4] Angela Kuberski, ed., *Wir treten aus unseren Rollen heraus: Dokumente des Aufbruchs Herbst '89*, Theaterarbeit in der DDR 19 (East Berlin: Zentrum für Theaterdokumentation und -information, 1990).

[5] *Stilles Land*, directed by Andreas Dresen (ex picturis, 1992, Filmgalerie 451, 2007); Barbara Honigmann, *Alles, alles Liebe!* (2000; Munich: DTV, 2003) (hereafter cited in text as *AAL*); Emine Sevgi Özdamar, *Seltsame Sterne starren zur Erde: Wedding — Pankow 1976/77* (2003; Cologne: Kiepenheuer & Witsch, 2004) (hereafter cited in text as *SS*).

[6] See Paul Cooke, *Representing East Germany since Unification: From Colonization to Nostalgia* (Oxford: Berg, 2005), 14.

34 ◆ LAURA BRADLEY

[7] Anklam had, however, experienced a period of notoriety from 1982 to 1984, when Frank Castorf was its chief director. See Laura Bradley, *Cooperation and Conflict: GDR Theatre Censorship, 1961–1989* (Oxford: Oxford UP, 2010), chapter 6.

[8] On *Das Leben der Anderen* see Thomas Lindenberger et al., "Dealing with the GDR Past in Today's Germany: *The Lives of Others*," *German Studies Review* 31, no. 3 (2008): 557–610.

[9] "Arbeitslosenzahlen in den alten und neuen Bundesländern 1975–2008," accessed 26 October 2009, http://www.sozialpolitik-aktuell.de/arbeitsmarkt-datensammlung.html.

[10] *Stilles Land*, DVD 1, undated interview with Andreas Dresen.

[11] Massimo Locatelli, "Ghosts of Babelsberg: Narrative strategies of the Wendefilm," in *Textual Responses to German Unification: Processing Historical and Social Change in Literature and Film*, ed. Carol Anne Costabile-Heming, Rachel J. Halverson, and Kristie A. Foell (Berlin: Walter de Gruyter, 2001), 211–24, here 215.

[12] For a brief discussion of the reception of the film see Laura G. McGee, "How Do We Tell Stories of What We Could Never Imagine? First East-West Encounters in German Feature Films from the Early 1990s by Andreas Dresen, Andreas Kleinert and Peter Kahane," *Colloquia Germanica* 40 (2007): 54–55.

[13] Kristie A. Foell, "History as Melodrama: German Division and Unification in Two Recent Films," in Costabile-Heming, *Textual Responses to German Unification*, 233–52, here 233.

[14] Undated interview with Dresen (see note 10).

[15] Wolf Biermann, "Noch," in *Mit Marx- und Engelszungen: Gedichte Balladen Lieder* (West Berlin: Klaus Wagenbach, 1976), 79.

[16] Heinrich von Kleist, *Der zerbrochne Krug* (Stuttgart: Philipp Reclam jun., 1993), 17.

[17] Anthony S. Coulson, "New Land and Forgotten Spaces: The Portrayal of Another Germany in Post-Unification Film," in *The New Germany: Literature and Society after Unification*, ed. Osman Durrani, Colin Good, and Kevin Hilliard (Sheffield: Sheffield Academic Press, 1995), 213–30, here 229.

[18] Seán Allan, "*Ostalgie*, Fantasy and the Normalization of East-West Relations in Post-Unification Comedy," in *German Cinema since Unification*, ed. David Clarke (London: Continuum, 2006), 105–26, here 113.

[19] Brecht explains the "Nicht, Sondern Prinzip" as follows: "Der Schauspieler soll bei allen wesentlichen Punkten zu dem, was er macht, noch etwas ausfindig, namhaft und ahnbar machen, was er nicht macht. Er sagt z. B. nicht: ich verzeihe dir, sondern: das wirst du mir bezahlen. . . . Gemeint ist: der Schauspieler spielt, was hinter dem Sondern steht; er soll es so spielen, daß man auch, was hinter dem Nicht steht, aufnimmt." See Bertolt Brecht, "Anweisungen an die Schauspieler," in *Werke: Große kommentierte Berliner und Frankfurter Ausgabe*, ed. Werner Hecht et al. (Frankfurt am Main and Berlin: Suhrkamp and Aufbau, 1993), 22.2:667–68, here 667.

[20] Gisela Rüß, ed., *Dokumente zur Kunst-, Literatur- und Kulturpolitik der SED 1971–1974* (Stuttgart: Seewald, 1976), 287.

[21] Moray McGowan, "Turkish-German Fiction since the Mid-1990s," in *Contemporary German Fiction: Writing in the Berlin Republic*, ed. Stuart Taberner (Cambridge: Cambridge UP, 2007), 196–214, here 201. For a discussion of the significance of *Der Bürgergeneral* in *Seltsame Sterne* see McGowan, "'Sie kucken beide an Milch Topf': Goethe's *Bürgergeneral* in Double Refraction," in *Language — Text — Bildung: Essays in Honour of Beate Dreike*, ed. Andreas Stuhlmann and Patrick Studer in cooperation with Gert Hofmann (Frankfurt am Main: Peter Lang, 2005), 79–88.

[22] Gabriele Eckart, "Barbara Honigmanns Briefroman *Alles, alles Liebe!*: Ein Beitrag zur García Lorca-Rezeption in der DDR," *Glossen 14* (2001), accessed 26 October 2009, http://www.dickinson.edu/glossen/heft14/geckart.html.

[23] Philippe Lejeune, *Le Pacte autobiographique* (Paris: Seuil, 1975).

[24] Barbara Honigmann, "Eine 'ganz kleine Literatur' des Anvertrauens," in *Das Gesicht wiederfinden: Über Schreiben, Schriftsteller und Judentum* (Munich: Carl Hanser, 2006), 7–29, here 26.

[25] For a fuller discussion of *Seltsame Sterne* as an example of life-writing, see Laura Bradley, "Recovering the Past and Recapturing the Present: Özdamar's *Seltsame Sterne starren zur Erde*," in *New German Literature: Life-Writing and Dialogues with the Arts*, ed. Julian Preece, Frank Finlay, and Ruth J. Owen (Berne: Peter Lang, 2007), 283–95.

[26] See Margaret Littler, "Cultural Memory and Identity Formation in the Berlin Republic," in Taberner, *Contemporary German Fiction*, 177–95, here 183. A similar concern to document the rapidly disappearing world of East Berlin can be seen in postunification publications comparing photographs of the city before and after unification. See Lyn Marven, "'Souvenirs de Berlin-Est': History, Photos and Form in Texts by Daniela Dahn, Irina Liebmann, and Sophie Calle," *Seminar* 43 (2007): 220–33.

[27] See for example Hermann Kurthen, Werner Bergmann, and Rainer Erb, eds., *Antisemitism and Xenophobia in Germany after Unification* (Oxford: Oxford UP, 1997).

[28] Simone Barck, "'Grundfrage: Antifaschistischer Widerstand': Zur Widerstandsrezeption in der DDR bis 1970," in *Frauen erinnern: Widerstand — Verfolgung — Exil 1933–1945*, ed. Inge Hansen and Beate Schneichel-Falkenberg (Berlin: Weidler, 2000), 216–32, here 217.

[29] John Pizer, "The Continuation of Countermemory: Emine Sevgi Özdamar's *Seltsame Sterne starren zur Erde*," in *German Literature in a New Century: Trends, Traditions, Transitions, Transformations*, ed. Katharina Gerstenberger and Patricia Herminghouse (New York: Berghahn, 2008), 135–52, here 135. Pizer notes but brushes aside one encounter between the narrator and "an East German racist," ignoring, for example, an anti-Semitic conversation that the narrator overhears between two elderly ladies (Pizer, 146; *SS*, 66).

[30] See Matthias Braun, *Drama um eine Komödie: Das Ensemble von SED und Staatssicherheit, FDJ und Ministerium für Kultur gegen Heiner Müllers "Die Umsiedlerin auf dem Lande" im Oktober 1961* (Berlin: Ch. Links, 1995).

[31] Barbara Honigmann, "Das Schiefe, das Ungraziöse, das Unmögliche, das Unstimmige," in *Das Gesicht wiederfinden*, 151–65, here 154 (hereafter cited in text as DS).

[32] Jürgen Gosch's planned production of Goethe's *Stella* was dropped in Schwerin after twenty-eight rehearsals in November 1975. See Bradley, *Cooperation and Conflict*, 136–37.

[33] See, e.g., Volker Ebersbach, "Brief vom 30. Dezember 1992," in *Fragebogen Zensur: Zur Literatur vor und nach dem Ende der DDR*, ed. Richard Zipser (Leipzig: Reclam, 1995), 108–11, here 109–10; and Klaus Frühauf, "Die neue, alte Zensur," in Zipser, *Fragebogen Zensur*, 147–48.

2: Melancholy and Historical Loss: Postunification Portrayals of GDR Writers and Artists

Anna O'Driscoll

THE POSTUNIFICATION ERA has seen a surge in melancholy sentiment and a renewed interest in the melancholy tradition and melancholy discourse, particularly in Germany.[1] This essay will analyze the melancholy evident in a number of narratives by former East German authors in conjunction with the notion of historical loss that has become dominant since the fall of the Berlin Wall. The texts — Christoph Hein's novel *Frau Paula Trousseau* (2007), Monika Maron's novels *Endmoränen* (2002) and *Ach Glück* (2007), and Christa Wolf's diary publication *Ein Tag im Jahr* (2003) — deal with both the pre- and postunification periods in East Germany either directly or indirectly. I will examine the protagonists' response to the changes brought about by unification (including Wolf's own reaction in *Ein Tag im Jahr*), as well as the effect these changes have had on their lives. Along with the melancholy subjectivity of the individual, a prevailing atmosphere of melancholy is evoked in these texts. However, the dominance of melancholy sentiments is not a phenomenon that has suddenly emerged in the postunification period; it was also in evidence in the former East Germany. Left-wing intellectuals, especially those in western Germany, some of whom retained an idealistic view of the GDR, lamented the loss of ideology following the fall of Communism. This loss of ideology has been accompanied by the concept of the end of history. The critical attention that has focused on this phenomenon is significant to our understanding of the aforementioned texts, but in an analysis of both Hein's and Wolf's narratives one must also take into account the sense of disillusionment and despair engendered by the lack of social and political progress in the GDR.

A brief examination of theoretical approaches to melancholy as it relates to historical experience will help to elucidate its manifestations in each of the texts under discussion. A changed relationship to historical time and an adherence to the idea of historical loss define the modern era. As Ludger Heidbrink suggests, the melancholy of the modern age following the French Revolution resulted from the emptiness engendered by a lack of control over historical time:

> Es wird sich zeigen, daß der Wille zur Einheit und die Sehnsucht nach dem Absoluten, die der Melancholie an der Moderne zugrunde lie-gen, von Anfang an in sich gebrochen sind. Die Herausbildung der Geschichte zu einem einheitlichen Prozeß . . . bedeutet . . . daß der Mensch . . . *der Herrschaft der historischen Zeit* ausgeliefert wird. . . . Die utopischen und verfallsgeschichtlichen Programme der Moderne sind gleichermaßen gegen die Leere der historischen Zeit gerichtet.[2]

A similar moment of historical disillusionment in our own times can be observed where postmodern art has abandoned political engagement in favor of a self-reflexivity that could be interpreted as neo-romantic: "Die postmoderne Kunst, von Ausnahmen abgesehen, ist weniger durch Zuversicht gekennzeichnet als durch politische Orientierungslosigkeit, Flucht in die Innerlichkeit und die Erneuerung romantisch-religiöser Mythologeme."[3] According to Heidbrink, since the fall of Communism the inability to find any future direction has become increasingly pro-nounced in the West. He considers Western capitalist society to have become ever more complex, but also more meaningless and monotonous due to the loss of fundamental sociopolitical progression; the belief in the possibility of a political utopia has been destroyed, and this has led to mel-ancholy becoming the dominant tone in social discourse, as well as repre-senting an individual approach to the present situation.[4] The break with the past at the turn of the nineteenth century may have been experienced as more profound and more disturbing than the caesura represented by the fall of the Berlin Wall; however, the sense of being trapped in an endlessly repetitive present, without the prospect of future progress, has reignited melancholy sentiments since the fall of the wall.

The loss of orientation following the collapse of the GDR has been addressed in different ways by each of the aforementioned authors, their perspectives and those of their protagonists being predicated on their experiences and perceptions of both GDR authoritarianism and the nature of political developments after 1989. The melancholy evident in their texts reflects their disillusionment with the lack of progress toward a more equal society and the continuing dominance of anti-humanistic materialism. Both Wolf and Hein were part of the minority who, following the collapse of East German institutions, called for a "Third Way" — a reformed Socialist state as an alternative to unification with West Germany. Maron, conversely, sided with the majority of East Germans, who looked forward to the prosperity that unification was expected to bring. Her increasing disenchantment with the realities of a market-driven economy and its effect on society is thematized in the novels under examination. The pro-tagonist of Maron's two novels and Hein's eponymous protagonist are both middle-aged women whose lives in reunified Germany are character-ized by lethargy and stagnation. However, just as each had very different experiences under totalitarian rule, so each protagonist's postunification sense of loss has divergent causes. It is significant that these are both female protagonists, their physical isolation in the East German country-side signifying their exclusion from the nucleus of power in Berlin. Yet gender is not the primary factor in the characters' sense of isolation: both Maron's Johanna and her husband, Achim, feel that the new, fast-paced society does not regard them as valuable citizens, and the disillusionment of Hein's Paula with the political system is due to the disadvantages she experienced as an artist rather than as a woman. Unlike these fictional protagonists, Wolf had always been involved in political life and partici-pated in the "Round Table" (*Runder Tisch*) discussions in Berlin following the fall of the wall. She is also old enough to have experienced the Second World War and to have taken part in efforts to build a Socialist society. Her basic ideals have not changed, which makes her dismay at witnessing the effects of rampant capitalism all the greater.

Endmoränen, Monika Maron

The experience of melancholy boredom in postunification society is appar-ent in Monika Maron's *Endmoränen*. The protagonist, Johanna, has retreated to the summerhouse among the end moraines of the East German countryside that she and Achim had acquired several years earlier. While she habitually spends the summer here, this is the first year in which she resists returning to Berlin at the end of the season. She feels weighed down by the meaninglessness of her life, which is connected to the approach of old age and her position as an older person in the new postu-nification society. Johanna thus falls into a lethargic state from which she is unable to free herself. Having abandoned her work on a biography of Wilhelmine Enke, the mistress of Friedrich Wilhelm II, she spends her days looking out at the natural world around her. The narrative is characterized by a distinct absence of significant events and is dominated by the repeti-tive routine of a character who has lost all sense of purpose and direction. Ironically, it was Wilhelmine Enke's sense of purpose and determination, maintained over a lifetime of struggle against her adversaries, that origi-nally attracted Johanna to her. She felt that by studying Enke's life she could better understand her own, in particular why she was unable to make the most of the new opportunities available to her. However, two years later Johanna can no longer find any connections between her own life and that of her subject.

The connections between melancholy, repetition, and boredom were first illuminated by Kierkegaard in *Repetition* (although this kind of existential boredom, brought about by the sense of endless monotony, is directly related to the ancient concept of *taedium vitae*) and are expressed from a psychopathological point of view in the analysis of the psychiatrist Johann Glatzel: "Der Stillstand der erlebnisimmanenten Zeit und das zwanghafte Auf-der-Stelle-Treten, das Nicht-abschließen-Können des Zwangskranken, begegnen als lähmende Wiederholung, als Wiederkehr des ewig Gleichen in der Verfassung der Langeweile."[5] The association between repetition and boredom is obvious in Johanna's life, as is her inability to find a way out of her inertia: "An den Abenden, die schon lang waren, sehnte ich mich nach der Stadt. Einmal beschloß ich, am nächsten Morgen abzureisen, und dann blieb ich doch."[6] The melancholic type becomes isolated from the outside world due to the sense that it is moving ever faster while his/her life has come to a standstill. Furthermore, the protagonist feels that she no longer has a significant role to play in contemporary society. As she nears old age she feels her value to society has greatly diminished: "Für uns [beginnt] bald diese öde lange Restzeit . . ., zwanzig oder dreißig Jahre Restzeit, in der wir nur noch als Zielgruppe von Verkäufern aller Branchen und als katastrophaler Kostenfaktor für die Krankenkassen wichtig sind und sonst von skandalöser Unwichtigkeit" (*E*, 55–56).

The protagonist's detachment from the present highlights a further melancholy association, namely the ability to conjure ghosts from her past. However, her exchange with these ghosts has positive implications, for it leads her to a better understanding of herself. It could thus be considered as a metaphor for a communication with her inner self: "Plötzlich habe ich einen Satz im Kopf, der vorher nicht darin war . . . so beten die armen Gottlosen, andere gehen zum Therapeuten oder in die Selbsthilfegruppe" (*E*, 216). Hence this is also a spiritual experience for Johanna, an alternative to religious belief. The subjective appropriation of religious or spiritual beliefs is a mark of the postmodern period, as seen above. In the context of the narratives under discussion, this can be regarded as a facet of a melancholy subjectivity more narrowly defined by the postunification era in the former East Germany.

The protagonist's experience of inwardness and inertia is accordingly not set within an ahistorical space. While there is the sense of a romantic orchestration in Johanna's melancholy suffering, it is grounded within the historical reality of the loss of Communism in East Germany. Her lethargy and boredom represent not merely a diffuse sentimentality but a response to her position within postunification eastern German society. Her profession as a biographer provides a vehicle through which the experience of historical rupture can be explored. The primary reason for Johanna's difficulty in making progress with her work seems to be that she has lost her connection to the past and to the notion of historical continuity that enabled her to identify with her biographical subjects. In researching the lives of others she previously found historical precedents for her own experiences and could see her life grounded within a logical continuation of historical time. She can no longer find these connections with the past, however, and her interest in Wilhelmine Enke's life subsides: "Ich muß wohl gehofft haben, irgendein zufällig gefundener Satz, entsprungen einer ebenso zufälligen Eingebung eines längst gestorbenen oder noch lebenden Menschen, könnte . . . das Muster wieder sichtbar werden lassen, in das ich meine Erlebnisse und Gedanken bis vor kurzem noch verwoben hatte und die nun durch meinen Kopf schwirrten wie Atome, denen ihr Kern abhanden gekommen war" (*E*, 151–52).

The lack of historical continuity in her own life is analogous to the lack of historical progression in the postunification period. The individual loss of future orientation has been engendered by a sociopolitical lack of direction and any meaningful alternatives to the present system. Despite the GDR's political stagnation, many retained the hope that the regime would one day be ousted; however, the visions of a better future that sustained the majority of East Germans no longer carry weight in reunified Germany. Johanna's disillusionment with conditions in the new society is highlighted by her choice of career. Before the *Wende* her work provided her with a sense of importance and a feeling of excitement: she could express her opposition to the GDR regime through the inclusion of secret subtexts in her biographies and in this way connect with other like-minded individuals. It might seem "eine ganz idiotische Wichtigkeit" (*E*, 57), as the protagonist herself admits, but many writers in the GDR were held in high regard by the general public, as Maron has shown in "Das neue Elend der Intellektuellen" (1990):

> Die Schriftsteller in der DDR waren eine besonders verwöhnte Gruppe ihres Berufsstandes. Damit meine ich weniger die von der Obrigkeit gewährten Privilegien als eine allgemeine Verehrung, die ihnen zuteil wurde, selbst von Menschen, zu deren Lebensgewohnheiten das Lesen von Büchern nicht gehörte. . . . Selbst wer der Zensur anheimfiel, wußte sich im anderen Deutschland um so aufmerksamer gelesen und auch im eigenen Land genossen als die verbotene Frucht.[7]

This is a somewhat one-sided and trivial view of the experience of the writer in the GDR. The effects of censorship may not have distressed those who were content merely to court fame; however, those who maintained a belief in the true ideals of Socialism and were committed to contributing to public life conceivably found it difficult to accept their continuing exclusion from public discourse, as is evident in the case of Christa Wolf, whose melancholic despair at the stagnating conditions of life in the GDR will be discussed below.

As for Johanna, the nature of her relationship to this society can be discerned through the lens of her chosen genre. That writing biographies is a vicarious occupation is here borne out in the protagonist's recourse to the experiences of historical subjects to comprehend her own life. By seeing her life as part of a historical continuum she could imbue it with meaning, despite the absurd restrictions imposed by the dictatorial regime. Cheating the censor, a small-scale deceit that she felt connected her to those who would read and understand the subtext of her words, previously gave her life some meaning. It was lived in the shadow of her biographical subjects since she worked in the service of their immortality. Following the collapse of Communism, writing biographies quickly becomes a mundane activity, and Johanna can find no replacement in the new society for her former negative attachment to the GDR regime. The euphoria with which she greeted the fall of the Berlin Wall soon dies away due to her own lack of motivation to embrace the opportunities now open to her, as well as her disillusionment at the lack of a socially progressive alternative to the old system.

The Search for a New Beginning in *Ach Glück*

Ach Glück, the sequel to *Endmoränen*, relates the experiences and viewpoints of both Johanna and her husband, Achim. It is set within a single day — the day on which Johanna leaves for Mexico and Achim is left alone to wander the city and wonder when or if she will come back. Much of the narrative is taken up with their retrospective musings on the changes that have occurred in their lives in the last four months since the fateful appearance of Bredow, the dog that Johanna found at the side of the highway at the end of the previous novel. She believes that the dog was left for her as a sign that she needs to make changes in her life. She also believes that the dog is communicating a message to her about the simplicity of achieving happiness:

> Ich frage mich, ob bei mehr als neunzigprozentiger Übereinstimmung der Gene sich nicht auch in mir etwas finden lassen müsste von der rätselhaften Fähigkeit dieser Kreatur, ob es nicht auch mir gelingen könnte, wenigstens mir selbst als Sinn zu genügen und froh zu sein, weil es mich gibt, wie der Hund froh ist, dass es ihn gibt.[8]

The author is doubtless aware that the dog holds a significant position within the melancholy tradition, having long been considered the companion of the melancholic type, and that this association seems to cast a shadow over the protagonist's hopes for the future or even to parody them. On the one hand Bredow is portrayed as having a wholly positive influence over Johanna's life, her relationship with him having rekindled her belief in destiny as well as her communion with nature and with the spiritual realm. On the other hand these preoccupations facilitate a continuing withdrawal from objective reality and increased alienation from her husband.

Johanna's life has been stagnating for some time as was already evident in *Endmoränen*, and she yearns for some future direction. She regards the dog as a sign but also sees him as much more than a messenger. Apart from enabling her to relate to her more primitive, instinctive self, Bredow's affection has opened her eyes to what has been missing from her life: "Liebe, hatte sie damals gedacht, es geht um Liebe" (*AG*, 106). Achim, the person seemingly unable to provide the love his wife needs, reads Johanna's relationship to the dog as marking the beginning of her withdrawal from him. He believes that she relates to Bredow not merely as an animal but as a higher being: "Als Hund mochte er ihn, wogegen Johanna ein höheres Wesen in ihm sah . . . das von Natur aus recht hatte, mit göttlicher Kompetenz ausgestattet" (*AG*, 30). It is only in retrospect, after Johanna has left for Mexico, that Achim realizes that it was her spiritual bond with the dog that had set his wife on a new course. He remembers the "absonderliche Geschichten" (*AG*, 31) she used to recount about her nightly excursions with Bredow, which led to the reawakening of a further link to the spiritual realm embodied in the communication with trees, an activity that Johanna had previously renounced due to Achim's ridicule. Her communion with ghosts was already depicted in *Endmoränen*, and she pursues this communication on another plane here. While this is for her a positive experience and represents an antidote to contemporary materialism, it also signifies her reluctance to come to terms in a rational way with the conditions of her life in postunification Germany. She has lost the sense of purpose that her opposition to the totalitarian regime of the GDR provided and has nothing to replace it but "öde, steppenähnliche Zeit" (*AG*, 106).

In order to escape the prospect of these endless, empty years, Johanna has decided to follow Natalia Timofejewna, a Russian acquaintance with whom she has been in email contact, to Mexico City. Natalia, in turn, is in search of her old friend Leonora Carrington. Johanna has been inspired by the indomitable spirit of both elderly women, which has been communicated through her correspondence with the former as well as the surrealist art of the latter (Carrington was romantically connected with Max Ernst earlier in her life). The novel ends with her arrival in Mexico, and so we never learn whether this trip will really change her life. It seems that she is unable to realize the "wunderlicher Anfang" that was anticipated at the end of *Endmoränen* and spends the duration of the novel in "diesem monströsen Blechbehälter," finding the experience of traveling between time zones, places, and languages the most unrealistic of possible states; only the expanse of clouds beneath the airplane, which resembles a covering of snow, affords the illusion of proximity to the earth (*AG*, 86). This unrealistic state further emphasizes the detachment from historical experience seen in the previous novel, and the title of the novel itself is ironic, as it appears to disparage any possibility of true happiness. The protagonist is suddenly aware of this at the point of her departure: "Sie hatte sogar flüchtig daran gedacht umzukehren, die ganze kindische Flucht abzublasen, weil auch ein paar Wochen Mexico nichts daran ändern konnten, dass sie alt wurde, dass ihrer beider Leben ein für alle Mal seine Richtung genommen hatte und ihre Wünsche nicht mehr die gleichen waren" (*AG*, 186).

So although *Ach Glück* purports to portray the hope of a new beginning, on closer inspection it is almost as melancholy as *Endmoränen*. Johanna's own awareness of the futility of her temporary escape from her life emphasizes this sense of melancholy, as does the knowledge that she and her husband are now too old to make any radical changes in their lives and will inevitably stay together, despite the fact that they no longer understand one other. Johanna accuses Achim of turning his back on the world and, more importantly, of turning his back on her; however, Achim does not believe that his wife will actually leave. It is only after he has waved goodbye to her at the airport that he wonders if Johanna has left him for good. He even compares this day to the day his mother died: "Den ganzen Tag war er gegen die Endgültigkeit angelaufen, an diesem Dienstag vor fast dreißig Jahren. Wie heute. Nur dass Johanna noch lebte" (*AG*, 205–6). The evocation of finality and the resigned tone in which it is expressed suggest that Achim is willing to reconcile himself to the loss of his wife. During the day, while looking at the Palast der Republik, he starts to reminiscence about their shared past: "Unsere ehemalige Jugend, dachte er, unsere ehemalige Jugend in diesem ehemaligen Staat" (*AG*, 91). By the close of the day it seems that their true lives have been relegated to the past, their present existence representing merely a barren end phase. However, nostalgia for the past entails nostalgia only for the hope and energy of youth, not for any aspect of the defunct GDR regime. Indeed, Achim and Johanna regard the subjugation to totalitarian rule as punishment for the crimes of the Holocaust. Consequently, they despise the attitude of those former West Germans who opposed unification and were happy to allow those in the East to suffer this punishment alone (*AG*, 198). Their jubilation at the collapse of the GDR dissipates once they recognize that the equal and fair society they had hoped for will not materialize. As East Germans their skills and experience are of little worth in the capitalist economy. Johanna fears that her areas of expertise are no longer relevant or important and thus will not be sufficient to sustain her in the years to come (*E*, 37), while Achim fails to gain promotion and must work under a mediocre boss who would never have secured his position as head of a renowned institute were he not from West Germany (*AG*, 166–67). Both nevertheless realize that they cannot hope for any change in their conditions, a realization that provokes Johanna's desire to escape.

Frau Paula Trousseau, Christoph Hein

Hein's novel relates the life story of the eponymous artist from her child-hood in the GDR in the 1950s to her death by suicide in about the year 2000. The narrative's key event is revealed at the beginning, which sets up an analytical framework within which the protagonist's eventual decision to commit suicide will be interpreted. The action takes place on two dif-ferent temporal levels, one of which deals with the protagonist's adult life and is related in the first person, the second of which reveals details of her childhood and adolescence and is related by a third-person narrator. Through this narrative strand the reader is immediately immersed in a childhood dominated by a father's unrelenting tyranny and a mother's despair. The child lives in fear of her father's verbal, and at times physical, abuse. She also lives in fear that her mother, who has already attempted to commit suicide a number of times, will one day succeed.

Through first-person narration we learn of Paula's later attempts to commit suicide. The episode that brought her closest to death took place in her mid- to late teens, following a painful rejection. At the age of nine-teen she agrees to marry Hans Trousseau although she does not love him. In fact, after her anguished experiences she vows never to fall in love again, a promise she will keep for the rest of her life. The marriage with Hans turns out to have been a disastrous mistake. She is much younger than he and he treats her as such, believing her desire to attend art college a child-ish whim that she will abandon once she has settled into marriage and motherhood. In order to speed up this process he replaces her contracep-tive pills with placebos, but when she becomes pregnant, Paula cannot be deterred from moving to Berlin to study art. As she tells her mother, "Das Malen ist für mich das Wichtigste, viel wichtiger als Heirat und Liebe. Ich sterbe, wenn ich nicht malen kann."[9] During divorce proceedings a couple of years later, Paula gives up her daughter as the price she feels she must pay for her freedom. Her subsequent relationships with men are conducted in a cold and calculating manner. By the end of her life her only meaning-ful relationships are with her son, Michael, and her lifelong friend, Kathi, the last one to see her before she departs for France, where she will soon after be found lying dead in a shallow river.

Paula's apprehension of the world is dominated by abiding emotional detachment, emphasized through the recurring melancholy motifs of cold-ness and numbness, as well as fear. The connection of these motifs with her experiences at the hands of men suggests that such experiences represent a primary source of the protagonist's melancholy. Certainly the continuing effects of patriarchal structures in contemporary society are an obvious preoccupation of the author. He has commented elsewhere that patriarchy is a hierarchical structure that subjugates men as well as women, a percep-tion that is reflected in a number of his novels.[10] However, a focus on the

effect of patriarchal dominance would elide the more particular phenomenon of an artist's life in the GDR — and a female artist at that. Accordingly,
the novel's references to the GDR's political and cultural stagnation are
more illuminating for an examination of this protagonist.

Following the fall of the Berlin Wall, Hein reiterated sentiments he
(and many others) had previously expressed regarding the inertia that
characterized the GDR: "Dieses Gefühl von Vergeblichkeit oder Auf-der-
Stelle-Treten, das in der DDR sehr stark war, diese soziale Geborgenheit,
aber gleichzeitig eine Unbeweglichkeit, die die Nähe zu versteinerten
Verhältnissen hatte. Und das wurde dann noch mit den entsprechenden
Parolen, dieses: Fortschritt, Fortschreiten, garniert. Das war etwas, was die
DDR gekennzeichnet hat." Hein does not directly thematize the sense of
futility at the lack of any historical progress, yet it constitutes the underlying tone throughout the novel. It is most directly expressed in the portrayal of how little the cultural and aesthetic values of the GDR elite
changed over time (*FP*, 250). The immediate negative reaction of Paula's
professors to her abstract portrayal of a snow-covered landscape demonstrates this further (*FP*, 275, 277), and this lack of progress is accompanied
by the hypocrisy of the GDR elite who constantly proclaimed the progres-
siveness of the state, as well as by the hypocrisy that many citizens, especially those in positions of authority, were forced to engage in. Consequently,
a profoundly cynical attitude dominates all levels of public life.

Paula encounters this cynicism with some surprise when she embarks
on a relationship with Professor Waldschmidt, one of her art professors.
She had thought that he and his colleagues believed their own rhetoric but
now finds that they, along with other prominent figures from various intellectual and artistic fields, are united in their contempt for the regime (*FP*,
228). This private opposition remains private of course, and is of no use to
Paula when her work flouts the established aesthetic conventions. Her
most accomplished piece of work during her time at the Kunsthochschule
is the aforementioned painting of a landscape that is barely perceptible
under a covering of snow. This "weißes Bild" is a significant motif in the
text as a symbol for the destruction of Paula's artistic potential through
censorship. Prof. Waldschmidt dismisses the painting as "modernistische
Scheiße," and she is warned to get rid of it immediately or both she and
her lecturers will face severe penalties. Her defiance nevertheless continues;
as a consequence of the views expressed in her final written exams Paula is
accused of cosmopolitanism and formalism, charges that were commonly
directed at those whose work or artistic conceptions did not correspond to
the realist norm. Having left college, Paula is forced to conform to the
aesthetic strictures in order to earn a living and finally loses the artistic
vision embodied in her white landscape, a vision of nothingness.

Living under such a repressive regime would have a profoundly negative effect on the protagonist's artistic potential, despite the fact that she

remains politically apathetic throughout the Communist era. However, it is only in the aftermath of unification that the personal consequences of both physical and cultural segregation from the West are really brought home to her. As Paula had never been able to see the originals of the paintings she admired, she was deprived of an important stimulus for her own work. She realizes that this was the price that she personally had to pay "für den Riss durch diese Welt" (*FP*, 515–16) and that she is now too old to regain what she has lost.

As for the portrayal of the postunification era in the novel, it is apparent that Hein has lost hope that this new society will lead to substantial improvements in the conditions of ordinary people. Following the fall of the Berlin Wall Hein had expressed the desire that the GDR would free itself from Stalinism and that Socialism would prevail in a more authentic form. The stagnation he feared would set in anew if this opportunity were squandered finds expression in this novel. It is specifically depicted in the situations of those who have lost their jobs and those who had to give up the professions that they were trained for and take on more capitalist-oriented occupations. There is no guarantee of success in these occupations, however, since capitalist enterprises had difficulty gaining a foothold in the immediate aftermath of unification, when most citizens of the former East still lacked personal wealth. For instance, Paula's neighbor Frau Dickert used to work as an agricultural economist and is now employed as an insurance agent. She tells Paula about the difficult situation she and her husband are in:

> Ich dachte anfangs, nun würde ich mit Menschen arbeiten, könnte ein paar Leuten helfen, aber ich muss jetzt sehr darauf achten, wo ich selbst bleibe. Ich brauche neue Abschlüsse, die Leute haben kein Geld mehr, und ich versuche, ihnen etwas einzureden. Mein Mann hat schon seit zwei Jahren keine Arbeit, er kommt am Morgen gar nicht mehr aus dem Bett. (*FP*, 530–31)

While the protagonist is able to continue in her profession, like many other artists at the time she has problems in selling her work after the *Wende*. She and Frau Dickert are now the youngest members of the community but, although only in their fifties, feel as if they are "uralt" (*FP*, 531). The fall of the wall seems to mark a kind of turning point for Paula, to represent the approach of old age. Visiting Berlin a week after the wall came down, she perceives the city as suddenly strange and sinister: "Ich war auf dem Wege, eine Dorftrine zu werden, die sich in der Großstadt ängstigt" (*FP*, 511). Consequently she views the upheavals of the time with interest but not with excitement (*FP*, 509–10).

The rapid changes following the fall of the Berlin Wall were evidently difficult for the older generations to come to terms with. Many of them were left alone as their children moved to the cities to find work, and those who would have liked to move themselves were trapped by the fact that they could not sell their homes (*FP*, 531–32). The difficulty of adjusting to the conditions of the new society in turn led those of middle age, such as Paula, to feel older than they were, like Maron's protagonist as well. Paula's lethargy is likewise reflected in a lack of interest in her work. She admits that, like Frau Dickert, she has difficulty getting up in the morning and does not feel the accustomed excitement when beginning a new composition. While this is a development that perhaps would have occurred even if unification had not taken place, it has been spurred on by the financial difficulties caused by the changeover to market capitalism and by the general sense of stagnation that exists in the postunification East. Moreover, the notion of historical loss is augmented by the realization of the personal loss caused by separation from the West. Before unification Paula had been content to compose her work in private, maintaining as little contact as possible with the outside world. Following the Berlin Wall's collapse, when she is able to see the originals of paintings she admires, she realizes the extent of her loss. So many sources of inspiration had been closed off to her and she is now too old to draw inspiration from them. While she embraces the freedom to travel to the West, it leads above all to a bitter confrontation with her lost potential.

Ein Tag im Jahr, Christa Wolf

Christa Wolf's diary gives an account of 27 September of each year from 1960 to 2000. She explains that this project was initiated when a Moscow newspaper called all writers of the world to describe their experiences of 27 September 1960 as precisely as possible. She was fascinated by the idea and decided to continue to chronicle the same day every year, which she was still committed to doing at the time of publication. By capturing everyday events and experiences as well as her perception of national and world affairs, Wolf hoped to fight against the inexorable loss of self (*Dasein*) that is brought about by forgetfulness. It is everyday occurrences and experiences that are most precious to her, since these everyday moments are the ones that retrospectively constitute "gelebte Zeit." Yet when looking back on one's life, one realizes that it amounts to more than just the sum of all of these moments. The question of principal interest for Wolf is therefore: "Wie kommt *Leben* zustande?" She writes

> Ist Leben identisch mit der unvermeidlich, doch rätselhaft vergehenden Zeit? Während ich diesen Satz schreibe, vergeht Zeit; gleichzeitig entsteht — und vergeht — ein winziges Stück meines Lebens. So setzt sich Leben aus unzähligen solcher mikroskopischen Zeit-Stücke zusammen? Merkwürdig aber, daß man es nicht ertappen kann. Es entwischt dem beobachtenden Auge, auch der fleißig

notierenden Hand, und hat sich am Ende — auch am Ende eines Lebensabschnitts — hinter unserem Rücken nach unserem geheimen Bedürfnis zusammengefügt: gehaltvoller, bedeutender, spannungsreicher, sinnvoller, geschichtenträchtiger.[11]

By attempting to describe one day a year in as much detail as possible, Wolf hopes to save at least a fraction of these moments in time from oblivion. She laments not only the fact that they are lost from memory but also that this loss brings with it a sense of transience and futility, described as "Zwillingsschwestern des Vergessens" (*ET*, 6). Both of these sentiments are closely associated with melancholy and with the melancholic relationship with time.

The philosophical realization that our lives are overshadowed by death brings about a sense of transience and futility. Throughout her life Wolf seems to have been haunted by the fear of self-destruction and by thoughts of death. A psychic mechanism of self-conjured fears protects her from the greater evils of the world outside (*ET*, 248) but does not protect against feelings of failure and the painful recognition that her efforts to commit herself to this society have been in vain: "Mein Bedauern über die viele verlorene Zeit, diese jahrzehntelange Anstrengung, mich 'hier' zu lösen, meine Unfähigkeit, 'drüben' eine Alternative zu sehn [*sic*]" (*ET*, 272). Following the death of a relative, which may have been at least partly due to medical negligence, Wolf undergoes a similar experience to that brought forth by an exhibition of *vanitas* art, except that it is marked by an acknowledgment of personal responsibility: "Nachts wurde ich mehrmals wach, schaudernd. Daß wir alle sterben müssen? Nicht nur das, glaube ich. Daß wir falsch gelebt haben und leben? Ja. Das vielleicht noch mehr" (*ET*, 414). This acknowledgment can be understood within the context of previous comments in which Wolf expresses a recurring sense of regret that she does not have the courage to put herself in danger by speaking out publicly against injustice, a failure she attempts to compensate for by sharing the prize money she regularly receives (*ET*, 410). While recognizing her failure, and perhaps that of other like-minded citizens, Wolf does not offer an alternative approach to life in the GDR, seeming rather to view a move to the West as the only option, albeit not one that she can entertain since she continues to consider herself a Socialist. As already mentioned, the predominant tone of Wolf's diary is of futility. The growing realization that there is nothing she can do to effect real changes in society provokes this sentiment to a greater extent than her personal fears, which also express the hopelessness and futility of her existence but act primarily as a protective shield from the greater dangers of the world outside.

In the early years of the GDR Wolf was burdened by an increasing disillusionment with the gap between the elite and ordinary citizens, and with the elite's blindness to the disastrous state of affairs that prevailed in both a practical and an ideological sense. On the one hand she witnessed the life-endangering shortcomings that existed in the state's hospitals (to name but one example); on the other hand the overemphasis on material interests led to a lack of ideas and of ideals among the people. This absence of intellectual or moral engagement with social or political issues led to widespread mental torpor, the extreme consequence of which was a complete numbing of the senses: "Da kann der Patient weder Schmerz noch Freude empfinden, sondern ist eben stumpf, beklagt sich darüber in bewegten Worten, *empfindet* aber den Verlust eigentlich nicht mehr, sondern beklagt ihn nur aus der Erinnerung" (*ET*, 94). While this is an expression of a pathological condition, similar symptoms could be observed among the population at large, according to Wolf, which seemed to illustrate the collective experience of living under a tyrannical regime (see *ET*, 94). This deadening of the emotions was intermingled with a general lack of hope for the future and a tendency toward forgetfulness, all of which were regarded as being caused by the conditions of GDR society. While observing people as they went about their daily lives Wolf asked herself what they hoped for, or whether they had any hopes for the future at all, either for themselves or for their children. She wondered if their apparent apathy was due to the fact that they had become tired of hoping (*ET*, 279). Forgetfulness is likewise caused by lethargy, but it is also the result of an excess of negative stimuli, as the author notes in her diary from 1981: "Nicht nur die oft genannte Überflutung mit Reizen, auch die *Art* der Reize mag den Gedächtnisinstrumenten, die ja keineswegs neutral, sondern emotional geladen sind, zuwider sein" (*ET*, 285).

Wolf eventually accepted her powerlessness and resigned herself to the status quo. This was signaled above all by the purchase of a summerhouse in Mecklenburg in 1973, which functioned as a place of retreat not only for the Wolfs but also for a number of their friends. Following the furor caused by the Wolf Biermann expatriation, her need for detachment reached its peak (see *ET*, 223). However, she realized, of course, that such a safe haven did not really exist and that she would always remain trapped between two fronts, between those who considered her too outspoken or critical of the GDR regime and those who believed that she was not critical enough. With the publication of *Was bleibt* in 1990 and the subsequent release of the files that implicated her as an IM (*Inoffizieller Mitarbeiter*) of the Stasi from 1959 to 1962,[12] the attacks against her became most virulent. Those commentators in the FRG who had previously considered her a dissident now declared her to be a *Staatsdichterin*.

Wolf sought consolation and meaning in her increasing attachment to a spiritual conception of the interaction between mind, body, and soul. In her emphasis on transcendent experiences she resembles the protagonist of Maron's novels. However, her interest is in investigating the way in which mind, body, and soul interact rather than in communing with ghosts or spirits. Her belief in the transcendent has to do with the power of the human being to transcend the constraints of material existence. The description of an out-of-body experience, for which its author is neither able nor willing to provide proof, is reminiscent of Wolf's own sentiments: such phenomena cannot be explained within accepted paradigms, since these paradigms do not allow for such experiences in the first place (*ET*, 313–14).

The interaction between mind, body, and soul continued to interest Wolf after the fall of the Berlin Wall, which did not lead to the more humanistic or holistic outlook that she might have hoped for. She had recognized that the primacy of a materialistic, rationalistic worldview had led to mental and emotional stagnation not only in the GDR but also in West Germany. Both societies had lost sight of their ideals of an equal and fair democracy, the former having become fixated on the oppressive control of all areas of public life and the latter on possession and consumption to the detriment of the rights of ordinary citizens (*ET*, 440). However, the demise of the GDR did not result in the formation of an alternative Socialist state, but instead gave way to a society dominated by narrow-minded greed: "Alles [läuft] auf den heutigen utopiefreien Zustand zu, in dem die einzelnen Interessengruppen durch ihr zähes Ringen um Vorteile, um Pfennig und Mark, zusammengehalten werden und Worte wie 'Gemeinsinn', 'Solidarität' nur noch hohl klingen und unverbindlichen Sonntagsreden vorbehalten sind" (*ET*, 624).

The continuing disregard for the personal needs of the individual is something that Wolf wishes to counteract in this diary. For her the engagement with subjective experience is the only means of countering the objectification of the human being (*ET*, 7–8). The assertion of her own subjectivity in this publication signifies a multilayered attempt to address the unbridled consumerism of contemporary society and to save from oblivion both the seemingly insignificant incidents of daily life and historical events. Wolf further wishes to prevent the events of recent history from being reduced to easy, manageable formulas and to facilitate the reexamination of preconceived ideas (*ET*, 8).

Conclusion

A key issue in the above considerations is the portrayal of the caesura of 1989 in the texts. The authors and protagonists occupy varying positions in relation to the loss of Communism and to unification. Monika Maron's protagonist, Johanna, regards the *Wende* as "ein Wunder" but becomes disenchanted with the materialistic society that quickly develops, as did Maron herself. Christoph Hein and Christa Wolf, while welcoming the demise of the GDR regime, regret that the opportunity to establish a new Socialist state was lost. In fact Hein's protagonist, Paula Trousseau, maintains her indifference to politics throughout her life. Her melancholy, like Wolf's, is equally connected with the loss of political development during the Communist era and the continuing stagnation of the postunification period, whereas the postunification melancholy of Maron's protagonist is conditioned by a sense of redundancy: her former activities and abilities have suddenly become irrelevant and unimportant under the new conditions. In none of the texts are the events of 1989 marked as the seismic shift that they represented for most East Germans. For the middle-aged women of the novels the *Wende* did not bring about any meaningful changes to their circumstances. Indeed unlike Wolf, who in late 1989 took part in discussions to establish a new constitution for East Germany, they are portrayed as being at a remove from the nucleus of historical change, which was negotiated largely by men.[13] There is no sense that they desire a functioning role in shaping political change; nevertheless, the awareness of their irrelevance to society engenders the feeling of being old before their time.

Notes

[1] A renewed surge in melancholy discourse is evidenced by Lutz Walther's anthology of writings on melancholy *Melancholie* (Leipzig: Reclam, 1999) and Wolf Lepenies's sociological study *Melancholie und Gesellschaft, mit einer neuen Einleitung: Das Ende der Utopie und die Wiederkehr der Melancholie* (Frankfurt am Main: Suhrkamp, 1998), as well as the philosophical analyses of Ludger Heidbrink, including his *Melancholie und Moderne* (Munich: Wilhelm Fink, 1994) and *Entzauberte Zeit: Der melancholische Geist der Moderne* (Munich: Hanser, 1997). Engagement with the melancholy tradition has also gained prominence in the realm of visual art as demonstrated by the exhibition "Saturn, Melancholie, Genie," which was staged at the Hamburger Kunsthalle 31 March–31 May 1992, and the exhibition "Melancholy — Genius and Madness in the West," which was held at the Galeries Nationales du Grand Palais, Paris, October 2005–January 2006 and in the Neue Nationalgalerie, Berlin, February–May 2006.

[2] Heidbrink, *Melancholie und Moderne*, 22; italics in the original.

[3] Heidbrink, *Melancholie und Moderne*, 16.

[4] Heidbrink, *Melancholie und Moderne*, 18–19.

[5] See, respectively, Søren Kierkegaard, *Repetition: An Essay in Experimental Psychology*, trans. Walter Lowrie (London: Oxford UP, 1942); Ludwig Völker, *Langeweile: Untersuchungen zur Vorgeschichte eines literarischen Motivs* (Munich: Fink, 1975), 133–35; and Johann Glatzel, *Melancholie und Wahnsinn: Beiträge zur Psychopathologie und ihren Grenzgebieten* (Darmstadt: Wissenschaftliche Buchgesellschaft, 1990), 95.

[6] Monika Maron, *Endmoränen* (2002; Frankfurt am Main: Fischer, 2005), 151–52 (hereafter cited in text as *E*).

[7] Monika Maron, *Nach Maßgabe meiner Begreifungskraft* (Frankfurt am Main: Fischer, 1993), 84–85.

[8] Monika Maron, *Ach Glück* (Frankfurt am Main: Fischer, 2007), 62 (hereafter cited in text as *AG*).

[9] Christoph Hein, *Frau Paula Trousseau* (Frankfurt am Main: Suhrkamp, 2007), 24 (hereafter cited in text as *FP*).

[10] See Christoph Hein, "'Mut ist keine literarische Kategorie': Gespräch mit Alois Bischof, aus Anlaß einer Aufführung von 'Die wahre Geschichte des Ah Q' in Zürich (1985)," in *Christoph Hein: Texte, Daten, Bilder*, ed. Lothar Baier (Frankfurt am Main: Luchterhand, 1990), 87–100, here 99.

[11] Christa Wolf, *Ein Tag im Jahr* (Munich: Luchterhand, 2003), 5 (hereafter cited in text as *ET*).

[12] See *Akteneinsicht Christa Wolf: Zerrspiegel und Dialog. Eine Dokumentation*, ed. Hermann Vinke (Hamburg: Luchterhand, 1993).

[13] The position of middle-aged women in the new *Bundesländer* is explored in a number of other narratives including Julia Schoch's *Mit der Geschwindigkeit des Sommers* (Munich: Piper, 2009) and Angela Krauß's recent prose work. For an empirical examination of the position of women in the east since unification, see Elizabeth Boa and Janet Wharton, eds., *Women and the Wende: Social Effects and Cultural Reflections of the German Unification Process*, proceedings of a conference held by Women in German Studies, University of Nottingham, 9–11 September 1993 (Amsterdam: Rodopi, 1994).

3: Literary Portrayals of the GDR by Non-GDR Citizens

Stuart Parkes

IN 1964 FOLLOWING A VISIT TO THE GDR, a number of journalists from *Die Zeit*, including the newspaper's subsequent editor Marion Gräfin Dönhoff, published a book about the country and their experiences there. This visit found its way into GDR literature, being clearly referred to in the novel *Das Impressum* of 1972 by Hermann Kant, who, as a favored son of the GDR, was presumably one of the journalists' interlocutors. The egregious Kant, however, wins no prizes for subtlety in renaming Dönhoff Lehndorff and in his main figure's characterization of her as — because of her pleasant manner — the most dangerous of enemies.[1] In this context what is significant is the title given to the volume: *Reise in ein fernes Land — Wirtschaft und Politik in der DDR*.[2] If one recalls Neville Chamberlain's infamous characterization of Czechoslovakia as "a far off country of which we know little," then the implications of this title become clear. Although many West Germans continued to visit the GDR, especially to see members of their family, until that state's demise, it is fair to say that it played a very limited role in intellectual discourse once division appeared sealed by the construction of the Berlin Wall. Hence in the 1980s Peter Schneider, as a resident of West Berlin, complained about the loss of a direction on the compass, meaning the GDR and points east,[3] while at the time of unification Patrick Süskind willingly admitted that, as a citizen of the Federal Republic, remote parts of Western Europe, such as the Outer Hebrides, felt closer to him than the GDR.[4] There are inevitably exceptions, for example Thorsten Becker's 1985 story *Die Bürgschaft* with its GDR setting.[5] Nevertheless one wonders with hindsight whether the stir caused by this work had more to do with what at the time was an exotic setting than with its literary qualities.

Since unification there has been a change. This chapter will consider three novels with a significant GDR setting written by westerners since unification. The first, *Die Verteidigung der Kindheit* (1991),[6] is by Martin Walser, born in 1927 and hence an author old enough to have memories of a single Germany. The second, *Nachglühen* (2008),[7] is by the much younger Jan Böttcher, born in 1973 and therefore with no such experience; and the third, *La maîtresse de Brecht* (2003),[8] by the French author

Jacques-Pierre Amette (born in 1943), shows that interest in the GDR has spread beyond Germany.

Die Verteidigung der Kindheit

From the late 1970s Martin Walser began to acquire a reputation for nationalism as he repeatedly expressed his dislike of the division of Germany.[9] Before that he had shown only limited interest in the eastern part of the country. Even his expressions of sympathy for the German Communist Party in the early 1970s had little to do with the ideology of the Party's GDR paymasters; in fact, he bemoaned the way the Party had failed to establish a western identity.[10] Given his subsequent change of direction, it must have been a happy coincidence that he was able to witness some of the events of autumn 1989 firsthand in Dresden. A year earlier he had been given a large quantity of biographical material relating to a lawyer, a native of Dresden, who had recently died in the Federal Republic. This was to form the basis for a novel for which research in Dresden was necessary, hence his presence there at the time of the GDR's disintegration.

Die Verteidigung der Kindheit is the story of Alfred Dorn. Like the real-life figure on whom he is based, he is a lawyer from Dresden. After failing a part of his legal studies course in Leipzig — he thinks because of his "bourgeois" background, his father being a dentist — he moves to West Berlin. Besides his studies his overwhelming priority is to maintain contact with Dresden, in particular with his beloved mother, whom his father has abandoned for a younger woman. Following his mother's death, which occurs after she has gone to live with her son, he becomes obsessed with acquiring artifacts that relate to his childhood, something that inevitably requires continuing contact with Dresden and the GDR. It is through the narration of visits and of Dorn's efforts to recapture the past that Walser provides a picture of the East German state.

The major issue in this connection is undoubtedly the restrictions increasingly placed by the GDR on freedom of movement between the two parts of Germany. This applies to the movement not only of people, but also of goods. The text — presumably authentic and written in stilted bureaucratic language — of a post office circular informing Dorn that he is no longer allowed to send washing back to Dresden, for instance, is included in the novel. When he is handed this leaflet, Dorn also observes the GDR authorities confiscating a goose destined for West Berlin from a "Bauersfrau aus der Zone" (*VK*, 146). Official documents are also quoted in connection with Dorn's projected visits, for example when he notes that more and more questions are being asked such as "*Waren Sie nach 1945 noch in der DDR wohnhaft?*" (*VK*, 106; italics in original). The answers to these questions provide reasons to refuse a visa. Increasingly Dorn finds it difficult to obtain such visas, not least for major holidays and initially even for his father's seventieth birthday. It is only after the latter, who is still working and active in society, threatens to withdraw from his professional association and the FDGB trade union (Freier Deutscher Gewerkschaftsbund) that the ban on his son is lifted through the intervention "*einer höheren Person*" (*VK*, 342; italics in original). Whether this person is a high-ranking Party official or someone from the Stasi is not made clear. In any case the impression given is of a closed, authoritarian state where decisions are made on an arbitrary basis. In fact this is stated explicitly when Dorn's Aunt Lotte, having reached retirement age, is allowed to move to the Federal Republic through the statement: "Dieser Staat schaffte Gnaden-Effekte, wie sie nur in absoluten Monarchien vorkamen" (*VK*, 424).

This comment is made by the novel's implied narrator. Unusually for Walser, *Die Verteidigung der Kindheit* is not written solely from the perspective of the protagonist. It also falls to the narrator to make the most vituperative comments about the GDR's restrictions on freedom of movement as manifested at its frontiers. The checks by frontier police to make sure nobody is hiding underneath a train are described on one occasion as "Idiotenballett" and the use of dogs for the same purpose with bitter irony as "Hundeschnulze" (*VK*, 392). The narrator also intervenes when Dorn and fellow passengers have goods confiscated. Nobody says anything because, it is suggested, they assume the action must be legal (*VK*, 142). Such acceptance provokes the phrase "Das deutsche Laster," which recurs throughout the novel as a comment on people's willingness to accept division and its consequences. At the same time there are a few occasions in the novel where this kind of negative portrayal is counterbalanced. When Dorn is leaving the GDR, the transport policeman, a man from Saxony, whose job it is to find potential refugees, is diverted by a book about the beauty of the Dresden Zwinger and ceases to question Dorn about his destination (*VK*, 12). On another occasion, when Dorn is bringing back an old plate from Dresden to West Berlin, the customs man does eventually let it through without any proof that it is worth less than the 30-mark limit for presents acquired in the GDR (*VK*, 149–50). One of the employees at the East Berlin office where applications for visas are made comes to recognize Dorn as a regular visitor and is even friendly (*VK*, 230–1), but such episodes are very much the exception. Although their inclusion may seem to run counter to the overall negative portrayal of the GDR, they do possibly imply the artificial nature of division by invoking common interests and common humanity across the divide.

Another aspect of the GDR that plays an important role in *Die Verteidigung der Kindheit* is the shortage of consumer goods, along with the perceived poor quality of those that are available. During one visit to Dresden, for example, Dorn's mother gives him a whole list of things to send to her, mainly everyday items such as toothpaste, coffee, and lemons (*VK*, 110). His father, too, asks for basic goods, in particular razor blades and seasoning for soup (*Suppenwürze*), because he is sick of GDR food (*VK*, 391). As for his young wife, on her visits to West Berlin before the construction of the wall she is desperately keen on Western fashions (*VK*, 130). One specific area mentioned on a number of occasions is that of medicines. To treat her blood pressure, Martha Dorn prefers the Western drug Raupina to the GDR's Hypernol. She is also convinced that her doctor believes she is right, although she knows he cannot admit it (*VK*, 109–10). Moreover, medicines are one of the items that cannot be imported, and Dorn's mother's supply is confiscated on one occasion (*VK*, 140).

There are very few times in the novel when there is a counterbalance to this picture of shortages and inferior goods. On one visit to Berlin Dorn's father shows great enthusiasm for his new Wartburg car, or at least talks at length about it (*VK*, 202). What is more, there is one member of the family, Tante Gustchen, who not only expresses scorn for those GDR citizens who seek Western currency to spend in the Intershop, but also maintains that there is no shortage of essential goods in the GDR, although she does make the exception of (good-quality) coffee, which she regards as a medicine (*VK*, 457). How far the validity of her argument is reduced by her self-confessed preference for a simple life is not commented on except in relation to Dorn, who expresses agreement with her but also with his stepmother's desire for Western products. This inconsistency is in keeping with his weak character although, in the case of his stepmother, he is anxious to maintain friendship with her so that she can help in obtaining the artifacts for his "childhood project" over the border.

A third area of the GDR that comes increasingly to the fore in *Die Verteidigung der Kindheit* is the built environment. The destruction of Dresden in 1945 is undoubtedly a contributory factor to Dorn's desire to recapture the past; at the same time he is shown to be horrified by what GDR planning and architecture are doing to the city. A good decade after the end of the war it is still a city of ruins, with Dorn feeling the need to compensate for this reality through what he calls "sein inneres Dresden," that is to say "Eindrücke von früher" (*VK*, 185). When the ruins are cleared, leaving gaping holes in the cityscape, he is led to the conclusion, "Vielleicht gab es Dresden gar nicht mehr" (*VK*, 371). As for the eventual rebuilding, it creates a desert, a "Reihe toter Riesenriegel" (*VK*, 439). Equally, the "marxistische Verblendung" (*VK*, 454) of those in power means that no effort is made to preserve what escaped the 1945 bombing.

Finally, it is not surprising that there are also passing references to the cultural policy of the GDR, in particular the attempts to keep out Western culture. One of the people Dorn visits in Dresden is a long-standing acquaintance, Heribert Priebe, a writer and music broadcaster. During one visit he complains to Dorn about official attempts to stop Western records reaching the GDR, although he also seems to see his attempts to thwart the authorities as an amusing game (*VK*, 362). Dorn becomes his supplier, with the result that on a later visit Priebe can boast to him that he now has the largest Bob Dylan collection in Eastern Europe. Protest music is one of his favorite subjects, but excessive public interest in his talks on this area has led to their being banned by the state (*VK*, 446). That Priebe is a homosexual and asks Dorn to send works by Klaus Mann and Hubert Fichte does not seem to have helped him either, despite official decriminalization.

The question that inevitably springs to mind is the fairness of Walser's extremely negative portrayal of the GDR. In certain areas there is little that can be said to be incorrect. GDR controls on the movement of goods and people were increasingly severe, and there were shortages of material goods. Nevertheless, it does not follow that a full picture is being given. The question is also more open when it comes to areas where there is a subjective element, for example the quality of GDR products. That GDR citizens, as in the novel, had a penchant for Western goods was clear at the time of unification. On the other hand some Eastern products have prospered subsequently, not least the once decried Rotkäppchen Sekt, which can now be bought in supermarkets throughout Germany. As for GDR architecture, while most would agree with Dorn, this too is an area where the subjective plays a role. Ultimately any attempt to determine how far Walser is right in his criticisms will founder on this question of subjectivity, not to mention personal political preference.

In the literary context the more important question to ask is how far the negative portrayal fits in within the novel. In his controversial 1998 speech when being awarded the Peace Prize of the German Book Trade, Walser replied to those critics who had drawn attention to the lack of references to Auschwitz in *Ein springender Brunnen*, his novel of the previous year, by claiming that the first rule of narrative was perspective.[11] If one takes the perspective of Alfred Dorn, it is totally credible that the themes discussed above loom large. As a lover of Dresden he wants to be able to visit the city, and as someone with fond memories of old Dresden he abhors the changes wrought by the GDR. As for Western goods, they no doubt played a major role in the life of many GDR citizens. In her 1982 book on East Germans Irene Böhme, a former citizen, speaks of their being taken "(o)hne Scham" and then discusses the whole psychology of intra-German gift-giving.[12]

Walser is on shakier ground when he abandons his rule of perspective and uses the narrator figure to comment on the GDR or the division of Germany. Here he comes close to expressing personal opinion, something he has frequently castigated, for example in the 1998 speech where he spoke disparagingly of certain intellectuals as "Meinungssoldaten."[13] Some examples have been given above. One particularly crass example is when it is said of the two city governments in Berlin, "West-Senat und Ost-Magistrat bewiesen, daß Deutsch keine Sprache mehr war" (*VK*, 139). At this point an expression of Walser's own political anger about the perceived willing acceptance by Germans of division and, by implication, of policies against the national interest intrudes into the literary text. That both West and East are targeted does not make any difference. It might also be pointed out that even in a non-fictional context many of Walser's political comments on the German Question might be classified as "Meinung." Unsurprisingly he expressed delight when the Berlin Wall fell, albeit in a controversial way. His comment — "Jetzt ist die Zeit, glücklich zu sein, sich zu freuen, daß Deutschen auch einmal Geschichte gelingt" — seemed to sweep aside previous German history in a somewhat cavalier manner.[14]

Nachglühen

As with Dresden in *Die Verteidigung der Kindheit*, Jan Böttcher's *Nachglühen* has a setting endowed with a particular significance, namely the five-kilometer-wide restricted zone (*Sperrgebiet*) created by the GDR authorities along its border with the Federal Republic. Certainly an original setting, this GDR specificity did not feature much, if at all, in GDR literature, particularly that which reflected official ideology; and despite the "kleiner Grenzverkehr" made possible by the 1972 Basic Treaty, the area was largely unknown to outsiders. The principal location here is the fictional border village of Stolpau on the eastern bank of the River Elbe, which marked the border and has now become part of the "western" state of Lower Saxony. The primary narrative takes place a good fifteen years after unification when Jens Lewin, now in his mid- to late thirties, gives up his job as a journalist in Göttingen to reestablish, along with his wife Anne, the inn his parents had run before the GDR's border regime required its closure. This enterprise, however, proves to be anything but a runaway success, because the past of the area continues to affect the attitudes of its inhabitants, a state of affairs reflected in the metaphor of the title and most importantly in the events described in the novel.

One example is provided by the recurring references to the expulsion of those citizens who were deemed a security risk when the border area was established in 1952. In the case of one family, the Wulfs, their former land has remained unclaimed since unification. The expulsion issue is one over which those who remain have cast a veil of silence. When after unification a flood appears to threaten the village, someone jokes that a repeat of the expulsions might be imminent. When nobody laughs, it is "wahrscheinlich aus lauter verräterischem Selbstekel" (*N*, 271). It is also noted at this juncture that none of the seven families expelled has returned. The disgust felt by the remaining inhabitants toward themselves would appear to be shared by their former neighbors toward them.

At the end of the novel the westerner Böttcher expresses his thanks to a number of people who gave him insights into the history of and everyday life in the restricted zone. The details given in the text of the more trivial restrictions imposed on its inhabitants could well be based on the information thus gained. It is difficult to lay hands on a ladder while permission to have a waterbarrel, in the case of one inhabitant at least, means inserting a middle support so that it cannot be misappropriated and used as a means of escape across the Elbe. Restrictions also mean that the inhabitants have to provide proof of identity every time they reenter the zone, something that irritates the adolescent Jens and prompts him to comments intended to annoy the border police, such as "Ganz schöner Westwind heute, was?" (*N*, 212).

At the other extreme many are happy to cooperate with the GDR authorities, not least the Brügemanns, the other main family in the novel. In contrast to Jens, the Brügemann boy of the same age, Jo — the similarity of their first names is surely no coincidence even if he is dark and Jens blond — is an apologist for the GDR border regime. He is willing to accept his father's explanation that the guards are only doing their duty. Moreover his father, an active supporter of the state, acts as a "*freiwilliger Helfer der Grenztruppen*" (*N*, 212; italics in original), keeping an eye on suspicious movements. That he applies his talents after unification to make an inventory of the birds that appear in the area is an ironic and, for some, disconcerting reminder of the past. As for Jo, he even acts as a go-between when trouble breaks out between local youths and border guards, for whose difficult role he continues to have understanding, suggesting that their repetitive lives consist of smoking and counting the days until the end of their military service (*N*, 116). Anne wonders why Brügemann has said this. The implication is that neither she, nor ultimately he, is convinced by the argument, which appears to absolve border guards from responsibility for their actions, something that, since unification, has never been accepted by the courts when former guards have been tried for shooting would-be refugees.

Jens's youthful rebelliousness has consequences on two occasions. He uses an event staged to celebrate the thirty-sixth anniversary of the GDR, for which cultural contributions are sought, to present a satirical puppet show in which the two characters are the traditional clown figure "Kasper(le)" and a minister. Their dialogue is mainly concerned with the future, with the minister predicting the transition from Socialism to Communism and Kasperle speaking of the end of Socialism. The other major topic raised is the desire of the minister to know what is going on in workers' and peasants' heads. He demands of Kasperle, "Finde alles heraus!" (*N*, 97), a requirement that smacks of Stasi minister Erich Mielke, though no name is mentioned. Although Jens's show attracts few spectators, not least because of the pouring rain, he is soon arrested. During the interrogation it is suggested that he has been incriminated by Jablonski, an eccentric photographer, who only comes into his own professionally after unification (*N*, 130). During GDR times Jablonski is something of an outcast living in primitive conditions and, as such, seems an unlikely inhabitant of the border zone. It is not entirely clear how far he is to be seen as embodying the typical GDR intellectual as viewed by Western detractors — apparently a rebel and thus able to exploit this status after unification, but in reality a loyal GDR citizen.

Jens's act of rebellion in 1985 does not have very serious consequences; however, the memory remains with him. When he returns to the site of his interrogation, now long after unification a ruin, someone has sprayed — out of awareness either of the place's past or appreciation of Nirvana's seminal album title — "NEVERMIND" [*sic*] on the wall, at which he smiles and thinks, "Das hätte man ihnen gern an den Kopf geworfen" (*N*, 130). How great a role betrayal played in these events is not made entirely clear. In the case of the second incident, there are no doubts: Jo is centrally involved in Jens's arrest and imprisonment, which extends into the period of the events of autumn 1989 and means that he is not present when the frontier fortifications are torn down.

In the narrative the full story emerges only at the end of the novel, after an account of a visit by Jo to Prague to meet the now famous Jablonski, during which the photographer's exact role in the first incident is not entirely clarified but Jo's betrayal of Jens is clearly referred to by him (*N*, 159). What exactly happened? As someone who understands technology, Jo told Jens that he knew how to tap into the border troops' telephone network, which provided Jens with the opportunity to use his very different talents to create another subversive text. This time there was only one main character, a border guard who inevitably spoke in a broad Saxony dialect, telling of his sexual exploits with a would-be refugee whom he claimed to be helping to cross to the Federal Republic. Through his technical know-how Jo made it possible for Jens to play his text; however, he had disappeared when his "friend" was arrested. Moreover, no action was taken against him, even though his voice was also on the tape played over the telephone network, which began with groans representing orgasmic pleasure.

When Jens returns to Stolpau, Jo is living in Hamburg and working for the police, but because of his grandfather's poor health, he returns home frequently. This does not lead to any meeting between the two men. Instead there are two meetings between Anne and Jo, the second of which leads to the unhappy dénouement of the novel. On the first occasion Anne, as a newcomer, asks Jo for some information about the village, a question he evades by saying that she will know everything in three weeks. Thereafter he tells her something about Jablonski and suggests that the carer he wants to employ for his grandfather might also work a little in her bar.

Before their next encounter there has been a series of problems with Jens and the inn. A fully booked Thanksgiving party flops because two thirds of those who had booked live in the West and cannot come because of a ferry breakdown. There is a suspicion that this supposed breakdown is an act of malice. When Jens investigates, his only reward is to come home soaking wet and be greeted by the schadenfreude of some of the regular drinkers, including Jo's father, whom he immediately bans from the bar. Thereafter he loses interest in his business, starts taking drugs, and falls ill with a bad cold. In her disillusionment Anne arranges a trip to Hamburg with Jo. It ends with them having sex in the tower where the border guard incident took place. When all is finished, the narrative becomes somewhat melodramatic. Jo's first comment — the expression of the wish that they had not made love there of all places — is introduced as the words "die ihre Welten blitzartig zerteilten" (*N*, 209). Shortly afterwards, Jo realizes that Jens has revealed nothing of previous events there to his wife. Her reaction, once she learns the truth from her mother-in-law and realizes that Jens has never taken her into his confidence, is to travel to a cousin in Sweden. She leaves behind the address along with the request that Jens should write if he has something to say. The future of the couple is thus left open.

The literary forbear of *Nachglühen* that springs to mind is Günter Grass's *Katz und Maus*. Böttcher too has written of youthful betrayal under an oppressive regime. At the same time the novel stands convincingly in its own right. Böttcher skillfully evokes the landscape and climate of his chosen setting, where the sky at any time of the year may show "sein ganzes Talent" (*N*, 127) — that is to say, it may be not only black, white, gray, and blue within a single day, but also several shades of these colors. Equally noteworthy as the evocation of the setting is the structure of the novel: the way the GDR past is only slowly revealed so that the reader is in a comparable position to that of Anne, who also must gradually discover the secrets of the area where she now lives. As noted above, the most important event of the story, the act of betrayal, is revealed almost at the end of the narrative.

It is also important to stress that *Nachglühen* aspires to be more than a novel about a specific corner of the GDR where living conditions were particularly difficult. Early in the novel Jo is the subject of a police disciplinary procedure at the end of which he is transferred to the radio department. Given what happened in the past this is highly ironic although, because of the non-linear narrative, the reader is only aware of this much later. During his disciplinary interview Jo quotes one of his grandfather's favorite maxims, a statement by Frederick II of Prussia: "*Wie ein Land an der Grenze funktioniert, so funktioniert ein Land*" (*N*, 21; italics in original). He goes on to claim that the border regime has forged his somewhat dour character. Unless this quotation is read simply as a convenient excuse offered by a fictional character — which, given the italics and the reference to the lack of understanding of his interlocutors, would seem to underestimate its importance — then the implication is that the restrictive conditions at the borders encapsulated the essence of the GDR and that the legacy of that state is the atmosphere Jens, now seen as an outsider, frequently encounters. While sick in bed with the illness referred to earlier, he ruminates on the citizens of Stolpau, their silence, their mistrust, and, in the case of Brügemann senior, his justification of previous conditions on the grounds of the security they provided. As there was such a large state presence, it was never necessary to lock doors, hence Jens wonders whether this kind of security can be regarded as "des Lebens Sinn und Qualität" before concluding his thoughts with a play on words on *Passierschein*: "sollte der am Ende die Sicherheit geben, dass alles nur *scheinbar passierte*?" (*N*, 192; italics in original).

Given the events of the novel, the cover of *Nachglühen* is correct to highlight the themes of "Schuld, Scham, Verrat." The text itself describes the GDR as an experiment, in the first case one comparable to the chemical kind (*N*, 70–86). The link to the kinds of issue that have been widely raised since the events of 1989–90 is obvious. Specifically, the main question remains that of the significance of the border regime for the GDR as a whole. While it is impossible to think of the GDR without being aware of its ever more rigid border controls, it remains a matter of debate whether the whole state can be reduced to them. When the Berlin Wall was built, Günter Grass contentiously compared the state to a concentration camp; only slightly less provocatively Böttcher, it would appear, compares it to a giant border control system.[15]

La Maîtresse de Brecht

While the events of *Nachglühen* take place in the last years of the GDR, *La Maîtresse de Brecht* is set in the state's first decade with the exception of the final chapter, which refers to the life of the eponymous main character after she has left the GDR. Maria Eich, a fictional figure, is an Austrian actress who is employed by the Stasi to gain information about the famous dramatist Bertolt Brecht, whose loyalty to Communism and the GDR is in question. She is willing to cooperate because she thinks that her father's and husband's Nazi links will make her vulnerable in the West and because she needs money to pay for expensive American medicines for her daughter, who lives in West Berlin and suffers from asthma. The Stasi is not only unconcerned about this reliance on the West, but is also willing to provide her with consumer goods, such as coffee and sugar, which are in short supply.

The picture of Brecht that emerges from the novel is varied. His physical weakness is referred to when it is noted that Maria has to organize his taking of medicines for heart problems (*MB*, 91–92). Despite this he retains his interest in young women. When she sees Maria for the first time, Helene Weigel, Brecht's wife, speaks of "a lamb for a wolf" (*MB*, 42), while on one occasion Brecht himself thinks of her as a "fool" (*MB*, 100). In political terms he remains anti-capitalist, reflecting on his return to Berlin in 1948 that "financiers" now interested in rebuilding the city were responsible for its destruction in the first place (*MB*, 15). This does not mean that he is an uncritical supporter of the GDR. He often expresses disillusionment with the state, which in his view, besides the bragging of Walter Ulbricht, displays "the one and only German bureaucratic aridity" (*MB*, 200). The novel also makes reference to his infamous declaration of loyalty to the GDR at the time of the June 1953 insurrection, with Maria seeing in him a kindred spirit in betrayal, only to ask "of what? of whom? And why?" (*MB*, 278). It is only with regard to theater that he is shown to maintain consistency and enthusiasm. He hopes, for instance, that his version of *Antigone* will surpass previous productions and be appropriate for the time (*MB*, 44).

Given Maria's assignment and the space devoted to how she is able to accomplish it, it is inevitable that the picture of the GDR that emerges from the novel is dominated by the Stasi. There are two main Stasi figures, Théo Pilla and his superior officer Hans Trow. The pair are presented very much in the popular culture tradition of "good cop" and "bad cop." Trow is from a bourgeois background steeped in German culture. Now he seems to be a convinced supporter of the GDR while at the same time retaining a certain humanity, especially toward Maria. When he first instructs her in connection with her assignment, it is with the manner of "a thoughtful teacher" (*MB*, 37). Later he admits his love for Maria and, toward the end of the novel, advises her to move to the West (*MB*, 244–45). It is small wonder that he achieves the authorial accolade of being, in keeping with the best French tradition of civility, "un honnête homme," the equivalent of the British gentleman (*MB*, 222).

Pilla, who comes from a simple farming background, is a much coarser individual. When he realizes that Trow has strong feelings for Maria, he asks why he does not have sex with her, even though his superior has told him that he does not have sexual relationships with agents. Pilla's response is to suggest that Trow take her to West Berlin and do the deed there. Inevitably he uses the crude word "baiser" (fuck; *MB*, 132). As an autodidact Pilla also has strong views on actors and the world of the theater. Unlike Trow he sees theater as "the art of disorder" (*MB*, 80), while actresses are nothing more than whores. It seems entirely logical that at the end of the novel he is bound for Moscow and subsequently, no doubt, professional advancement.

Pilla and Trow, whose personal observation of Brecht complements that of Maria, are not the only Stasi figures to appear in the novel. The reports on Brecht go to the ministry, specifically to someone code-named General Orlow. Orlow seems depressed by the nature of his work. Rather than passing on what he has read to Prime Minister Grotewohl, he would apparently prefer to be talking to the head of the American forces, General Clay. Reading about Brecht and his "gang" is nothing more than an irksome duty (*MB*, 156). The attention paid by Amette to the Stasi undoubtedly reflects the importance attached to this organization following unification. As with Böttcher's frontier zone, it remains a matter of debate how far the GDR can be characterized by one aspect of its existence. While the significance of the Stasi cannot be denied, the refinement of its system of surveillance undoubtedly came in the era of Erich Mielke, who became responsible for it in 1957, the year after Brecht's death.

In addition to the Stasi, Amette refers to other negative aspects of the GDR. When Helene Weigel is to be spied on, Trow receives a confidential paper telling him that it is because of her Jewish origins. Although this order comes as a result of Soviet demands, the question of anti-Semitism in the GDR is still raised. How far the GDR's anti-Zionism was in fact anti-Semitism remains a very contentious issue, although again it should be noted that it was mainly in later decades that the GDR and its allies pursued anti-Israel policies. There is a more general condemnation of the GDR towards the end of the novel, albeit very much from Maria's perspective. Her complaints range from the climate to more political questions. In a passage lasting over two pages she speaks, among other things, of a "world of puppets and automata, of endless trials, reports, commissions, obligatory signatures" (*MB*, 258). After she has left the GDR, she retains her interest in Marxism, but in the way people are interested in "gangrene" (*MB*, 297), an unpleasant analogy it would be hard to surpass.

It is no surprise that Amette's novel did not find favor with some in the eastern part of Germany. Reviewing it in *Freitag*, Sabine Kebir is able to point to various errors.[16] The newspaper of the Soviet occupiers becomes the *Taglische* [*sic*], rather than the *Tägliche Rundschau* (*MB*, 160), and one assumes that Brecht's colleague at the Berliner Ensemble "Peter Patzlich" is in reality Peter Palitzsch, later to be a distinguished theater director in the Federal Republic (*MB*, 149). Another objection raised by Kebir, for which Amette cannot be blamed, is the way French critics have seen Maria Eich as symbolizing exploitation in the GDR. This does seem excessive, given the references to her lot in the Nazi era. Since she does not achieve real happiness in the Federal Republic either — on the final page of the novel she is described as a "phantom" and an "absence" (*MB*, 301) — it would seem more logical to regard her more specifically as a woman deprived of the opportunity to create her own identity. This, along with the portrait of Brecht, is where the literary interest of the novel lies.

Conclusion

All the three novels discussed in this essay present a similarly negative portrayal of the GDR, and the possibility that these might be one-sided has been discussed in relation to each. As Roger Woods has pointed out, GDR biographies were varied enough to make negative generalizations run the risk of being simplistic.[17] What is beyond dispute is that the GDR remains a contentious topic that is likely to interest writers — and not only those with a GDR background — for a long time, even if it may never spawn as many volumes, both fiction and non-fiction, as the French Revolution or the Third Reich. Even if their literary qualities are beyond dispute, that two of the three novels can be linked to major literary prizes might well have to do with the attention the GDR has attracted since its demise.

Amette's novel was awarded the Prix Goncourt in 2003. Its subject matter includes two topics of major continuing interest in relation to authoritarian and totalitarian societies. The first is the behavior of writers and intellectuals in such societies. The conduct of Brecht, a major figure in world literature, has always been a bone of contention considered in biographies such as Martin Esslin's *Brecht: A Choice of Evils* and in literary works such as Günter Grass's play *Die Plebejer proben den Aufstand.* Following unification the whole question of the attitudes of GDR writers to that state came to the fore in what became known as the "deutsch-deutscher Literaturstreit." The issue has remained topical, as evident in the polemics engendered in 2007 by the election of Volker Braun to be chair of the literature section of the Academy of Arts. The author Gert Loschütz accused Braun of having produced the "widerlichsten Hervorbringungen" in defense of the Berlin Wall in his poem "Die Mauer." That the attack was based on a misunderstanding of the poem, an ironic juxtaposition of Western and Eastern propaganda dating from the mid-1960s, does not mean the issue of writers' attitudes to the GDR is any less sensitive.[18]

The second issue concerns the Stasi. For a time after the events of 1989–90 that institution arguably vied with Romania's Securitatae for international media attention but might now be said to have left its counterpart behind. Why this has been the case is ultimately a matter for speculation; however, certain suggestions can be made, for example the influence of portrayals of its activities in the film *Das Leben der Anderen* (2006), which achieved international acclaim. This success can in turn be attributed to widespread concern in many countries about the adoption of methods of surveillance readily associated with the Stasi, even if the GDR did not possess the technological tools now available and increasingly used even — or especially — in advanced democratic countries.

Böttcher won the Ernst Willner Prize at the 2007 Ingeborg Bachmann Competition for the story "Freundwärts," which is linked to the subject matter of *Nachglühen*. Its achievement is to concentrate on an aspect of the GDR, life in the restricted zone, that has received little attention but is linked to a phenomenon of the GDR that is as notorious as the Stasi and can be subsumed under the general heading "Berlin Wall." This too was a topic that has been at the center of public and literary interest both before and since the GDR's demise. Examples from the early 1980s include Peter Schneider's *Der Mauerspringer* (1982) and the satirical portrayal of the fall of the wall by Thomas Brussig in *Helden wie wir* (1995), one of many works by East German authors about the collapse of their state.

This momentous event brought into literary debates the idea, borrowed more or less ironically from the concept of the Great American Novel, of the Great German Novel inspired by what happened in 1989/1990. Walser's *Die Verteidigung der Kindheit* was an early contender for this unofficial title. Alongside the historical events Walser's interest in national questions as outlined above and his specific interest in Dresden brought about not only by the biography of the person on whom the figure of Dorn is based, but also by his study of the life and works of the linguistic scholar Victor Klemperer, produced a happy combination. Walser's literary horizons became broader. After a series of novels based on the personal tribulations of similar individuals, the two decades since unification have seen works, beginning with *Die Verteidigung der Kindheit*, on a greater variety of topics. For Walser especially, though far from exclusively, the end of the GDR and unification have provided new literary opportunities. What this essay has tried to show is how these opportunities are reflected in three works by authors of different generations and nationalities.

Notes

[1] Hermann Kant, *Das Impressum* (Berlin: Rütten & Loening, 1972), 107.

[2] Marion Gräfin Dönhoff et al., *Reise in ein fernes Land — Wirtschaft und Politik in der DDR* (Hamburg: Nannen Verlag, 1964).

[3] Peter Schneider, "Über das allmähliche Verschwinden einer Himmelsrichtung," *Deutsche Ängste* (Darmstadt: Luchterhand, 1988), 54–64.

[4] Patrick Süskind, "Deutschland, eine Midlife-crisis," *Der Spiegel*, 17 September 1990, 116–25.

[5] Thorsten Becker, *Die Bürgschaft* (Zurich: Ammann, 1985).

[6] Martin Walser, *Die Verteidigung der Kindheit* (Frankfurt am Main: Suhrkamp, 1991) (hereafter cited in text as *VK*).

[7] Jan Böttcher, *Nachglühen* (Berlin: Rowohlt, 2008) (hereafter cited in text as *N*).

[8] Jacques-Pierre Amette, *La maîtresse de Brecht* (Paris: Albin Michel, 2003) (hereafter cited in text as *MB*).

[9] An early expression of Walser's condemnation of division is found in a 1977 speech in which he states, "Wir dürften, sage ich vor Kühnheit zitternd, die BRD sowenig anerkennen wie die DDR." The somewhat self-conscious pose adopted does not ultimately detract from the message. See Martin Walser, "Über den Leser — soviel man in einem Festzelt darüber reden soll," in Martin Walser, *Wer ist ein Schriftsteller?* (Frankfurt am Main: Suhrkamp, 1979), 94–101, here 101.

[10] See, for instance, Martin Walser, "Wahlgedanken," *Wie und wovon handelt Literatur* (Frankfurt am Main: Suhrkamp, 1973), 100–18.

[11] Martin Walser, "Erfahrungen beim Verfassen einer Sonntagsrede," in *Die Walser-Bubis-Debatte*, ed. Frank Schirrmacher (Frankfurt am Main: Suhrkamp, 1999), 7–17, here 12.

[12] Irene Böhme, *Die da drüben* (Berlin: Rotbuch, 1982), 11.

[13] Walser, "Erfahrungen beim Verfassen einer Sonntagsrede," 15.

[14] Martin Walser, "11. November 1989," *Über Deutschland reden* (Frankfurt am Main: Suhrkamp, 1989), 115.

[15] Günter Grass, "Und was können Schriftsteller tun?," *Die Zeit*, 18 August 1961. Also in *Die Mauer oder Der 13. August*, ed. Hans Werner Richter (Reinek: Rowohlt, 1961), 64–66.

[16] Sabine Kebir, "Brechts Maîtresse," *Freitag*, 16 January 2004, http://www.freitag.de/2004/04/04041702.php.

[17] Roger Woods, "Retold lives," in *Dislocation and Reorientation. Exile, Division and the End of Communism in German Culture and Politics*, ed. Axel Goodbody, Pól Ó Dochartaigh, and Dennis Tate (Amsterdam: Rodopi, 2009), 245–55, here 246.

[18] For more details of this affair see Stuart Parkes, *Writers and Politics in Germany 1945–2008* (Rochester, NY: Camden House, 2009), 160.

4: Screening the Stasi: The Politics of Representation in Postunification Film

Nick Hodgin

> *Describe the communist state, and the historian conjures up an image of illiberal surveillance and the manipulation of fear and privilege. Describe the communist society, and one can end up with a trivialization of coercive mechanisms.*
> — Charles Maier, "What Have We Learned since 1989?"

WHEN IN 2006 THE DDR MUSEUM opened on Unter den Linden, the prestigious Berlin address that is home to a range of expensive boutiques, up-market hotels, and embassies, its (western German) director, Robert Rückel, was accused of treating GDR history rather too lightly, a charge that both he and the museum's head of research, the respected (eastern German) historian Stefan Wolle, rejected. That the museum sought to provide insight into the GDR in ways that would "combine education and entertainment" was criticized as an inappropriate approach to the representation of the East German state, though the museum was also nominated for the European Museum of the Year Award in 2008.[2] By contrast *Das Leben der Anderen*, Florian Henckel von Donnersmarck's film, a drama following a devoted Stasi officer's transformation and redemption, which had premiered just three months before the museum's debut, was widely praised as an authentic view of life in the East German state. Writing in *Der Spiegel*, Susan Stone considers the museum with reference to recent debates about German history and in the context of the continuing appeal of *Ostalgie*. Although Stone concedes that the museum does in one of its rooms acknowledge "the troublesome past," it has, she suggests, fallen to films such as *Das Leben der Anderen* to remind audiences what the GDR really was "a terrifying police state that monitored and persecuted tens of thousands of its citizens."[3]

On its release the film, which the director originally had trouble financing due to German producers' apparent lack of interest in the subject matter (it was eventually produced by Wiedemann and Berg Filmproduktion and distributed by Disney's influential Buena Vista), was quickly endorsed by an array of public figures. Shortly after its triumph at the Oscars (one of the many awards it won) the CDU politician Friedbert Pflüger stressed the pedagogical significance of Donnersmarck's film and called for it to be used in classrooms in order to ensure a continued focus on and analysis of Germany's "second dictatorship." Pflüger's commentary also stressed that the film finally enabled audiences to see the dictatorship as it really was and that such scrutiny was imperative given the "zunehmende Relativierung der DDR-Diktatur."[4] Implicit in Pflüger's claim is that the film provides a more accurate and thus much-needed portrait of the GDR than has hitherto been the case. This opinion, which is indicative particularly of the right wing's view of the East German state, is by no means uncommon: German reviewers especially have regarded the film as a necessary corrective to the *Ostalgie* narratives that enjoyed considerable success in previous years. Conferring the Friedenspreis des Deutschen Films on Donnersmarck, Hans Dietrich Genscher, the former vice chancellor of Germany and one of the architects of *Ostpolitik*, clearly spelled out the film's significance in countering *Ostalgie*: "Dieser Film kommt zur richtigen Zeit, er gibt den Opfern ein Gesicht in einer Zeit, in der DDR-Nostalgie wie eine Art geschichtlicher Weichspüler zu wirken beginnt."[5]

Ostalgie and Film

Such an assessment of *Ostalgie* is a reaction to its kitsch commercialization and to what is perceived to be a selective, invariably sentimental review of the GDR. Critics of *Ostalgie* — and Genscher's is not a lone voice — are inclined to view the trend in terms specifically of eastern Germans' nostalgic celebration of the past, which has led to a general playing-down or trivialization of the GDR. Originally disregarded as an ironic and iconoclastic celebration of East Germany, which was possible only once the state had ceased to exist, *Ostalgie*'s subsequent development in terms of its commercial and media presence and its influence on and reflection of the politics of remembrance has led to continued criticism. The German vice chancellor and chairman of the FDP Guido Westerwelle, for example, was blunt in his assessment of the GDR's current status: "Ich finde die Romantisierung der DDR von einigen Intellektuellen zum Kotzen. Die DDR stand nicht für Gerechtigkeit, sondern für Mord an der Mauer, Unterdrückung, eine wirtschaftliche und ökologische Katastrophe."[6] Evaluations of this kind are among the complex reasons why many eastern Germans persist in guarding private memories and experiences from what they perceive as an all-encompassing and equally selective narrative, one that is dominated by western discourse.[7]

But *Ostalgie* is not limited to those with firsthand experience of the SED state. A general interest in the Eastern Bloc has led to the current vogue for Communist chic that has seen a renaissance of the Soviet style in advertising and the ironic use of Communist imagery and design — and not just in the former East. With its ideology defused by history, much of the iconography has been recycled by postmodern culture. Temporal and historical distance makes such appropriation possible. A mock Soviet star above a city-center bar specializing in vodka is unlikely to cause offence given how far removed it is from the original context. With the symbols' ideological origins largely consigned to history, the referents have been destroyed, allowing them to be recontextualized. There is also evidence of the Communist past enjoying new, tamer usage in its original sites. Certain SED phrases and captions have been borrowed by eastern German businesses (a bar called Planwirtschaft — Planned Economy — opened in Dresden soon after the state's collapse, and the Stasi-themed café Zur Firma — a reference to the Stasi's sobriquet "the firm" — which opened in 2008 in the eastern Berlin district of Lichtenberg, a borough that was previously home to a high number of Stasi employees), is as tasteless as it was inevitable.[8]

Ostalgie's double appeal can be seen in the reception of two key postunification films, *Sonnenallee* (Leander Haußmann, 1999) and *Good Bye, Lenin!* (Wolfgang Becker, 2003). While the former enjoyed considerable success, despite its inclusion at numerous international festivals its appeal was limited to Germany and in particular to the new *Bundesländer*. Becker's film, meanwhile, broke box-office records and went on to find significant international acclaim, at that time still a rare feat for German film. Following the contentious debates surrounding the proposed reconstruction of the eighteenth-century Berlin City Palace (Berliner Stadtschloss) at the site of the former Palace of the Republic (Palast der Republik), East Berlin's showcase cultural venue and where the East German government once sat, the journalist Klaus Hartung noted that "obwohl sich vor allem Architekten besonders heftig beteiligten, war der Schlossstreit eines nicht: eine Architekturdebatte."[9] The reviews of *Sonnenallee* and *Good Bye, Lenin!* were likewise often less about the films than about their context. Many reviewers recognized *Sonnenallee*'s significance for eastern Germans' relationship to their own past. Skeptics might have anticipated that the review in *Neues Deutschland*, the former SED organ, would consider the film "keine Verklärung der DDR aber ihre Entdämonisierung," but similar lines were taken by other papers whose readership did not traditionally consist of former GDR citizens.[10] The film's "'ostalgische' Perspektive" was pejoratively noted by the reviewer for the *Frankfurter Rundschau* but also rationalized as a response to the "massive Entwertung der Ost-Biografien nach dem Fall der Mauer."[11] Other reviews were hostile and less prepared to see Haußmann's film as anything other than a banal comedy, whose celebration of East German adolescence was remiss in its failure to acknowledge the GDR's dictatorial nature, an approach that was even more evident in his conscription comedy *NVA* (2005). Scholars have been more judicious in their treatment of *Sonnenallee*, seeing it less as a nostal-

gic narrative than as a text whose "main concern is to examine the underlying tensions competing within the phenomenon of *Ostalgie* itself."[12]
While these analyses are convincing, they fail to explain the film's popularity with audiences who, judging from the many comments on website
forums and DVD reviews, react more to the film's comic-grotesque portrayal of the GDR, its generic details — the pop soundtrack, the protagonists' teenage concerns, the generational conflict — than they do to any
subtle critique of rival master narratives.[13]

The explanations that Thomas Brussig, the author of the novel
Sonnenallee, and Haußmann have given for making the film have not been
entirely consistent. In early interviews Haußmann took issue with those
who accused him of providing a false picture of the GDR and emphasized
his subjective approach: what he had made, he stressed, was "nicht nur
einen Film über die DDR, sondern auch einen Film über das, was wir erinnern."[14] But while both Brussig and Haußmann frequently argued that the
film brought some balance to the depictions of the GDR, that it enabled
eastern Germans to remember their past without being obliged to reference the state's many failings and abuses, both filmmaker and author
repeatedly and unequivocally asserted their opposition to the SED state
(not least, one suspects, because of certain flippant remarks to which the
director in particular was prone): "Die DDR war miefig, es roch nicht gut"
and "Die DDR war ein Scheißsystem."[15] Both the academic assessment of
the film as a careful critique and the response of those who enjoy the film
at face value would suit the filmmakers, who have in dozens of interviews
over the years sought to contextualize it as a defense of the East Germans'
right to remember and simultaneously stressed its deconstruction of nostalgia.

Becker's film enjoyed a much broader appeal, extending far beyond
German cinemas. But where the international reviews rarely made mention
of its contribution to or reflection of unification debates, discussions in
Germany focused primarily on its approach to *Vergangenheitsbewältigung*,
with most reviewers agreeing that *Good Bye, Lenin!* was a film less concerned with *Ostalgie* than with providing a normalized view of the GDR.[16]
Although some could not resist mentioning that the most successful
Wendefilm was a western production (both the scriptwriter and the director were western Germans), most reviewers felt that in contrast to
Sonnenallee Becker's film might go some way to improving relations
between eastern and western Germans. Its depiction of the GDR was
regarded as more evenhanded: it referenced the state's tyrannical side but
also acknowledged that a ground-level commitment to the Socialist rather
than the SED cause had existed, as personified by the protagonist's mother.
While the narrative follows the protagonist's attempts to recreate the GDR
(by recovering original East German artifacts and faking news reports) and
thus spare his bedridden mother the shock of discovering that the state has

collapsed during her eight-month coma, the film's subtext has commonly been seen as concerning the corruption of an ideal, namely Socialism on German soil, which went some way to permitting and explaining the eastern Germans' continued yearning for the past's unrealized future.

Screening the Stasi

One of the arguments guiding the reception of *Das Leben der Anderen* was that it provided a much-needed examination of the Stasi, something that had been lacking in the recent filmic portrayals of the GDR. Donnersmarck was both unequivocal and constant in his criticism of such nostalgia narratives:

> When *Good Bye, Lenin!* came out — and this was just one in a series of films of *Ostalgie* — I felt that it was becoming even more important for me to make the film, because these things did distort the way that the GDR is viewed and that the whole Communist dictatorship is viewed. People like that — just the idea that it was just this funny place.[17]

Whether those films do indeed distort perceptions of the GDR is, as I have indicated, debatable. The implication that the inquiry into the East German state has somehow ignored its dictatorial features is, however, refutable. It needs to be: anyone reading the *Boston Globe*'s review headline "A Forbidden Topic Captivates Nation" could be forgiven for thinking that Donnersmarck was the first director to turn his attention to the Stasi.[18] The *Boston Globe*'s reviewer was not the only person to make such a claim: even the reviewer in the respected film journal *Sight and Sound* concluded that the film was "notable as one of the first films to have looked back at the legacy of the GDR without nostalgia or ironic humor."[19] A report on the keynote speech given by Donnersmarck at a market research congress also noted, "Oppressed as they were by a totalitarian regime, they are grateful that . . . *The Lives of Others* offers the world a rare glimpse of their dark past," before acknowledging the director's own view: "I think they're glad that I took their concerns seriously without judging them or turning them into a caricature."[20]

After its demise interest in the SED state very quickly focused on the lengths to which the regime had gone in order to exert its control over the population. This interested eastern Germans, for whom the Stasi's coercive methods had been a taboo subject in the GDR, as much as it did those in the west, for whom the Stasi was endlessly fascinating. For reasons that were both political and practical, little was known about the Stasi's methods before 1989. Even if scholars had been able to gain access to Stasi archives it was, as Norman Naimarck notes, "considered politically inap-

propriate for West German scholars in particular to dwell on the totalitarianism of the East and the mechanisms of repression that East German
citizens were forced to endure."[21] The subsequent access to the Ministry
for State Security's (MfS or Stasi) records and employees changed that and
has sustained an unwavering public and media interest that is not only
historical or personal; in Germany and abroad there is a prurient fascination with the Stasi's more eccentric and immoral methods. This has been
evident, for example, in the British dailies: in 2009 the *Daily Mail* reported
on a "Stasi propaganda film which used children to simulate realistic war
games found in archives";[22] the year before, the *Independent* was among a
number of papers around the world to announce, "Stasi's Official
Pornography Department Finally Exposed."[23]

Investigations into the Stasi's files had and continue to have consequences, most notably following revelations concerning previously respected
public figures' (alleged) collaboration. Christa Wolf famously found herself
embroiled in such a scandal in 1993, and there has been a steady stream of
accusations and rumors involving other writers, poets, and artists. It is not
just those in the cultural sphere who have been caught up in the web of
accusations; politicians and civil servants have also been associated, whether
accurately or not, with the Stasi. Examples include the SPD politician Dirk
Stieger, the former federal minister of transport Manfred Stolpe, a large
number of police officers including two of Angela Merkel's guards, and
even the chancellor herself, while Gregor Gysi, the garrulous chairman of
Die Linke, is just one of a number of his party to have been linked to the
Stasi (not altogether surprising given Die Linke's direct lineage from the
SED). Reputations have been ruined — rightly so, in some cases. Articulate
and self-analytical, Wolf was able to survive the furor surrounding her neg-
ligible relationship with the Stasi; others, such as Gysi, who was accused of
involvement with the Stasi by Marianne Birthler, the then Federal
Commissioner for the Records of the State Security Service of the former
GDR, have been more vociferous in their denial, with Gysi accusing the
media of inaccurate and unprofessional reporting and contending that the
allegations were politically motivated. In a few cases the allegations proved
too much to bear: the former SPD politician Bodo Thomas committed
suicide in 1995, as did the journalist and Berlin chairman of the Federation
of Taxpayers Felix-Erik Laue. The enormous numbers of people directly or
indirectly connected with the Stasi naturally meant different levels of
involvement, and the burden of guilt varied. For this reason Barbara Miller
rightly concludes that though "a differentiated approach was required . . .
Such a moral reckoning was, however, never feasible."[24]

Despite claims to the contrary, the Stasi has been a source of near
constant interest not only in documentaries and television histories, but
also in feature films: both television productions such as *Die andere Frau*
(Margarethe von Trotta, 2003), *Der Stich des Skorpion* (Stephan Wagner,

2004), *Die Nachrichten* (Matti Geschonneck, 2005), and *Ich wollte nicht töten* (Dagmar Hirt, 2006), and cinema releases such as from Alexander Zahn's short, satirical, low-budget grotesque *Die Wahrheit über die Stasi* (1992), Michael Gwisdeck's claustrophobic psychodrama *Abschied von Agnes* (1994), and Sebastian Petersen's satire *Helden wie wir* (1999). A common theme is the Stasi agents' successful life since unification, which reflects postunification debates about eastern Germans' failure to face up to their GDR past and to punish those who are culpable, an issue that has further encouraged the problematic and much-contested comparison between the two German dictatorships. Rather than abating, the issue of culpability continues to provoke debate and acrimony as was evident in the response to the revelation that as many as 17,000 former informers are now working as civil servants.[25] Other themes include Stasi victims' continuing trauma and incomprehension, issues that have been explored in documentary films such as *Jeder schweigt von etwas anderem*, directed by Marc Bauder and Dörte Franke (2006), and their earlier *Keine verlorene Zeit* (2000), and the consequences for friendships and relationships following revelations that expose Stasi contacts — a topic that was explored in some of the first post-GDR Stasi films such as *Der Blaue* (Lienhard Wawrzyn, 1994) — or the state's manipulation of individuals as in *Der Verdacht* (Frank Beyer, 1991).

Though dozens of films made in the first decade after unification and since have sought to engage with important, contemporary issues, including the Stasi's legacy, these seldom have made any significant impact on German audiences, whose interest in filmic portrayals of the east (before and after 1989) has favored melodramas and comedies over social critical dramas.[26] One can speculate as to the reasons for the audiences' lack of enthusiasm. Eastern audiences may not have had much appetite for films that addressed precisely the problems that they themselves faced and in which they were implicated; western audiences, meanwhile, may not have been encouraged by either the subject matter or the choice of genre. These films were not fast-paced thrillers about the GDR's clandestine operations but pessimistic accounts from the east, which highlighted further economic challenges and the unforeseen social disintegration of eastern communities and, in the case of the Stasi, signaled an unwelcome contribution to the ever-uncomfortable question of *Vergangenheitsbewältigung*, albeit related to the GDR past.

It was not just the films' content but also their style that kept audiences away. One such example, which demonstrates the restrained approach to an issue that was so often seen as the stuff of high drama, is Andreas Höntsch's *Die Vergebung* (1995). Höntsch's film travels across the eastern German landscape and across time, alternating between the GDR past and the postunification present, a complex narrative in which, as the opening voiceover warns, "nichts ist wie es ist." As with other films of this period, *Die Vergebung* considers the consequences of state policy on the eastern German population even after its demise. In particular the film considers the threat to individuals' physical health and to the environment as a result of irresponsible manufacturing processes, and the psychological effects wrought by the state's security forces. But it is neither an environmental drama nor a simple critique of the Stasi. The Stasi's effect on people's lives is evident, and yet the menacing Stasi figures familiar to other postunification films are seldom in sight. Their absence may be explained by Höntsch's desire to avoid a portrayal that relied on "schwarz-weiß-Malerei."[27] The eastern German director's aversion to such formulaic representation also explains his focus on effect rather than cause. Höntsch's film therefore ignores the state security's *modus operandi*, preferring to examine how the state's mistreatment of individuals continues to have repercussions on people, relationships, and communities even after unification.

It is the harm done to individuals who are unable to forget or to forgive that is central to the film. Victims remain scarred by their memories. Sylvester Groth, who plays the principal character (credited simply as "Der Mann"), communicates both the pain and the bewilderment suffered by individuals detained by the state (a role he reversed for *Abschied von Agnes*, in which he plays a Stasi officer). Unsure as to the reasons for his imprisonment and reluctant to believe that his brother-in-law (revealed to be a former Stasi employee) may have betrayed him, he remains intense and introspective, unable to communicate with his family and unwilling to question anyone directly. His wife, meanwhile, tries desperately to discover the collaborator, for only the truth can initiate the healing process and effect reconciliation as Höntsch's film repeatedly stresses: "Was heißt jeder hat jeden verraten? Wo ist die Wahrheit? Wo die Wahrheit ist, da ist die Lösung. Wo die Lösung ist, da ist der Frieden. Wo der Frieden ist, da ist die Wahrheit."

While access to the Stasi's reports was made possible following the state's collapse, the truth, according to Höntsch, cannot be so easily supplied. He is therefore reluctant to adduce information and the plot relies as much on implication as exposition, but the truth finally remains elusive. The narrative thread that follows the wife's efforts to identify her husband's betrayer entwines different characters without conclusively discovering the true villain — and, in an unexpected twist, the wife realizes that she may have been the unwitting informer. While she attempts to remember details that might bring to a close her investigation, others prefer to repress the past. Paradoxically, the truth that she feels is necessary if she and her family are to move on is evaded by others for the same reason. Where the victims remain burdened by their memories, former Stasi apostates strive to divest themselves of the past — "die Zeiten sind vorbei," one tells the couple optimistically.

The Politics of Representation

How best to represent the Stasi has, then, been as fraught a debate as have the wider discussions concerning the GDR. Rarely has any film on this topic received uniform praise. Höntsch's received mixed reviews and only limited distribution, and more than fifteen years on, the director has yet to make another feature film. Disagreements typically arise in response to the films' choice of perspective. Some offer an ostensibly objective historical account such as a number of television series that have thematized the GDR, including the two popular Mitteldeutscher Rundfunk (MDR, the eastern German regional broadcaster) series "Das war die DDR" (Gitta Nickel, Wolfgang Schwarze et al., 1994) and "Damals in der DDR" (Karsten Laske, 2004); others have opted for a more unconventional approach, eschewing the straight chronology and provision of fact that have characterized the television accounts, and they have not always been well received. Early documentaries that set out to investigate the Stasi, such as Sybille Schönemann's highly personal *Verriegelte Zeit* (1990) and Johann Feindt and Tamara Trampe's *Der schwarze Kasten: Versuch eines Psychogramms* (1992) may have been appreciated by critics (Marc Silbermann describes the latter as a "nonexclusionary form of public psychotherapy"[28]), but went largely unseen. A number of documentaries, such as Thorsten Trimpop's *Der Irrationale Rest* (2005) and Thomas Heise's *Mein Bruder — We'll Meet Again* (2005) and his earlier *Barluschke* (1997), continued to focus on the consequences that the truth brings (in the latter case, the revelation that the eponymous Barluschke was a Stasi spy, something not even his wife suspected). While critics were often fascinated and appalled by the double lives that Stasi employees lived, some objected to documentary films such as Jan Lorenzen and Christian Klemke's *Das Ministerium für Staatssicherheit: Alltag einer Behörde* (2002) for allowing former Stasi officers to narrate their own past. It was not only columnists who were indignant; according to one report, fights almost broke out among audience members when the film was first screened.[29] Some praised *Wir lieben euch doch alle* (Eyal Sivan and Audrey Maurion, 2004), which also considers the ministry's activities from the perspective of the Stasi, in this case a former employee whose monologue (read by the actor Axel Prahl) accompanies a montage of original Stasi footage, as an original and thought-provoking account; others found it too stylized, the tone not sufficiently serious.[30] What concerned the detractors most was not the aesthetics but the content and its potential impact on audiences' understanding of the GDR. To focus on the perpetrators and not their victims was for several reviewers questionable, even irresponsible.

Other films received more hostile attention. In 2008 Hubertus Knabe, the director of the memorial site at the former Stasi prison in Berlin's Hohenschönhausen district, rebuked the national broadcaster ARD for showing Connie Walther's *12 heißt: Ich liebe Dich* (2008), criticizing the film, which traces the relationship between a Stasi prison officer and one of the inmates, as both unrepresentative and deeply insensitive to the victims of the Stasi, and questioning the veracity of the real-life story on which the film was said to be based. Though the station did not yield to the demands made by Knabe, victims' groups, or public (online) criticism, it did revise its schedule to include a short Stasi documentary, *In den Fängen der Stasi* (Bettina Renner, 2008), a series of interviews with victims of the Stasi, following the feature.[31] This tactic was reminiscent of the furor surrounding the broadcast of Marvin J. Chomsky's *Holocaust* television series in 1979, when programmers likewise felt obliged to include discussion shows and documentaries in order to provide some balance to Chomsky's historical melodrama. Walther's film did not generate the attention that *Holocaust* did but Knabe's condemnation was widely covered, and the coverage again showed how sensitive the discussion and representation of East German history was.

It was interesting that *12 heißt: Ich liebe Dich* generated such criticism when both the book by the actual protagonists, Regina Kaiser and Uwe Karlstedt, and an earlier documentary film about the couple, *11 und 12* (Till Harms, 1999), had not provoked any such disapproval.[32] Indeed, the latter had been praised for the "behutsame Einblicke" it offered while a reviewer for *Horch und Guck*, the journal whose remit is the critical appraisal of the GDR regime, claimed, "Aus der sogenannten Täterperspektive ist hier sicher das bislang ehrlichste, sensibelste und offenste Buch gelungen," and commended it as a valuable contribution to the "Aufarbeitung der DDR-Vergangenheit."[33] Despite the negative attention surrounding Walther's adaptation, the film received good reviews and went on to win a number of awards including the German Television Award.

Das Leben der Anderen: Criticism and Endorsement

Knabe had been equally critical of Donnersmarck and had refused the director permission to film in the former Stasi prison at Hohenschönhausen, explaining, "Die Geschichte des Films handelt davon, wie ein Stasi-Offizier einen kritischen Schriftsteller überwacht und sich am Ende auf dessen Seite stellt. Das hat es — leider — nicht gegeben. Der Stasi-Vernehmer als Held: Das verletzt die Gefühle vieler Opfer und führt die Zuschauer in die Irre."[34] The unprecedented actions of the Stasi officer risked compromising the film's claims of authenticity. But while insisting that the details were accurate and placing emphasis on the considerable research he had undertaken — factors that are naturally intended to underline the authenticity of the film as a kind of historical document — the director also emphasized his role as a storyteller rather than as a historian or politician. He later refined this argument in the course of many interviews, referring to the endorsement of the film in *Stern* magazine by Joachim Gauck (the former Federal Commissioner for the Stasi files), highlighting the article's title "Ja so war's," and acknowledging permission granted by Gauck's successor, Marianne Birthler, to film in the Stasi archives. He also conceded that if the film was not entirely accurate — a concession that followed the numerous factual anomalies that were noted in reviews — it did capture the East German experience "in essence."[35]

Gauck does indeed praise the film. He concludes that it serves as a "Medikament gegen Nostalgie," an assessment that corresponded with many German reviews.[36] The title of Reinhard Mohr's piece in *Der Spiegel*, for example, "Stasi ohne Spreewaldgurke," included a clear reference to that East German product, which long eludes the protagonist of *Good Bye, Lenin!* and which had come to serve as a signifier of East German identity.[37] The contrast with *Ostalgie* narratives was inevitable. In addition to the film's somber mood and milieu, which sets it apart from the contested *Ostalgie* narratives (though few reviewers seemed able to recall that *Helden wie wir* is a close, albeit satirical, study of the Stasi that subscribes to the view of the Ministry as a "kleinkarierter Laden voller Ignoranten"[38]), Donnersmarck's film contains a number of details and markers that announce its own position opposing *Ostalgie*'s apparent neutralization of the East German regime. The most obvious is the film's *mise-en-scène*, which was widely praised as realistic and meticulous in its attention to detail, often by people who may never have actually known East Berlin in the early 1980s (it was routinely mentioned in international reviews, for example). Whether the GDR was as — or even more — colorless and drab has not just been an issue discussed by critics and scholars, but one that has prompted dozens of responses from the public on various online sites (in response to reviews of the film on retail sites, for example). For all the debates concerning its authenticity/artificiality the fact remains, as Owen Evans rightly notes, that "it seeks to represent how the GDR is *remembered* now, rather than how it truly *looked* at the time."[39] The film is thus less a reflection of the past than it is of the present's relationship's to that past.

Donnersmarck acknowledges and defends other lapses in authenticity: he and the costume designer, Gabriele Binder, decided for example that the kind of clothes typically worn in the GDR in the mid-1980s risked being seen as comical and, if included, would compromise the film's serious tone. The clothing, then, was more typical of the late 1970s, and each character's outfit was chosen to symbolize and accentuate aspects of their personality, be it Wiesler (Ulrich Mühe), the rigid Stasi protagonist memorable in his cement-gray jacket ("ein hermetisch abgeriegelter Kasten," whose superfluous buttons are intended to represent "zusätzliche Augen"), or the playwright Dreyman (Sebastian Koch), comfortable in his worn corduroy suit (an incorrect choice, according to Timothy Garton Ash, who argues that Dreyman looks more like a "West German intellectual from Schwabing" than an East German writer).[40] Binder is rather more frank in explaining their approach to design and concedes a more subjective attitude, noting that they asked themselves, "Was mögen wir? Wie wollen wir die Menschen sehen?" Instead of using original period garments the costume designer relied on a volume of photographs of Croatian artists from 1978 to 1983. The garments were also to correspond with cinematographer Hagen Bogdanski's somber color palette, which consists mainly of browns, grays, and other pale and desaturated colors. This palette also differentiates the film from the color frequently associated with *Ostalgie* films (but not the garish *Ostalgie* shows on television), though reviewers' and audiences' memories may conflate and confuse those films' vibrant mood with their visual composition and color schemes.

Do these liberties with surface detail undermine the value and worth of *Das Leben der Anderen*? This is not, after all, the first historical drama to include anachronisms and inaccuracies. In his discussion of contemporary German Second World War-dramas, Matthias Fiedler suggests that where audiences expect history books to be "true to historical facts, we do not have the same expectation of historical feature films."[41] Certainly historical films are more widely seen than history books are read. While audiences may view such films with some awareness that these are products of the entertainment industry and not faithful accounts or the result of careful scholarship, the fact remains that history films are for many people an influential source of information.[42] Close scrutiny of the film's details is justified precisely because the director has been so fervent in his description of the film's authenticity and because of the official endorsement of the film and its perceived educational significance. In omitting or altering certain details Donnersmarck naturally exposes himself to criticism. The indignation provoked by some of the liberties taken is not simply a question of eastern German pedants or revisionists spotting inaccuracies and anachronisms and thus wishing to undermine the film (though this was motivation for some). As a text that is relevant to ongoing debates about identity, memory, and history, *Das Leben der Anderen* would inevitably be analyzed as much by historians and politicians as by film critics. This does not apply exclusively to the GDR past, for the moment a (German) filmmaker makes a film about German history, especially recent, highly contested, history, s/he must expect to attract such analysis. *Der Untergang* (Oliver Hirschbiegel, 2004), *Valkyrie* (Bryan Singer, 2008), and *Der Baader-Meinhof-Komplex* (Uli Edel, 2008) all generated varying degrees of controversy. The fact that Donnersmarck was so willing to discuss the film and the GDR provoked more responses than might otherwise have been the case. In Germany the frequent reference to Donnersmarck's privileged upbringing was sometimes less an issue of biographical detail than it was a means of questioning his right to comment on the GDR, a suspicion that reflected the argument within post-GDR discourse that analysis could never supersede lived experience. The recurring issue of who is qualified to narrate GDR history reflects the salient struggle between history and memory, a conflict that is often characterized as one between east and west, between subjective experience and objective analysis. The journalist Christoph Dieckmann has, for example, highlighted the fact that the GDR past is often narrated by western Germans: "Manchmal schickt der Westen einen Auslandskorrespondenten herüber, zur vertiefenden Verallgemeinerung des Bekannten: Arbeitslosigkeit, Stasi, Ausländerhaß. Mehr und mehr wird auch mein Osten ein mir westlich vermitteltes Summarium altbundesdeutscher Medien."[43] As one *Spiegel* interviewee put it, "Wir wollen uns nicht von den Westlern an der Hand führen lassen. Das ist unsere Vergangenheit."[44]

Perhaps conscious that his film would become mired in *Vergangenheitsbewältigung* debates, which risked obscuring its considerable artistic achievements, Donnersmarck sought to justify some of the film's fictions; so while he stressed that "part of the quest for authenticity went into shooting in as many original locations as possible," he also added that he did not want to lose himself "in historical details but to tell a story about real people with an emotional viewpoint."[45] This point is served well enough by the film and largely corresponded with the international reception, which focused primarily on the film's generic pleasures, its melodramatic qualities, its espionage-thriller tension. Some reviews barely considered the specific socio-historical or national context of Donnersmarck's film, looking instead at what it revealed about dictatorships or contemporary surveillance debates in general. For others it was the film's central conceit, namely Wiesler's conversion from a man of hard principle to a man softened by conscience, that made the film so fascinating and so appealing. These reviews concentrated on Wiesler's redemption, which follows his vicarious appreciation of the music and poetry enjoyed by those under his surveillance, and his mounting discomfort with the personal, rather than professional, motives of his superiors (Stasi *Oberstleutnant* Grubitz and Minister Hempf) for monitoring the playwright Georg Dreyman and his lover, Christa-Maria Sieland (Martina Gedeck). But not everyone was convinced by this conversion. The film critic Jonathan Romney was among those for whom this development did not ring true: "Given how minutely the film establishes Wiesler as a hard-liner and a technocrat, his seemingly easy discovery of compassion undermines the film's point about the terrible thoroughness of the Stasi system. Von Donnersmarck dilutes an otherwise very substantial film by choosing to send us home on a nobly affirmative note in keeping with the reassuring 'closure' that makes international cinema Oscar-eligible."[46] Whether or

not Wiesler's transformation is plausible or his ability to manipulate the
Stasi operation credible — and a number of commentators have pointed
out that there is no precedent for the former and that the latter would have
been impossible — was clearly not important to audiences, few of whom
presumably have any detailed knowledge of Stasi protocol.

The tendency is to view Wiesler's transformation in terms of redemption: his exposure to art (Brecht's poetry, music, and, one might add, the
art of living — the subjects under surveillance are passionate, vital figures
and thus the complete antithesis of the man in gray) precipitates a fundamental change in him, a dawning realization and not, as some see it, a
sudden epiphany, that he is on the wrong side. Much less is said about
Dreyman. To date, only Slavoj Žižek has commented on the characterization of this figure:

> Why wasn't he considered at least a little bit problematic by the
> regime, with his excesses tolerated because of his international fame,
> as was the case with famous GDR authors like Bertolt Brecht, Heiner
> Müller and Christa Wolf? The film takes place in 1984 — so where
> was he in 1976 when the GDR regime did not allow Wolf Biermann
> to return from a West German tour, leading nearly all great East
> German writers to sign a petition protesting this measure[?][47]

Biermann himself was rather positive about the film, though he did
acknowledge that his reaction was in part a sentimental response to a familiar milieu.[48] Dreyman's position is far more awkward than most reviewers
are willing to credit, and this myopia is strange given the various criticisms
of him that the film contains. The first of these is, on the face of it, rather
innocuous: Grubitz (Ulrich Tukur), Wiesler's superior, admonishes him
for being suspicious of the celebrated playwright, friend of Margot
Honecker, and *Nationalpreisträger*, noting that "für ihn ist die DDR das
schönste Land der Welt." The comment may be interpreted in a number
of ways. It can be seen as a criticism of those *linientreue* artists to whom
Dreyman ostensibly belongs and whose fealty in real life earned them certain privileges, for the SED knew to reward as well as to punish — an
approach Charles Maier terms "*Privileg oder Prügel*."[49] Using culture in
order to further legitimize the state was important to the Party even if
Donnersmarck's Minister Hempf (Thomas Thieme) is a boorish and
uncultured character and the Stasi figures are ignorant of art and music
and literature. The GDR may not be Dreyman's ideal — early scenes demonstrate his discomfort in having to deal with the odious Hempf — but by
East German standards he leads a gilded life. Grubitz's comment can also
be seen as a reminder to those mesmerized and misinformed by *Ostalgie*
that the GDR was not "das schönste Land der Welt"; the fact that it is
uttered by a Stasi officer spying on an essentially loyal citizen further
underlines this irony. It also echoes the closing line uttered by Micha,

Haußmann's protagonist in *Sonnenallee*, who reflects on his East German adolescence as "die schönste Zeit meines Lebens, weil ich war jung und verliebt." But where Micha's comment facilitates a normalized view of life in the GDR, Grubitz's observation alerts contemporary audiences to how misguided such a view is. After the death of Jerska, a close friend driven to suicide by his despair at not being allowed to work, Dreyman's comfortable existence is more directly criticized by his friend the journalist Paul Hauser, for whom the playwright's stance is increasingly untenable: "Du bist so ein jämmerlicher Idealist, dass du schon fast ein Bonze bist. Wer hat denn Jerska kaputt gemacht? Genau solche Leute: Spitzel, Verräter und Anpasser. Irgendwann musst du Position beziehen, sonst bist du kein Mensch!"

Hauser's moral judgment is directed at Dreyman but it also applies to Wiesler, who is covertly monitoring the conversation from his attic hideaway. Although both Dreyman and Wiesler do finally take a stand (the former secretly writes a critical report about suicide in the GDR that is published in the West; the latter doctors his reports in order to conceal this and thus protect the playwright and his partner), most reviewers focus on Wiesler's moral recovery, which is the more dramatic of the two (and arguably the least plausible). Hauser's criticism of his friend is in fact a criticism — voiced in some postunification debates — of those many East Germans who, if not "Spitzel" or "Verräter," were at least "Anpasser" willing to tolerate an intolerable regime (a *Spiegel* report acknowledged this sentiment as early as 1989 when it included a photo of western graffiti declaring, "Kritische Mitbürger aus der DDR willkommen! Anpasser + Lohndrücker Nein Danke"[50]). That each man makes the right decision is confirmed by other parties: though ignorant of his real identity, Sieland recognizes Wiesler to be a "guter Mensch," and Dreyman's rehabilitation as such is confirmed by his friends' renewed support and by the *Spiegel* editor, who congratulates him on his article, commenting that it will expose "das wahre Gesicht der DDR."

While the facts about the GDR's high suicide rate and the regime's refusal (from 1977) to make the data available are true, there are two aspects of this development in Donnersmarck's plot with which one might take issue. One is the implication that state repression (here in the form of the unspoken *Berufsverbot* imposed on Jerska) explains the high number of suicides in the GDR. In the context of the film it is entirely feasible that the SED's ill-treatment of the director has expedited his death, but the long-held assumption that it was the state's repressive policies that were the principal cause for the GDR's suicide rates is a view that has been challenged in recent years.[51] The second is the *Spiegel* editor's claim. Though it refers specifically to Dreyman's article, the assertion is equally revealing of the filmmaker's repeated determination to show the GDR "as it really was." Given the chronology of postunification debates, one can see how and why Donnersmarck is interested in balancing those nostalgic accounts of life in the East and in reminding audiences of the SED's abuses and repression, but the film reinstates the binary approach to East German history — that is, of perpetrator/victim, *Mitläufer/Anpasser* — with which so many eastern Germans have struggled in postunification debates, even if the main protagonist performs an unprecedented shift from one side to the other. This GDR is populated almost exclusively by victims and villains. The list of characters can be separated into Stasi employees (from Stasi students to high-ranking officers) and artists (who are either deemed to be *Staatsfeinde* and are under surveillance by the Stasi, or who are colluding with the MfS). There are some minor, anonymous characters — a handful of people in a bar, briefly seen neighbors, some children — but they are seldom given any voice and serve only to confirm the Stasi's pervasive menace or underscore Dreyman's humanity. Donnersmarck would presumably argue that more characters would detract from the main protagonists (he has explained that the set design was intentionally minimal in order not to distract the viewer), but for some eastern Germans the absence of ordinary citizens is an absence too hard to bear. Andreas Dresen, for example, a highly respected filmmaker whose socially engaged films have chronicled the lives of ordinary eastern Germans, took exception with the pedagogical value accorded Donnersmarck's film as a serious and realistic portrayal of the GDR noting, "dieser Film [hat] mit der DDR so viel zu tun wie Hollywood mit Hoyerswerda."[52]

Dresen objects to Donnersmarck's stylized GDR — the very portrayal that for so many rang true — and especially the Stasi employee imagined by Donnersmarck. Wiesler, whom one reviewer described as "ein spießig-asketischer Mönch der DDR-Staatsreligion," is for Dresen too singular a figure to represent the thousands of people who worked for the MfS or reveal anything of their motives, their dilemmas, or their ordinariness.[53] With over 90,000 employees and 170,000 informants, the MfS was sufficiently well staffed to monitor, exploit, and persecute the East German population. Many of those who worked for the Stasi were, as satires such as *Helden wie wir* and documentaries such as *Ministerium für Staatssicherheit* demonstrate, rather unexceptional figures living ostensibly conventional lives with their families and were probably less committed to their métier than is Wiesler (the director chose to delete from the film, but not the DVD, a scene in which Wiesler begins spying on his neighbors from his own apartment, which emphasizes his commitment to rooting out the state's enemies and his lack of any individual life). It is the lives of these others, the ordinary perpetrators, the everyday victims, that directors such as Dresen would like to investigate further.

Conclusion

Good Bye, Lenin!, *Sonnenallee*, and to a lesser extent *Helden wie wir* each presents a GDR abounding with period artifacts with which many eastern Germans especially can identify. Though more critical of *Ostalgie* than is often assumed, their nostalgic appeal undoubtedly lies with what Brussig astutely terms the "Wiedersehensfreude mit dem Inventar, mit dem man aufgewachsen ist."[54] Such appeal, however, is not exclusive to those with direct memory of the East German state since the films also satisfy those who are simply curious about the GDR. Brussig's explanation indirectly aligns the films with the exhibitions on everyday life in the GDR that proliferated in the years of the films' release. The criticism directed at the best-known of these exhibitions, the DDR Museum in Berlin, echoed that directed at the films and *Ostalgie* in general. The misgivings about the museum are partly due, one suspects, to its location: its proximity to some of the city's long-established and celebrated museums and galleries (the Altes Museum, the German Historical Museum, the Pergamon, and so on) confers upon it a degree of authority and legitimacy that its critics find troublesome, even if the museum lacks its neighbors' international status.

Equally problematic is the authority accorded *Das Leben der Anderen* as a sober assessment of the GDR's oppressive reality. Donnersmarck's film may engage the same material and themes used and explored in a host of other Stasi narratives, be it documentaries, films, or history texts, but it continues to be discussed as a response to *Ostalgie* films not least because it eschewed precisely those trifling period relics that tempt visitors to GDR exhibitions and draw audiences to *Ostalgie* films and shows. Whilst Donnersmarck's film counters what the director calls the eastern Germans' "understandable but definitely dangerous" nostalgia, the success and endorsement of *Das Leben der Anderen* arguably relates to a different kind of nostalgia — not for the good old days of the GDR but for the bad.

Politicians and historians endorsed the film because it serves to remind audiences of the horrors of the East German dictatorship, and in Germany, as the country approached the twentieth anniversary of unification, the need to address the selective view of the state, its rebranding into something more harmless, had become more urgent. School children's ignorance of the SED state in particular was a cause for concern, and this lack of knowledge was often attributed to *Ostalgie*'s trivialization of the GDR (a screening of the film for school children in Saxony in 2007 with the title "Gegen das Vergessen — Das Leben der Anderen," organized under the patronage of CDU politician Veronika Bellmann, exemplifies the instrumentalization of certain narratives — that is, the attempts to establish the film's historical authority and to use it to combat nostalgia and omniscience). The revelation that Ulrich Mühe's former wife, the DEFA actress Jenny Gröllmann, had allegedly worked for the Stasi, which resulted in an acrimonious court case, seemed to lend Donnersmarck's film even greater legitimacy — not least because Gröllmann's former Stasi controller later admitted that he had concocted some of his reports and that the actress was ignorant of her IM status.[55]

But one might also argue that the film relates a version of the GDR that indulges the "public's enduring fascination with the subject of secret surveillance and the dark medial side of power" through its carefully recreated Stasi milieu.[56] Where *Good Bye, Lenin!* and *Sonnenallee* are to some extent analogous to the aforementioned museums of the everyday, there are aspects of Donnersmarck's film that are reminiscent of exhibitions displaying the tools of the Stasi trade. It is worth noting that the DVD menu includes an option that allows the viewer to inspect a gallery of Stasi gadgets used for espionage, images reminiscent of the photos on view at the 2003 exhibition "Duell im Dunkel: Spionage im geteilten Deutschland" at the Haus der Geschichte (German National Museum of Contemporary History) in Bonn.[57] Unlike the East German consumer goods advertising a past material culture in other films (from lentils to lousy furniture), these props are not mnemonic prompts intended to signal the East German *Alltag* (unless perhaps for former MfS employees). As with the lingering close-ups of Stasi equipment and the emphasis on procedure and protocol — from the listening devices used to the collection of suspects' odor samples to methods of interrogation — they underline the GDR's oppressive past. This is not simply a fascination with the state's mechanisms of control but also, arguably, a yearning for a time when the ideological lines were clearer and the West's triumph over Communism was a battle waiting to be won. Focusing on the iniquities of state Socialism, such a view exposes the GDR's guiding ideology as morally bankrupt and emphasizes *Ostalgie* as fiction; at the same time it serves as an indirect reminder of the benefits and superiority of the Western system, which may reassure or further exasperate, a point that the psychologist Hans Joachim Maaz also makes when he suggests, "Die reine Negativdarstellung der DDR wirkt auf viele Ostdeutsche nicht aufklärerisch, vielleicht eher wie eine Schönfärbung der Bundesrepublik."[58]

That *Das Leben der Anderen* was chosen in the USA as the best conservative film of the last twenty-five years by the right-wing *National Review* provides a further clue as to this nostalgic appeal and perceived significance. The publication offers only a sketchy explanation noting, "Conservatives enjoy these films because they are great movies that offer compelling messages about freedom, families, patriotism, traditions, and more."[59] More revealing are the journal's other reviews, one by its late founder, William F. Buckley Jr., who describes the film as a much-needed "holy vessel of expiation," given the eastern Germans' "corporate national shame at the betrayal of life, as so brazenly done by so many millions."[60] Another review from the same journal declares quite simply, "Donnersmarck has created a film that will be remembered longer than East Germany itself."[61] For some this may be the film's great achievement; for others its success and the significance accorded it may prove to be a further obstacle in coming to terms with the GDR past. Reflecting on the film, Wim Wenders acknowledged his misgivings: "Traurig bin ich ein bisschen darüber, dass das nun als der ultimative Film zu diesem Thema behandelt wird. Als ob es jetzt nichts mehr zu erzählen gäbe über die DDR."[62] Whether such pessimism is warranted remains to be seen.

Notes

[1] Charles Maier, "What Have We Learned since 1989?" *Contemporary European History* 18, no. 3 (2009): 253–69, here 266.

[2] See the DDR Museum website, accessed 1 June 2010, http://www.ddr-museum.de/en/media/faqs/.

[3] Susan Stone, "DDR Living. Museum Offers 'Ostalgic' Look at East Germany," *Der Spiegel*, 20 July 2006, http://www.spiegel.de/international/0,1518,427579,00.html.

[4] CDU-Fraktion des Berliner Abgeordnetenhauses, accessed 10 June 2010, http://www.cdu-fraktion.berlin.de/Aktuelles/Presseerklaerungen/Oscar-praemierter-Film-Das-Leben-der-Anderen-sollte-in-Schulunterricht-integriert-werden.

[5] Cited in Manfred Wilke, "Wieslers Umkehr," *Die Politische Meinung* 442 (2006): 25–32, here 31.

[6] Guido Westerwelle, "'Es gibt wieder zu viel DDR in Deutschland,'" interview by Claus Christian Malzahn and Anna Reimann, *Spiegel Online*, 11 November 2007, http://www.spiegel.de/politik/deutschland/0,1518,516296,00.html.

[7] See Thomas Ahbe's essay in this volume for an in-depth analysis of *Ostalgie*.

[8] Similar trends are observable in other former Soviet Republics, including Russia. See T. Sabonis-Chafee, "Communism as Kitsch," in *Consuming Russia. Popular Culture, Sex and Society since Gorbachev*, ed. Adele Marie Barker (Durham, NC: Duke UP, 1999), 362–82. Only in Georgia, Stalin's birthplace, could a cigarette packet featuring the Soviet dictator be named "Prima Nostalgia."

[9] Klaus Hartung, "Eine Stadt hofft auf Heilung," *Die Zeit*, 19 July 2001, http://www.zeit.de/2001/30/Eine_Stadt_hofft_auf_Heilung.

[10] Gunnar Decker, "Freiheit zu lachen," *Neues Deutschland*, 6 October 1999.

[11] "Der surreal existierende Sozialismus," *Frankfurter Rundschau*, 7 October 1999.

[12] Paul Cooke, *Representing East Germany since Unification: From Colonization to Nostalgia* (Oxford: Berg, 2005), 112.

[13] One might have expected *Helden wie wir* (1999), Sebastian Peterson's adaptation of Brussig's celebrated unification satire, to be as successful as Haußmann's film, but this was not the case (the former attracted under 200,000 visitors, the

latter more than ten times that figure). Despite its comic take on the GDR, positive press reviews, and the coinciding release date, the Brussig script failed to generate anywhere near the same level of interest. One explanation may be that the film is far more skeptical of the GDR and of the ways in which the state is remembered.

14 Quoted in Katharin Tiedemann, "Helden des Alltags," *Freitag*, 1 October 1999.

15 Rüdiger Schaper and Jan Schulz-Ojala, "Der Osten war eine Orgie," *Der Tagesspiegel*, 5 October 1999; Leander Haußmann, "'Es kam dicke genug,'" *Der Spiegel*, 8 September 2003, http://www.spiegel.de/spiegel/print/d-28530391.html.

16 See for example Jan Schulz-Ojala, "Eins, zwei, drei," *Der Tagesspiegel*, 20 February 2003.

17 Quoted in Vadim Rizov, "Lives in His Hands," *The Reeler*, 7 February 2007, http://www.thereeler.com/features/lives_in_his_hands.php.

18 Colin Nickerson, "German Film Prompts Open Debate on Stasi," *Boston Globe*, 29 May 2006.

19 Geoffrey Macnab, "The Lives of Others," *Sight and Sound* 68 (May 2007).

20 Robert Heeg, "Market Research Got It Absolutely Right," ESOMAR Research World Article, accessed 1 June 2010, http://www.esomar.org/uploads/pdf/research-world/RW0709_InterviewF.HenckelVonDonnersmarck.pdf.

21 See Norman M. Naimark, *To Know Everything and to Report Everything Worth Knowing: Building the East German Police State, 1945–1949* (Washington, DC: Cold War International History Project, Woodrow Wilson International Center for Scholars, 1994), 1.

22 Alan Hall, "Stasi Propaganda Film Which Used Children to Simulate Realistic War Games Found in Archives," *Daily Mail*, 27 November 2009, http://www.dailymail.co.uk/news/article-1231220/Stasi-propaganda-film-used-children-simulate-realistic-war-games-archives.html.

23 Tony Paterson, "Stasi's Official Pornography Department Finally Exposed," *Independent*, 28 March 2008, http://www.independent.co.uk/news/world/europe/stasis-official-pornography-department-finally-exposed-801774.html. A typical example from Germany can be found in an article in *Focus* that details the exploits of "Horizontal-Agentin" Monika Lustig, a Stasi call girl, in 1997. See Wilhelm Dietl, "Die Flotte Moni," *Focus*, 7 July 1997, http://www.focus.de/politik/deutschland/ddr-flotte-moni-von-der-stasi_aid_166367.html.

24 Barbara Miller, *The Stasi Files Unveiled: Guilt and Compliance in a Unified Germany* (New Brunswick, NJ: Transaction Publishers, 2004), 139.

25 "Desk Jobs for Secret Police," *Der Spiegel*, 7 September 2009, http://www.spiegel.de/international/germany/0,1518,635230,00.html.

26 For a detailed account of the different responses to unification in film in the years since 1989, see Nick Hodgin, *Screening the East: Heimat, Memory and Nostalgia in German Film since 1989* (Oxford: Berghahn, 2011).

[27] Andreas Höntsch, "Ungeheure Bilder zum Nachdenken: *Die Vergebung* — Ein Gespräch mit den Filmschöpfern," interview by Dorothee Trapp, *Schweriner Volkszeitung*, 9 November 1995.

[28] Marc Silberman, "Post-Wall Documentaries: New Images from a New Germany?" *Cinema Journal* 33, no. 2 (1994): 22–41, here 32.

[29] Robert Ide, "Die innerste Sicherheit," *Berliner Zeitung*, 22 April 2004, http://www.tagesspiegel.de/kultur/tagestipps/art135,2168491.

[30] Andreas Busche, "Fragwürdig, aber beeindruckend," *die tageszeitung*, 11 February 2004, http://www.taz.de/1/archiv/archiv/?dig=2004/02/11/a0238.

[31] See Joachim Huber, "Trauter feind," *Der Tagesspiegel*, 16 April 2008, http://www.tagesspiegel.de/medien-news/Liebesgeschichte;art15532,2513760.

[32] Regina Kaiser and Uwe Karlstedt, *12 Heisst "Ich Liebe Dich": Der Stasi-Offizier und die Dissidentin* (Cologne: Kiepenheuer & Witsch, 2003).

[33] Johannes Beleites, "Die Schöne und das Biest?," *Horch und Guck*, 42 (2003): 85–86, http://www.horch-und-guck.info/hug/archiv/2000-2003/heft-42/04222/; and RJB, "Stasi-Opfer liebt Stasi-Täter," *Die Welt-Online*, 9 October 1999, http://www.welt.de/print-welt/article586982/Stasi_Opfer_liebt_Stasi_Taeter.html.

[34] Claus Christian Malzahn und Severin Weiland, "Das Problem liegt bei der PDS," *Der Spiegel*, 15 September 2006, http://www.spiegel.de/politik/deutschland/0,1518,437210,00.html.

[35] Florian Henckel von Donnersmarck, "*Das Leben der Anderen / The Lives of Others*," interview by Michael Guillen, *The Evening Class* (blog), 20 January 2007, http://theeveningclass.blogspot.com/2007/01/das-leben-der-anderen-lives-of.html.

[36] Joachim Gauck, "'Ja, so war es!,'" *Stern*, 7 August 2006, http://www.stern.de/kultur/film/das-leben-der-anderen-ja-so-war-es-558074.html. The issue of authenticity is also important to Becker's film. The deluxe *Good Bye, Lenin!* DVD package includes a documentary, *Genau so war's* (Elena Bromund, 2002), in which the director stresses the production's focus on staging an authentic GDR. See Nick Hodgin, "Aiming to Please? Consensus and Consciousness-raising in Wolfgang Becker's *Good Bye, Lenin!*," in *New Directions in German Cinema*, ed. Paul Cooke and Chris Homewood (London: I. B. Tauris, 2011).

[37] Reinhard Mohr, "Stasi ohne Spreewaldgurke," *Der Spiegel*, 15 March 2006, http://www.spiegel.de/kultur/kino/0,1518,406092,00.html.

[38] Cited in Jens Giesecke, *Die hauptamtlichen Mitarbeiter der Staatssicherheit* (Berlin: Links, 2000), 12.

[39] Owen Evans, "Redeeming the Demon? The Legacy of the Stasi in *Das Leben der Anderen*," *Memory Studies* 3 (2010): 164–77, here 171.

[40] See "Interview mit Gabriele Binder," *vierundzwanzig.de*, http://www.vierundzwanzig.de/kostuem/interview_mit_gabriele_binder#; and Timothy Garton Ash, "The Stasi on Our Minds," *New York Review of Books*, 31 May 2007, http://www.nybooks.com/articles/archives/2007/may/31/the-stasi-on-our-minds/.

[41] Matthias Fiedler, "German Crossroads: Visions of the Past in German Cinema after Reunification," in *German Memory Contests: The Quest for Identity in Literature, Film and Discourse since 1990*, ed. Anne Fuchs, Mary Cosgrove, and Georg Grote (Rochester, NY: Camden House, 2006), 127–43, here 143.

[42] Owen Evans makes a similar point in his article "Redeeming the Demon?," 163.

[43] Christoph Dieckmann, *Das wahre Leben im Falschen: Geschichten von ostdeutscher Identität* (Berlin: Ch. Links, 2000), 15.

[44] In H. M. Broder, "Wir lieben die Heimat," *Der Spiegel*, 3 July 1995.

[45] Emmanuel Levy, "Lives of Others — Florian Henckel von Donnersmarck," *Cinema 24/7*, accessed 1 June 2010, http://www.emanuellevy.com/search/details.cfm?id=3826.

[46] Jonathan Romney, "The Lives of Others," *Independent*, 15 April 2007, http://www.independent.co.uk/arts-entertainment/film-and-tv/film-reviews/the-lives-of-others-15-444821.html.

[47] Slavoj Žižek, "The Dreams of Others," *In These Times*, 18 May 2007, http://www.inthesetimes.com/article/3183/.

[48] Wolf Biermann, "Die Gespenster treten aus dem Schatten," *Die Welt*, 22 March 2006, http://www.welt.de/print-welt/article205348/Die_Gespenster_treten_aus_dem_Schatten.html.

[49] Charles S. Maier, "What Have We Learned since 1989?," *Contemporary European History* 18, no. 3 (2009): 253–69, here 266.

[50] "Fettleibig mit Dauerwelle," *Der Spiegel*, 23 October 1989.

[51] See Udo Grashoff, *"In einem Anfall von Depression . . .": Selbsttötungen in der DDR* (Berlin: Ch. Links, 2006). Though mostly well received, the review in *Die Welt* appears both disappointed in and skeptical of Grashoff's conclusion that the high suicide rate was due to the region's Protestant heritage and not the GDR's political terrors. See Lars-Broder Keil, "Warum sich im Osten mehr Menschen als im Westen umbringen," *Die Welt*, 2 November 2006, http://www.welt.de/politik/article91841/Warum_sich_im_Osten_mehr_Menschen_als_im_Westen_umbringen.html.

[52] Andreas Dresen, "Der Falsche Kino Osten," *Die Zeit*, 16 May 2009, http://www.zeit.de/2009/17/Dresen.

[53] Rainer Gansera, "In der Lauge der Angst," *Süddeutsche Zeitung*, 23 March 2006, http://www.sueddeutsche.de/kultur/2.220/film-das-leben-der-anderen-in-der-lauge-der-angst-1.894518.

[54] See for example the DDR Museum Malchow, which opened in 1999 (http://www.ddr.museum.ist.online.ms/). Other exhibitions that year included "Typisch DDR? Personen und Gegenstände" at the Museum für Thüringer Volkskunde Erfurt and "Die andere Vergangenheit — 40 Jahre Leben in der DDR" at the Stadtmuseum in Dresden.

[55] See Regina Mönch, "Selbstvergiftung," *Frankfurter Allgemeine Zeitung*, 18 April 2008, http://www.faz.net/s/Rub475F682E3FC24868A8A5276D4FB916

D7/Doc~E8D6486E9276448F194D87E25C9EAACFD~ATpl~Ecommon~Scon
tent.html.

[56] Eva Horn, "Media of Conspiracy: Love and Surveillance in Fritz Lang and
Florian Henckel von Donnersmarck," *New German Critique* 103 (Winter 2008):
127–45, here 130–31.

[57] Florian Henckel von Donnersmarck, dir., *The Lives of Others* (Lions Gate Home
Entertainment, 2007), Region 2 DVD.

[58] Hans Joachim Maaz, "Viele Ostdeutsche sind nicht geheilt," interview by
Stefan Berg and Michael Sontheimer, *Spiegel Online*, 14 August 2009, http://
einestages.spiegel.de/static/authoralbumbackground/4748/_viele_ostdeutsche_
sind_nicht_geheilt.html

[59] John J. Miller, "The Best Conservative Movies," *National Review Online*, 23
February 2009, http://nrd.nationalreview.com/article/?q=YWQ4MDlhMWRkZ
DQ5YmViMDM1Yzc0MTE3ZTllY2E3MGM=.

[60] William F. Buckley Jr., "Great Lives," *National Review Online*, 23 May 2007,
http://article.nationalreview.com/316273/great-lives/william-f-buckley-jr.

[61] Louis Wittig, "Back in the Old GDR," *National Review Online*, 9 February
2007, http://article.nationalreview.com/305283/back-in-the-old-gdr/louis-wit-
tig.

[62] Wim Wenders, "Wer hätte gedacht, dass sich das Kino selbst verabschiedet,"
interview by Christopher Keil, *Süddeutsche Zeitung*, 11 August 2006, http://www.
sueddeutsche.de/kultur/2.220/wim-wenders-im-interview-wer-haette-gedacht-
dass-sich-das kino-selbst-verabschiedet-1.430978.

Part 2: Remembering the GDR through Museums and Memorials

5: "The Spirit of an Epoch Is Not Just Reflected in Pictures and Books, but Also in Pots and Frying Pans": GDR Museums and Memories of Everyday Life

Silke Arnold-de Simine

NEW MUSEUMS AND MEMORIALS IN BERLIN form the focus of controversial and politically charged public debates regarding the aesthetics of remembrance. Berlin is dense with reminders of difficult pasts, with the historical and architectural legacy of the National Socialist and the GDR periods, whose relationship not only to the present but also to each other needs to be negotiated and formulated. But even if the landscape of memory in Berlin has its own distinct features, it is still necessary to contextualize these debates in a wider global landscape of remembrance that informs and therefore helps to understand the contests taking place in Germany.

Twenty years after the fall of the Berlin Wall the debates concerning the question of how to remember the GDR are as fierce as ever. The GDR memorial landscape is clearly divided: museums, documentation centers, and memorials focus either on state oppression or on everyday life in the GDR and its consumer culture. State funding and media coverage both fuel this polarization of the debate on remembrance of the GDR. The two sides cannot easily be divided into east versus west or left-wing versus right-wing politics. The lines are also drawn between two very different museal approaches: on the one hand is the idea of the museum based on a collection in which everyday material culture is preserved because the disappearance of these (historical) objects would be perceived as a cultural loss. A very different kind of institution focuses on the narratives as well as the material evidence of state oppression. The latter is not only more prominent because it receives political support and public funding, but also because it is based on the memory of a group of people who have an active and vested interest in giving voice to their own experience of oppression in the GDR. I would argue that museums such as the Berlin Wall Documentation Center in Bernauer Strasse (established in 1999, and with a revised exhibition set to be completed in 2012) and the Berlin-Hohenschönhausen Memorial (1994), the former remand prison for people detained by the Ministry of State Security (Stasi), have to be seen in the context of the global phenomenon of the "memorial museum," defined by Paul Williams as "a specific kind of museum dedicated to a historic event commemorating mass suffering of some kind."[1] Williams identifies a trend but his definition is too limited, because it does not account for a range of museums not necessarily concerned with atrocities but with political persecution and oppression, which could still be described as "memorial museums," not least because they combine the function of a memorial and a museum, encouraging reflection and remembrance in their visitors. This type of museum, which relies on authentic sites and eyewitness accounts, is increasingly popular and therefore caters not to a specific community of memory, but to international tourists who flock to these sites.[2]

In contrast to the "memorial museums," the Dokumentationszentrum Alltagskultur der DDR (Documentation Center of Everyday Culture in the GDR), established in 1993 in Eisenhüttenstadt, and the DDR Museum, which opened thirteen years later in Berlin, are not site-specific and are not first and foremost concerned with remembering a difficult past. Given that they are both exhibiting such seemingly mundane topics as everyday life, consumer objects, material culture, and memories of daily routine, it might be surprising that their representations of the GDR are nevertheless contentious. However, it is exactly this emphasis on "normality" that attracts criticism, because both museums are accused of ignoring the political dimensions of the GDR. The criticism directed toward these museums ranges from accusations of blatant nostalgia for the GDR to a more differentiated skepticism regarding the museums' forms of representation. The Dokumentationszentrum Alltagskultur der DDR was seen as a maverick enterprise and as a rival to the official presentation of post-1945 German history in the Haus der Geschichte in Bonn (opened in 1994) and later also the Zeitgeschichtliches Forum (Forum of Contemporary History) in Leipzig (opened in 1999). In 2006 the museal representation of the GDR was already more diversified, and the DDR Museum was criticized most of all because it was perceived to be riding the crest of the *Ostalgie* wave. The Sabrow report, among others, claimed that public interest in GDR everyday culture should not be left to such "unofficial" channels but addressed, for example, by the German Historical Museum (Deutsches Historisches Museum) in Berlin, as seen in its temporary exhibition "Parteidiktatur und Alltag in der DDR" (30 March–29 July 2007).[3]

Opponents to this approach voice concern that the museal presentation of everyday life steers museum visitors away from the political oppression and severe constrictions that shaped life in the GDR. The director of the Hohenschönhausen Memorial, Hubertus Knabe, claims that in these museums the GDR is presented as "sozialpolitisches Großexperiment und nicht als menschenverachtende Diktatur."[4] The response to this criticism is that daily life in the GDR cannot be uncoupled from the political regime or vice versa.

Neither of these museums of everyday life in the GDR was initiated by eastern Germans determined to preserve objects with which they grew up or eager to share their memories of life in the GDR, but by western Germans with a professional interest in the exceptional process of a material culture vanishing from the public and often also from the private sphere more or less overnight. The historian Andreas Ludwig campaigned for funding to set up the Dokumentationszentrum Alltagskultur der DDR and then became its director. The ethnologist and businessman Peter Kenzelmann had the idea for the DDR Museum after failing to find exhibitions on the GDR's everyday culture while visiting Berlin. Neither institution receives state funding, but whereas the DDR Museum is a commercial enterprise (DDR Museum Berlin GmbH) with private sponsors,[5] funded by entrance fees and merchandise, the Dokumentationszentrum Alltagskultur does receive financial support from the Brandenburg Ministry for Science, Research, and Culture, the administrative district Oder-Spree, and the city of Eisenhüttenstadt.

Although these museums focus on the material culture of the GDR, they also claim to address the discrepancy between individual experiences of life in the GDR and public representations of the GDR after its demise — that is, the gap between individual and communicative memory on the one hand and political or cultural memory on the other.[6] Political and cultural memory are attempts to differentiate the contested notion of "collective memory" in which the term "memory" does not stand for the mental ability of an individual to recall personal experiences, but for a range of social and cultural practices by which a collectively shared sense of the past is generated, negotiated, and communicated. Such practices enable people to extend their memory beyond events they have experienced themselves. Therefore it is important to distinguish between (1) the memories of an individual that are only shared with his/her immediate environment (communicative memory), (2) the collectively organized acts of remembrance as vital features of societies (political memory), and (3) the cultural articulations and representations of individual and collective memory in different media and institutions (cultural memory).

According to Aleida Assmann's definition, "political" and "cultural memory" denote ways in which human relationships to the past are actively constructed by social institutions such as the government, schools and universities, and publishing houses "with the aid of memorial signs such as symbols, texts, images, rites, ceremonies, places, and monuments."[7] Museums are institutions that "engender and consolidate social *practices*" of remembrance.[8] The crucial question here is not only what means are deployed to remember the past, but what is gained for the present from doing so. It is therefore important to investigate the underlying implications of recent changes in the "basic grammar of the construction of collective political memory"[9] and in the institutions concerned with the construction and presentation of the past.

What has been described as the global "memory boom" means that representations of the past do not aim first and foremost to further knowledge, but more importantly to generate a sense of belonging to a past that requires emotional investment and identification,[10] sometimes to an extent that suggests the imaginative reliving of events — even by people who did not experience those events personally. Memory is seen as more than a process of necessary simplification and distortion that cannot be trusted,[11] and historiography's ideals of objectivity and detachment and its insistence on a clear distinction between past and present appear heartless, even a betrayal of the victims of state repression and violence. To relegate something completely to the realm of historical knowledge seems nothing short of shying away from a moral responsibility toward the past. In oral testimonies the voices of the victims are retrieved from silence to enable later generations to empathize with them. This form of confrontation with the past comes with the moral obligation to engage with past experience and especially with suffering on a personal and emotional level through identification and empathy. This change in the global landscape of remembrance asks nations and their citizens to remember not only times of glory or martyrdom, but also the more inassimilable pasts of perpetration and guilt on the one hand, victimhood and suffering on the other. In regard to the German situation, unification has certainly contributed to this development by complicating an already difficult situation: not only did East and West Germany have very different perceptions of the National Socialist past that needed to be negotiated, but the legacy of the GDR produced its own discourse of perpetrators and victims. At present the political Right instrumentalizes this discourse to divert from or to relativize National Socialist crimes and interprets the suffering of GDR citizens as a heroic sacrifice for unification.

The competition between different media as to which can provide the best access to this past is another reason for the boom of "empathic memory" in the museum context: historical museums find themselves competing for audiences with feature films that claim to tell "true" stories through the eyes of individuals and therefore invite identification. In response to that competition, museums increasingly highlight individual case stories and explore the combined potential of various media such as personal photographs and objects, documentaries, interviews, and oral testimonies.

In the last twenty years, the museum has gone through a period of redefining its role and its function in society. In response to postmodern and postcolonial critiques of the museum apparatus, objects, collections, and processes of musealization have been resignified and redefined, and these changes in museological thought have resulted in new types of museums. One of them is the so-called memory museum, which could be described as a new form of historical museum. For Susan Sontag "memory museum" is the generic term for the United States Holocaust Memorial Museum in Washington, DC (1993), the Jewish Museum in Berlin (2001), and the museum at the Yad Vashem memorial site (new Holocaust History Museum, 2005). She claims that "the memory museum in its current proliferation is a product of a way of thinking about, and mourning, the destruction of European Jewry in the 1930s and 1940s."[12] However, the genre is by no means restricted to Holocaust museums, but can be seen to address very different historical events and periods.

The genre of the memory museum diversifies into a range of sub-genres that concentrate on the experience of the "people." Museums as varied in topic and location as the Immigration Museum in Melbourne (1998), the Imperial War Museum North in Manchester (2002), and indeed the DDR Museum in Berlin (2006) aim to create memories for those visitors who may not have any direct experience of those historical events.[13] By granting a voice to everyday experiences and to what has been left out in the dominant discourses of history, these memory museums adopt a mode of representation that has so far been the domain of art, and specifically literature. In this way the museum has allegedly left behind its vertical and disciplinary mode of organization, providing a democratic sphere that seems to allow the collective recovery and reconstruction of memory and community.

These recent developments are not simply exciting new projects in the global memorial landscape, which provide a public forum for individual and conflicting memories, they also entail various problems that need to be addressed in regard to GDR remembrance culture:

(1) To give a voice to the communicative memory of the people who experienced the GDR firsthand seems to guarantee the democratization of the record of the past, but existing exhibitions often fail to represent different communities whose memories are — at least partially — incompatible and who are competing for financial support, for media attention, and for endorsement in the public sphere. Communicative memory might appear to be "bottom-up" and therefore more authentic than an authoritative "top-down" narrative, but there are still political interests at play, which means that some memory communities, for example the SED victims' associations, are better represented through state funding in the memorial landscape and consequently receive more media attention than former GDR citizens who defied GDR authorities in one way or another but in retrospect cannot, or do not want to, claim victim status. This deepens and cements the already existing gulf between these memory communities.

(2) Memory does not simply grant access to the past, but engages with relationships between past and present. Memory scholars are interested in how people experience their past in the here and now. This is one of the reasons "memory" has become such an important concept in subjects such as literary and film studies, which are concerned with representations, with memory texts, rather than with the question of "how it really was." The existing polarization in GDR remembrance culture between the focus on the everyday and the focus on political repression is a symptom of very different political and ideological interest in the present. To state that this polarization is an unjustified simplification does not help to understand why it is so persistent and which interests it serves.

(3) The split in GDR remembrance culture between what is seen as everyday nostalgia and the commemoration of the GDR as an *Unrechtsstaat* tends to rely on the assumption that concern with the everyday is inherently unpolitical and bound to sentimentalize and banalize the GDR.[14] In contrast, to focus on the wall, the Stasi, and the repressive character of the state is seen to form the basis for a critical and intellectually viable approach. This assumption endorses a clear distinction between the private and public spheres and chooses to ignore that the personal is always political.

Andreas Ludwig, director of the Dokumentationszentrum Alltagskultur der DDR, claims that "public representations [of the GDR] still focus on political history with a strong emphasis on repression and resistance."[15] He argues that the museums of GDR everyday life have to be seen as part of a diversified landscape of remembrance in which most memorials and documentation centers do indeed deal with the border regime, the Stasi, and political imprisonment.[16] To back up his claim, he refers to a controversial report by a committee of experts appointed by the SPD-Green coalition (1998–2005) that voiced recommendations regarding the future of GDR remembrance culture and its institutions. The committee was convened by Martin Sabrow, the director of the Research Center for Contemporary History (ZZF) in Potsdam, and consisted of scholars, experts in GDR history, and members of the former GDR opposition movement. The report of the so-called Sabrow Commission discussed the allocation of government subsidies for the *Aufarbeitung* of the GDR and offered advice regarding potential oversights and neglected aspects.[17] The fact that they chose the term *Aufarbeitung* (meaning to "reappraise" or "examine" the past) rather than *Vergangenheitsbewältigung* (commonly translated as "coming to terms with the past") signals a clear differentiation between the two difficult pasts that resists and tries to go beyond a simple equation of the "two totalitarian dictatorships." It was intended to provide a basis to improve the coordination of existing initiatives and organizations dealing with oppression and opposition within the GDR. The report, published in May 2006, suggested that there was a need for a stronger emphasis on resistance and opposition — something they felt was underrepresented in the GDR memory landscape.[18] The commission called for state subsidies to establish a more balanced landscape of memory (*Erinnerungslandschaft*), and isolated initiatives were to be regrouped around three topics: regime-society-opposition, surveillance and persecution, and division and border.

The Sabrow Commission also criticized the "trivialization of the GDR" in the "uncritical collection of GDR everyday culture" by the DDR Museum and the Dokumentationszentrum, advocating a new museum that would deal with everyday life in the GDR under the dictatorship.[19] However, when the report was published on 15 May 2006, the Commission itself was accused of a "Verniedlichung der DDR"[20] and the new minister of culture under the CDU-SPD Grand Coalition (2005–9) Bernd Neumann (CDU) distanced himself from the report. The very term *Alltag* (everyday life) seemed to indicate to the SED victims' associations that an attempt was being made to trivialize life in the GDR. The establishment of the Bundesstiftung zur Aufarbeitung der SED-Diktatur (government-funded organization devoted to the examination and reappraisal of the SED dictatorship in East Germany) was the main result of the commission's work. This organization sees its role as contributing "to a complete reappraisal of the causes, history, and impact of dictatorship in the SBZ (Soviet zone of occupation) and the GDR. It aims to testify to the injustice of the SED-regime and its victims, to further the anti-totalitarian consensus within our society, as well as to strengthen democracy and German Unity."[21]

Museums of Everyday Life in the GDR: Dokumentationszentrum Alltagskultur der DDR, Eisenhüttenstadt

The Dokumentationszentrum Alltagskultur der DDR, opened in 1993, is the oldest museum to focus on the preservation and presentation of everyday life in the GDR. It is located not in Berlin but in Eisenhüttenstadt, quite some distance south of the capital, and well off the tourist track. This is reflected in their visitor numbers, which remained constant at around six thousand per year between 2007 and 2009. One third of the visitors come from the region, another third are Berliners, and only about 10 percent are visitors from abroad. The federal state of Brandenburg was willing to finance the museum, which explains its location. Its director, Andreas Ludwig, believes its significance lies in collecting, preserving, and interpreting material culture that "represents the diversity of societies rather than giving a distinct narrative of history."[22] The permanent exhibition (over 250 square meters), which was put together by Ludwig and the graphic designer Helga Lieser in 2001, is not chronological but focuses on topics such as politics, economy, social welfare, and education. In contrast to the DDR Museum, however, it distinguishes between the different decades and their key features and provides comparisons to other countries.

The temporary exhibitions (over 200 square meters) take their inspiration from current public debates: the first exhibition, "Tempolinsen and P2" (1993), for example, considered whether GDR everyday culture had survived the demise of the country in the private sphere and, if so, how this had been achieved. One of the aims was to show how seemingly innocuous objects have a political dimension: convenience food such as quick-cooking lentils (*Tempolinsen*), for example, were introduced to reduce the time women had to spend in the kitchen in order to enable them to join the workforce.

The museum houses 150,000 objects donated to the museum by 2,000 former citizens of the GDR. It also includes photographs, films, and audio documents. It is clearly object-centered rather than narrative-centered, its core function being preservation rather than narration. Instead of presenting visitors with a master narrative, the aim is to allow them to make up their own minds. It forces them to "read between the lines" and assume responsibility for an interpretation that might change over time. All donated objects are catalogued by provenance, and interviews are conducted with donors to document and archive the meaning of these objects for their owners. According to Andreas Ludwig, however, the stories told by donors of objects usually digress rather quickly from the objects, which are used as props and serve as a trigger for life stories associated with those objects. The basic assumption is that stories accrue around objects and that one task of the museum is to salvage those (hi)stories instead of using the objects as illustrations for preconceived narratives.

Objects can trigger memories of everyday life in the GDR, and in this capacity they form a part of its communicative memory. Currently around one third of visitors to the museum have a GDR background and are therefore likely to have firsthand experience of the exhibits. The visitor books contain comments that describe objects in the exhibition as starting points for accounts of life in the GDR. According to Ludwig, the ideal scenario for a visit would be a group consisting of three generations (with different experiences of the GDR or — in the case of the youngest — none at all) for whom the objects serve as a catalyst for discussion. However, these conversations are only possible if family members have firsthand experience of the GDR, which means that visitors from the former FRG or from abroad are automatically excluded from this approach. While the DDR Museum has to rely on entrance fees from (international) tourists, the Dokumentationszentrum's location mainly attracts visitors who either live in the surrounding area or who have a particular interest in GDR everyday culture.

Around one hundred interviews with donors were recorded to transform their individual memories into more durable — if necessarily mediated — cultural memory. These stories are transcribed but do not form part of the exhibition, in which the displays are accompanied by only minimal textual explanations in captions to allow for the visitors' own interpretation. In the interviews all the donors are asked why they chose to give these specific objects; however, they usually fail to answer that question and expand instead on the — seemingly more objective — reasons why these objects should be preserved, and in so doing invariably reveal a rather defensive desire to portray a positive image of the GDR.

In the permanent exhibition "Life in the GDR," traditional glass cases and platforms are deliberately used as distancing devices. Rather than integrating the objects into dioramas of reconstructed living environments, the installations are a constant reminder that they are representations of the past.[23] Their expressed function is to prevent visitors from immersing themselves in that past. In each room text panels expand on the curators' take on the topic and offer background information on the GDR. This is supposed to allow visitors to form their own interpretation of the relationship between the political regime and everyday life. The proclaimed aim of the museum is to encourage critical distance, providing the basis for "Bildung und Forschung" and enabling "Anschauung und Kommunikation zwischen Ost- und Westdeutschen, zwischen den Generationen und Kulturen."[24] However, it is difficult to imagine how this communication not only between generations but also between different cultures and between eastern and western Germans could be facilitated if the conducted interviews do not form part of the exhibition. This problem will become even more pressing when the communicative memory of the GDR has come to an end — that is, when there is nobody left with firsthand experience of the GDR and the three-generational family group envisaged as the ideal visitor scenario is a thing of the past.

Museums of Everyday Life in the GDR: The DDR Museum, Berlin

In contrast to state-funded remembrance projects, most of which focus on the regime's control of its borders and the activities of the SED and the Stasi, the DDR Museum is a private and commercial enterprise. It is located in the center of Berlin, opposite the neo-baroque cathedral and the currently empty space that once housed the Berlin City Palace (partly destroyed in the Second World War and demolished in 1950) and later the Palace of the Republic (opened in 1976 and demolished between 2006 and 2009). Its prominent location enables the museum to attract a large number of (international) tourists. Numbers rose from fifteen thousand in 2006 to fifty thousand in 2009. In 2008 the museum was nominated for the European Museum of the Year Award.[25]

The museum is seen to be part of the *Ostalgie* phenomenon,[26] which ironically enough is first and foremost a thriving nostalgia industry that flourishes on the basis of a material culture and its associated lifestyle that literally vanished overnight. After unification East German commodities were discarded en masse or found a new home in museums. Both the German Historical Museum (founded in 1987) in the West and the Museum of German History (Museum für deutsche Geschichte, 1952–90) in the East launched public appeals for donations with the slogan: "Die DDR ins Museum!" (Put the GDR in a museum!). The aim was to collect everyday objects that constituted a vital part of people's socialization and would otherwise be irretrievably lost. Their effort to collect as many objects as possible was a race against time as the post-*Wende* jump in the quantity of household waste being thrown away in the former East Germany made only too clear.[27] Objects were saved from the scrapheap and transferred to the museum as if it were Noah's ark: each a representative of a whole species. Exhibitions of GDR everyday objects presented many eastern German visitors with displays of domestic scenes that were similar to their own homes and featured the kind of furniture that many of them had just discarded in favor of new products from the West. The effect is ambivalent: on the one hand, one's own ordinary life seems somehow ennobled; on the other, this can only be achieved by rendering it obsolete.[28]

Nostalgia for everyday life in the GDR set in barely a decade after the demise of the country and mainly afflicted defiant eastern Germans who had fond memories of their lives in the GDR and associated them with certain consumer goods not (readily) available anymore: "Despite — or perhaps because of — the abrupt 'secularisation' of GDR artefacts, where they no longer embody the dreams of a prosperous present and a hopeful socialist future, they now serve as repositories of private histories and sentimental reflection."[29]

The revival and success of former GDR products rested on their popularity with eastern Germans and a fascination on the part of the West: the *Ostalgie* phenomenon includes a range of novelty goods associated with the GDR that are popular with western tourists (the *Ampelmännchen* products, for example, which feature the figures shown on traffic lights at pedestrian crossings in the former GDR) or deemed cool by young (eastern and western) Germans who never experienced the GDR.[30] Only 37 percent of visitors have firsthand experience of the GDR: most are either too young to have experienced the GDR or are tourists from other countries. The DDR Museum nevertheless aims to be part of a process in which these artifacts of East German material culture are transformed into repositories of memory.[31] Even before the museum was officially opened, its website announced: "The spirit of an epoch is not just reflected in pictures and books, but also in pots and frying pans." The guidebook explains that the authentic artifacts can provide visitors with a "hands-on experience" of what life was like back then:

> Everyday life is lived history — only comprehensible if you as a visitor experience it, too. This is exactly what the exhibition of the GDR Museum Berlin enables you to do: visitors are encouraged to handle the exhibits. You can rev the Trabi's engine, explore a typical kitchen or lounge in authentic GDR movie chairs to watch a documentary. Various themed sections invite visitors to learn about topics in a playful way. And in the thematic area "Stasi," they can even gain a firsthand experience of what being spied on was like — from the perspective of the perpetrator and the victim.[32]

According to the director of the museum, Robert Rückel, its aim is to satisfy a general curiosity about history.[33] It promises an almost indiscreet peek through the keyhole: "A concrete-slab flat with living room, kitchen, and bathroom, designed in original 70s style, invites you to rummage through someone else's cupboards."[34] This form of interactive engagement with the diorama could be described as a museum equivalent of reality TV, but in this GDR-specific context it is also highly problematic as an activity that mimics the Stasi's intrusion into the private sphere without being thematized as such.

When criticized for an excessively benign, highly selective view of a dictatorship, the curators of the DDR Museum claimed that as a memory museum it showcases what had been neglected by the "top-down" approach to history by representing the memories of people for whom political and ideological issues were simply not that important. The head of research, Stefan Wolle, clearly champions this perspective of memory as a less restricted and more comprehensive and democratic way of presenting the GDR:

> The historians have made up their minds and their central points seem to be conclusive. The GDR was a satellite state at Moscow's mercy. The security apparatus was the iron fist that held everything together. . . . But there are still some points that cannot be easily explained. The GDR was more than just an artificial product of ideology and power — for millions of people it was their life. . . . Sometimes, it was quite easy to forget all about politics and ideology.[35]

Yet as long as the museum does not incorporate representations of varied and contrasting experiences of the GDR, this approach does risk turning a proclaimed "majority experience" into a master narrative.

The exhibition (over 400 square meters) is not organized chronologically but subdivided into themes such as fashion, consumption/products, transportation, and youth.[36] It was designed by the architect Frank Wittmer, the designer Constantin Bänfer, and Robert Rückel. The objects are presented in display cabinets, which also function as partitions. The cabinets are wooden miniatures of the kind of prefabricated apartment blocks associated with the GDR of the 1970s and 1980s. In order to assuage their critics, the curators have incorporated reminders of the GDR's omnipresent state security by encouraging visitors to use working Stasi equipment to listen in on the conversations of other visitors in the reconstructed (bugged) living room on display. However, the transgression into the private sphere can never be simulated in a public sphere: the visitors might not at first realize that their conversations in the mock living room can be overheard by other visitors using Stasi observation equipment, but nobody ever leaves the public space of the museum, which is shared with other visitors, and therefore one's private sphere is never invaded and the whole exercise seems harmless enough, even fun. This kind of voyeurism is without consequences for the "spies" or those being spied on and is little more than a parlor game. The exhibition also displays a diorama of the death strip, which in scale and presentation resembles a toy-train landscape. The attempt to include reminders of state oppression in the exhibition of the DDR Museum is impeded by the museum's focus on providing an experiential and playful encounter with an exhibition that is supposed to be inviting to visitors of all ages and backgrounds. That said, the ideal visitor scenario, according to Stefan Wolle, is the guided tour that complements and comments on the exhibition.

Although the museum is clearly popular with visitors and does not rely on public funding, it has tried to address criticism voiced in the media with plans to extend and reorganize the permanent exhibition and to include temporary exhibitions as well as events such as readings. The new exhibition, which opened in October 2010, incorporates more information on the SED and on the Stasi. For example it includes a reconstruction of a prison cell and interrogation room in which visitors can listen to audiotapes of narrated interrogation protocols. For this the museum is working in close cooperation with the Bautzen Memorial (1993). This does not result, however, in its losing its lighthearted approach: the revamp also includes a museum restaurant that offers meals based on GDR favorites.

One might say that the term "museum" in its traditional sense is somehow misleading here, as the main purpose of the DDR Museum is not to collect objects of material culture in order to further historical knowledge.[37] Text-based information is kept to an absolute minimum and visitors are allowed to handle objects, which obviously runs counter to the museum's task of preservation. The curators are not so much trying to analyze the objects in their collection as working toward furnishing a master narrative: on their website they appeal to the public in their search for specific objects needed to complement the sensual and tactile experience of a coherent narrative.[38] They aim to provide visitors with an experience rather than with detailed information, with "infotainment" rather than knowledge, with a theme park rather than a museum.

Difficult pasts that are still remembered firsthand by a fair percentage of visitors present a challenge to conventional museological concepts that do not seem to encourage a moral or experiential engagement with this past. But the response of modern memory museums is also deeply problematic because the logical consequence of their mission would be to showcase the multitude of different memory communities whose narratives are mutually exclusive and cannot easily be integrated into one coherent master narrative.

Conclusion

The polarization of the GDR memorial landscape is the result not only of a clash of interests between different communities of memory or between a "top-down" official narrative and a variety of personal (unheard) stories, but of two very different approaches that are reflected in the museal landscape:

(1) For former GDR citizens who suffered under the regime and want to voice their memories of repression and opposition, authentic places such as the former Stasi prison at Berlin-Hohenschönhausen and authentic objects serve to illustrate their stories and also act — even more importantly — as visual evidence of their accounts. This approach has gained currency because it also ties in with the global development of the so-called memorial museums. Recent memory discourses have tended to fall into two dominant modes: remembering victimization, and remembering in order to come to terms with the legacy of the perpetrators. This binary can stand in the way of thinking through the complexities and ambiguities of politics both social and subjective, and it can limit the capacity to grasp the gray area between the "done to" and the "doing." The fact that German as well as global memory culture is focused on perpetrator-victim narratives means that stories that conform to this template are more likely to be heard. The problem is that this approach ignores what some of the critics of the Sabrow report termed the "correlation between the regime and society ranging from acceptance to revolt, enthusiasm to disdain, discontented loyalty to *Nischenglück* [withdrawal from society into a group of like-minded people]."[39]

(2) Compared to the "memorial museums," the attempts of historians to preserve the material traces of the GDR in museums seem old-fashioned, belonging to a time when the museum was criticized as a dusty

storage space. In addition, such attempts became equated with the phenomenon of *Ostalgie* that set in several years after unification. Museums
such as the DDR Museum and the Dokumentationszentrum Alltagskultur
der DDR do not seem to fit into the traditional museum landscape: they
exhibit banal everyday objects such as pots and frying pans rather than
focusing on high culture (such as art galleries) or providing a chronological historical account (like historical museums). A collection of everyday
objects is usually associated with local history or heritage museums. Nor
do the two museums discussed here fit in with the modern "memorial
museums": they were not conceived by former GDR citizens desperate to
tell their stories or to fill the gap between individual experience and public
representation. In fact they started out with the material remains — with
the objects themselves rather than with people's memories. These objects
might now provide visitors from the former GDR with the opportunity to
present their own versions of life in the GDR, but this can only work as
long as they and their stories are still around. Once the opportunity for
direct communication with people who have firsthand experience of the
GDR is gone, those memories will only be available in their mediated (and
fixed) form as recorded interviews.

Some of the criticism directed at the DDR Museum, which attempts
to defy its image as a mere tourist attraction exploiting nostalgia for everyday GDR culture and the West's fascination with the "exotic" East, is
certainly justified. But the assumption that nostalgia is necessarily uncritical
and the result of a failure to engage with one's history in a meaningful way
has been challenged very convincingly by Svetlana Boym's notion of
"reflective nostalgia." Boym argues that, apart from a restorative function
in which a longing for something lost is expressed, nostalgia can also have
a critical reflective function.[40] In this sense it is no accident that former
GDR consumer objects are at the center of the *Ostalgie* phenomenon.
These objects denote shared experiences rather than highlighting the differences between various memory communities. Because of their longevity
they bind together different generations, standing for both the private
(consumption) and the public (production) and therefore — in retrospect
at least — holding the utopian promise of a reconciliation between subjectivity and collectivity.[41] This form of projection speaks of a need to establish a community of memory of former GDR citizens that is not divided
but united. *Ostalgie* can also be seen as an attempt to regain agency in the
decision of what should be left behind and what should be preserved, but
in its favoring of former GDR goods it is not least a veiled critique of a
capitalist system that has failed to address the implications of the social,
economic, and cultural challenges of German unification.

Notes

¹ Paul Williams, *Memorial Museums: The Global Rush to Commemorate Atrocities* (Oxford: Berg, 2007), 8.

² "In 2009 the Memorial could reach a new record with more than 314,000 visitors in total and 50 percent of these being students. Since the Foundation came into effect in July 2000, the number of visitors is more than three times higher (figures as of 06.01.2010). Tours of the prison are usually led by former inmates, who provide first-hand details on prison conditions and the interrogation methods employed by the GDR's Ministry of State Security (MfS)." See Gedenkstätte: Berlin-Hohenschönhausen, accessed 10 March 2010, http://en.stiftung-hsh.de/document.php?cat_id=CAT_231&special=0.

³ See further discussion of the so-called Sabrow Commission later in this article.

⁴ Hubertus Knabe, *Die Täter sind unter uns: Über das Schönreden der SED-Diktatur* (Berlin: Ullstein, 2007), 8.

⁵ About 600,000 euros were needed to plan and install the permanent exhibition, with most of the work being done by volunteers and laypeople.

⁶ For the definition of these formats of memory see Aleida Assmann, "Memory, Individual and Collective," in *The Oxford Handbook of Contextual Political Analysis*, ed. Robert E. Goodin and Charles Tilly (Oxford: Oxford UP, 2006), 210–24, here 215.

⁷ Aleida Assmann, "Four Formats of Memory: From Individual to Collective Constructions of the Past," in *Cultural Memory and Historical Consciousness in the German-Speaking World Since 1500*, ed. Christian Emden and David Midgley (Oxford: Peter Lang, 2004), 19–37, here 26.

⁸ Williams, *Memorial Museums*, 5; italics in the original.

⁹ Assmann, "Memory, Individual and Collective," 219.

¹⁰ Geoffrey Cubitt, *History and Memory* (Manchester: Manchester UP, 2007), 1.

¹¹ Elisabeth Loftus, "The Reality of Illusory Memories," in *Memory Distortions: How Minds, Brains and Societies Reconstruct the Past*, ed. Daniel L. Schacter (Cambridge, MA: Harvard UP, 1995), 47–68.

¹² Susan Sontag, *Regarding the Pain of Others* (London: Penguin Books, 2004), 77. Also see Katrin Pieper, *Die Musealisierung des Holocaust: Das Jüdische Museum Berlin und das U.S. Holocaust Memorial Museum in Washington, D.C. Ein Vergleich* (Cologne: Böhlau, 2006).

¹³ Alison Landsberg has coined the term "prosthetic memory" for this process and talks about "experiential museums." See Alison Landsberg, *Prosthetic Memory: The Transformation of American Remembrance in the Age of Mass Culture* (New York: Columbia UP, 2004), 33.

¹⁴ See Michael Schwartz and Hermann Wentker, "Die Debatte in den Fachzeitschriften," in *Wohin treibt die DDR-Erinnerung? Dokumentation einer Debatte*, ed. Martin Sabrow (Göttingen: Vandenhoeck & Ruprecht, 2007), 373.

[15] Andreas Ludwig, "Views on the Recent Past. Interpretations and Contradictions in Museum Representations about the GDR" (unpublished manuscript 2007, quoted with the author's permission).

[16] The most important examples are the Information and Documentation Center at the Office for the Records of the State Security Service of the Former GDR (IDZ), the Stasi Museum Berlin (1990), and the Berlin-Hohenschönhausen Memorial (1994).

[17] Empfehlungen der Expertenkommission zur Schaffung eines Geschichtsverbundes "Aufarbeitung der SED-Diktatur," May 2006, http:/www.zeitgeschichte-online. de/site/40208626/default.aspx.

[18] Sabrow, "Zur Entstehungsgeschichte des Expertenvotums," in Sabrow, *Wohin treibt die DDR-Erinnerung?*, 7–9, here 9.

[19] Sabrow, "Die Empfehlungen der Expertenkommission zur Schaffung eines Geschichtsverbundes 'Aufarbeitung der SED-Diktatur,'" in Sabrow, *Wohin treibt die DDR-Erinnerung?*, 17–45, here 20 and 35.

[20] Michael Schwartz and Hermann Wentker, "Erinnerungspolitik auf dem Holzweg. Zu den Empfehlungen der Expertenkommission für eine künftige 'Aufarbeitung der SED-Diktatur,'" in Sabrow, *Wohin treibt die DDR-Erinnerung?*, 369–74, here 373.

[21] Bundesstiftung zur Aufarbeitung der SED-Diktatur, "Remembrance as Duty," January 2010, http://www.stiftung-aufarbeitung.de/downloads/pdf/english.pdf ?PHPSESSID=558eed57a59c452de9e43ac92acb936e.

[22] Ludwig, *Views on the Recent Past*, 10.

[23] Part of the museum, though not in the building itself, is a historically reconstructed apartment from 1957 (Historische Wohnung, Straße der Republik 29, Eisenhüttenstadt); see http://www.alltagskultur-ddr.de/pages/aus/aus.html, accessed 10 March 2010.

[24] See http://www.alltagskultur-ddr.de/pages/dok/dok.html, accessed 10 March 2010.

[25] DDR Museum, accessed 10 March 2010, http://www.ddr-museum.de/de/ presse/statistiken/.

[26] See Ruth Reiher and Antje Baumann, eds., *Vorwärts und nichts vergessen: Sprache in der DDR. Was war, was ist, was bleibt* (Berlin: Aufbau, 2004); Thomas Ahbe, "Ostalgie als Laienpraxis: Einordnungen, Bedingungen, Funktionalität," *Berliner Debatte INITIAL* 3 (1999): 87–97; and Thomas Ahbe, "Arbeit am kollektiven Gedächtnis: Die Fernseh-Shows zur DDR als Effekt vergangenheitspolitischer Diskurse seit 1990," *Deutschland Archiv* 36, no. 6 (2003): 917–24.

[27] Gerd Kuhn and Andreas Ludwig, "Sachkultur und DDR-Alltag: Versuch einer Annäherung," in *Alltag und soziales Gedächtnis: Die DDR Objektkultur und ihre Musealisierung*, ed. Gerd Kuhn and Andreas Ludwig (Hamburg: Ergebnisse Verlag, 1997), 13–24, here 20–21.

[28] Other examples include photo books on GDR design such as Georg C. Bertsch and Ralf Ulrich, *DDR Design East German Design: 1949–1989* (Cologne: Taschen 2004).

[29] Paul Betts, "The Twilight of the Idols: East German Memory and Material Culture," *The Journal of Modern History* 72 (2000): 731–65, here 754–57.

[30] Martin Blum, "Club Cola and Co.: *Ostalgie*, Material Culture and Identity," in *Transformations of the New Germany*, ed. Ruth A. Starkman (New York: Palgrave Macmillan, 2006), 131–49, here 132.

[31] At the same time these consumer products are redesignated as signifiers of potential resistance because they come to stand for disillusionment with the promises of Western consumerism.

[32] http://www.ddr-museum.de/en/exhibition/topics/, accessed 10 March 2010.

[33] Robert Rückel, "A Friendly Welcome," in *The GDR Museum: A Guide to the Permanent Exhibition — A Hands-on Experience of Everyday Life*, ed. Robert Rückel (Berlin: DDR Museum Verlag, 2006), 4–5, here 4.

[34] http://www.ddr-museum.de/en/exhibition/layout/, accessed 10 March 2010.

[35] Stefan Wolle, "The Human Being Is at the Centre of Attention: Life and Dictatorship in the GDR," in Rückel, *The GDR Museum*, 11.

[36] The sixteen topics are border, Berlin, traffic, youth, education, work, consumption, state security, building, living, family, media, fashion, free time, culture, and holidays.

[37] Museological standards as laid down in the ICOM Code of Ethics for Museums are clearly not the priority of the DDR Museum; see http://icom.museum/code2006_eng.pdf, accessed 10 March 2010. It has reacted to criticism by introducing online access to its object database, which visitors can now browse, and it also invites those who lived in the GDR to add information and stories about the objects.

[38] http://www.ddr-museum.de/de/museum/wir-suchen/, accessed 10 March 2010.

[39] Schwartz and Wentker, "Erinnerungspolitik auf dem Holzweg," 373.

[40] "Restorative nostalgia puts emphasis on *nostos* and proposes to rebuild the lost home and patch up the memory gaps. Reflective nostalgia dwells in *algia*, in longing and loss, the imperfect process of remembrance . . . Restorative nostalgia manifests itself in total reconstruction of the past, while reflective nostalgia lingers on ruins, the patina of time and history, in the dreams of another place and another time." See Svetlana Boym, *The Future of Nostalgia* (New York: Basic Books, 2001), 41.

[41] Betts, "The Twilight of the Idols," 753, and Daphne Berdahl, "'(N)Ostalgie' for the Present: Memory, Longing, and East German Things," *Ethnos* 64, no. 2 (1999): 192–211, here 199.

6: Remapping the Wall: The Wall Memorial in Bernauer Strasse — From an Unloved Cold War Monument to a New Type of Memorial Site

Günter Schlusche

Bernauer Strasse Today

MANY VISITORS WHO COME to Bernauer Strasse today expecting to see a brutal, terrifying, and insurmountable bulwark will be amazed to encounter instead a somewhat secluded and strangely innocuous urban landscape. A broad strip of undeveloped land runs along Bernauer Strasse like a pathway cut through the city; in the adjoining districts, meanwhile, urban life appears to go on as normal. The more attentive visitors may be puzzled by this marked schism or feel a sense of unease or wonder. When visitors come across the now weather-beaten sections of the former Berlin Wall and notice the construction work in progress on the undeveloped land, they perhaps gain a clearer sense of the historical significance of this area. Once they have arrived at the Wall Memorial — a section of the original border fortifications placed between two seven-meter-high rust-colored steel walls — or discover the unusual oval-shaped Chapel of Reconciliation (Versöhnungskapelle) located unassumingly in the background, they realize that world history casts a shadow across this area, for this was once the location of the Berlin Wall, which divided East and West Berlin for many years, and which split a country and a continent into two opposing blocs.

Between 1961 and 1989 the stretch of Berlin Wall along Bernauer Strasse divided an urban residential area that, despite war and destruction, had remained largely intact since it was established at the beginning of the nineteenth century. The construction of the wall on the orders of the SED regime had an acute impact on the everyday lives of the residents of this area. The street became the focus of public attention after 13 August 1961 (the date of the construction of the Berlin Wall) because of the unusual way that the border was drawn here — the fronts of the apartment blocks constituted the border. It was here that dramatic escape attempts occurred, where the first deaths at the wall took place, where more than two thousand residents were driven out of their homes in the buildings along the border. For many years the ghostly appearance of the walled-up houses formed the border to the West, until the construction of "Border Wall 75," the most advanced design, in 1980. The death strip also crossed the grounds of the old Sophien-Friedhof (graveyard). The graves were relocated from 1967 and the neighboring Church of Reconciliation (Versöhnungskirche) stood isolated in the middle of the no man's land at the border before being demolished in 1985.

The fact that Bernauer Strasse was a place of both protest and commemoration of the victims between 1961 and the fall of the wall demonstrates its historical significance within the memory of the city. It also explains why the memorial to the Berlin Wall and its victims had to be located here. The dramatic events following the construction of the wall cemented this site in the collective memory of many Germans and many Berlin residents, and its drastic impact on the everyday life of the city and on the lives of many families and neighborhoods was much more tangible here than, for example, at the Brandenburg Gate or Checkpoint Charlie.

The Berlin Wall as Symbol

The Berlin Wall symbolized the SED regime and its violation of human rights; moreover, it had international significance as an integral feature of the Communist sphere of influence, and its meaning and symbolic impact go far beyond GDR history. The construction of the wall confirmed the boundless arrogance of the SED regime, which believed that by implementing a perfectionist vision of a border system patrolled by the military it could secure long-term control over the population of the GDR and rob it of its desire for freedom. At the same time the construction of the Berlin Wall was tantamount to a declaration of failure by the SED leadership, which was unable to maintain power without the use of force and repression. For the citizens of the GDR the wall meant continued helplessness, fear, and pressure to conform. Only a few were able to escape.

In this context memory of the Berlin Wall is also always associated with the idea of freedom. The popular view of the fall of the wall is that it was a rare moment in German history, when "das Volk der DDR . . . in einer Revolution die Demokratie in seinem Lande erzwang."[1] The wall's collapse, initiated by a relatively small citizens' movement, finally came to represent a global symbol of the defeat of Communism, and in the process the wall gained a broader significance: "im Zustand ihrer Überwindung" (Andreas Nachama) it became a symbol of the desire for freedom and the universality of human rights. It is precisely this dual function that makes the wall a unique cultural and historical monument and the "bekanntesten Bauwerk der DDR, das wahrscheinlich auch sehr viel bekannter ist als die meisten jener Anlagen, die auf der UNESCO-Welterbeliste stehen."[2]

At a time when it has almost completely disappeared, the Berlin Wall attracts more international attention than perhaps ever before. For many years an increasing number of visitors have come to Berlin to gain their own impressions of the "myth" surrounding it. The number of visitors to the Berlin Wall Documentation Center alone has increased from 38,000 when it opened in 2000 to over 370,000 in 2009, when the memorial site at the former Stasi prison in the Hohenschönhausen district of Berlin had 248,000 visitors and the privately run Checkpoint Charlie Museum had as many as 850,000 visitors. Opened just a few years ago, the DDR Museum, also privately run, had around 308,000 visitors in 2009. The events of that year marking the twentieth anniversary of the fall of the Berlin Wall had a strong international presence and again clearly underlined its significance. For at least the past decade there has also been considerable international and interdisciplinary research into the construction, function, and impact of the border fortifications.

Developments from 1989 to the Present

The demolition of the border fortifications began just a few months after the opening of the wall in November 1989. The process officially began on 13 June 1990, when those between Ackerstrasse and Bernauer Strasse were dismantled, and by November of that year the work was almost complete. At the same time the center of Berlin saw an unparalleled development boom and enormous numbers of building projects. In some areas barely a brick remained. The vast expanse of land previously taken up by the border fortifications, some of it measuring up to three hundred meters from front to back, was viewed as a welcome reserve of land for new development, especially the sections in the heart of the city, which shot up in value following new real estate criteria and had good links to the surrounding infrastructure. Removing everything connected with the border in this area thus became a priority. Up to October 1990 the work was carried out by GDR border guards, commissioned by a now democratically elected East Berlin government, and later by the Berlin Senate that represented the unified city. Those calling for at least part of the border fortifications to be preserved and protected only succeeded in a few cases. The ones in Bernauer Strasse were among those to be preserved, but here — as in the other Berlin locations earmarked for preservation — these measures met with strong political and local resistance.[3] Following pressure from the parish of the Sophien-Kirche, a section of the wall along Bernauer Strasse was even removed in 1997. It was suspected that war graves were located in this area, and there was resistance to this section of the wall being preserved and designated a listed historical site.

The more difficult it was for residents of Berlin to recall where the wall had once stood and what it had looked like, the greater was the need to preserve the few remaining stretches and to obtain accurate information about its impact on the lives of residents on both sides. A turnaround came in 2004 with a temporary art installation near the former border at Checkpoint Charlie to remember the deaths at the wall. The installation was designed by Alexandra Hildebrandt, director of the adjacent, privately run Checkpoint Charlie Museum. It was of poor artistic quality, drew on unsound theories, and cited inaccurate figures, and was removed after a few months. However, it served as a catalyst, for in the same year the German Bundestag launched an initiative to establish an information center on the Berlin Wall and German division at the Brandenburg Gate, and the Berlin Senate established a working group to draw up a concept for the project. The Berlin Wall memorial site concept was not adopted by the Senate until 2006, but it provided an appropriate response to the change in the significance of the wall evident for more than ten years. The concept is decentralized in that it covers all of the main locations of the former wall and of the German-German border where authentic remains and traces of the border fortifications are still to be found. These are variously integrated into a memorial site concept and targeted at different types of visitor. The individual elements of the concept will be developed and funded in a process that in some cases will take many years. The Berlin Wall Memorial in Bernauer Strasse, the south side of which was the location of the wall for twenty-eight years, has a key role in this concept, which was adopted by the Berlin Senate in close consultation with the federal government and Bernd Neumann, the federal minister responsible.

Because Berlin has been governed by a left-wing coalition of the SPD and Die Linke since 2002, there were heated political disputes from 2002 to 2007 before and during the implementation of this concept. As the successor party to the SED, Die Linke still faces strong criticism for glossing over the legacy of the GDR and because of the stance of important party members before 1989 not just in Berlin but also in the five new *Bundesländer*. It was surprising, given this background, that responsibility for the overall Berlin Wall memorial site concept was then given to Senator Thomas Flierl, a member of Die Linke. Despite ongoing party disputes, the Berlin Senate's political decision to implement the concept has, how-

Fig. 6.1. The western section of the Berlin Wall Memorial with the remaining sections of the front wall (top right), the Window of Remembrance for the Victims of the Wall (below), the hinterland wall (bottom), the new visitor center (top left), and the housing estates of the district of Wedding in former West Berlin (summer 2010). Copyright © Günter Schlusche/Stiftung Berliner Mauer.

ever, met with widespread cross-party and expert support. Political disputes on remembering the wall have since been defused somewhat, partly because the Berlin Wall Foundation, which was established by the Berlin Senate, has been working tirelessly on the implementation of the individual elements of the concept for the past two years — with tangible results.

The sheer scale of the former border fortifications that once existed within the city is overwhelming. The 44-kilometer stretch between East and West Berlin comprised a good quarter of the 156 kilometers occupied by the border around West Berlin. Up to 1989 the border fortifications in Berlin covered an area of 330 hectares, or 3,300,000 square meters.[4] These figures underline the extensive and unmitigated impact of the construction and expansion of the border on the city's infrastructure, but they also emphasize how misleading it is to reduce the border fortifications to the 16-centimeter-thick concrete structure constituting the border wall itself, which, constructed on the GDR side along the actual state border, was and still is the dominant image of the Berlin Wall in the minds of western Germans and their visitors. However, this was only the final element in a complex and multilevel border system that was constantly perfected during its twenty-eight-year existence and that was predominantly inward-facing, that is, directed against its own population.

Today there are three distinct urban planning approaches to dealing with the former East-West border zones in Berlin. Those for some areas have transformed the architecture and function, realigning with their uses prior to the construction of the wall or even prior to 1945. Examples of this first approach are centrally located, prominent areas such as Potsdamer Platz or the bend in the River Spree (near the Reichstag), which now serve as symbols of the "new Berlin," and also inner-city residential areas such as the Dresdener Strasse in the Kreuzberg district. The second approach is to leave sections of the former border zone in an empty and undeveloped state and adopt a discreet approach to their development. Examples include open spaces such as the park at Nordbahnhof, completed in 2009, and the Mauerpark, opened back in 1995, a large inner-city park that evokes its former status as a border zone through both its name and its layout. The Holocaust Memorial, a giant, abstract sculpture that stands for a new type of memorial site without ignoring its history as part of the no man's land in the former border zone, counts as a unique example. The horizontal form of the Field of Stelae, which covers an area of approximately two hectares, transforms the former barrier function of the border zone into a historically charged space for reflection, which shows the historical caesuras in the development of Germany. Finally, a lack of funding or unresolved questions concerning ownership mean that some wasteland areas remain disused despite the existence of plans and design concepts. These areas — mainly in outlying urban districts — include the former border zone in Bernauer Strasse.

The situation regarding ownership of the land belonging to the former border zone mirrors the history of two German dictatorships, which are both particularly apparent in Bernauer Strasse. Privately owned property was expropriated by the GDR government after 1961 and now often belongs to the federal government, its legal successor. However, a special law gives the former owners, including many Jews who had their property expropriated before 1945, the opportunity to buy back their land under particularly favorable conditions. However, this leads to an extremely convoluted legal situation where ownership is often split among many heirs because of the time periods concerned. The price of the land is a further disputed issue. Although some of these estates have only just gone back to private ownership, following the decision to establish the memorial site at Bernauer Strasse the aim is to reacquire them and ultimately transfer ownership to the memorial site, which will require extremely complex negotiations. Nonetheless, over the past three years agreements have been reached with the owners of over two thirds of the land concerned in Bernauer Strasse, and this land is now available to the Berlin Wall Foundation for the construction and running of the open-air exhibition. In addition to the actual building costs incurred in extending the memorial site, the acquisition of land in the former border zone represents a major cost factor, which is to be borne by both the federal and the Berlin government.

The Development of the Berlin Wall Memorial
and the Chapel of Reconciliation

In early 1990 the "Round Table" in the Mitte district of Berlin and the parish of the Church of Reconciliation in the Wedding district called for the preservation of a representative section of the border fortifications in Bernauer Strasse and the establishment of a memorial site, and the (East) Berlin *Magistrat* (Council) placed the section of wall located between Ackerstrasse and Bergstrasse under a preservation order on 2 October 1990. On 13 August of the following year the Berlin Senate voted to establish a memorial site there, and in 1994 the German Historical Museum launched an open competition to find a design. Even in these preparatory stages conflict emerged over plans to construct a new road to channel traffic through Bernauer Strasse, the architectural uses of the former border zone, and even with the parish of the Sophien-Kirche, which wanted the graveyard to be fully accessible again.

After a lengthy delay, the winning design by the Stuttgart architects Kohlhoff and Kohlhoff was completed in 1998. The memorial consists of two seven-meter-high steel walls enclosing an original seventy-meter-long section of the border strip, which visitors are not permitted to enter. It has attracted some criticism for its purist form. The documentation center opposite is located in the parish hall of the Church of Reconciliation at Bernauer Strasse 111. Designed by the architect Franke and completed in 1965, this building was itself a reaction by the parish to the enforced loss of the church and parish hall, which were then located behind the wall. On 9 November 1999, the tenth anniversary of the fall of the Berlin Wall, the Verein Berliner Mauer (Berlin Wall Association), a small but committed citizens' initiative founded the previous year, opened its first exhibition in this building; however, the exhibition proved to be too small, and there were soon plans to extend it. The new documentation center, which was designed by the Berlin architects Hapke/Zerr/Nieländer and opened in June 2003, contains an extended exhibition and the newly built viewing platform.

The new Chapel of Reconciliation, which was consecrated on 9 November 2000 at the site where the church once stood, stands 150 meters from the parish hall in the former border zone. Designed by the Berlin architects Reitermann and Sassenroth, this is an exceptional construction and not just in the architectural sense. Twenty-five years ago it would have been inconceivable that a new church would again stand in this location, once home to the neo-Gothic, brick Church of Reconciliation, built in 1894 and featuring a seventy-five-meter-high spire. GDR border guards demolished the spire and nave on 21 and 28 January 1985 in order to increase "security, order, and tidiness along the state border with West Berlin," as the official GDR statement put it. The demolition sparked widespread protest, particularly among the parish of the Church of Reconciliation itself, which, powerless, had to observe these developments from the West.

Since 13 August 2005 there have been daily memorial services in the chapel for those who died trying to flee to West Berlin, drawing on information from a book of mourning featuring the biographies of the victims.[5] National and regional representatives annually mark the construction of the Berlin Wall and its impact on people in Germany and Berlin at ceremonies at the memorial for the victims of Communism on the corner of Bernauer Strasse and Ackerstrasse.

The Background to the Contemporary Culture of Remembrance

After 1945 the culture of remembrance in both German states was characterized by the common experience of National Socialism and the Holocaust: "Auch nach 1989/90 hat der Holocaust im vereinigten Deutschland letztlich die Diskussion über die jüngste Geschichte in Deutschland dominiert — trotz des Zusammenbruchs der kommunistischen Systeme."[6] Nonetheless there were and continue to be marked differences between the cultures of remembrance in the two German states. Memory of the Berlin Wall and German division therefore has to be viewed in light of these differences.

After initial attempts at a differentiated approach, commemoration in the GDR increasingly became a matter for the state. Victims' associations' ideas about remembrance were replaced by an anti-Fascist ideology conceived as justification for the foundation of the second German state, and remembrance of National Socialism was restricted to the Communist resistance against the "Hitler Fascists." The ruling SED party thus took charge of the development of the large memorial sites such as those at Buchenwald, near Weimar, and Sachsenhausen, near Oranienburg. Consequently, the culture of remembrance degenerated into an increasingly codified *raison d'état* that dominated the everyday life of GDR citizens from an early age. The Holocaust and Jewish victims were practically non-existent in the culture of remembrance. It was only from the mid-1980s that GDR leaders took tentative measures toward acknowledging and compensating Jewish victims, having realized that such measures were necessary if they were to improve their international reputation.

Developments in the Federal Republic took a different course. In the administration and economy of postwar West Germany an astonishing pragmatism emerged with regard to the presence of former National Socialists. The attitude of state institutions to the culture of remembrance, however, was predominantly reticent or even hostile. This stemmed perhaps from the National Socialist era, when commemorative rituals had been regulated down to the last detail and the state had usurped artistic freedom to an unparalleled extent. In accordance with the view that remembrance was a private or ideological concern, initiatives to establish monuments or museums came from victims' associations or churches, and it was not until the 1960s that the first memorial sites were built, for example in Bergen-Belsen and Dachau. In the architectural and artistic sense these sites were characterized by careful additions to the existing topography of suffering in the form of new churches or chapels and small-scale artworks, mainly depicting human figures.

From the late 1970s, and against the background of the student movement that emerged in 1965, new tendencies emerged in the Federal Republic, one central concern being a reappraisal of authentic sites. Countless citizens' initiatives researched specific places, people, and traces of events related to the period 1933 to 1945 (inspired by the "Dig where you Stand" movement in 1970s Sweden), which resulted in a new civil dimension and a highly differentiated approach to the culture of remembrance. When it came to the layout of historical sites, autonomous artistic statements sometimes lost significance. The priority was rather to "let the site speak" by protecting inconspicuous or insignificant traces, adding factual information, and researching and involving survivors and eyewitnesses (oral history). An example of such a memorial site is the Topography of Terror in the former government quarter of Berlin, which has developed since the early 1980s and which presents a new approach to perpetrator-oriented documentation and research on National Socialist history.

The conventional understanding of monuments as fixed and affirmative structures came to be viewed with increasing suspicion. The task now was to establish sites but not to create objects. Examples of memorial sites with a strong aesthetic message include the "Library" on Bebelplatz in Berlin, which recalls the National Socialist book burning on this square on 10 May 1933; and the memorial wall by Karol Broniatowski at the Grunewald S-Bahn station in Berlin, which, along with the neighboring "Platform 17" memorial by the architects Wandel, Hoefer, Lorch, and Hirsch, is located at the place where deportation trains left Berlin for the concentration camps. This phase saw a preference for evolving forms of remembrance that provoked an active response in the observer. Examples include works such as Horst Hoheisel's "negative form monument" in Kassel, a sunken fountain (designed as a monument to "Aschrott's Fountain," originally constructed by a German-Jewish company and destroyed by the Nazis), and Jochen Gerz's "2146 Stones — Monument against Racism" on the square in front of Saarbrücken Castle (the seat of the regional parliament). The stones of the latter were engraved with the names of Jewish communities that no longer exist and set into the square with the text underneath. James E. Young has coined the term "counter-monument" for these artistic concepts that radically question our conventional understanding of monuments.[7]

The aim of letting authentic sites "speak" can result in reconstruction concepts with interesting spatial and artistic approaches in cases where there are few authentic traces of the past or where these are inconspicuous and difficult to interpret. Examples of this type of memorial site include the monument designed by Dani Karavan in Gurs in the south of France, the redesigned memorial at "Station Z," the former National Socialist execution site at Sachsenhausen, and the project "Zeichen der Erinnerung" (Signs of Memory) in Stuttgart. The striking memorial site at the former extermination camp at Bełzec (Poland) and the "Umschlagplatz" monument ("Collection Point," that is, marking the area where Jews assembled for deportation), built in 1988 in Warsaw, also fit into this category. The latter, resulting from an initiative by the opposition movement, also serves to criticize the one-sided heroism that characterized official monuments under real existing Socialism. The "Path of Memory," which was established in conjunction with the "Umschlagplatz" memorial, consists of nineteen points placed throughout the former Warsaw ghetto. Such contextualization within a public environment represents an additional tendency in the contemporary art and architecture of monuments. The memorial in the Bayerisches Viertel (Bavarian Quarter) in Berlin, consisting of street signs featuring anti-Jewish legislation enacted by the Nazis, the "Spiegelwand" (Mirrored Wall), a memorial to the Jews deported from the Steglitz district of Berlin, and the "Homomonument" in Amsterdam are all examples of memorials that make a strong impact not only because of their unusual aesthetics, but also as a result of their "anti-monumental" locations and their presence in everyday surroundings. These monuments do not provide visitors with easy answers but rather require them to actively interpret and decode the artistic message.

Contemporary artistic approaches to monuments frequently involve interaction with a topographical or urban setting. This is the case both for memorial sites at authentic locations — for example Bergen-Belsen, where the new documentation center marks the start of a topographical passage through the former camp grounds, now barely recognizable as such — and for monuments at non-authentic, urban locations such as the Memorial for the Murdered Jews of Europe in the heart of Berlin, which blends seamlessly with the urban environment.

Another important feature of contemporary artistic approaches to monuments is their explicit reference to the victims. There are various ways of achieving this, for example by listing the full names of all the victims of a specific site or from a specific group, or mentioning the most accurate possible number of victims. The memorial to the murdered Czech Jews at the Pinkas synagogue in Prague, designed in the mid-1950s, incorporated the full names of the victims. This approach was in contrast to the tendency at that time to commemorate nameless heroes rather than individual victims. The individualization of victims draws an important distinction between these memorials and German war memorials to the First World War or the monuments established by dictatorships, which use the cult of the anonymous victim to gloss over and establish a heroic view of death.

Over the past twenty years documentation and visitor centers have become a key feature of memorial sites and places of remembrance. Because they were established earlier, memorial sites to the victims of National Socialism served as forerunners in this respect, but the trend can also be noted with memorial sites to the second German dictatorship. One reason is that the aura of authentic relics and traces is fading and their meaning is obviously not clear enough for younger generations. Some accompanying or clarifying commentary therefore becomes necessary. The development of educational programs at memorial sites over the past twenty years can also be linked to this tendency.

To sum up, one can say that the contemporary culture of remembrance is essentially a civil culture for both those who initiate and those who visit the memorials concerned. Over the past twenty years most national and local remembrance projects have been the result of citizens' initiatives. This applies both to memorial projects concerning the National Socialist dictatorship and those remembering the GDR. It is the task of the state and of administrative departments to promote this civil engagement, to organize and professionalize the development of these sites, to push forward the decisions on which events should be remembered and where, and to secure the design and funding of the sites chosen for memorialization.

Over the past fifteen years, the funding of memorial sites remembering the Nazi and SED dictatorships has shifted from being purely the responsibility of the respective institution or federal state to a joint national and regional task. This can be seen in the federal government's memorial site concept, which was implemented in 1999 and is proof of the professionalization of the work of memorial sites. The new memorial site concept, adopted in 2008, created a balanced structure for the funding and responsibility for important memorial sites remembering both dictatorships while also giving the federal states the main remit for developing and funding these sites. This has not meant a decrease or withdrawal of citizens' involvement. The citizens' initiatives responsible for the establishment of memorial sites continue to play an important role in the decision-making processes of practically all memorial sites, either as trustees or through their input in the exhibitions.

The contemporary culture of remembrance is based on three pillars. The rational-cognitive pillar presents objective facts and context and thereby applies the classic method of transmitting information through pictures, text, and documents. The emotional-artistic pillar uses aesthetic and design-based features and appeals to the subjective emotions of the individual with unusual forms, materials, and configurations. The educational-pedagogical pillar focuses on the acquisition and understanding of complex historical facts and aims to generate empathy and moral receptiveness, and to stimulate action among visitors. Each memorial project must define and, if necessary, redefine the balance between these three pillars.

The Main Principles for Memorializing the Berlin Wall

The concept for the Berlin Wall memorial site and its expansion was developed in this context. Following initial resistance, it has grown over a number of years through committed citizens' initiatives in close and successful cooperation with the Berlin state administration. The concept can be summed up as follows:

(1) The main objective of the memorial site is to link historical events with the authentic location. Many events and images connected with the Berlin Wall are still present in collective and individual memory; however, they have become largely disassociated from the actual context of the wall's development and are influenced by selective and ideological approaches, which can lead to inaccuracies. The aim of the memorial site is to locate and contextualize events accurately by explaining them and providing information.

(2) The authentic remains and traces of the border fortifications are extremely important and have to be protected, preserved, and presented according to conservation principles. Only by maintaining the authenticity of the original substance can the memorial site guard against pathos and inaccuracies and secure the value of the original features as testimony to the past. This in turn will guarantee the longevity of the memorial site. The meticulous preservation of original features is thus crucial. Later additions to the site must be identified as such and kept distinct from the original features.

(3) Individual histories and biographies clarify the history and impact of the wall and the division of Germany, and the memorial site has to give scope to individual commemoration of the victims of the wall. One of its central objectives is thus to honor the at least 136 people who died trying to flee the to the West between 1961 and 1989.

(4) It is important to emphasize the complex structural nature of the border fortifications and the urban division and physical destruction of the city that were a consequence of their construction. This includes consideration of the development of the wall from a raw, improvised construction to the perfected "border system," inconspicuous but deadly, that had an impact on practically all aspects of city life. The history of the Berlin Wall

and the division of Germany thus cannot be communicated at one single site but require different contexts.

(5) The conservation principles adopted for the Berlin Wall cannot involve reconstruction but instead the notion of "conservation as found." Even the most perfect reconstruction is not able to recreate the deadly nature of the wall and the immobilizing impact of the border fortifications, which were guarded and illuminated day and night. Any attempt at reconstruction encounters the problem of deciding which stage should be reconstructed. Moreover, the history of the wall did not stop in 1989.

(6) East and West German views of the Berlin Wall and a divided Germany must be given equal status. The iconic image of the graffiti-covered border wall with people dancing on top is familiar throughout the world, but it embodies the view from the West and the liberating confrontation with the wall once it had fallen. The wall was not directed against the West, however, but against the population in the East. Residents of the GDR were to be intimidated physically and psychologically by a multilevel and ever-present border system.

(7) The memorial site is intended as a new type of commemorative space that neither focuses on authoritarian, one-sided "schwarze Pädagogik"[8] nor presents an easily "consumable" product, but rather aims to evoke an active and reflective response from visitors. The protected remains and traces and the carefully presented information are meant to encourage, but not enforce, reflection on the part of the visitor. They are part of an undemonstrative space that does not explain everything or provide conclusive answers but instead leads visitors to think about issues themselves.

(8) The memorial site aims to make remembrance of the Berlin Wall and German division a feature of an everyday culture that seeks to strengthen freedom and individual responsibility. In "post-heroic society"[9] memorial sites and places of remembrance are becoming part of the daily lives of different generations and are no longer isolated locations, but rather public spaces that encourage visitors to spend time there and to contemplate their meaning.

The Design of the Memorial Site

Over the years the number of visitors to the documentation center, to the Chapel of Reconciliation, and to the memorial has steadily increased. Experts estimate a further rise in visitor numbers in the future given the growing public and tourist interest in the Berlin Wall, which is possibly the best-known construction in Berlin after the Brandenburg Gate, even though it has almost completely disappeared from the urban landscape. The site's popularity was one of the reasons behind the decision to adopt a development concept to be implemented in several stages. The first of these was the construction of the new documentation center on the corner of Gartenstrasse and Bernauer Strasse, which opened recently. The enlargement project will also result in the development of the area around the former stretch of wall along Bernauer Strasse that is 1.3 kilometers long and covers an area of 4.4 hectares. An open-air exhibition will be established here as part of the Berlin Wall Memorial. The final stage of the development will be the renovation of the existing documentation center at Bernauer Strasse 111 to house the necessary extension to the permanent exhibition and pedagogical facilities.

An international competition was launched in 2007 to find a design for the planned developments up to 2012. The remit of the competition posed several challenges: How does one remember something that has disappeared? How does one protect the numerous but unprepossessing remains and traces of the border fortifications, which only rarely express a clear meaning? How does one communicate to today's visitors something of the once deadly characteristics of this high-security border, which was closely guarded day and night? How can one create a worthy place to commemorate those who died here or at other places along the Berlin Wall? And how can one design this "Insel der Leere"[10] so that it is not perceived as an alien feature of the urban environment but rather brings together and connects neighboring districts? These were the main questions raised in the competition tender, which was jointly produced by the memorial site and the Berlin Senate administration in 2007.

The winners of the international competition were the architects Mola/Winkelmüller, Sinai Faust.Schroll.Schwarz (landscape architects) and ON architektur C. Fuchs (exhibition design). They produced a convincing response to this difficult task by designing simple but effective features that create a specific commemorative space and a layout that is both striking and makes the existing remains and traces of the border fortifications easier to understand. The team uses rust-colored Cor-Ten (weathering steel) as the main material in the outdoor areas to add to the existing traces and to mark places of memory and the scene of certain events, as well as for the façade of the visitor center. Cor-Ten steel was used for the external surfaces of the two tall steel walls of the memorial built in 1998 and also for the information posts marking the course of the wall within the city. It obtains its characteristic color through natural corrosion, which also functions as a protective layer, and is therefore extremely weather-resistant.

The course of the former border wall between Gartenstrasse and Brunnenstrasse is marked by a close succession of thin posts made of Cor-Ten steel. These create a spatial impression of the former wall, but visitors and pedestrians can pass between them. This design concept provides an authentic impression of the dimensions and extent of the

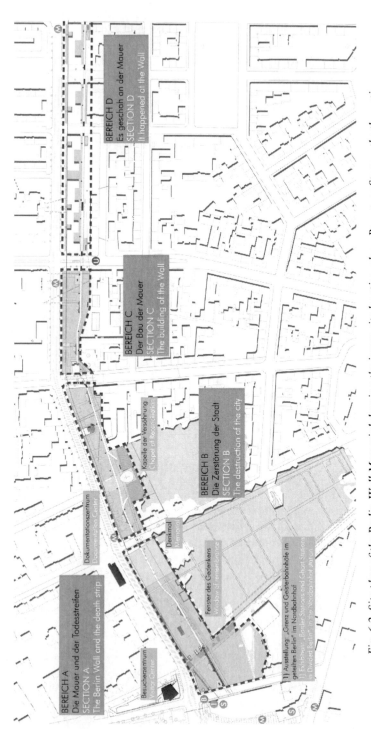

BEREICH D
Es geschah an der Mauer
SECTION D
It happened at the Wall

BEREICH C
Der Bau der Mauer
SECTION C
The building of the Wall

Kapelle der Versöhnung
Chapel of Reconciliation

BEREICH B
Die Zerstörung der Stadt
SECTION B
The destruction of the city

Dokumentationszentrum
Documentation Center

Denkmal
Memorial

BEREICH A
Die Mauer und der Todesstreifen
SECTION A
The Berlin Wall and the death strip

Besucherzentrum
Visitor Center

Fenster des Gedenkens
Window of Remembrance

1) Ausstellung: „Grenz und Geisterbahnhöfe im geteilten Berlin" im Nordbahnhof
1) Exhibition „Border Stations and Ghost Stations of Divided Berlin" in the Nordbahnhof station

Fig. 6.2. Site plan of the Berlin Wall Memorial showing the inner-city location along Bernauer Strasse, the thematic structure of the open air exhibition, and other elements (e.g. the Chapel of Reconciliation and the Window of Remembrance). Copyright © sinai/Stiftung Berliner Mauer.

former border fortifications without falling into the trap of producing a reconstruction, which can never appear as real as the original. At the same time it avoids the confusion that frequently arises over what is original and what has been added later — the original remains of the Berlin Wall and all elements added to the border fortifications until 1989 are made of concrete.

The memorial site's visitor center is on the corner of Bernauer Strasse and Gartenstrasse — where the Berlin Wall formed a sharp angle up to 1989 — and will serve as a signpost to all parts of the extended memorial site. Because of its excellent public transport links and its recognizable location in the city, the visitor center will be the main arrival point for visitors; moreover, from there one can still make out the former course of the wall at Bernauer Strasse and in the park at Nordbahnhof. Visitors arriving at the memorial site by S-Bahn can see a small exhibition in the neighboring Nordbahnhof S-Bahn station. This exhibition, which opened in October 2009, deals with a further aspect of the Berlin Wall and German division: the border stations and "ghost stations" that arose as a result of the division of the S-Bahn and underground network after 1961.

The prize-winning design for the visitor center by the Berlin architects Mola und Winkelmüller gives particularly clear expression to its role as a point of orientation. The ground floor of the two-story construction faces Gartenstrasse, while the upper floor, turned at an angle of thirty degrees, faces the course of the wall in Bernauer Strasse. At the same time this design creates a protected external area that can also function as a meeting or information point during bad weather or outside opening hours.

The visitor center provides basic information on the different elements of the memorial site, guiding visitors to where they can obtain in-depth information on various aspects. It also indicates links to other sites of memory in Berlin such as the East Side Gallery, Checkpoint Charlie, the "Parliament of Trees" memorial in the Bundestag library in Marie-Elisabeth Lüders House, the Invalids' Cemetery, which was divided by the East-West border, and the former border crossing at Bornholmer Strasse. The upper floor of the visitor center contains seminar rooms for school groups and for political education activities, which are in ever greater demand at the site. Here visitors can watch a short introductory film on the Berlin Wall and obtain concise information on its national and international aspects.

The New Open-Air Exhibition

A key feature of the new memorial site will be the open-air exhibition along the former border zone, the construction of which began in 2009.

Fig. 6.3. Aerial view of Bernauer Strasse (center). To the left is the former border strip, which is being converted into the Wall Memorial, and the inner-city district of Mitte (former East) and Wedding (former West). Copyright © Jürgen Hohmuth, zeitort/Stiftung Berliner Mauer.

It will be open twenty-four hours a day and cover an area of 4.4 hectares, the central area between Gartenstrasse and Brunnenstrasse encompassing the area between the former border and the hinterland wall, which remains empty apart from one building. The extension to the exhibition between Brunnenstrasse and Schwedter Strasse includes the five- to ten-meter-wide former patrol area, which remains largely intact. The Berlin landscape architect company Sinai will lay a new, hard-wearing grass surface over this area, which will expose and indicate the historical remains and traces of the border fortifications. Flat panels or strips of Cor-Ten steel will replace those that have disappeared or are severely damaged, and archaeological findings will be identified and preserved using frames or outlines made of Cor-Ten steel. The spatial evocation of the former border wall between Gartenstrasse and Brunnenstrasse with the rows of thin Cor-Ten steel posts will be of particular significance, for the steel reinforcements will give some impression of the wall's strength and physical presence; but being able to pass between the posts will also emphasize its impermanence.

The unassuming design of this commemorative space includes a range of exhibition features made of Cor-Ten steel which ON, the company responsible for the exhibition layout, has designed in accordance with the overall concept. These include a system of exhibition panels with varying combinations of text, photo, and video, which will be positioned at the approximately twenty information points where visitors can learn more about various themes such as forced resettlement, border patrols, and the development of the border fortifications. There will also be steel plates set into the ground to show the course of the underground tunnel dug from the West Berlin side to enable people in the East to flee. Finally, numerous points mark the scene of historic events that are strongly anchored in public memory, such as protests, successful escapes, and escape attempts resulting in death.

One particularly important element of the open-air exhibition is the commemorative site for the at least 136 people who died trying to cross the Berlin Wall. This will be located on the former death strip that previously crossed the Sophien-Friedhof. The exhibition architect Fuchs has designed a "Window of Remembrance" for this memorial in the form of a steel wall. A window is devoted to each victim, containing their name, dates of birth and death and, where possible, a photograph. This concept creates a worthy site of memory for all victims of the Berlin Wall, enabling both individual mourning and public commemoration.

Implementation and Future Perspectives

The Berlin Wall Foundation, a foundation under public law, is responsible for implementing these challenging and complex expansion plans in the years to come. It works closely with the real estate agencies of the federal and Berlin governments on the process of land acquisition. The Berlin Senate's department for cultural affairs and urban development and Grün Berlin GmbH, the Berlin agency for park planning and maintenance, provide considerable support in terms of the planning and construction process. Some of the most important elements, such as the visitor center and the southwest corner of the exhibition grounds between Gartenstrasse and Ackerstrasse, are already complete. The open-air exhibition will be largely finished by 2012 and will be followed by the renovation of the house at Bernauer Str. 111. Both before and during the building process it is necessary to obtain funding from various budgets for many other factors such as sourcing land, building and planning regulations, and other specific measures. The construction and land acquisition costs alone will exceed twenty million euros. Funding for the extension of the memorial has come from a broad range of sources, including various Berlin finance programs, the national budget for culture, and the EU's Regional Development Fund. The coordination of these funds over an implementation period of at least five, if not six or seven, years is a daunting task.

Fig. 6.4. The entrance to the Berlin Wall Memorial showing the remapped course of the front wall and a commemorative stele for the Berlin Wall victim Otfried Reck. Copyright © Jürgen Hohmuth, zeitort/Stiftung Berliner Mauer.

The objective remains to create a memorial site that has a particular impact based on its dual character as both an authentic site that explains historic events and a place of commemoration and reflection. The human rights violations and terror of the border regime controlling the Berlin Wall and the militarized force of the death strip make a particular impression here. At the same time this site can also express the joy at the fall of the Berlin Wall and the "peaceful revolution" that put an end to German division. Finally, the still diverging eastern and western German memories of the wall, particularly in terms of everyday life and individual experience, are given expression and placed in relation to one another. German history and also that of other countries show that sites that allow an exchange of experience, learning, and the communication of various perspectives can continue to serve a constitutive and reconciliatory function within society decades after their construction.

Translated from the German by Caroline Pearce

Notes

[1] Klaus-Dietmar Henke, "1989," in *Revolution und Vereinigung 1989–90: Als in Deutschland die Realität die Phantasie überholte*, ed. Klaus-Dietmar Henke (Munich: DTV, 2009), 45.

[2] Axel Klausmeier, "Ein Memorialort neuer Prägung," *Deutschland Archiv* 42 (2009): 892.

[3] Gerhard Sälter, "Das Verschwinden der Berliner Mauer," in Henke, *Revolution und Vereinigung 1989–90*, 353.

[4] See Manfred Zache and Helmut Zempel, *Stadtplanerische Dokumentation zum ehemaligen Grenzstreifen der Mauer in Berlin: Gutachten im Auftrag der Senatsverwaltung für Stadtentwicklung* (Berlin: Senatsverwaltung für Stadtentwicklung, 2000), and Axel Klausmeier and Leo Schmidt, *Mauerreste — Mauerspuren* (Berlin: Westkreuz Verlag, 2005).

[5] Zentrum für Zeithistorische Forschung/Stiftung Berliner Mauer, *Die Todesopfer an der Berliner Mauer 1961–1989: Ein biographisches Handbuch* (Berlin: Ch. Links, 2009).

[6] Michael Faulenbach, "Diktaturerfahrungen und demokratische Erinnerungskultur in Deutschland," in *Orte des Erinnerns: Gedenkzeichen, Gedenkstätten und Museen zur Diktatur in SBZ und DDR*, ed. Anne Kaminsky (Berlin: Ch. Links, 2007), 17.

[7] James E. Young, *At Memory's Edge* (New Haven, CT: Yale UP, 2000), 90.

[8] See Katharina Rutschky, *Schwarze Pädagogik* (Munich: Ullstein Taschenbuch Verlag, 1977), and Alice Miller, *Am Anfang war Erziehung* (Frankfurt am Main: Suhrkamp, 1980).

[9] Herfried Münkler, "Militärisches Totengedenken in der postheroischen Gesellschaft," in *Bedingt erinnerungsbereit: Soldatengedenken in der Bundesrepublik*, ed. Manfred Hettling and Jörg Echternkamp (Göttingen: Vandenhoeck & Ruprecht, 2008), 22.

[10] Romuald Loegler, Gruppe Planwerk, *Stadtidee: Verfahren und Ergebnisse* (Berlin: Verlag Dirk Nishen, 1992).

7: Commemorating the Berlin Wall

Pertti Ahonen

GERMAN UNIFICATION IN 1990 ARRIVED with high expectations and big promises. Chancellor Helmut Kohl predicted "blooming landscapes" for the former GDR, and in the early euphoria of unity the path forward seemed clear to many: the victorious liberal democracy of the Federal Republic would extend itself over its defeated Socialist rival, and a nation arbitrarily divided by the legacies of the Nazi era and the vicissitudes of the Cold War would grow together again.[1]

In reality unification turned out to be a much more conflictual affair. Economic crisis rather than blossoming affluence promptly enveloped the former GDR, bringing with it a variety of accompanying social and political problems. The government's attempts to address these and other pitfalls linked to the GDR's legacies fueled disputes and divisions, particularly between former East and West Germans, *Ossis* and *Wessis*. The sources of controversy were many: subsidies and transfer payments aimed at resuscitating eastern Germany's moribund economy, attempts to return private property nationalized under Communist rule to its previous owners, efforts to grapple with the Stasi's toxic legacy and to prosecute East German officeholders and functionaries for various actions defined as criminal.[2] Yet ultimately unified Germany's east-west divisions were rooted in something deeper and more fundamental: clashing self-perceptions, memories, and mentalities. Although the militarized boundary that had divided the two Germanys had been dismantled, Peter Schneider's prediction about its most visible and symbolic section proved prescient: the "Wall in [the] heads" between former *Ossis* and *Wessis* was to take much "longer to tear down" than the concrete structure of the Berlin Wall itself.[3] The wall continued to haunt and divide unified Germany in general and Berlin in particular long after its physical disappearance.

This chapter will examine the public commemoration of the wall in postunification Berlin. These efforts and the accompanying controversies are important in themselves as a key factor in the evolution of the public remembrance of the GDR at a crucial site of recent German memory. But they also illustrate the broader trajectory through which the commemoration of the GDR evolved in the two decades following German unification. The initial rush to unity yielded a wave of Western triumphalism that translated into a sustained prioritization of the western perspective on the wall, reflected in part in a tendency to sweep the barrier aside as quickly and comprehensively as possible. This trend in turn provoked prolonged tension, primarily along the east-west axis. A more inclusive history of division that incorporates certain elements of the GDR's public narrative about the wall and possibly provides a way forward to a more balanced memory culture only began to emerge well after the turn of the millennium.

The Western-Led Drive to Demolish the Wall

In the context of the GDR's final crisis and Germany's swift unification at the beginning of the 1990s, the most notable development vis-à-vis the Berlin Wall was the rush to demolish it. The initial decision to remove the barrier was made by the reformed East German government in late 1989, and GDR work crews carried out the bulk of the dismantling, with the work finished by November 1990, well ahead of schedule. The wall's speedy removal was in large part reflective of a consensus among the majority of Berliners that the fortifications that had divided the city for nearly three decades had to go as quickly and comprehensively as possible. But at a deeper level the demolition also underscored the spirit of Western triumphalism — or at least a clear prioritization of the Western Cold War perspective — that characterized official attitudes toward the wall in early postunification Berlin. Revealingly, the component of the former border fortifications slated for the speediest removal — and typically defined as "the wall" in contemporary public discourse — was the westernmost element, the structure that had faced West Berlin and assumed iconic significance, particularly outside the Communist Bloc. The removal of this particular part of the complex barricade system was widely equated with the disappearance of the wall as a whole, despite the fact that many other components, located further back on former GDR terrain, were dismantled much later or not at all. The East Berliners' perspective on the wall, in which the final west-facing structure had been an invisible and practically unreachable entity at the end of a long series of fences and other fortifications that had started with the so-called hinterland wall — the initial barrier blocking access from East Berlin into the border strip itself — remained almost completely marginalized in this vision.[4]

Another — rather ironic — indicator of the seemingly comprehensive triumph of the Western perspective on the inter-German Cold War rivalry was the extensive commodification that accompanied the wall's rapid disappearance. To be sure, most of the barricades vanished quietly and anonymously, with fences and other components dismantled and discarded and the bulk of the westward-facing wall ground into pieces of aggregate and subsequently used for street construction. But as ever-larger segments of the wall disappeared, the value of the best remaining bits rose, roughly in keeping with capitalist laws of supply and demand. As a result, the "quintessential symbol of Communism was transmuted into a highly desirable capitalist commodity," to quote one author's apt formulation.[5]

This development was made even more ironic by the fact that the primary actor seeking to profit from the sales of wall segments was the disintegrating East German state itself. During their last months in power GDR officials authorized a state-owned firm to market hand-picked segments of the westward-facing wall to foreign buyers. The result was a brief but lively international trade in these massive Cold War mementos as particular parts of the barrier — many of them notable for their graffiti art — were sold to the highest bidders, most prominently at an exclusive Monte Carlo auction in June 1990.[6] Interestingly, one of the private individuals who purchased a chunk of the wall as a personal memento of sorts was the granddaughter of Winston Churchill, whose famous "Iron Curtain" speech of 1946 had been instrumental in popularizing the notion of a strict political division of Europe that the Berlin Wall subsequently came to embody. A piece of the wall in the hands of the Churchill family provided a potent symbol of the comprehensive Western victory in the European Cold War.[7]

The most obvious indication of the primacy of the Western perspective on the wall in the early postunification period was the fate of the competing commemorative sites and practices that had been established in the city's two halves during the Cold War. The East German government had portrayed the wall as a defensive necessity, erected to preempt aggression from the hostile West. It had also invested heavily in the public commemoration of a particular group of the wall's victims: GDR guards killed at it in the line of duty, often in unclear circumstances, in connection with East-West escape attempts. It had stylized the fallen guards into "hero-victims of the Socialist frontier," exemplary citizens victimized by Western treachery whose lives and deaths were supposed to provide a model for other East Germans, promoting mobilization and building legitimacy among the population.[8]

After unification the various East Berlin memory sites that the GDR government had set up to accentuate its official interpretation of the wall and its Socialist hero-victims disappeared quickly. In 1992 the Berlin Senate established an independent commission composed of representatives from both halves of the city to deliberate on what to do with "political monuments of the postwar era in former East Berlin." The commission recommended that "[all] monuments and memorials to the remembrance of GDR border guards killed on duty . . . be removed without substitution." While repudiating any desire to "censure . . . those who died," the commission emphasized that "after the fall of the wall and the reunification of Germany there [could] no longer be any justification for regarding [the border guards] as heroes and for honoring a service that was by no means honorable."⁹ These recommendations were then implemented quickly, as the various GDR-era monuments dedicated to dead border guards, most of which had already fallen into disrepair as a result of postunification neglect and vandalism, were systematically dismantled and removed. By the late 1990s all such memorials had disappeared from Berlin despite some scattered opposition, primarily from former East German officials.

Other public reminders of the GDR's erstwhile hero-victims of the Socialist frontier also vanished promptly following unification. The vast majority of the many schools, youth clubs, sporting facilities, and other objects named after the fallen guards were promptly renamed something less controversial. This was especially true in Berlin itself, where action typically ensued more quickly and comprehensively than in some more remote regions of the former GDR. A particularly symbolic step was the systematic renaming of streets in former East Berlin during the 1990s, whereby a wide array of Communist-era celebrities of different kinds, ranging from SED functionaries to Communist pioneers of the Weimar and Nazi periods, found themselves expunged from street signs. Some of the earliest — and least controversial — renamings involved prominent fallen border guards, who disappeared from Berlin's streetscape as early as 1991 amidst some muted protest from the former East.¹⁰

While the GDR's memorials and commemorative practices were rapidly marginalized, the traditions that had prevailed in former West Berlin continued largely unaltered. The well-established public narrative of the wall as an embodiment of Communist oppression reasserted itself. The memory sites set up to honor the wall victims prioritized in the Cold War West — East German escapees and other civilians gunned down by GDR guards — maintained their prominence. A highly formative event took place on 13 August 1990, during the final transition to unified Germany, as West Berlin's Senator for Internal Affairs spoke at a wreath-laying ceremony at the memorial to Peter Fechter, a young East Berliner shot at the wall in August 1962. Admonishing his audience to "remember the many people . . . who were injured or even killed at the wall," the Senator called for a continuation of West Berlin's well-established commemorative practices.¹¹ The venue for his address — the memorial for the wall's best-known victim in the West that had provided a key location for West Berlin's annual remembrance ceremonies for nearly three decades — pointed to a strong desire for continuity, which quickly translated into reality. Very similar ceremonies, performed at the same venue on each anniversary of the wall's construction, dominated the public commemoration of the wall and its victims in early postunification Berlin.

Significantly, however, these rituals of public remembrance were subject to clear limits, thereby perpetuating the restricted élan that had characterized similar West Berlin activities from the 1970s onwards. The official ceremonies were confined to particular sites and times — primarily a few select memorials on each 13 August — and the commemorative practices were highly choreographed, even ritualized. Representatives of the government, the mainstream parties, and select other organizations would appear, deposit wreaths and flowers, and read brief, prepared statements about the importance of remembering the wall's victims and ensuring that similar cruelties would not recur. The inhumane boundary and the authoritarian East German regime behind it were thereby stylized into comparative object lessons in the virtues of present-day liberal democracy. At the same time the negative comparator to the new Berlin Republic was presented as an entity enclosed in the past. The bad days of the GDR and its brutal border regime were gone, and although an evocation of the wall's evils was desirable, within carefully defined limits, a more comprehensive public preoccupation with the barrier's victims was not. The key task was instead to pull together and build a new Berlin oriented toward a bright, united future rather than a murky, divided past.[12]

The drive to modernize and revamp Berlin in search of a new, unified, and more dynamic image was evident all over the city in the early to mid-1990s, most notably in the massive building projects that seemed to crop up everywhere. Many of the projects gave the impression of wanting to bury the most problematic aspects of the city's recent past behind a new, business-friendly façade of concrete, steel, and glass. This spirit was most evident in the area around the iconic Checkpoint Charlie, the site of numerous Cold War tragedies, including the shooting of Peter Fechter. In the early 1990s the Berlin Senate decided to turn the surrounding area into an "American Business Center," a redeveloped commercial district that was supposed to attract big business into the heart of Germany's new capital. The plan was to have private investors construct five large building complexes, called Quarters (*Quartiere*), composed of offices and retail outlets, which in turn were expected to transform the deprived border strip into a wealthy, bustling urban neighborhood. Remembrance of the wall and its victims played only a marginal role in this vision. Admittedly, the projected new commercial district was supposed to include "a suitable area for an open-air wall memorial," according to the agreement signed between the city government and the building contractors in 1992. But the practical details remained vague, and the actual construction activity focused on the business complexes while neglecting any memory sites.

East-West Memory Conflicts and Other Problems

The comprehensive, forward-looking, and decidedly Western modernization drive promoted by Berlin's ruling elites in the early 1990s, often at the expense of nuanced commemoration of the wall and its victims, soon ran into problems, however. Some of the obstacles were of a purely practical nature. The American Business Center, for example, quickly proved a step too far for the financially strapped city. As investments failed to pour in anywhere near the expected levels, the ambitious building plans were scaled back. Only two of the projected business complexes reached completion, and the open-air memorial to the wall's victims never materialized.[13]

Other obstacles to a radical removal of the physical reminders of the city's division were directly linked to the barrier itself. The key factor was countervailing pressure in favor of preserving some of the wall fortifications that emerged during the GDR's final months. The East Berlin Institute of Conservation listed certain wall segments as monuments of historic significance and tried to protect them from demolition, with patchy success.[14] Various individuals also advocated preserving parts of the barrier then and later, none more prominently than Willy Brandt, who first raised the issue in November 1989.[15]

Despite these exhortations, most of the westward-facing wall was torn down promptly in 1990, and the bulk of the other border fortifications was also removed in keeping with the largely west-driven agenda for reshaping the city's image and identity. Although a handful of sizeable wall segments did remain *in situ*, the key point of debate after late 1990, once the demolition of the wall strip as such had been completed, became whether — and how — to commemorate the former border zone. This issue proved highly conflictual, with the most obvious dividing line again running between east and west, and the outcome of the disputes highlighted the primacy of the western perspective on the erstwhile barrier.

Several initiatives by former East Germans called for turning the entire border zone — or at least a major segment of it — into an environmental memorial of sorts. One proposal advocated the planting of thousands of lupines in the death strip, while another sought to convert the former no man's land into a "green belt" of trees whose growth would symbolize the gradual healing of a historic scar.[16] Neither suggestion found favor with the city government; however, by the mid-1990s the Berlin Senate, too, had come around to the view that the former boundary line needed to be marked in some fashion, at least in certain areas. At a formal hearing in 1995 the most balanced proposal — put forward by an artist from the former GDR — envisaged the laying of two lines of mosaic into the ground through the city center: a red line to mark the location of the initial border fence on the East German side and a blue one to denote the westward-facing wall.[17] But this idea, too, was quickly rejected, and instead the authorities chose to mark just the final barrier that had faced West Berlin, and only in selected areas. Lines were drawn in the pavement using different materials in different places: concrete plates in the vicinity of the Reichstag, a band of copper near the city parliament, and a double row of cobblestones in some other areas.[18] The eastern perspective on the border fortifications received no acknowledgment in this characteristically western-dominated project.

The primacy of the western viewpoint on the wall was also evident in postunification Berlin's main effort to create a new, central memory site for the barrier and its victims. The campaign in question was the attempt to establish an official wall memorial in the symbolically significant Bernauer Strasse, one of the streets that had itself been divided as a result of the building of the wall, with the East-West boundary running along one side of the pavement. Although the initiative was broached by GDR officials in the summer of 1990 and quickly endorsed by key authorities in unified Germany, nearly a decade passed before the main memorial finally opened on a date of high symbolic significance: 13 August 1998, the thirty-seventh anniversary of the wall's construction.

The reasons for the delay lay in the vocal opposition that the project provoked. Many of the objections reflected the prevailing western-oriented public mood of the early to mid-1990s, according to which the promotion of new, forward-looking image for Berlin took priority over addressing problems of the past and commemoration of the wall and its victims — although desirable as a lesson in the evils of the GDR's state Socialism and the benefits of West German liberal democracy — was to be continued in the limited, largely ritualistic fashion familiar from the West Berlin of the previous decade. Accordingly city planners sought to veto the project, claiming that what Bernauer Strasse needed was not a wall memorial but a new inner ring road to channel traffic through the area. Representatives of a nearby old people's home maintained that the residents would be better off without a fresh reminder of the pain that the barrier had inflicted. Others argued that the city's existing memory sites more than sufficed to commemorate the wall and its victims.[19]

The finished memory site also reflected the primacy of a west-centric interpretation of the wall. Admittedly, on one level the Bernauer Strasse memorial strove to provide a relatively even-handed portrayal of the barrier and its human consequences. Its physical installations reconstructed the entire East German border zone, including not only the final west-facing barrier but also the eastern hinterland fence and the death strip in-between. More intriguingly, physical and visual access to the border strip was blocked by an additional structure on either side of the installations, so that visitors could only peek into the exclusion zone through small holes in the hinterland fence, from former GDR terrain. This provided a corrective to the usual postunification fixation on the west-facing wall, even if the viewpoint on offer failed to match the authentic experience of East German citizens; controls stretching far back into East Berlin would have made it impossible for anyone to take a leisurely peek into the border zone through the hinterland barrier prior to late 1989. Similar dispassion also shone through in the Documentation Center that was unveiled next to the memorial proper in 1999. The diverse materials on display eschewed overt western triumphalism and sought to portray the wall and its impact from multiple perspectives.

On closer inspection, however, the Bernauer Strasse memorial, too, remained ultimately west-centric. Although the Documentation Center's exhibitions and publications steered clear of pronounced anti-Communism, they nevertheless stressed the barrier's inhumanity and "terror," often with a particular emphasis on individuals who had lost their lives in failed escape attempts.[20] To be fair, in many ways such conclusions reflected common sense about the wall and its tragic human consequences. But the power of a particular interpretation to impose itself was evident in the changes made to the initial conception of the Bernauer Strasse site in response to specific social pressures. The original inscription at the memorial's entrance, which simply read "in memory of the division of the city from 13 August 1961 to 9 November 1989 and in remembrance of the victims," aroused the ire of GDR victims' organizations, with the result that the revised, final inscription refers to the "remembrance of the victims of Communist tyranny."[21]

Equally revealingly, visitor complaints about the confusing nature of the displayed border installations led to the construction of a viewing platform next to the Documentation Center, on former West Berlin territory.[22] This adjustment restored a bird's-eye perspective on the wall that was fundamentally western, dating back to the observation towers erected along the wall in West Berlin during the Cold War. The unfamiliar, faux-GDR view through cracks in the hinterland fence had to yield to the hegemonic western perception of the borderline, even at the semi-official wall memorial.

Preserving and Commemorating
the Wall's Remnants

While the predominant public perception of the wall was reasserting itself in Bernauer Strasse around the turn of the millennium, another key aspect of postunification Berlin's western-dominated culture of wall commemoration was gradually eroding. As suggested by the establishment of the new Wall Memorial, the previously dominant tendency to sweep the wall out of the cityscape in favor of forward-looking urban structures was being tempered by a growing interest in preserving and commemorating the barrier. This gradual shift in priorities was in good part an outgrowth of economic pressures emanating from the tourist industry. As unified Berlin became an increasingly popular travel destination in the 1990s, the wall featured as a theme of great fascination for tourists, who generated a growing demand

for wall tours, guidebooks, and various mementos, contributing significantly to the revival of interest in the vanished border that was evident by
the end of the decade.

The booming tourist trade was not the only cause of that revival, however. A decade after unification some of the passions that had accompanied
the wall's sudden collapse had subsided, and a growing proportion of
Berlin's population and officialdom felt that urban clearance in the border
zone had been too swift and sweeping. There was a strong sentiment that
the surviving components of this part of the city's historical legacy had to
be preserved, not least among members of the young, post-Wall generation that lacked clear personal memories of the barrier. The most ambitious preservation advocates even launched a campaign for UNESCO
World Cultural Heritage status to be granted to the remnants of the wall.[23]
Although most others were less sanguine about the chances of a destroyed
Cold War symbol to be listed among humankind's most treasured accom-
plishments alongside the Acropolis and the pyramids of ancient Egypt, a
growing consensus emerged in favor of enhanced attention to the wall, not
least as a counterpoint to the wave of *Ostalgie* — or GDR nostalgia — that
was rising at the time, partly in reaction to the western triumphalism of the
early postunification years. Disappointed with their lot in united Germany,
considerable numbers of former East Germans started to view the pre-
1989 past through rose-tinted glasses, reminiscing about the positive
aspects of the GDR's everyday life and culture while blending out the sup-
pression and coercion that had loomed in the background.

But there was an obvious problem with these plans. The vast bulk of
the former boundary across Berlin had simply disappeared, and previously inflicted damage could not be undone. Admittedly, those who
cared to search for traces of the border fortifications could have found
them in numerous locations, but primarily in radically altered settings
that made them difficult to recognize. Some former patrol roads had
been transformed into cycle paths, for example, and in certain areas
floodlights from yesteryear's death strip now illuminated parks and other
public facilities.[24]

More recognizable remnants of the GDR's border fortifications had
grown very scarce. Segments of the westward-facing barrier were particularly rare. By the twenty-first century only three pieces still stood at their
original locations: a 15-meter remnant in Liesenstrasse, an unglamorous
side street; a 212-meter segment adjoining the new Wall Memorial in
Bernauer Strasse; and a somewhat shorter remnant in Niederkirchner
Strasse, near Potsdamer Platz and next to the former Gestapo headquarters, whose ruins house the Topography of Terror memorial, dedicated to
documenting the horrors of the Third Reich. Thanks to its close juxtaposition of the material legacies of two different dictatorships, the Niederkirchner
Strasse site in particular attracted a steady stream of visitors — and con-

fused some, including a foreign tourist who was heard to comment, "I didn't know Hitler built the Berlin Wall."[25]

Traces of East Berlin's hinterland wall were somewhat more numerous. Chunks of varying sizes survived in various areas, but none could match the prominence of the so-called East Side Gallery, an almost mile-long stretch of the hinterland wall that ran along the Spree River, near the Oberbaum Bridge. Originally built to shield the menacing border installations from the view of foreign dignitaries who were chauffeured between the East Berlin city center and Schönefeld Airport along an adjoining road, this piece of the hinterland wall had possessed the white, smooth appearance usually reserved for the structure facing West Berlin. In spring 1990 it was transformed overnight as over one hundred artists from twenty-one countries painted a wide variety of motifs on its eastern face, creating the East Side Gallery, a world-renowned experiment in public art.[26]

The East Side Gallery testified to the growing public attention to the wall that had become evident in Berlin by the turn of the millennium. By then the entire strip had been placed under historical protection while city authorities, conservationists, and business representatives engaged in prolonged debates about how best to restore and maintain it.[27] Similar intent was also evident at various other locations. The most important surviving components of the border fortifications had become increasingly valued urban landmarks, with several joining the East Side Gallery on the city's list of historically protected sites.

At the same time several new memorials to the wall and its victims emerged. Near the Reichstag, inside the new parliamentary library, a row of original wall segments placed where the westward-facing wall had once stood was painted with numbers to indicate the number of people killed at the barrier year-by-year from 1961 to 1989. The resulting wall memorial at the Marie-Elisabeth Lüders House opened in 2005.[28] Just a stone's throw away, on the southern bank of the Spree, along which the East-West border used to run, another new memorial, composed of seven white crosses inscribed with the names of individuals killed at the wall, was unveiled two years earlier.[29] At various other locations privately organized campaigns yielded memory sites dedicated to particular victims in the early years of the new millennium. Günter Litfin, for example — the first GDR escapee shot at the wall, in late August 1961 — received two different memorials in central Berlin and a side street named after him in the eastern Berlin district of Weissensee, his old neighborhood, thanks primarily to the persistent activism of his younger brother, Jürgen.[30]

In many ways the enhanced attention to the wall and its victims evident by the turn of the millennium highlighted yet again the dominance of the western perspective and the continuity of western-style commemorative practices. The wall memorial at the Marie-Elisabeth Lüders House, for example, was visible from a predictable angle: eastward-facing observers could inspect the wall segments and the information painted on their western façade much as West Berliners would have been able to peruse the wall with its graffiti during the Cold War. The nearby crosses along the Spree essentially replicated an earlier West Berlin memorial of white crosses erected at the same spot in the early 1970s. The particular victims commemorated there and at the new individual memory sites around the city were all of the kind honored in the former West Berlin — that is, East Germans killed during East-West escape attempts or West Berliners mowed down in the GDR border strip. The GDR's favored victims, particularly its fallen border guards, had no place in the commemorative landscape. Predictably, east-west resentments therefore continued to smolder and periodically they erupted into open strife. The renaming of Strasse 209 in the eastern Berlin district of Weissensee as Günter-Litfin-Strasse in August 2000, for example, faced strong initial opposition from the post-Communist PDS party's local representatives, one of whom denounced Litfin as an economic opportunist who did not deserve "canonization." Although the PDS subsequently reversed course and officially supported the name change, reservations lingered, also among the local population. Revealingly, a little boy who lived in the area confided to a journalist that, according to his mother, Litfin had been "a thief or something."[31]

Although long-standing divisions between *Ossis* and *Wessis* have typically been the dominant source of tension in disputes about the remembrance of the wall in contemporary Berlin, other factors have also fueled the flames of controversy. The commemoration of the wall and the East German system that created it has never been far removed from ongoing memory politics vis-à-vis the Third Reich. Attempts to promote particular public memories of the GDR have continued to be linked to the more extensive campaigns to commemorate the Nazi era and its victims in an at least implicitly competitive fashion. Several issues have divided advocates of the two causes, even if those issues have rarely been fully articulated. There have been disagreements about the prioritization of particular projects, rivalries over funding resources, and broader controversies about the similarities and differences between the two dictatorships.[32]

To complicate matters further, the advocates of commemorating the wall in terms that comply with the prevailing western paradigm have also been far from united. The most significant rivalry has pitted the newly established, largely publicly funded Bernauer Strasse memorial against the much longer-standing, by now privately financed Checkpoint Charlie Museum, whose exhibitions and other campaigns aimed at exposing the injustices of the wall and the GDR regime reach back to the early 1960s. Although the two institutions have officially denied any competition, they have in fact vied against each other in several ways. Both have tried to attract the sizable number of tourists — and locals — interested in the wall, a contest in which the Checkpoint Charlie Museum has tended to prevail, attracting well over half a million visits a year, considerably more than its unofficial rival, which by 2008 had reached an annual visitor total of 305,000.[33] The two institutions also operate on contrasting principles. Whereas the Bernauer Strasse memorial strives for a dispassionate, relatively balanced presentational style, the Checkpoint Charlie Museum has remained something of a Cold War relic, its exhibitions and publications still frequently reflecting a crusading anti-Communist spirit with a flashy, "touristy" undertone.

The clearest public expressions of these underlying differences have been the mutually incompatible calculations of the total number of wall victims sponsored by the two institutions. The Checkpoint Charlie Museum has continued its Cold War tradition of issuing lists of confirmed or surmised deaths at the inter-German border before each anniversary of the wall's construction. For a long time the numbers showed a remarkable tendency to increase, jumping from 372 in 1992 to 728 in 2005, with deaths at the wall constituting a large proportion of the total.[34] In 2001, for example, the museum's figure of the wall dead was 254.[35] The Bernauer Strasse memorial hosted a rival attempt to determine the number of the wall's victims. In 2009 this multi-year project arrived at the much lower — and more reliable — figure of 136, which reflected stricter selection criteria and better research.[36] In reaction the Checkpoint Charlie Museum also began to lower its own numbers somewhat, but in August 2009 they still stood at 245.[37]

The Checkpoint Charlie Museum has also proved divisive in other ways. Its hard-hitting publicity campaigns have occasionally stoked major controversy. In October 2004, for example, the museum erected a short segment of imitation Wall fortifications, painted white and accompanied by over a thousand white crosses, in its vicinity, justifying the construct as a temporary work of art in honor of wall victims. Critics denounced the new monument, which was not an accurate replica of the former wall in terms of either its structure or its precise location, as a "fast food version of the wall" suited only for "quick visual satisfaction" and a "striking photo for the souvenir album," while some victims' organizations praised it as a much-needed addition to the existing memorial landscape. After prolonged public controversy city authorities finally removed the entire structure in July 2005, against the museum's wishes.[38]

While the Checkpoint Charlie Museum actively courted controversy in this instance, on other occasions it has become the involuntary object of divisive or downright embarrassing publicity. In summer 2004, for example, it engaged in a prolonged squabble with three male strippers who took turns dressing in East German uniforms, posing at the rebuilt American border-guard hut that stands in front of the museum, and charging tourists for photographs. As the men refused to leave despite repeated warnings, museum staff wrapped the entire guardhouse in blue plastic, creating an eyesore. The strippers responded by posing further, covered in thick layers of toilet paper. After a few weeks the conflict was resolved as the men agreed to leave, but the whole episode hardly enhanced the prestige of the Checkpoint Charlie Museum or, by extension, of the broader effort to commemorate the wall and its victims with appropriate dignity.[39]

Toward a More Integrated Memory Landscape?

Prompted partly by a desire to preempt similar strife and, more importantly, by a broader interest in providing general direction for the wall's commemoration, Berlin's authorities have grown more involved in coordinating relevant activities. Experts have vocalized a desire to transcend existing conflicts and to fuse different perspectives into a comprehensive "history of division" encompassing eastern and western views.[40] As a move in this direction the Berlin Senate promulgated its "Memorial Concept" for the wall in 2005. Following extensive consultation with interested parties from east and west, the working group charged with drafting the new concept criticized the hasty, piecemeal approach to the commemoration of the city's Cold War division that had prevailed in the early postunification years and recommended a more coordinated strategy for the future. The Bernauer Strasse memorial featured as "the central [commemorative] site" in this broad blueprint, to be expanded both externally, with the incorporation of additional parts of the surrounding former border zone, and internally, with more inclusive and differentiated displays that should also address the experiences of "the young East Germans" who "performed their military service" at the border. Other public and private sites within the city's "decentralized . . . commemorative landscape" were also to be respected, however, and allowed to evolve further, with improved coordination and information. In other words, the memory landscape of the wall was to grow more integrated and user-friendly, with the fiftieth anniversary of its construction in 2011 as the deadline for implementing many of these ideas.[41]

The recommendations have started to yield tangible results. Proceeding from them, the Berlin Senate produced more concrete plans for the wall's commemoration in summer 2006, and practical action has ensued.[42] The Bernauer Strasse site has entered a period of intensive development, acquiring official status as the official, government-endorsed Berlin Wall Memorial in August 2008. An ambitious redesign of the surrounding area, which aims to integrate the surviving traces of the former border installations into an extensive outdoor wall memorial, is to be concluded by the fiftieth anniversary of the barrier's erection, in 2011. Other public and private memory sites dedicated to the wall and its victims have been maintained and redeveloped, and individual sites have been linked in innovative ways. Central Berlin boasts a special wall walking route ("Geschichtsmeile Berliner Mauer") that follows the former border and includes twenty-nine information stations packed with details about the wall and particular incidents at it.[43] There is also a much longer bicycle route, known as the wall path ("Mauerweg"), which snakes through 160 kilometers of former border terrain in and around Berlin and provides similar information.[44] The city has invested in accompanying high-tech applications as well. Berlin's official web pages include a special wall portal with links to numerous relevant sites, and since spring 2008 visitors have been able to use a novel gadget: a portable multimedia guide to the former borderline, replete with historic film clips and eyewitness reports.[45]

While the memory landscape around the wall has thus grown better integrated and more accessible, the content of at least some memory sites has also become more comprehensive, with enhanced attention to eastern German perspectives. In a change from the previous decade, in parts of central Berlin, including the area around Potsdamer Platz, the pavement markings that denote where the wall once stood now include not only the westward-facing element but also the hinterland barrier.[46] Fallen GDR border guards have started to feature at some memory sites, not as East German hero-victims but as individuals who also lost their lives in divided Berlin. The inner-city pedestrian route, for instance, provides information about the violent deaths of at least three East German guards. More strikingly, a specific memory site to one of them — the twenty-one-year-old non-commissioned officer Egon Schultz, shot during a mass tunnel escape from East to West Berlin in October 1964 — has again been established, thanks to an initiative from the Bernauer Strasse memorial. A plaque on the building inside which Schultz was killed gives a lengthy account of the key events, including the tunnel escape, during which fifty-seven East Germans made their way to West Berlin, its discovery, the ensuing shootout that culminated in Schultz's death, and the GDR authorities' subsequent efforts to blame his killing on Western agents, fully cognizant of the fact that Schultz had, in fact, been accidentally shot by one of his comrades.[47] With the public display of such carefully weighed information about a particularly controversial incident, the culture of wall commemoration appears to be moving toward the kind of multifaceted history of division that some observers have been advocating for some time.

None of this means that the memory of the wall has been politically neutralized, of course — or that past conflicts have been forgotten. The Berlin Senate's general plan for the commemoration of the wall continues to highlight the barrier's significance as "the symbol" of "political repression and structural weakness" and of "the denial of elementary human rights" in the GDR. With a similar nod to the long-standing western discourse about the GDR's general illegitimacy, the plan also portrays the wall as a symbol of something much more positive, primarily in the context of

November 1989: the ultimate futility of a rogue regime's efforts to sup-
press its citizens' desire for "democracy and human rights" of the kind
guaranteed by the Federal Republic of old and the united Germany of
today.[48] The wall and its commemoration remain highly politicized,
despite the more dispassionate and inclusive forms that much of the commemorative effort has begun to assume.

This political edge was evident yet again in the key anniversary year of
2009. The official celebrations on both 13 August, the forty-eighth anniversary of the wall's construction, and particularly 9 November, the twentieth anniversary of its figurative collapse, portrayed the wall as an
embodiment of the injustices of the East German regime and celebrated
the peaceful liberation sparked by the events of 9 November 1989, in
keeping with the Berlin Senate's commemorative blueprint. Although
much of that macro-level narrative could be described as commonsensical
twenty years after the GDR's demise, its underlying political accents not-
withstanding, polarized disputes rooted in long-standing east-west divisions remained acute in particular local contexts.

The most revealing incident took place on the eve of the 9 November
celebrations in Strausberg, a small town just outside of Berlin that had
been the seat of the East German defense ministry. While preparations for
the official "Festival of Freedom" in the nearby capital reached their final
stages, a long-brewing, symbolically charged east-west dispute in Strausberg
entered its latest embittered round. It was the only town in former East
Germany that retained a street named after one of the GDR's hero-victims
of the Berlin Wall: Peter Göring, killed in a May 1962 shoot-out in which
the West Berlin police fired back at GDR guards to protect a severely
wounded fourteen-year-old East German escapee.[49] Repeated postunification campaigns to change the street name had come to naught, largely
because of stonewalling by the locally strong post-Communist PDS party.
Frustrated with their political failures, local activists now resorted to direct
action. They used a self-designed paper sticker to turn Peter-Göring-
Strasse into Michael-Gartenschläger-Strasse in honor of a prominent but
controversial anti-Communist campaigner ambushed and killed by a special Stasi commando in 1976 while trying to dismantle an automatic
shooting device on the Eastern side of the inter-German boundary. The
renaming succeeded, but only for one night. The next morning city officials removed the sticker and restored Peter Göring to the street sign.[50]

In many ways this Strausberg episode was highly exceptional, reflective
of a perspective on the history of German division that is diametrically
opposed to the prevailing national norm because of very unusual local
conditions. But the events also highlighted broad continuities in ongoing
German memory politics vis-à-vis the Berlin Wall and the related legacies
of the GDR, showing once again how politicized and potentially divisive
some of these issues remain even twenty years after the barrier's physical

disappearance. The metaphorical wall in the heads of former East and West Germans has not yet fully disappeared, and it is likely to manifest itself again in the run-up to the next major pertinent commemoration — the fiftieth anniversary of the wall's construction in August 2011.

Notes

For a fuller version of many of the points developed here see Pertti Ahonen, *Death at the Berlin Wall* (Oxford: Oxford UP, 2011), chapter 8.

[1] Helmut Kohl's television speech of 1 July 1990, reprinted in *Bulletin des Presse- und Informationsamtes der Bundesregierung*, 3 July 1990, 741.

[2] See for example A. James McAdams, *Judging the Past in Unified Germany* (Cambridge: Cambridge UP, 2001); Andrew H. Beattie, *Playing Politics with History: The Bundestag Inquiries into East Germany* (New York: Berghahn, 2008); and Roman Grafe, *Deutsche Gerechtigkeit: Prozesse gegen DDR-Grenzschützen und ihre Befehlsgeber* (Munich: Siedler, 2004).

[3] Peter Schneider, *The Wall Jumper* (Chicago, IL: U of Chicago P, 1983), 119.

[4] Polly Feversham and Leo Schmidt, *Die Berliner Mauer heute/The Berlin Wall Today* (Berlin: Verlag Bauwesen, 1999), 66–70; Gerhard Sälter, *Der Abbau der Berliner Mauer und noch sichtbare Reste in der Berliner Innenstadt* (Berlin: Verein Berliner Mauer, 2004), 7–12; and Gerhard Sälter, *Mauerreste Berlin/Relicts of the Berlin Wall* (Berlin: Verein Berliner Mauer, 2007), 10–17.

[5] Feversham and Schmidt, *Die Berliner Mauer Heute*, 126.

[6] Thomas Flemming and Hagen Koch, *Die Berliner Mauer* (Berlin: be.bra, 2001), 127–28.

[7] Edgar Wolfrum, "Die Mauer," in *Deutsche Erinnerungsorte*, ed. Etienne François and Hagen Schulze (Munich: Beck, 2001), 1:566–67; Wolfgang Rathje, "W:rbert Mayer, ed., ersial — re-'Mauer-Marketing' unter Erich Honecker," PhD dissertation (Kiel University, 2001).

[8] Ahonen, *Death at the Berlin Wall*, especially chapters 3 and 4.

[9] Feversham and Schmidt, *Die Berliner Mauer heute*, 146.

[10] Brian Ladd, *The Ghosts of Berlin* (Chicago, IL: U of Chicago P, 1997), esp. 208–15; Herbert Mayer, ed., *Wegweiser zu Berlins Strassennamen: Umbenennungen — Die neuen Strassennamen seit der Grenzöffnung* (Berlin: Luisenstädtischer Bildungsverein, 1992), 55–56; *Lexikon: Alle Berliner Strassen und Plätze — Von der Gründung bis zur Gegenwart* (Berlin: Verlag Neues Leben, 1998), 1:466; 3:444; 4:63.

[11] "'Jetzt die Mauern in den Köpfen der Menschen einreissen,'" *Frankfurter Allgemeine Zeitung*, 14 August 1990.

[12] On Western commemorative practices see Ahonen, *Death at the Berlin Wall*.

[13] "Dokumentation: Gedenkkonzept Berliner Mauer," *Netzeitung.de*, 18 April 2005, esp. 4.

[14] Sälter, *Der Abbau der Berliner Mauer*, 8, 16; Feversham and Schmidt, *Die Berliner Mauer heute*, 68–70.

[15] Sälter, *Mauerreste Berlin*, 15.

[16] *Berlin Wall: Memorial Site, Exhibition Centre and the Chapel of Reconciliation on Bernauer Strasse* (Berlin: Jaron, 1999), 23; Feversham and Schmidt, *Die Berliner Mauer heute*, 148.

[17] Eberhard Elfert, ed., *Markierung des Mauerverlaufs: Hearing am 14. Juni 1995 — Dokumentation* (Berlin: Senatsverwaltung für Bau- und Wohnungswesen, 1995).

[18] Sälter, *Mauerreste Berlin*, 25; Sälter, *Der Abbau der Berliner Mauer*, 14–15; Joachim Schlör, "'It has to go away, but at the same time it has to be kept': The Berlin Wall and the Making of an Urban Icon," *Urban History* 33 (2006): 89–92; Feversham and Schmidt, *Die Berliner Mauer heute*, 148; Patrick Major, *Behind the Berlin Wall: East Germany and the Frontiers of Power* (Oxford: Oxford UP, 2010), 276–78.

[19] See for example *Berlin Wall: Memorial Site*, 19; Feversham and Schmidt, *Die Berliner Mauer heute*, 174–76; Gerd Knischewski and Ulla Spittler, "Remembering the Berlin Wall: The Memorial Ensemble Bernauer Strasse," *German Life and Letters* 59 (2006): 283–84.

[20] Knischewski and Spittler, "Remembering the Berlin Wall," 288–89; *Berliner Mauer Dokumentationszentrum* (Berlin: Verein Berliner Mauer, 2002), 8–9.

[21] Feversham and Schmidt, *Die Berliner Mauer heute*, 180; Knischewski and Spittler, "Remembering the Berlin Wall," 285; Major, *Behind the Berlin Wall*, 279–83.

[22] Knischewski and Spittler, "Remembering the Berlin Wall," 284–85.

[23] Schlör, "'It has to go away, but at the same time it has to be kept,'" 103–5.

[24] Alex Klausmeier and Leo Schmidt, *Mauerreste — Mauerspuren* (Berlin: Westkreuz, 2004).

[25] Feversham and Schmidt, *Die Berliner Mauer heute*, 140; Klausmeier and Schmidt, *Mauerreste*, 26–27, 100–111, 122–29, 158–65; Sälter, *Mauerreste Berlin*, 31–41.

[26] Feversham and Schmidt, *Die Berliner Mauer heute*, 74, 79; Klausmeier and Schmidt, *Mauerreste*, 194–99; Sälter, *Mauerreste Berlin*, 35–39; *Mauerkatalog: "East Side Gallery"* (Berlin: Oberbaum, 1991).

[27] Dirk Verheyen, *United City, Divided Memories? Cold War Legacies in Contemporary Berlin* (Lanham, MD: Lexington, 2008), 249–50.

[28] "Die Mauer führt durch die Bundestagsbibliothek," *Berliner Zeitung*, 24 February 1995; Anne Kaminsky, *Orte des Erinnerns: Gedenkzeichen, Gedenkstätte und Museen zur Diktatur in SBZ und DDR* (Bonn: Bundeszentrale für politische Bildung, 2007), 105.

[29] Kaminsky, *Orte des Erinnerns*, 87–88.

[30] Jürgen Litfin, *Tod durch fremde Hand* (Husum: Verlag der Nation, 2006), 134–47; "Strasse wird nach Günter Litfin benannt," *Berliner Zeitung*, 29 June 2000.

³¹ "Adenauer siegt in Weissensee," *Jungle World*, 18 October 2000.

³² On Nazi legacies see for example Caroline Pearce, *Contemporary Germany and the Nazi Legacy: Remembrance, Politics and the Dialectic of Normality* (Basingstoke: Palgrave Macmillan, 2008); and Karen E. Till, *The New Berlin: Memory, Politics, Place* (Minneapolis: U of Minnesota P, 2005).

³³ Feversham and Schmidt, *Die Berliner Mauer heute*, 186; Verheyen, *United City, Divided Memories?*, 241, 231; Christine Richter, "Nichts darf vergessen werden," *Berliner Morgenpost*, 9 November 2009.

³⁴ Hans-Hermann Hertle and Gerhard Sälter, "Die Todesopfer an Mauer und Grenze," *Deutschland-Archiv* 39 (2006): 667–76.

³⁵ "109 oder 254 — wie viele starben an der Mauer?," *Der Tagesspiegel*, 5 August 2001.

³⁶ Hans-Hermann Hertle and Maria Nooke, *Die Todesopfer an der Berliner Mauer 1961–1989* (Berlin: Links, 2009).

³⁷ "Weiter Streit um Zahl der Mauertoten," *Potsdamer Neueste Nachrichten*, 11 August 2009.

³⁸ Maren Ullrich, *Geteilte Ansichten: Erinnerungslandschaft deutsch-deutsche Grenze* (Berlin: Aufbau, 2006), 26; Schlör, "'It has to go away, but at the same time it has to be kept,'" 87–88.

³⁹ "Checkpoint Charlie, jetzt eine Geschmacksgrenze," *Süddeutsche Zeitung*, 12–13 June 2004.

⁴⁰ Knischewski and Spittler, "Remembering the Berlin Wall," 290–92; Feversham and Schmidt, *Die Berliner Mauer heute*, 180.

⁴¹ Thomas Flierl, *Gedenkkonzept Berliner Mauer* (Berlin: Senatsverwaltung für Wissenschaft, Forschung und Kultur, 2005), 11–19; "Dokumentation: Gedenkkonzept Berliner Mauer" (see note 13).

⁴² "Gesamtkonzept zur Erinnerung an die Berliner Mauer," June 2006, http://www.berlin.de/mauerdialog/site/pictures/gesamtkonzept.pdf.

⁴³ "Geschichtsmeile Berliner Mauer," accessed 27 May 2010, http://www.berlin.de/mauer/geschichtsmeile/index.de.html.

⁴⁴ "Berliner Mauerweg," accessed 27 May 2010, http://www.berlin.de/mauer/mauerweg/index/index.de.php.

⁴⁵ "Berlin resurrects vanished Wall with GPS guide," *Spiegel Online*, 5 June 2008, http://www.spiegel.de/international/germany/0,1518,551559,00.html.

⁴⁶ http://www.berlin.de/mauer/orte/potsdamer_leipziger_platz/index.de.php#1, accessed 27 May 2010, author's visit.

⁴⁷ Kurt Frotscher and Horst Liebig, *Opfer deutscher Teilung* (Cologne: GNN, 2005), 136; Ahonen, *Death at the Berlin Wall*, chapter 4.

⁴⁸ "Gesamtkonzept zur Erinnerung an die Berliner Mauer," 4–5 (see note 42).

⁴⁹ See Ahonen, *Death at the Berlin Wall*, chapter 3.

⁵⁰ "Schilderkampf in Strausberg," *Berliner Zeitung*, 9 November 2009.

8: The Evolution of Memorial Sites in Mecklenburg-West Pomerania since 1990

Andreas Wagner

THE EASTERN GERMAN STATE of Mecklenburg-West Pomerania (Mecklenburg Vorpommern) was originally founded in 1945 comprising the state of Mecklenburg and the part of the Prussian province of Pomerania that remained under German administration after the war. The suffix West Pomerania was dropped in 1947. Following its administrative reform of 1952, the Socialist Unity Party (SED) replaced Mecklenburg with three districts. The Rostock district was located along the stretch of Baltic Sea coast belonging to the GDR, the Schwerin district was in the west of the region, and the Neubrandenburg district in the east. The federal state of Mecklenburg-West Pomerania was reestablished shortly before the unification of Germany in 1990. As part of the Soviet zone of occupation after 1945 and then part of the GDR from 1949, the culture of remembrance in Mecklenburg-West Pomerania was predominantly state-controlled and gradually taken over by the ruling party, the SED. This centralized culture of remembrance focused on distancing the East German state from the National Socialist regime and the Second World War and honoring Communist heroes. The aim was to legitimize the SED regime and to present a "superior" version of history to that in West Germany.[1] The state-regulated politics of memory lasted until the collapse of the SED regime in 1989, and with its accession to the Federal Republic of Germany in 1990, the former GDR was faced with the task of developing a new, democratic culture of remembrance. Memorial sites play a significant role in this respect and have undergone substantial changes since unification. These changes will be discussed in this article with a focus on developments in Mecklenburg-West Pomerania.[2]

The period after 1989–90 saw a reevaluation of the past, just as there had been after 1945. This was accompanied by changes to a memorial landscape established over the course of forty years, changes with regard to existing memorial sites and exhibitions, plaques, monuments, and cemeteries, but also street names and the names of businesses and other institutions. Remembrance of the victims of German Fascism had played a key role in the memory politics of the SED; Communists were depicted as leading figures in the resistance and Communist victims were made into heroes and instrumentalized for the political agenda of the SED. In the process other victims' groups — such as the victims of National Socialist racial policy — were marginalized, discriminated against, ignored, or considered much less important. Under the influence of Stalinism, people and events that did not correspond to the dominant historical interpretation became taboo. As well as focusing on the history of the Communist movement, the SED created a version of historical progress in which revolutionary social movements played a key role. This was reflected in monuments to leading figures from the 1848–49 revolution and the workers' movement in the nineteenth century, to victims of the 1920 Kapp Putsch, and to members of the workers' movement murdered by the National Socialists. In many respects this memorial landscape was linked to the sites of historic events.

The East German culture of remembrance allowed little scope for diversity; however, citizens' initiatives were able to address some previously repressed themes in the 1980s. For example a memorial to Count Schwerin von Schwanenfeld, who was executed for his involvement in the plot to assassinate Hitler on 20 July 1944, was erected in 1987 in his former home village of Göhren, near Neustrelitz, and 1988 saw many events to commemorate the persecuted and murdered Jews as well as the establishment of plaques and memorials. The perestroika movement in the Soviet Union also encouraged emboldened citizens to address previously unanswered questions relating to their own history.

Those involved in the "peaceful revolution" of autumn 1989 wanted the ruling party to stop dictating the way they confronted the past. There was a need to fill in the numerous "gaps" in contemporary history; moreover, there was a painful distinction between private and public memory and a desire for the end of the obvious manipulation of history for political agendas in the present. The storming of the Ministry for State Security in early December 1989 finally stripped the East German secret police (Stasi) of their power and secured access to the files that would expose the all-encompassing nature of the surveillance system. It also gave people in the GDR a part of their history back.[3] The extent to which the East German security service had destroyed lives, manipulated events, and persecuted and disciplined people became horrifyingly apparent. Confrontation with this aspect of the GDR was initially impaired by its focus on Stasi informants; however, the process is still ongoing in the context of debates on East German history. It is significant that the people took control of the buildings and sites connected to the Stasi, moving these out of the shadows and into the glare of public debate.

After unification Mecklenburg-West Pomerania was the only one of the new *Bundesländer* to launch a government committee of enquiry

(Enquete-Kommission). This committee, "Life in the GDR, Life After 1989 — Confrontation and Reconciliation," operated between 1995 and 1997 and sought ways of reconciling "victims" and "perpetrators" by investigating the past. Through commissioning research projects and organizing public hearings, representatives from five political parties — the CDU, SPD, PDS, FDP, and Bündnis 90/Die Grünen — aimed to establish an accurate account of GDR history, to provide a public catalyst for confrontation with the past, and to avert attempts to repress or play it down. The committee wanted an inclusive debate but set itself restrictive boundaries as decisions had to be adopted by consensus. The dispute over whether to show an exhibition by the Federal Ministry of Justice titled "In the Name of the People? State Justice in the SED State" in Mecklenburg-West Pomerania demonstrated just how little consensus there was in terms of confronting the GDR past: the exhibition's objective of highlighting the injustice of the regime and those responsible for it was not universally supported. In 1997 three CDU representatives and one from the FDP resigned as a result of this dispute, including the former chairman of the Mecklenburg-West Pomerania branch of the Association for the Victims of Stalinism (*Vereinigung der Opfer des Stalinismus*). The committee of enquiry was unable to satisfy the justified claims for compensation from the victims of persecution and discrimination under the SED regime; however, its work did pave the way for research into regional GDR history and for public debate.[4]

Mecklenburg-West Pomerania also differs from the other new *Länder* in its decentralized approach to memorial sites. Unlike in the other states of the former GDR, no foundation was established there to preserve the central ones, the responsibility for coordinating them being given to the Mecklenburg-West Pomerania *Landesfachstelle* (department) for memorial sites, part of the organization Politische Memoriale e.V., founded in 1996. Its task is to provide expert support for memorial sites and remembrance projects and advice on organization and funding. It also runs staff training programs and is responsible for publicity and disseminating research. Cooperation between the *Landesfachstelle* and memorial sites is on a voluntary basis, but the former has become a central feature of the network of monuments and memorial sites relating to the history of National Socialism and the Communist regime in Mecklenburg-West Pomerania. It also advises the Landeszentrale für politische Bildung (Regional Center for Political Education) there, along with other regional bodies that work with memorial sites.

The memorial landscape in Mecklenburg-West Pomerania has evolved in many different ways. Old memorial sites have been dismantled, extended to include explanatory information, and renamed; the impetus for these developments has come from citizens' initiatives and the local administration. In addition, new memorials have been established to places or people that were not previously commemorated for various reasons. Some forgotten memorials have been revived and thereby attained a completely new significance.

Confrontation with the Communist regime, the commemoration of those persecuted by the Soviet secret police and the SED regime, and the remembrance of resistance and everyday life under the dictatorship continue to provide the impetus for the redevelopment of the memorial landscape. The past twenty years have seen an increased focus on the workings of the GDR regime and the "asymmetric parallel histories" of the two postwar German states.[5] Nonetheless, the memory of repression, victimhood, and resistance remains an integral feature of the confrontation with the East German dictatorship, irrespective of which political party is in power. For most citizens of the former GDR, this confrontation process is connected with the need to reflect self-critically on their lives in their GDR, for they carried the system and adapted to it, even if they did so reluctantly. It is a common psychological tendency to avoid such self-analysis.

Memorial Sites to the Victims of Stalinist Persecution under the Soviet Occupation

Due to its close links with the Soviet Union, the SED constantly avoided any investigation of the crimes carried out during the Soviet occupation. Sites where Germans were persecuted by the Soviet secret police and discussion of this persecution remained taboo until 1989. With the Waldheim Trials of 1950, a legal farce where GDR judges meted out draconian sentences to prisoners handed over to them by the Soviets, the GDR judiciary not only perpetuated Stalinist terror but also gave it belated legitimation. When it came to memory politics, the SED leadership wanted to stand on the side of the victors of the Second World War, and after 1956 there were no more than tentative efforts to confront Stalinist crimes.

However, there were many people in the GDR who had been arrested and tortured by the Soviet secret police after 1945 and imprisoned for years in camps and prisons. These individuals were forced to remain silent, and they held their tongues for fear of further persecution. The families of the many victims who died in the camps were kept in the dark about what had happened to their relatives. In the 1980s Dieter Krüger from the then Neubrandenburg District Historical Museum conducted research into the history of the World War Two prisoner-of-war camp Stalag II-A. In the process he came across its later use as a detention camp by the Soviets. The former camp grounds and cemetery, which contained a memorial erected in the late 1950s, lay in a restricted military zone that had fallen into disrepair and vanished from public memory. A citizens' initiative led by

Krüger, the Fünfeichen Bürgerinitiative, attempted to change this situation in 1990 and discovered the mass graves of thousands of prisoners from the Soviet Speziallager Nr. 9. Reports on this discovery at the end of March 1990 attracted considerable public interest, and additional special camps and mass graves were identified at a later stage. Many of those affected by these findings subsequently tried to find out what had happened to their fellow prisoners or family members or recounted their own experiences; moreover, people could now obtain memoirs and reports that had been published in the Federal Republic.

The Neubrandenburg regional museum and town archive began to document the history of former prisoners of Soviet Speziallager Nr. 9 in Fünfeichen, which existed between summer 1945 and the end of 1948. April 1991 saw the establishment of the Arbeitsgruppe Fünfeichen, an association of victims and relatives of former prisoners of the special camp. A simple memorial was inaugurated in November 1991, funded by the German War Graves Commission (Volksbund deutsche Kriegsgräber-fürsorge), the town of Neubrandenburg, the Federal Ministry of the Interior, and donations, and a newly designed memorial site was opened on 25 April 1993, responding to the challenge of addressing both phases of the Fünfeichen camp — its use as a prisoner-of-war camp from 1939 to 1945 and as a Soviet special camp from 1945 to 1948. The site includes all three cemeteries — that is, the cemetery for the prisoners of war and the two containing the mass graves of the camp. The Fünfeichen memorial site was further developed in subsequent years, primarily on the initiative of the Arbeitsgruppe Fünfeichen. In 1999, for example, several bronze plaques with the names of over 5,000 victims of the special camp were inaugurated in the southern cemetery. In addition to extending the site, the working group has produced a documentary on the history of the Soviet special camp, provides support to survivors and relatives of the vic-tims, and organizes tours of the site and cemeteries. The regional museum in Neubrandenburg also has a small exhibition on the various camps that existed in the area during National Socialism, and the town archive gathers artifacts and organizes school projects.[6]

The activity of the Soviet military tribunals was a further aspect of the GDR regime to come under scrutiny with the revelation of details of the fate of the Rostock law student Arno Esch (1928–51). These tribunals issued harsh sentences, above all to critics of the new system in the Soviet zone of occupation and in the early years of the GDR. As a leading mem-ber of the Liberal Democratic Party in the Soviet zone, Arno Esch fell victim to Soviet military justice after publicly calling for democracy and opposing a Communist transformation of East German society. On 18 October 1949 he was arrested by the Soviet secret police. He was sen-tenced to death by the Soviet military tribunal in Schwerin and after being sentenced again in Moscow on 24 July 1951, he was executed there. He was one of over nine hundred German citizens shot dead between 1950 and 1953 as the result of sentences passed by Soviet military tribunals in Moscow, and thousands more were deported to Soviet forced labor camps.[7] Former political prisoners from the West German association of former Rostock students (VERS) submitted a request to the Soviet authorities for the rehabilitation of Arno Esch in the late 1980s, and they ultimately complied in May 1991. On 24 February 1990 a memorial plaque to Esch was erected in the main building of Rostock University next to the plaque for a scientist murdered by the National Socialists that had been put up during the GDR period. The inscription reads:

> DEM STUDENTEN ARNO ESCH
> geb. am 6. Februar 1928
> hingerichtet am 24. Juli 1951
> UND ALLEN OPFERN UND VERFOLGTEN
> DES
> STALINISMUS
> AN DIESER UNIVERSITÄT
> ZUM MAHNENDEN GEDENKEN.

Streets were named after Arno Esch in Rostock, Grevesmühlen, and Schwerin, and there are regular commemorative events in Rostock.

There is one particularly significant site commemorating those sentenced by Soviet military tribunals in Mecklenburg and West Pomerania. The main remand prison of the Soviet secret police there was located on Demmlerplatz in Schwerin. Soviet military tribunals issued political sentences in the court next door, and deportations to the special camps started there.[8] From 1954 the Schwerin district branch of the Stasi was housed in the court and remand prison. At the end of 1989 the buildings were occupied by a citizens' committee (*Bürgerkomitee*), and since unification the district and regional courts have been located in the imposing building, originally constructed in 1916. Following an initiative from the Association for the Victims of Stalinism, a memorial plaque was put up next to the entrance of the court in 1994. There was a long dispute concerning the use of the prison wing as a place of learning and commemoration, and the Commissioner for the Records of the State Security Service of the Former GDR (Beauftragte für die Unterlagen des Staatssicherheitsdienstes der ehemaligen DDR) in Mecklenburg-Western Pomerania pushed for the establishment of a memorial site and exhibition in the building. The judiciary was using the entire prison complex at that stage, and political consensus was required before a memorial site could be established, so the dispute went on for several years. Following the debate initiated by the committee of enquiry "Life in the GDR — Life after 1989," in 1998 the Mecklenburg-West Pomeranian government voted to establish memorial sites and research facilities in the former Stasi remand prisons in Rostock and Schwerin. The

Fig. 8.1. The Document Center Demmlerplatz in Schwerin is located in part of a former prison that was used by the Nazis, the Soviet Secret Police (1945–53), and the East German State Security Service (1954–89). A comprehensive exhibition about the history of the building is housed in its cells and interrogation rooms. Photo from 9 October 2008, courtesy of Politische Memoriale e.V.

documentation center at Demmlerplatz in Schwerin was inaugurated on 6 June 2001 and is funded by the state of Mecklenburg-West Pomerania. The exhibition, which is divided into three sections, documents the abuse of rights under National Socialism, the Soviet occupation, and the GDR.

Alongside the central sites remembering persecution by the Soviet secret police at Neubrandenburg-Fünfeichen and Schwerin-Demmlerplatz, plaques or memorials were erected at other small prisons in the 1990s, for example in Parchim, Güstrow, Malchow, and Alt Strelitz. There are also plaques remembering specific victims. For example the former grammar school in Parchim put one up in 1993 to commemorate two brave teachers who promoted democracy and warned pupils of their impending arrest so that they could escape in time. They were arrested by the Soviet secret police in 1951, and the Soviet military tribunal in Schwerin sentenced each of them to twenty years of forced labor for spying. One of them died in a Soviet camp in 1951, and the other returned in poor health in 1955. Then in 2002, following an initiative by a relative, Penzlin town council voted to erect a memorial to a group of young people who were arrested by the Soviet secret police in late 1945 and accused of being part of the Nazi Werewolf combat force. They were tortured until they confessed and subsequently received harsh sentences from a Soviet military tribunal; five of the nine did not survive their imprisonment. The town inaugurated a memorial and plaque in the cemetery on the People's Day of Mourning (*Volkstrauertag*) in 2003.

There are around fifteen documented memorials to the victims of persecution by the Soviet secret police in Mecklenburg. The impetus for these came largely from survivors of the camps and prisons and from relatives of the victims. The need to finally have a place of mourning and to inform people about the actual conditions of their imprisonment played a decisive role.

Memorial Sites to the Victims of Political Persecution by the SED Regime

The victims of political persecution during the GDR are mainly remembered at the sites where they were persecuted and imprisoned, namely the Ministry for State Security and its remand prisons. At an early stage victims' associations called for plaques to be put up at former Stasi buildings, and in 1995 the Association for the Victims of Stalinism had one put up at the building that housed the Stasi headquarters for the Rostock district from 1959. However, the plaque was immediately destroyed by unidentified perpetrators and had to be replaced, this time under a pane of reinforced glass. Plaques were put up at the former Stasi premises in Schwerin and Stralsund in 1994 and 1996 respectively. One was also erected at the former local headquarters of the Stasi in Greifswald on the tenth anniversary of the storming of the building, but here the aim was different: to proudly commemorate the "peaceful revolution" that brought an end to the repressive regime without bloodshed. The buildings at Lindenberg that housed the Stasi headquarters for Neubrandenburg from the 1970s were converted into council offices in 1990, and one of the many institutions now located there is the Neubrandenburg branch of the Federal Office for the Records of the State Security Service of the former GDR.

In 2008 a series of information points on "GDR Security at Lindenberg" was established in Neubrandenburg with the support of the Mecklenburg-West Pomerania Commissioner for the Records of the State Security Service of the former GDR and the organization Politische Memoriale. Six information points explain the former use of these buildings by the Stasi, and the clear focus is on using the historic site as a place of learning. The Neubrandenburg branch of the Office for the Records of the State Security Service of the former GDR provides pedagogical staff who run tours of the site and develop educational programs; the information points can also be accessed by individual visitors. Up to 1987 the Neubrandenburg branch of the Stasi was based at the remand prison in the neighboring town of Neustrelitz, which was later used by the police and the judiciary. In 2006 pupils from Neustrelitz grammar school, groups of citizens, and experts started to investigate the history of the prison, charting the biographies of former inmates and intending to set up a memorial site. A documentary film from 2007 recounts the story of three prisoners and the role of the Stasi remand prison as a place of persecution.[9]

The most important memorial site related to the history of the Stasi in Mecklenburg-West Pomerania is the Documentation Center and Memorial Site in the former Stasi remand prison in Rostock, where an exhibition opened in 1999 providing information on the work of the Stasi in the Rostock district. It is staffed by employees of the Rostock branch of the Federal Office for the Records of the State Security Service of the Former GDR, who also oversee the content of the exhibition. This memorial site is associated with the Documentation Center for the Victims of German Dictatorships in the Twentieth Century in Mecklenburg-West Pomerania, founded in 1998, and cooperates with the Historical Institute of Rostock University. The history of the GDR's State Security Service forms one of the three sections of the Demmlerplatz documentation center, opened in 2001 in Schwerin, which contains details of many individual victims and in-depth historical information.

Confrontation with the regional history of the Stasi is a crucial factor in dealing with the history of the GDR because it was fundamental to the GDR's system of repression and oppression. In the vast majority of cases political prisoners were arrested and interrogated by the Stasi, and the remand prisons were frequently the first stage on the way through the

GDR prison system. While former prisoners successfully called for the sites concerned to be identified in the mid-1990s, political wranglings over the establishment of sites of remembrance and learning in the former prisons were much more drawn-out. Not only was a political majority required to implement such proposals, but plans by the administration to convert the buildings had to be overturned and funding secured. The 1998 decision by the Mecklenburg-West Pomeranian government facilitated the development of exhibitions and educational programs in the former remand prisons in Rostock and Schwerin, and support for these plans from the Commissioner for the Records of the State Security Service of the Former GDR in Mecklenburg-Western Pomerania was instrumental in this decision. This small institution was established in 1993 to provide advice and support to citizens before and after they consult their Stasi files. A further objective is to advise public institutions that screen personnel and to promote political and historical education on the history of the GDR. From the start it has also had the important task of supporting remembrance projects and the work of existing memorial sites. This body plays a significant role as an intermediary between citizens' initiatives and victims' associations and the government and administration of Mecklenburg-West Pomerania.[10] The work of the three regional branches of the Federal Office for the Records of the State Security Service of the former GDR in Neubrandenburg, Rostock, and Schwerin thus cannot be underestimated. Although their main task is to open up the Stasi files and secure access to them, they also cooperate closely with memorial sites and have a productive influence on the network of remembrance projects and memorial sites in organizing events and developing touring exhibitions.

Along with sites recalling Stasi repression, there are memorial sites dealing with many other aspects of the GDR regime on both sides of the former German-German border, some of those on the western side having been established before 1989. These memorials address a broad range of themes, for example the development of the inhuman GDR border regime, forced resettlements between 1952 and 1961, everyday life in the exclusion zone at the border, escape attempts, the fall of the Berlin Wall, and the end of German division. Between 1999 and 2001, a small museum project was established at the former checkpoint at Sector Four (Ortsteil Vier) in Boizenburg. The concept was developed by a regional employment agency to provide meaningful work for the unemployed and to realize a project of public interest. It deals with the existence of two histories on one site: the history of the sub-camp of a concentration camp from 1944–45 and the local history of the German-German border. Between 1952 and 1972 Boizenburg lay in the exclusion zone at the border and was only accessible with a special permit. The checkpoint was on the transit road directly in front of the Lauenburg-Horst border crossing. In 2008–9 the exhibition was completely revised and the themes presented

Fig. 8.2. In Schlagsdorf, a village on the former border between East and West Germany, a local association runs a small museum (opened 1999) about the local history of the border. It has an open-air exhibition where parts of the East German border installations from different periods have been reconstructed. Photo from 27 August 2009, courtesy of Politische Memoriale e.V.

separately in order to highlight the differences between the two histories of the site. The most important exhibition on the history of the German-German border in Mecklenburg-West Pomerania is located in the "Grenzhus" in Schlagsdorf, near Ratzeburg Lake, where a small exhibition on everyday life at the border was opened in 1999. A local association is responsible for the upkeep of the museum and runs guided tours, and there is an outside area containing a reconstruction of original features of the GDR border fortifications.

In addition to these small museums there are memorials marking the former GDR border fortifications and pointers to further traces of the border, for example the watchtower in Kühlungsborn, to the west of Rostock. Although the German-German border is still alive in public memory, it is not common knowledge that the GDR's entire Baltic Sea coast served as a border area and was subject to specific security measures. Border troops patrolled the beaches, there were watchtowers spaced at regular intervals, and the use of motorboats was strictly regulated. The only remaining feature of this border is the watchtower at Kühlungsborn.

A small local initiative has made efforts to preserve this watchtower and provide information on the border regime in that area. In 2000 a memorial to those who attempted to escape via the Baltic Sea was erected in the resort of Boltenhagen.[11]

A further element of the repression under the SED regime is remembered in Bützow: the GDR penal system. Political opponents of the SED regime, dissidents, the victims of purges and expropriations, and other "troublesome" individuals were imprisoned there, especially in the 1950s. Bützow prison, the largest and oldest prison in Mecklenburg-West Pomerania, played a particularly important role in "Operation Rose" at the beginning of 1953. This was an expropriation order carried out by the army general staff in the Rostock district, during which 447 restaurant and hotel owners were arrested and imprisoned at Bützow-Dreibergen. In a show trial a specially appointed criminal division of Bützow district court handed out prison sentences to those arrested and stripped them of their property. Most of those imprisoned through Operation Rose were released following the uprisings of 17 June 1953, and from the late 1960s the conditions of imprisonment and the profile of the prisoners changed. Bützow became a prison for serious offenders, and political prisoners — arrested mainly for attempting to flee the GDR — were the exception. At the end of 2002 a new documentation center on the political abuses of the penal system in Bützow was opened in the Krummes Haus, a historic building with a library and the local history museum. This small permanent exhibition was the product of academic research and local debates that led to the decision to completely redesign and revise the memorial site to the victims of National Socialism in Bützow, which was established in 1985 but increasingly subject to criticism after 1990 as it did not present the history of persecution after 1945. The new exhibition provides information about the political abuses of the local penal system from the nineteenth century up to 1989. It has received widespread regional support for charting the history of political prisoners detained there both between 1933 and 1945 and in the postwar period. This exhibition presents facts rather than opinions and addresses the question of responsibility.

Since 2003 former political prisoners of the Bützow penal system under the GDR and other interested parties have organized an annual meeting and a public forum for the critical confrontation with GDR history.[12] Following an initiative by former political prisoners the town launched a competition to design a monument to the political prisoners of the Bützow penal system. The striking construction was inaugurated during the 2008 meeting, and there are now memorials in front of the Krummes Haus commemorating the political prisoners at Bützow during the National Socialist period, the Soviet occupation, and the GDR.

In addition to these memorial sites and monuments to specific victims or groups of victims at sites connected with certain types of persecution, there are also general memorials "to the victims of war and tyranny," an inclusive formula agreed on by those responsible that, however, fails to differentiate between different types of victimhood and to address the causes and consequences of war and persecution under different political systems. The memorials concerned are mainly simple stones or plaques placed in the center of a town or village or in the local cemetery. Many of the monuments constructed in the 1920s and 1930s to remember those who died in the First World War had fallen into disrepair and been forgotten about prior to unification, but these monuments attracted renewed interest after 1990. New plaques were added to commemorate those who died in the Second World War or all victims of war and tyranny. Two examples from the Ludwigslust district deserve attention here. In 1994 the municipality of Rastow restored the monument to those who died in the wars of 1870–71 and 1914–18, adding a plaque with the inscription, "Wir gedenken der Opfer des 2. Weltkrieges 1939–1945. Die Einwohner der Gemeinde Rastow." The war memorial in Bahlsdorf to those who fell in the First World War was also renovated in the 1990s to include two new plaques featuring a list of the names of residents who died in the Second World War. The additional text "Unser Gedenken gilt auch den ungenannten Opfern" points to other groups of victims. The problem with the restoration of these war memorials is that it gives credence to the original dedications, which were sometimes nationalist and misleading. Far-right extremists are quick to use these monuments to support a view of history that relativizes National Socialist crimes.

There are only a few memorials dedicated to the resistance against the SED regime and to the "peaceful revolution" of 1989. All former sites of repression touch on the history of the resistance; however, they focus on the persecution, imprisonment, and suffering of the victims, and the reasons for persecution play a secondary role. This approach can be explained partially by the negative experience of the GDR period, when a distinction was drawn between active resistance and victimhood. Moreover, there is an increased tendency to highlight victimhood, and not just in terms of National Socialist history. There are just three memorials in Mecklenburg-West Pomerania that focus on resistance itself. The first recalls the uprisings of 17 June 1953 in Stralsund and Rostock, where the town squares have been named to commemorate where shipyard workers went on strike and called for political change in the GDR. The second can be found at Greifswald University, where there is a plaque in the stairwell of the building housing the lecture theaters that recalls the medics' strike of 1955, when over two hundred students protested against plans to make Greifswald a center for training military doctors. The strike led to a compromise whereby both civilian students and military medics could study at the Faculty of Medicine of the University of Greifswald until the end of the

GDR. The third example is the "Round Table" monument in Schwerin, designed by the Lübeck sculptor Guillermo Steinbrüggen in 1990. The Runder Tisch was established as a result of the "peaceful revolution" and accompanied the transition from dictatorship to democracy in all political spheres of the GDR. The Schwerin branch held its first meeting on 12 December 1989 in the Catholic parish hall, and the members included representatives from various parties and the citizens' movement. It managed the break-up of the Stasi, uncovered official abuses and corruption, and dealt with many other problems. In 1995 the artist added color to the metal sculpture and it was placed in a new location accessible to the public.

It is surprising that there are only a few memorials in Mecklenburg-West Pomerania recalling the courageous protests of autumn 1989 that led to the fall of the SED regime. There are plaques remembering the peaceful protests in Rostock, Schwerin, and Waren, but there are far more memorials and plaques to German unification on 3 October 1990 (at least thirteen) than there are to the "peaceful revolution." The fall of the Berlin Wall evokes positive memories among citizens of the former GDR, while those who experienced the "peaceful revolution" have diverging interpretations of it, depending on their individual stance toward the SED system.

Memorial Sites to the Victims of National Socialism

The end of Communism also changed perspectives on the history of National Socialism. Questions were raised that had previously been repressed or left unanswered, which led to new challenges. It was necessary to address sites, themes, and victims' groups that had previously been ignored, but also the ideology of anti-Fascism, which had been the standard form of remembrance in the GDR. At first public interest in these sites and themes fell dramatically. Many citizens of the former GDR associated remembrance of the victims of National Socialism with the SED regime, which they had just rejected. Very few people attended remembrance ceremonies or visited the sites, which lost credibility and legitimation. In addition there was an increased tendency to trivialize or play down the National Socialist regime, especially on the part of far-right groups.[13] Moreover, difficulties in addressing individual responsibility during the SED dictatorship had an impact on the confrontation with the attitudes of the generations that had lived through National Socialism. Those who were reluctant to analyze their own lives self-critically also tended to view life under National Socialism in a far less critical light and to subscribe to exculpatory viewpoints, which resulted in a number of debates and controversies. These made it clear to the leaders of Mecklenburg-West Pomerania that it is impossible to discuss the period between 1933 and 1945 without reference to the terror of the National Socialist regime.

The opening up of former military zones following the end of the GDR and the withdrawal of Russian troops shed light on the military legacy of the GDR but also the historical sites related to the National Socialist period. The best-known internationally in this respect is the village of Peenemünde, in the north of Usedom Island, where in 1936 the National Socialists started to build an enormous research facility designed to develop modern armaments technology, especially guided missiles. Other important sites that only became accessible after 1990 include Prora, a planned seaside health resort for the Kraft durch Freude (Strength through Joy) movement,[14] and Alt Rehse, the location of the former SS Reichsärzteführerschule.[15] Following the collapse of the GDR and the withdrawal of the military, attempts were made in Peenemünde to establish a new identity and new employment opportunities. The National Socialist history of the area seemed ideal for the purpose, and on 9 May 1991 the Association for the Promotion and Development of a Historical and Technical Museum in Peenemünde — the Birthplace of Space Travel opened its first provisional exhibition in the former control bunker outside Peenemünde power station. The organizers were taken aback by the number of visitors and the national interest it attracted. Their efforts to concentrate on the technical side of missile development corresponded to the interests of the federal air and space industry, as well as various politicians who wanted to celebrate the fiftieth anniversary of the successful launch of the type A4 missile on 3 October 1942 as marking the birth of space travel. The motive was to present the invention of missile technology as unrelated to the political aims of the National Socialists.

These plans provoked an international controversy that, however, ultimately led to a responsible confrontation with the National Socialist past in Peenemünde with the support of the Mecklenburg-West Pomeranian government.[16] The Project Group to Redesign and Extend the Peenemünde Museum was founded in 1996 and both produced a new concept for the museum and developed a detailed exhibition titled "Gravity's Rainbow" ("Die Enden der Parabel") in the former power station, which is the most significant remaining part of the National Socialist army research center. The first part of the exhibition opened in 2000. In 2003 the decision to show "Crimes of the Wehrmacht. Dimensions of a War of Annihilation, 1941–44," an exhibition devised by the Hamburg Institute for Social Research, at the museum hit the headlines when a regional association was formed in support of the exhibition in order to counter protests from the far right. The Historical Technical Museum in Peenemünde has since become an internationally significant museum of contemporary history. In the future the confrontation with the legacy of missile development in

Peenemünde will continue to focus on historical and critical analysis of the National Socialist regime and its war of ideology and annihilation.[17]

Along with these "perpetrator sites" dealing with National Socialism and its appeal among individual professional groups or sectors of society, other previously unknown or marginalized sites were developed after 1989. Free from the ideological constraints imposed by GDR anti-Fascism, confrontation with Jewish history and the persecution and murder of Jews from Mecklenburg and Pomerania began, new memorials emerged, and historical remains were preserved. Contact with Holocaust survivors and their families led not just to emotional encounters but also to a new understanding. The free access to Israel and Western Europe was a prerequisite for this. The Max-Samuel-House, a center for Jewish history and culture, was established in 1991 in Rostock and provides historical information as well as details on contemporary Jewish culture. Two historic synagogues have become places of remembrance and learning. A citizens' initiative restored a synagogue in Röbel-Müritz and opened a youth center on the site. In 2006 an exhibition on Jewish history opened in east Mecklenburg and has since organized many school projects. In Hagenow the buildings of the former Jewish community have belonged to the museum since 2001, and it has restored the synagogue, which was re-opened to the public in 2007 and holds events and presents school projects and exhibitions. The revival of the Jewish community since 1990 has been very important for Mecklenburg-West Pomerania, and it now plays an integral role in the spiritual and religious life of this federal state.[18]

Remembrance of the victims of the National Socialist concentration camps is also a central feature of the memorial landscape in Mecklenburg-West Pomerania. Although there was no main concentration camp in the area, in 1942 and 1943 numerous sub-camps, mainly of Ravensbrück, were established there. Thousands of male and female concentration camp prisoners were deployed as forced laborers in the armaments industry for the Wehrmacht or at SS institutions, a past that is remembered at memorial sites and small exhibitions in Neustadt-Glewe, Barth, and Neubrandenburg. These also include the memorial site at Wöbbelin, to the south of Schwerin, where a sub-camp of the Neuengamme concentration camp existed between February and May 1945 to house prisoners evacuated from various concentration camps. Around one thousand of the prisoners crammed into this camp died as a result of the horrendous conditions.

During the GDR period there were memorials and commemorations for the victims of National Socialism in Mecklenburg-West Pomerania; however, after unification there was a need to free these commemorative practices from the restrictions of the anti-Fascist ideology of the GDR state. Memorial sites now focus closely on preserving and protecting original features, primarily the foundations of buildings and other architectural relics. In Wöbbelin and Barth, for example, architectural remains were documented, marked, and protected, and a new monument to those who died in the sub-camp of Neuengamme was erected in the former camp grounds in Wöbbelin. In Barth a local initiative established a series of information points in the former camp grounds between 2000 and 2002, detailing the history of the camp and its prisoners. There has also been a series of information points in Neubrandenburg since 2008 that focus on the history of National Socialist forced labor in the north of Neubrandenburg, a center for the armaments industry. Through numerous initiatives, especially international work camps and school projects, it has been possible to rediscover almost the entire network of sub-camps, including sites absent from public memory before 1990 such as Neustadt-Glewe, Gelbensande-Schwarzenpfost, Peenemünde, and Malchow. The remains of the camps have become places of remembrance providing visible testimony of the past, and opportunities to research and travel freely since 1990 have provided a major catalyst for information on the history of the individual camps resulting in numerous publications for the general public. This has paved the way for the redevelopment of certain sites (for example in Wöbbelin) and for initiatives to establish such exhibitions for the first time since 1945 (for example in Barth and Gelbensande). Memorial sites in these locations adopt a pluralist approach to remembrance, and their work includes organizing seminars, international work-camps, visits to memorial sites, and educational theatrical productions. The testimony of survivors and eyewitnesses is an important feature of the new exhibitions, which deal with all aspects of victimhood.[19]

Although academic research into contemporary history at the two universities in Mecklenburg-West Pomerania has tended to focus on the post-1945 period, knowledge of the regional history of National Socialism has increased enormously. This has shed light on previously marginalized sites related to National Socialist history, for example the former Wehrmacht prison in Anklam, where members of the Wehrmacht sentenced by military courts were imprisoned. There were several thousand prisoners here, many incarcerated for undermining military morale (*Wehrkraftzersetzung*), refusing to obey orders, desertion, and going absent without leave. Over 130 death sentences were issued. Although a research group of the GDR Cultural Association (Kulturbund) had carried out some extensive research here in 1960–61, a memorial site was not established because no evidence could be found of Communist resistance among the prisoners. Research was intensified after 1990 and in 2005, after fifteen years of neglect, the foundation Center for Peace took over the former prison, made it accessible to the public, and organized events and guided tours.[20] The historical dimensions of additional sites have been revealed through new research, for example the crimes against Soviet prisoners of war and the murder of patients in clinics and care homes in the course of the Nazi euthanasia program.

There is a further group of sites that were marginalized or not mentioned at all during the GDR period: the cemeteries for Germans who died during the Second World War or in the course of flight and expulsion from the former German territories in Eastern Europe at the end of the war. These cemeteries were established between 1945 and 1946 next to the quarantine and displaced persons camps. Many were rediscovered after 1990. The largest war cemetery in Mecklenburg-West Pomerania is at Golm, where thousands of victims were buried following the air raid on Swinemünde on 12 March 1945. For years the Protestant church was the only institution that saw itself responsible for the upkeep of the cemetery, and this work was impaired by state restrictions. In 1968 it became a memorial site and annual commemorations were held there, but these failed to mention the harsh fate of those who had fled or been expelled from Eastern Europe. After unification a citizens' initiative assumed responsibility for the memorial site and redesigned it but included the memorial erected during the GDR. In 2005 the German War Graves Commission took over responsibility for the memorial site and set up a German-Polish youth center in Kamminke, which has successfully run projects aimed at German-Polish reconciliation. Attempts by far-right organizations to use this memorial site for their political agenda have failed in the face of decisive opposition from the German War Graves Commission and the democratic forces in the region, but such attempts recur. Far-right groups portray the German casualties as victims of Allied terror and reject or trivialize German crimes. Until a few years ago far-right marches were always staged to coincide with the commemorations, and representatives from the far-right NPD party tried to join the remembrance ceremonies. For this reason these sites of memory must provide an accurate historical context and explain the causes of war and genocide as well as promoting international understanding and peace.

Conclusion

The memorial site landscape of Mecklenburg-West Pomerania began to evolve after unification, and the changes had made a considerable impact by the mid-1990s. Like all citizens of the former GDR, the citizens of this federal state have faced the dual task of addressing the challenges posed by the experience of two dictatorships and confronting both pasts. Over the past twenty years a varied and pluralistic memorial landscape has emerged as a result of the interplay of citizens' initiatives, administrative decisions, and a decentralized policy of regional funding.

Completely new memorial sites to the victims of persecution by the Soviet secret police and the SED regime were established after unification, sometimes in the face of considerable unvoiced opposition. The impetus for these memorial sites often came from citizens' initiatives and victims' associations; however, they would not have come into being without the administrative and financial support of state institutions, foundations, and educational bodies that ensured consistency and professionalism. In Mecklenburg-West Pomerania the Landeszentrale für politische Bildung, the regional branch of the Federal Office for the Records of the State Security Service of the Former GDR, and the regional department (*Landesfachstelle*) for memorial sites play a particularly important role in this respect.

Confrontation with the National Socialist past had to be liberated from the ideological constraints placed upon it during the GDR, and new memorials were established at sites that had been inaccessible to the public before 1990 and to commemorate aspects of persecution that had been ignored or marginalized. Exhibitions and pedagogical facilities at existing memorial sites recalling the National Socialist period were further developed with support from the state, which is important for the confrontation with far-right extremism in Mecklenburg-West Pomerania.

After twenty years the memorial landscape in Mecklenburg-West Pomerania faces a range of new challenges, so the Landeszentrale für politische Bildung began work on a memorial site concept for Mecklenburg-West Pomerania in 2009. The aim is to establish the focus of future activities, identify areas where more research is needed, and encourage the professionalism of educational programs. The concept should also define the role and function of the *Landesfachstelle* within the memorial landscape since the expectations placed on this institution have increased in line with the growing number of memorial sites to be maintained. In 2008 the memorial sites in Mecklenburg-West Pomerania formed their own representative body, the Mecklenburg-West Pomeranian Memorial Site Working Group, to face new challenges in view of increased temporal distance from the historic events. For example it is necessary to preserve architectural remains, ensure a scholarly approach to the work at certain sites, develop new exhibitions and pedagogical approaches, and secure organizational support. Research into the various historical layers of these sites will continue to underpin these measures. In contrast to the early 1990s it is now rarely necessary to convince people of the necessity of the work of memorial sites, but the debates on how this should be structured will undoubtedly continue.

Translated from the German by Caroline Pearce

Notes

[1] See Jürgen Danyel, ed., *Die geteilte Vergangenheit: Zum Umgang mit Nationalsozialismus und Widerstand in beiden deutschen Staaten* (Berlin: Akademie Verlag, 1995).

[2] Also see Wolf Karge, Hugo Rübesamen, and Andreas Wagner, *Bestandsaufnahme politischer Memoriale des Landes Mecklenburg-Vorpommern* (Schwerin: Projektgruppe Gedenkstättenarbeit in Mecklenburg-Vorpommern, 1998), and Anne Kaminsky, ed., *Orte des Erinnerns: Gedenkzeichen, Gedenkstätten und Museen zur Diktatur in SBZ und DDR* (Berlin: Forum Verlag, 2007).

[3] See Frank Rahel, Martin Klähn, and Christoph Wunnicke, *Die Auflösung: Das Ende der Staatssicherheit in den drei Nordbezirken* (Schwerin: Landesbeauftragte für Mecklenburg-Vorpommern für die Unterlagen des Staatssicherheitsdienstes der ehemaligen DDR, 2010).

[4] Rainer Prachtl and Manfred Rißmann, "Die Arbeit der Enquete-Kommission 'Leben in der DDR, Leben nach 1989 — Aufarbeitung und Versöhung,'" in *Mecklenburg-Vorpommern im Wandel: Bilanz und Ausblick*, ed. Jochen Werz and Nikolaus Schmidt (Munich: Olzog, 1998), 34–50.

[5] For an overview see Bernd Faulenbach, "Die DDR als Gegenstand der Geschichtswissenschaft," in *DDR-Geschichte vermitteln*, ed. Jens Hüttmann, Ulrich Mählert, and Peer Pasternack (Berlin: Metropol Verlag, 2004), 65–79.

[6] Tobias Baumann, "Das Speziallager Nr. 9 Fünfeichen," in *Sowjetische Speziallager in Deutschland 1945 bis 1950*, ed. Sergej Mironenko et al. (Berlin: Akademie Verlag, 1998), 1:426–44. Earlier research is presented in Dieter Krüger and Gerhard Finn, *Mecklenburg-Vorpommern 1945 bis 1948 und das Lager Fünfeichen* (Berlin: Verlag Gebr. Holzapfel, 1991).

[7] See Arsenij Roginskij et al., eds., *"Erschossen in Moskau . . .": Die deutschen Opfer des Stalinismus auf dem Moskauer Friedhof Donskoje 1950–1953* (Berlin: Metropol, 2005), and Horst Köpke and Friedrich-Franz Wiese, *Mein Vaterland ist die Freiheit: Das Schicksal des Studenten Arno Esch* (Rostock: Hinstorff Verlag, 1997).

[8] Anne Drescher, *Haft am Demmlerplatz: Gespräche mit Betroffenen* (Schwerin: Landesbeauftragte für Mecklenburg-Vorpommern für die Unterlagen des Staatssicherheitsdienstes der ehemaligen DDR, 2001).

[9] The film is titled *Einen Namen hast du da nicht gehabt: Die Stasi-Untersuchungshaftanstalt Neustrelitz in der späten DDR* (Jörg Hermann, 2007).

[10] See the annual report of the Mecklenburg-Vorpommern Office for the Records of the State Security Service of the former GDR, http://www.landesbeauftragter.de.

[11] Information about the exhibition can be found at http://www.ostseefluchten.de.

[12] *Politische Strafjustiz 1945–1989: Der Gefängnisstandort Bützow als Gedenk- und Lernort*, Reihe Beiträge zur Geschichte Mecklenburg-Vorpommern, no. 14 (Schwerin: Friedrich-Ebert-Stiftung, Landesbüro Mecklenburg-Vorpommern, 2008).

[13] See Regina Scheer, "Geschützte Leere: Ein Recherchebericht über politische Denkmäler in Brandenburg," in *Vielstimmiges Schweigen. Neue Studien zum DDR-Antifaschismus*, ed. Annette Leo and Peter Reif-Spirek (Berlin: Metropol, 2001), 127–51.

[14] See Joachim Wernicke and Uwe Schwartz, *Der Koloss von Prora auf Rügen* (Königstein: Langewiesche, 2006).

[15] Between 1935 and 1943 the Reichsärzteführerschule provided "ideological education" for doctors, pharmacists, and midwives from throughout Germany. See Rainer Stommer, ed., *Medizin im Dienste der Rassenideologie: Die "Führerschule der Deutschen Ärzteschaft" in Alt Rehse* (Berlin: Ch. Links, 2008).

[16] See Bernhard M. Hoppe, "Peenemünde. Ein Beitrag zur deutschen Erinnerungskultur," in *Peenemünde: Mythos und Geschichte der Rakete 1923–1989*, ed. Johannes Erichsen and Bernhard M. Hoppe (Berlin: Nicolai, 2004), 11.

[17] See Erichsen and Hoppe, *Peenemünde*.

[18] See Irene Diekmann, ed., *Wegweiser durch das jüdische Mecklenburg-Vorpommern* (Potsdam: Verlag für Berlin-Brandenburg, 1998).

[19] For an overview see Andreas Wagner, "KZ-Außenlager in Mecklenburg-Vorpommern: Zum gegenwärtigen Umgang mit der Vergangenheit und Erfahrungen aus der pädagogischen Arbeit," in *Die Außenlager der Konzentrationslager Sachsenhausen und Ravensbrück*, ed. Stiftung Brandenburgische Gedenkstätten (Oranienburg: Stiftung Brandenburgische Gedenkstätten, 2004), 42–56.

[20] Andreas Wagner, *"In Anklam aber empfängt mich die Hölle . . .": Dokumentation zur Geschichte des Wehrmachtgefängnisses Anklam 1940–1945* (Schwerin: Politische Memoriale e.V., 2000).

9: An Unequal Balance? Memorializing Germany's "Double Past" since 1990

Caroline Pearce

IN HER SPEECH AT THE BRANDENBURG GATE on the twentieth anniversary of the fall of the Berlin Wall, Angela Merkel referred to the momentous events of 1989 as "eine wahrhaft glückliche Stunde der deutschen und der europäischen Geschichte" and deemed 9 November a "Tag der Freude für uns alle." However, she added:

> Doch für uns Deutsche ist der 9. November auch ein Tag der Mahnung. Heute vor 71 Jahren wurde in der Reichspogromnacht das dunkelste Kapitel deutscher Geschichte aufgeschlagen: die systematische Verfolgung und Ermordung der europäischen Juden und vieler anderer Menschen. Auch das vergessen wir an diesem Tag nicht.[1]

This aspect of the speech was largely unreported in the national and international media, which focused primarily on the story of unification. Nonetheless, its inclusion was indicative of the dilemma surrounding commemoration of 9 November: the heroes of 1989 cannot be celebrated without mourning the victims of 1938. An editorial in the *Frankfurter Allgemeine Zeitung* maintained that it was possible to celebrate the fall of the Berlin Wall without forgetting or repressing the Nazi past.[2] And yet the organizers of an "anti-Fascist demonstration" on 9 November 2009 in Berlin to remember the anti-Jewish pogroms of 1938 indicated that remembrance of the two pasts is not so readily accommodated within a single narrative: "Durch die Behauptung, der Mauerfall 1989 stehe für die Überwindung 'zweier Diktaturen auf deutschen [*sic*] Boden', wird der Nationalsozialismus und seine Verbrechen relativiert."[3]

The year 2009 not only marked the twentieth anniversary of the fall of the Berlin Wall but also the seventieth anniversary of the outbreak of the Second World War and the sixty-fifth anniversary of the liberation of the concentration camps. The subsequent reappraisal of the Nazi and GDR pasts also considered their joint legacy. A group of historians, politicians, and intellectuals put their names to a feature in *Die Zeit* that discussed the significance of the Hitler-Stalin Pact of 1939 under the heading "Das Jahr 1989 feiern, heißt auch, sich an 1939 zu erinnern!,"[4] while Matthias Platzeck, Prime Minister of Brandenburg, sparked controversy by comparing the post-1990 rehabilitation of SED functionaries with that of members of the Waffen-SS in West Germany.[5] The postunification period has seen recurring and unresolved debates on how to remember the Nazi and GDR pasts in the attempt to shape a unified narrative on German history. The challenge is firstly which elements of both pasts to preserve in official memory, and secondly how to represent them without conflation, relativization, or hierarchization. Central to the discourse is the question of whether it is "permissible" to compare the two regimes. On the one hand such comparisons seem inevitable and indeed essential for understanding the Nazi and GDR pasts in their historical context; on the other hand there is the view that comparing the two merges them into one universalized totalitarianist narrative and erases their distinct features. This view is often coupled with the concern that the Holocaust may cease to be a defining feature of national remembrance in Germany. By the same token, victims of the post-1945 period may feel that their experiences are being downplayed.

In the first place interpretations of the Nazi and GDR pasts in unified Germany are colored by the varied biographical experience of either regime, which produces a range of distinct, and potentially conflicting, memory narratives. These narratives may of course differ from "official" historiography, which differed widely in East and West Germany. There is undoubtedly a political dimension to these interpretations. Conservatives and victims of Communism tend to find points of similarity between the two regimes. They prioritize "anti-Communist or collective anti-totalitarian commemoration" and are not opposed to commemorating former Nazis persecuted after 1945. By contrast left-wingers and victims of Nazism stress the differences and insist on the "pre-eminence of the Nazi past."[6] These differences are also apparent in the classification of the eras of persecution in question. This article uses the term "double past," which is commonly applied to describe the periods of National Socialist and Communist injustice in Germany, the latter from 1945 to 1950 or from 1945 to 1989,[7] although the term "double" should not be taken to mean that the two are mirror images. The term "triple past" possibly provides a more adequate distinction in additionally highlighting the period of Soviet occupation from 1945 to 1949. Some — mainly the advocates of an "anti-Communist" approach — perceive a single totalitarian era from 1933 to 1989,[8] which in implying continuity and similarity between the two regimes is often seen as downplaying the crimes of Nazism.

With the rapidly dwindling numbers of those with direct memory of the Third Reich and the increase in those too young to remember the GDR, the representation of the "double past" is progressively informed by the cultural memory shaped for example by the media, political debate, and education. Increasingly viewed as places of both remembrance and learning, memorial sites at locations with authentic links to the Nazi and the

Soviet and/or GDR periods are of particular interest in the debate on Germany's "double past." Approaches to these sites since 1990 illustrate the evolution and challenges of memorialization and the priorities accorded to the remembrance of each period. A number of national and regional strategies have been developed to shape and formalize memorialization of the "double past" in the new *Bundesländer*. This chapter will investigate these strategies and a range of associated controversies. It will show that despite the national importance ascribed to remembering both pasts, it is difficult to realize a balanced approach either within a written concept or at a memorial site. The problem is accentuated by the competing memories of different victims' groups, as well as conflicting political interests. The article will also consider the extent to which measures to deal with the "double past" in the new *Länder* are influenced by the conventional West German model of *Vergangenheitsbewältigung*, which was established prior to unification and focuses on remembrance of the victims of Nazism. In this respect Bill Niven has identified a "principle of hierarchy" that prioritizes the Nazi past.[9] However, some — generally more controversial — cases show the attempt to place an equal focus on both regimes, or to downplay their crimes, in what Andrew Beattie terms a "principle of equation."[10]

Uncovering the "Double Past" at German Memorial Sites

After the war, sites of Nazi persecution served very different purposes in East and West Germany. In the West a number of sites were initially used to house prisoners of war or expellees. Most were subsequently dismantled or neglected. With the exception of the memorial sites at Dachau, opened in 1965, and Bergen-Belsen (1966), it was not until the 1980s that sustained efforts were made to preserve and document sites of memory, usually as a result of citizens' initiatives but not without some public and political resistance. Two of the best-known sites of memory in Berlin, the Memorial to the Murdered Jews of Europe and the Topography of Terror, only came about following the efforts of such groups. In the East some of the former sites of Nazi persecution became Soviet special camps (*Speziallager*) after the war. These were used to incarcerate former Nazi functionaries, but also political opponents or those arbitrarily arrested. Tens of thousands died in harsh conditions before the final closure of these camps in 1950. The former Nazi concentration camps at Buchenwald, Ravensbrück, and Sachsenhausen were later designated as "National Sites of Warning and Memory" in 1958, 1959, and 1961 respectively. The layout and commemorative practice at these sites propagated a narrative of anti-Fascism, Communist resistance, and Socialist ideology. The topography of the grounds was altered for this purpose. At Sachsenhausen, for example, the former prisoner roll-call area was divided by a semi-circular wall, and the focal point of the site was no longer the "Tower A" entrance, but a much larger obelisk with a red triangle to symbolize political prisoners and an accompanying "Liberation" sculpture depicting a Soviet soldier and two camp survivors.[11]

Unification necessitated a review of these national memorial sites as well as research into sites that had previously silenced their role in Nazi or Communist persecution. There was a need to document the Holocaust, which had been marginalized or instrumentalized in East German historiography, as well as the history of the Soviet special camps, which had been taboo in the GDR and barely broached in the West. Confrontation with the special camps not only reawakened painful memories but raised awkward questions on how to classify these victims: some had undoubtedly been unjustly imprisoned, but many had been Nazi functionaries. These "schuldige Opfer,"[12] for example the doctor Friedrich Timm, known as the "Angel of Torgau" among his fellow inmates at the Torgau Soviet special camp but formerly an NSDAP member with professional links to the Buchenwald concentration camp,[13] blurred the conventional boundary between victims and perpetrators and made unified commemoration difficult. The addition of "forgotten" or formerly discredited victims to the commemorative discourse intensified struggles for representation and prioritization at memorial sites and led to often bitter disputes over whether victims' groups should be commemorated separately or jointly. In practical terms memorial sites had the task of distinguishing between various historical layers, which was difficult where authentic traces had been altered, re-utilized, or erased. The GDR memorial site at Sachsenhausen, for example, had incorporated just 5 percent of the original camp grounds, the rest being used by the military up to 1990. Finally, there was a need to revise commemorative practices, which had been heavily ritualized and politicized in the GDR.

Memorializing a Unified Past: The National Memorial Site Concept

The new *Länder* of Brandenburg, Thüringen, and Saxony set up foundations to administer their memorial sites in 1993, and similar organizations were founded later in Saxony-Anhalt (1995) and Mecklenburg-West Pomerania (1996).[14] Memorialization of the "double past" was, however, to attain national dimensions. While cultural policy is usually the remit of the individual *Länder*, the Unification Treaty indicated national support for the preservation and redevelopment of memorial sites in the former GDR.[15] The Bundestag established two committees of enquiry (Enquete-Kommissionen), operating from 1992 to 1994 and 1995 to 1998, to investigate strategies to confront the legacy of the GDR regime in unified Germany. The Enquete-Kommissionen's final report included an official political strategy for memorialization, with a focus on the new *Länder*. This memorial site concept (*Gedenkstättenkonzeption*) highlighted the importance of remembering the "double past." It deemed the Nazi and GDR pasts "eine Hypothek, die auch auf den nachgeborenen Deutschen lastet" and underlined the need for *all* Germans to remember both for the purposes of national and democratic self-understanding.[16] Memorial sites were considered to play an important role in this respect. The report defined these sites as places of remembrance and political education rather than state-dictated ritual, thereby signaling a departure from commemorative practices in the GDR (*SB*, 232, 237). It listed a number of sites of "national significance" that would receive 50 percent state funding, the other 50 percent to be provided by the respective *Land*. Some of these have a "double past," for example the three GDR national memorial sites and the prisons at Bautzen and Torgau.[17] Funding was restricted to Berlin and the new *Länder*, thereby prioritizing the development of the memorial landscape in the former GDR. To be eligible for funding, the projects and sites concerned had to be of national or international significance and historically relevant, and have a clear museological and pedagogical concept. The national importance ascribed to memorialization in this report was confirmed by the new left-wing SPD-Green coalition, which came to power in autumn 1998. It extended the program's original ten-year limit, raised the budget, and also opened up eligibility to memorial sites in western Germany.[18]

The national memorial site concept was significant not only in giving state recognition and financial backing to memorialization of both the Nazi and GDR pasts, but also in linking memorialization to the democratic development and perceived responsibility of unified Germany. It is interesting to note that no such committee of enquiry was held on the legacy of the Nazi past in post-1945 West Germany. In addition, no national memorial site concept existed in West Germany where, as mentioned, memorial sites attracted little interest until the 1980s, and even then mainly as a result of pressure from victims' associations and citizens' initiatives. Memorialization strategies were implemented much more quickly in the new *Länder* than they had been in the West. On the one hand memorial sites in the new *Länder* could benefit from the experience and research of established sites in the West, which certainly helped to rectify errors in the presentation of the National Socialist period. Yet on the other hand input from the West often ignored the specific challenges posed by the GDR past. There was a tendency to apply West German patterns of *Vergangenheitsbewältigung* to initial strategies to address the "double past" at memorial sites. For example the commissions established in 1991 to discuss new concepts for Sachsenhausen and Buchenwald were dominated by left-liberal historians from West Germany, which explains the subsequent focus placed on the victims of Nazism.[19]

The national memorial site concept stated the importance of remembrance for the "anti-totalitarian consensus." On the one hand this suggests an attempt by the Right to restore the anti-Communist approach of the early postwar period, which had been used to veil discussion of Nazi crimes. Beattie points out that the committees of enquiry were dominated by the Right and that early discussions displayed totalitarianist and equationist tendencies.[20] However, the memorial site concept was approved by all parties except the PDS and, as shown above, the focus on the Holocaust at memorial sites did not wane. The "anti-totalitarian consensus" in the national memorial site concept can be defined as a synthesis of left- and right-wing views on *Vergangenheitsbewältigung*. Hence, the right wing managed to secure an inclusive approach that placed importance on remembering Communism as well as Nazism, but the report also upheld the centrality of the Holocaust, reflecting left-wing views. Importantly, the 1998 report insisted on the importance of differentiating between the two regimes (*SB*, 245–55). Moreover, it alluded to the so-called "Faulenbach formula" attributed to the historian Bernd Faulenbach, which is frequently taken as a standard for remembering the "double past": "Die Erinnerung an das kommunistische Unrecht darf nicht zu einer Nivellierung des NS-Verbrechen führen, die Erinnerung an Verbrechen unter der sowjetischen Besatzung und SED-Herrschaft aber soll nicht unter Verweis auf das NS-Unrecht bagatallisiert werden."[21]

Such a balanced and non-hierarchical approach is laudable but difficult to implement. One past may be more "visible" or better-researched at a memorial site, overshadowing the other. Historical socialization will inevitably lead to comparisons between and value judgments of both regimes, conveying one as more important. The media portrayal of the two regimes undoubtedly has influence in this respect. The "Faulenbach formula" could be interpreted as granting all victims equal status, even if they are not equated, but political interests and the memory narratives of victims' groups automatically accord priority to one or the other past. The following examples will show the difficulty of achieving consensus and balance when memorializing the "double past."

Equation and Division: The Saxony Memorial Site Concept and the Torgau Controversy

The eastern German state of Saxony has many examples of sites with a "double past." The Saxony Memorial Site Foundation to Remember the Victims of Political Tyranny (Stiftung Sächsische Gedenkstätten zur Erinnerung an die Opfer politischer Gewaltherrschaft) was founded in

1994. The name already implies an equation of the Nazi, Stalinist, and SED regimes but could also be said to prioritize post-1945 injustice by mentioning political and not racial persecution. This was perhaps understandable in the immediate aftermath of unification, but almost ten years later, in April 2003, the government of Saxony provoked national controversy with a law granting the Foundation a legal status that endorsed this equationist approach and rejected the national consensus on memorialization. The law drew no distinction between the Nazi and GDR regimes, with formulations such as: "Die Stiftung hat die Opfer politischer Gewaltherrschaft und den Widerstand gegen die Diktaturen zu würdigen sowie die Strukturen und Methoden der jeweiligen Herrschaftssysteme . . . zu dokumentieren."[22] In January 2004 the Central Council of Jews in Germany and other groups representing the victims of Nazism broke ties with the Foundation, accusing it of a "Waagschalenmentalität" that trivialized National Socialist crimes by equating them with those of the Soviet and GDR regimes.[23] The latter claim was substantiated by the fact that all victims' groups were to be represented on the same committee. For the Association of Victims of the Nazi Regime — The Anti-Fascist Alliance (VVN-BdA), the scales were tipped too heavily to one side: it criticized the prioritization of sites dealing with GDR injustice and the victims of Stalinism.[24]

The controversy in Saxony was further highlighted by the ongoing dispute over the memorial at Torgau, which is funded under the national memorial site concept. This is an interesting example as it shows a struggle for prioritization between victim groups at a site that has a "double past" but is not explicitly linked with the Holocaust. During the Second World War Torgau was the site of two Nazi military prisons, the inmates including deserters and conscientious objectors. From 1943 it housed the Reich War Court, which issued around fourteen hundred death sentences during the war. After 1945 the former Fort Zinna prison served as a Soviet special camp and was later used as a prison by the GDR.[25] Following unification, conflict arose over the commemoration of two "forgotten" groups: the victims of Wehrmacht justice, who were not fully rehabilitated by the Federal Republic until 2009, and the victims of Stalinism, whose suffering had been silenced in the GDR. Both now sought commemoration as well as "legal and moral rehabilitation."[26] As Fort Zinna still functions as a prison, the space for commemoration was restricted to the parking lot outside. The victims of Stalinism called for a memorial in 1991. Their proposal was revised to include all "victims of tyranny," thus fitting the universalizing approach towards memorialization in Saxony. However, groups representing the victims of Nazism withdrew from the project and the subsequent memorial focused solely on the victims of Communism. Problematically, it presented all special camp prisoners — including former Nazi perpetrators — as "innocents" who had been "murdered."[27] In 1994 the government of Saxony appeared to change its approach by proposing a new memorial to Nazi, Stalinist, and GDR victims, but with a focus on the Nazi past. However, victims' groups failed to reach a consensus, arguing for example over the amount of space allocated to each group. The debate continued for another decade, gaining national attention in 2004 in connection with the controversy over the Saxony Memorial Site Foundation. A token gesture was made that year to commemorate the Wehrmacht victims with an information board referring to the persecution of this group. Finally, it was decided to divide the parking lot into two commemorative spaces separated by a hedge. The Foundation agreed to correct inaccuracies on the information boards regarding the postwar rehabilitation of victims of Nazi military justice, and to specify that some special camp prisoners had been Nazi judges or involved in the Nazi system of repression.[28]

The memorial was inaugurated in May 2010. One half commemorates the victims of Nazism with a sculpture bearing the inscription "Nie wieder Krieg." The other remembers the victims of Stalinist and GDR injustice and contains the wooden cross from the original memorial. The site's inauguration was marred by conflict between victims' groups, its most vociferous critic being Ludwig Baumann, a Wehrmacht deserter who was imprisoned at Fort Zinna for eighteen months and now chairs the Federal Association for the Victims of Military Justice. In his speech (which, interestingly, is absent from the list on the website of the Saxony Memorial Site Foundation) he described the memorial as a "Schandmal." The information boards had not been altered as agreed and, in another twist, the Torgau Association for the Victims of Stalinism had reinstalled a plaque to the former Nazi Friedrich Timm, which had been removed in 1996 following protests. Members of this association distributed flyers during the inauguration, refuting Baumann's views.[29] This dispute shows that while the Saxony Memorial Site Foundation may favor a "principle of equation," victims' groups advocate a "principle of segregation," underlined by Baumann's assertion that the hedge between the two commemorative areas was too low.

Baumann has also been involved in disputes with the Saxony Memorial Site Foundation over the exhibition "Traces of Injustice" ("Spuren des Unrechts"), which opened in 2004 in Schloss Hartenfels.[30] The Federal Association for the Victims of Military Justice has criticized the exhibition for failing to focus on the Third Reich, the fact that prison inmates after 1945 included former Nazi perpetrators, and discrimination against victims of Wehrmacht (in)justice in the Federal Republic. In this case there does appear to be a prioritization of post-1945 victimhood. Baumann was not allowed to speak at the exhibition's inauguration, and when he did try to voice his opinions he was silenced by Joachim Gauck, who refused to let Baumann cut short his own allocated speaking time.[31] In autumn 2009 the

Foundation agreed to review the exhibition although there are no firm plans to change it. Meanwhile, groups representing victims of Nazism tentatively resumed cooperation with the Foundation in 2010, but on the condition that the memorial site law be changed.[32]

Equation as Repression? The CDU-CSU Memorial Site Concept (2004)

While the conflict at Torgau has essentially been fought out between two specific victims' groups, the wider controversy in Saxony bears the hallmark of political instrumentalization of the past. According to Oliver Reinhard, "In Sachsen wiegen politische Interessen . . . bei der Aufarbeitung der Geschichte oft schwerer als das Gebot der Vernunft" and the CDU-led government in Saxony prioritizes confrontation with the GDR past.[33] For Reinhard one reason could be a concern to avoid public discussion of the Holocaust on account of the presence of NPD delegates in the parliament of Saxony. However, another could be the desire to pursue a memorialization strategy that focuses on the crimes of the GDR regime as a way of downplaying responsibility for the Nazi past. This would echo the normalizing approach to remembrance attributed to the Right before unification, which appeared to resurface at national level in November 2003, when the CDU-CSU group in the Bundestag drafted a new national memorial site concept "Promoting Memorial Sites on the History of Dictatorship in Germany — An Integral Concept for the Worthy Remembrance of All Victims of Both German Dictatorships."[34] Initiated by the former GDR civil rights activist Günter Nooke, the proposal mirrored the law in Saxony. It ignored the "Faulenbach formula" and instead called for a concept that remembered both dictatorships jointly. The Nazi and GDR pasts were presented as two sides of the same totalitarian coin, for example with the claim that the connection between the two was "evident" at sites with a "double past." The attempt to overturn the previous "anti-totalitarian consensus" seemed clear: the proposal made no mention of the uniqueness of the Holocaust and at the same time criticized the "marginalization" of national remembrance of the SED dictatorship.

The proposal met with strong criticism from political parties and victims' groups alike for equating the Nazi and GDR pasts under the umbrella term "history of dictatorship" and for pursuing an indiscriminate narrative of totalitarianism that ignored the specificities of the two regimes and relativized the Holocaust.[35] A further criticism leveled at the proposal was that it would increase the state's influence over memorialization and that such "renationalization" of remembrance would erase the necessarily European dimensions of the remembrance of National Socialism.[36]

The debate over this proposal evoked controversies over remembrance during Helmut Kohl's chancellorship in the 1980s and, notably, the re-dedication of the Neue Wache memorial in Berlin as the Federal Republic's "National Memorial to the Victims of War and Tyranny" in 1993. The absence of any explicit reference to National Socialism and a plaque that drew no distinction between victims and perpetrators, or between regimes, led to allegations that Kohl was attempting to whitewash Nazi crimes and merge the Nazi and GDR pasts into a single narrative of common victim-hood. The 2003 concept also appeared to favor an indiscriminate narrative of German victimhood by proposing the establishment of memorials to German victims of expulsion and Allied bombing raids during the Second World War.

The CDU-CSU proposal was withdrawn in January 2004 following the Saxony scandal. However, it was resubmitted that June with only minimal amendment: reference to the Saxony law was omitted and a token sentence added describing the Holocaust as a unique crime requiring a special form of remembrance.[37] Delegates at an open hearing of experts convened by the Culture Committee of the Bundestag in February 2005 warned against making the affair a political dispute on approaches to *Vergangenheitsbewältigung* or playing one dictatorship off against the other.[38] Yet the battlelines between "anti-Communist" and "anti-Fascist" interpretations of history continue to be drawn in debates on memorializa-tion. It is important to note the presence of eastern and western German voices in these debates. In May 2006 the outspoken CDU Interior Minister of Brandenburg Jörg Schönbohm delivered a speech marking the liberation of the Sachsenhausen concentration camp in which he declared that all victims of the camp should be remembered, including those imprisoned after 1945, who, he said, had been just as deprived of rights as the concentration camp prisoners. The subsequent controversy revealed the established West German left-liberal approach to *Vergangenheitsbe-wältigung*, which rejects such equation, but those of the Right might equally argue for adequate confrontation with post-1945 injustice. Werner von Bebber additionally identified an East German perspective unwilling to admit to the existence of postwar Soviet repression, a "verlautbarter DDR-Antifaschismus, der den roten Terror nicht wahrhaben will."[39]

A Return to the "Faulenbach Formula": The 2008 Memorial Site Concept

Unsurprisingly the CDU-CSU proposal was abandoned, but discussions over memorialization continued in the SPD-CDU Grand Coalition estab-lished in autumn 2005. The Coalition Treaty pledged to continue the 1999 memorial site concept to ensure "appropriate" remembrance of both dictatorships.[40] A new draft was presented by the CDU Culture Minister, Bernd Neumann, in summer 2007.[41] Described as a continuation of the 1999 concept, it was a clear departure from the 2004 proposal, stating the importance of remembering both the GDR and Nazi regimes but also of distinguishing between them. However, groups representing the victims of Nazism criticized some imprecise wording. The text referred for example to "beiden totalitären Systeme in Deutschland" and, after emphasizing the singularity of the Holocaust, appeared to contradict itself by asserting that SED injustice should be confronted "parallel dazu."[42]

A revised concept was adopted the following year under the title "Assuming Responsibility, Strengthening Confrontation, Intensifying Remembrance."[43] It recommended new sites for funding and increased the budget by 50 percent to thirty-five million euros for 2008 and 2009. The focus of the 2008 concept has shifted back to the postunification "consensus" on memorializing the "double past." Accordingly, it refers directly to the "Faulenbach formula" to promote differentiated remembrance of the two pasts (G, 2). An accompanying statement from the CDU-CSU was careful to reiterate "dass keine Diktatur gegen die andere ausgespielt wird, keine zu Lasten der anderen aufgearbeitet wird. Opfer und Opfergruppen werden nicht gegeneinander aufgerechnet, sondern individuell gewürdigt."[44]

At the same time a certain prioritization of the Holocaust can be discerned in the introduction, which emphasizes the singularity of the Nazi genocide (G, 1). The concept pledges to provide more support for memorial sites of "national significance" that remember the Nazi regime and its victims. However, it clearly states a second objective: to intensify confrontation with the Soviet occupation and the GDR regime, where it identifies a need to "catch up" (G, 7). Importantly, it deems the GDR period "Teil der gesamtdeutschen Geschichte" and therefore a "gesamtdeutsche Aufgabe" (G, 3). Along with increasing funding for memorial sites, an additional proposed measure is the establishment of a "Historical Association to Confront the Communist Dictatorship in Germany" to focus particularly on resistance and opposition in the GDR.

Political and media responses to the new concept were generally favorable. However, there was some reluctance on the part of groups representing the victims of Nazism to accept the "Faulenbach formula" and "share" commemoration. Somewhat unfairly Salomon Korn, vice-president of the Central Council of Jews in Germany, considered that the concept wrongly put both pasts on an equal footing and thereby trivialized the Nazi past. His response also indicated more practical motives behind the conflict over representation. Korn pointed out that 50 percent of the applications for tours of the Buchenwald memorial site had to be turned down due to a lack of staff. Clearly prioritizing its Nazi history, he asserted that sites remembering the GDR should take second place to those remembering Nazism as there was not enough money for both and, moreover, the survivors of National Socialism were rapidly dwindling while those of the GDR would be around for a long time yet.[45] Despite all the evidence suggesting gaps in knowledge of the GDR past, Volkhard Knigge of the Federal Association of Concentration Camp Memorial Sites hinted that there was now perhaps an overemphasis on post-1945 research, a point also raised by the Association of Victims of the Nazi Regime, which complained that the new memorial site concept only devoted two and a half pages to former Nazi sites but nine to former Communist sites. Knigge also drew attention to competition over funding, adding that there were already four funding bodies for GDR memorialization compared to two for Nazi remembrance.[46] And yet appearances can be deceptive: Regina Morch points out that in fact two-thirds of funding goes towards memorial sites remembering the victims of Nazism.[47]

Unified Memorialization, West German Memories?

The "Historical Association" mentioned in the 2008 concept was originally proposed by the SPD-Green coalition in May 2005. The so-called Sabrow Commission, led by the historian Martin Sabrow, was set up that year to examine the proposal and to make recommendations for memorializing the SED regime. Its final report, published in May 2006, praised the quantity and standard of research into the GDR, but rightly noted that there was still a division between eastern and western German interpretations, a lack of school education on the period, and a tendency to trivialize the GDR in the media. The commission proposed that memorialization of the GDR focus on three categories: "Regime, Resistance, and Society," "Surveillance and Persecution," and "Division and the Border."[48] These categories were put into the 2008 memorial site concept with the exception of the first, which was split into "Society and Everyday Life" and "Resistance and Opposition."

The Sabrow Commission's report aimed to promote a differentiated picture of the SED dictatorship and GDR society; however, it was not universally welcomed. The main criticism was that an increased focus on everyday life in the GDR would relativize the extent of repression under the regime. Hubertus Knabe, director of the memorial site at the former Stasi prison in Berlin-Hohenschönhausen, complained that this would indulge the *Ostalgie* trend, while Horst Möller, from the Institute of Contemporary History in Munich, asserted that it was the Stasi — not state childcare — that was typical for the GDR.[49] The opposing argument is of course equally valid: overemphasis on repression paints an incomplete picture of GDR society. This point was raised with regard to the 2008 memorial site concept. Sabrow said that attention needed to be paid to the interaction between regime, society, and everyday life. He made the valid point that both dictatorships tended to be reduced to their violent and criminal aspects, wherease it was important to demonstrate how each "auf erschreckende Weise auch Normalität produzierte."[50]

These debates on representation of the GDR again suggested the distinction between "anti-Fascist" and "anti-Communist" interpretations of history. Evoking the former, the Greens stated that implying that the entire GDR population suffered from repression and persecution ignored aspects such as loyalty and ideological conviction. They also considered the 2008 concept to place too much emphasis on the GDR past and called for more focus on Nazi crimes.[51] It is understandable that confrontation with the Nazi past at memorial sites in the new *Länder* was initially guided by established (left-liberal) West German patterns. However, more recent debates on representing the GDR also suggest western German claims on ownership of the past, but this time along right-wing, "anti-Communist" lines. Richard Schröder has noted a dominance of western, not eastern, German voices in this respect, along the lines of "Wir bewältigen euch eure Vergangenheit . . . wie wir es schon einmal getan haben."[52] The motive of the current CDU-led government is perhaps to cast the West German state (and its process of *Vergangenheitsbewältigung*) in a better light. Bernd Neumann stated that confrontation with the SED dictatorship must focus on the injustice of the regime and, moreover, "wir dürfen nicht zulassen, dass sich die Täter zu Opfern stilisieren."[53] Such insistence on the criminal nature of the SED regime calls for an attitude absent in the early years of the Federal Republic, when many Nazi perpetrators were rehabilitated.

A right-wing approach to history has also affected developments in the new capital. In January 2006 the Bundestag controversially voted to demolish the Palace of the Republic (Palast der Republik) in Berlin and replace it with a reconstruction of the Prussian palace that once stood on the site. This exemplifies the challenge of deciding which layers of history to preserve or highlight in the new capital. Yet one could also deduce an unwillingness to commemorate the GDR, or the desire for a more triumphant historical narrative that sidelines both the Nazi and East German regimes.

One Past Too Many? The Debate on the "Commissioner to Confront Dictatorships" in Brandenburg

The examples so far have shown the challenges of balancing remembrance of Germany's 1933–45 and 1945–89 pasts at sites where memories of both coexist. However, there are cases where reference to the "double" past may not be appropriate because reference to the one hinders confrontation with the other. Brandenburg is active in remembering the "double past," with the Brandenburg Memorial Site Foundation playing a prominent role. It is thus somewhat surprising that the Brandenburg government has proposed a new memorialization concept, "History Where It Happened," which could be said to equate the Nazi and Communist pasts in addressing a single period from 1933 to 1990.[54]

The problem here may be terminology rather than intention: the proposal insists on a pluralist approach and public consultation and also acknowledges the historical dominance of the Holocaust. However, the Brandenburg government did face substantial criticism for an apparently equationist approach to the "double past" in summer 2009 when the SPD and CDU tabled the "Law on the Brandenburg Commissioner for the Records of the State Security Service of the former GDR and the Reappraisal of the Consequences of Dictatorial Regimes" ("Gesetz über den Beauftragten des Landes Brandenburg zur Aufarbeitung der Unterlagen des Staatssicherheitsdienstes der ehemaligen DDR und von Folgen diktatorischer Herrschaften"). Brandenburg was the only state in the former GDR without a dedicated commissioner to deal with Stasi records, and the law was intended to address this deficit. The preamble states the aim of confronting both the Nazi and Communist dictatorships and evokes the "Faulenbach formula."[55] However, the controversy arose as a result of imprecise terminology and historical definitions as well as the remit of the post. The stated aim was to provide counseling for "alle Opfer diktatorischer Herrschaftsformen." The text referred to political persecution "in den verschiedenen Diktaturen" but failed to mention the victims of racial persecution. The pedagogical remit of the post was equally vague, the objective being to provide information on "verschiedener diktatorischer Herrschaftsformen." While focus was to be placed on the post-1945 period, the aim was to deal with "neuere Diktaturgeschichte," which was said to necessitate the inclusion of the National Socialist period: "Die Wirkungsbereiche diktatorischer Herrschaftsinstrumente reichten . . . weit in andere Bereiche hinein. Bei der Aufarbeitung der Wirkungsweise der MfS ist es vielfach notwendig, auch Bezüge zu anderen diktatorischen Herrschaftsformen herzustellen."

Such indirect references to the Nazi past may have been added to avert criticism and to balance left- and right-wing priorities, but they appeared to be an awkward afterthought. Moreover, the above statement diverges from the "Faulenbach formula" in suggesting that references to one regime can serve to highlight the other.

A public hearing on the bill was held in June 2009. Critics did not oppose the establishment of a post that would enlighten citizens about the GDR regime; however, they opposed its dual function. It is tempting to condemn the motives behind a law that appeared to draw no adequate distinction between the two regimes, but speakers at the hearing appeared to have the best of intentions, attempting to accommodate the needs of all victims' groups with restricted resources. On a practical level it was of course difficult to see how the post could manage such a vast remit with a planned four-member staff.

Reactions from groups representing the victims of Nazism rejected joint confrontation, emphasized the primacy of the Holocaust, and warned against relativization. At the hearing the historian Wolfgang Wippermann criticized the law for a "totalitarianist" approach that wrongly equated or compared the two regimes. He expressed amazement that it neglected to mention Jews or racial persecution and stressed: "Es gab viele Diktaturen aber nur einen Holocaust."[56] Hans Coppi, from the Association of Victims of the Nazi Regime, pointed out that victims' groups had not been consulted on the law and were upset and outraged that the two regimes had been "lumped together." Günter Morsch, director of the Brandenburg Memorial Site Foundation and the Sachsenhausen memorial site, stated that former Nazi victims from Germany and abroad felt like they were being treated as "second-class victims," a view usually voiced by the post-1945 victims of Communism in view of the primacy of Holocaust remembrance. He considered the law to be a step backwards for the consensus on memorialization achieved since unification.

By contrast, groups representing post-1945 victims had fewer problems with the dual concept, though the Union of Associations of Victims of Communism expressed concern that GDR victims might be sidelined and that joint counseling services might provoke conflict between victims' groups. Its solution was to limit the post to confronting the SED past. Rüdiger Sielaff, director of the Frankfurt (Oder) branch of the Stasi Records Office, agreed: in his view the reference to the Nazi past over-stretched the post. These representatives upheld a universal view of twentieth-century dictatorships in Germany; however, in most cases this did not seem to be an attempt to downplay the Nazi past but rather the view that this was intertwined with, if not equal to, the GDR past. For Jörn Mothes, the former director of the Stasi Records Office in Mecklenburg-West Pomerania and identified at the time as a likely candidate for the Brandenburg post, there were clear links between the two regimes and so no caesura should be drawn between them. During his work in Mecklenburg-West Pomerania most requests for counseling related to the period from 1945 to 1955. The biographies of those concerned thus spanned both regimes, with experiences pre-1945 impacting on life in the GDR. However, other contributions evoked an equationist approach. Gerhard Ruden, the director of the Stasi Records Office in Saxony-Anhalt, maintained that as both dictatorships had affected several generations in Germany, the crimes should be confronted together; after all, "Verbrechen sind Verbrechen." Michael Beleites, director of the Stasi Records Office in Saxony, justifiably provoked criticism with a flippant remark on the need for comparisons: "Wenn es sich eben um verschiedene Dinge wie Äpfel und Birnen handelt, so wird man das Differenzierungsvermögen zwischen Äpfeln und Birnen nicht dadurch schärfen, indem man den Obsthändlern vorschreibt, dass der eine nur mit Äpfeln und der andere nur mit Birnen handeln darf." Beleites also showed a disparaging approach to confrontation with the Nazi past, claiming that those responsible for "das deutsche Reinheitsgebot der NS-Aufarbeitung" were yet to propose a strategy for confronting the GDR past that would incorporate links to Nazi crimes "ohne dass damit gleichzeitig sich sozusagen NS-Aufarbeitung marginalisiert fühlt."

As a result of the dispute the law was amended to become the "Law on the Brandenburg Commissioner for the Reappraisal of the Consequences of the Communist Dictatorship" ("Gesetz über den Beauftragten des Landes Brandenburg zur Aufarbeitung der Folgen der kommunistischen Diktatur"). Direct references to the Nazi period were removed, although they do remain implicit. The aim of the post is to provide counseling for those persecuted from 1945 to 1949 and during the GDR, but this may include "biografische Bezüge, die vor das Jahr 1945 reichen." The second objective remains rather vague: to provide information on "die Wirkungsweisen diktatorischer Herrschaftsformen," though with a focus on the post-1945 period.[57] The law was passed by a majority in July 2009, and the former GDR civil rights activist Ulrike Poppe was appointed that December.

The dispute surrounding this law emerged from the fact that references to the Nazi past simply did not fit. The aim was to fill a gap in confrontation with the GDR past, and so an independent focus was required on the GDR but not on the Nazi or "double" past. The "Faulenbach formula" did not work in this case: reference to the Nazi past was inevitably seen to be trivialized or secondary as there was no clear justification for its inclusion. Reactions displayed further evidence that victims' groups may favor a segregated approach to commemoration. The dispute coincided with the inauguration of a Jewish cemetery at Lieberose, one of the former sub-camps of Sachsenhausen and later a Soviet special camp. In his speech the president of the International Sachsenhausen Committee, Roger Bordage, criticized the "empörendes Amalgam" of pasts presented in the law and said that it was "unworthy" to blur the history of the concentration camp prisoners with those of the special camp, who would of course have included former Nazi perpetrators.[58]

Reactions to the "Double Past" at Memorial Sites

Having explored regional and national strategies for memorializing the "double past," it is interesting to assess their impact on memorial sites in the new *Bundesländer*. Incidents such as the 1991 plans to build a super-

188 ♦ CAROLINE PEARCE

market by the entrance to the former Ravensbrück concentration camp (although these were never realized), and far-right arson attacks on the Jewish barracks at Sachsenhausen (1992) and the death march memorial at Belower Wald (2002) were seen as proof of a reluctance to confront the Nazi past in the early postunification years. Twenty years after unification memorialization of the "double past" still does not enjoy universal support in the new *Länder*. In 2009 for example, the Ravensbrück memorial site's application to build a new car park provoked opposition from citizens who said that they felt "distant" from this part of their history.[59] Yet if one compares the progress made with that in the first two decades of the West German state, when little memorialization took place, the speed and breadth of change has been impressive, particularly in view of the challenge of reviewing historical narratives and addressing the legacy of two pasts. There has been a marked professionalization of many memorial sites in the new *Länder*, with the development of modern museums and pedagogical facilities.

The confrontation with the "double past" has improved cooperation between memorial sites in the new and old *Länder*. The Federal Foundation for the Reappraisal of the SED Dictatorship in East Germany (Bundesstiftung zur Aufarbeitung der SED Diktatur) and the association "Against Forgetting, For Democracy" organize an annual seminar for representatives from both types of memorial site, and there is an international memorial site seminar in Kreisau for representatives from memorial sites in Eastern and Western Europe. Historical research into both periods has been enhanced with new research, for example into the Nazi euthanasia program at Pirna Sonnenstein (Saxony), and can provide a more nuanced understanding of victims and perpetrators in examining different forms of repression and victimhood.

Sachsenhausen is one of the most documented examples of "double past" memorial sites as it exemplifies confrontation with various historical layers. It has adopted a "decentralized" concept featuring a range of different exhibitions with no obvious hierarchy that explore the National Socialist, Soviet, and East German uses of the site. There are also continued efforts to address the authentic traces beyond the memorial site, for example with the opening of a "history park" at the former Nazi brickworks in Oranienburg. In theory this decentralized concept is a good way of adhering to the "Faulenbach formula." Yet in practice the site is best known as a former Nazi concentration camp, and Morsch concedes that this particular history is what prompts most visits to Sachsenhausen.[60] The postunification redevelopment of Sachsenhausen has prioritized remembrance of Nazi persecution. Plans adopted in 2004 foresee the demolition of the semi-circular wall built on the roll-call area during the GDR period, and the commemorative heart of the site is now the Nazi execution site "Station Z," clearly shifting the focus from Communist resistance to Nazi crimes. While it was necessary to abandon the one-sided commemorative practices of the GDR, the victims of the Soviet special camp may feel under-represented. The architectural competition for the special camp museum stipulated that the design should not resemble a memorial. Similarly, the special camp museum at Buchenwald was not to contain any "Trauerelemente," and the building is indeed overshadowed by the much larger storeroom for prisoners' belongings from the former concentration camp. In addition, groups representing victims of the special camp at Buchenwald were asked not to extend the area where they had placed memorial plaques.[61] This takes us back to the challenge of remembering the "guilty victims" implicit in the "double past."

However balanced the strategy for remembering Germany's "double past," it is important to note that no written memorialization strategy can — or should — dictate public perception, expectation, or preconceptions, which will vary depending on a range of factors including nationality (particularly whether one is from the east or west of Germany or Europe) and age. Through education and the media most visitors to memorial sites with a "double past" are familiar with the history of the Holocaust and expect to see evidence of the site "as it was" during the Nazi period. Many are unaware of the role of these sites after 1945 or their relevance to cultural remembrance of the GDR.[62] One reason is that the Soviet special camps in particular are not (yet) embedded in German or international cultural remembrance. There are, for example, no images of liberation such as those associated with the former concentration camps. Haase's point that those imprisoned after 1945 do not belong to established communities of memory to the same extent as those persecuted by the Nazis on religious grounds is a further contributing factor.[63] It is of course difficult to grasp the complex historical significance of memorial sites with a "double past." As Norbert Reichling points out: "Viele dieser Orte bergen eine solche Vielzahl historische Schichten und Geschichten, dass die Rezeptionsweisen des 'Durchschnittsbesuchers' gelegentlich überfordert sind. Manche BesucherInnen . . . verstehen einfach nicht, um welche Periode der Ortsgeschichte es gerade geht."[64]

Long before unification the concentration camps had become "icons" of cultural remembrance in West Germany as well as in Western Europe, and so it is perhaps inevitable that visitors from these areas will associate memorial sites with a "double past" exclusively with the Nazi past. This is despite the efforts of pedagogical staff. Daniel Gaede mentions a school group from Hessen that spent a week at the Buchenwald memorial site but barely mentioned the Soviet special camp in their project report, even though it was explained during the visit. Entrenched prejudices may also block effective confrontation with both pasts. Gaede also refers to a group from Duisburg where the teachers criticized an "over-emphasis" on

Communism.[65] One might expect groups from the former GDR to have a greater interest in the post-1945 elements of the "double past" due to their closer biographical links to the period. Annette Leo and Peter Reif-Spirek mention that the few groups who do visit the special camp exhibition at Buchenwald often find names of relatives in the lists of those who died, and yet they note that school groups from the new *Länder* also tend to prioritize the Holocaust. Although some of their teachers may still be influenced by GDR commemorative pedagogy, the school children do not identify with the resistance fighters but with Holocaust victims, and particularly the Jews: "Viele Schüler brachten Beschämung darüber zum Ausdruck, dass Konzentrationslager und Judenverfolgung zu ihrer Geschichte gehören."[66] Leo and Reif-Spirek remark that information on the former concentration camps draws comments such as "unfassbar" or "unvorstellbar," whereas the response to the special camps is more muted. The "aura" of the former Nazi concentration camps is perhaps stronger than the sites of Communist persecution, provoking a more vivid mental image and a more emotional response. Communist repression is perhaps also viewed in more abstract terms than the more individualized presentation of Holocaust victims. Of course not all "double past" memorial sites are at former concentration camps. Less familiar sites such as former prisons used by pre- and post-1945 regimes may be more successful in achieving a balanced historical understanding, particularly of the post-1945 period.

The first Oranienburg Tolerance Prize, awarded in 2010, also suggested a closer identification with the victims of Nazism. The prize was launched by the Brandenburg government, in association with the Brandenburg Memorial Site Foundation, to support projects promoting diversity and tolerance. It went to a joint initiative entitled "Learning and Working in the Former Sachsenhausen Concentration Camp" that was submitted by vocational colleges in Brandenburg and Bremen. The initiative involves students carrying out a week's voluntary work at the memorial site and reporting on their experiences. Focus is placed on the National Socialist history of the camp.[67]

The Holocaust may, then, be the dominant element of memorialization of the "double past" not because of any political strategy, but as a result of personal interpretation. The identification with the Holocaust is particularly interesting as the parents of young eastern Germans would have been socialized by a version of history that marginalized this factor. This "unified" focus on the Holocaust is perhaps due to the input of western historians, the internationalized nature of Holocaust remembrance, or the heavier focus on the Nazi past in schools. In an echo of the postwar repression of the Nazi past, a further reason could be that it is easier to deal with the more "distant" history of the Third Reich than with that of the GDR, which is still raw for many in the new *Länder*. Alternatively, identification with the Nazi past may have emerged as a result of skepticism toward the SED's version of history.

Conclusion: The Europeanization of the "Double Past"?

This chapter has so far examined German debates on memorializing the "double past," which of course has European rather than purely national dimensions. This was acknowledged in the 1998 memorial site concept, which referred to sites remembering Nazi victims as "Orte einer europäischen Erinnerungskultur" and underlined the Europe-wide significance of the Communist legacy (*SB*, 244). In February 1993 the European Parliament adopted a resolution on preserving memorial sites at former Nazi concentration camp sites and rejected the equation of the Nazi and Communist regimes.[68] However, this principle may be changing. During the hearing on the aforementioned law in Brandenburg, the Polish historian Kazimierz Wóycicki said that joint remembrance of Communism and Nazism was the norm in Poland, and the EU has introduced a similar approach. In September 2008 the European Parliament proposed an annual European Day of Remembrance for Victims of Stalinism and Nazism, to take place on 23 August (the anniversary of the Hitler-Stalin Pact). The aim is to remember the victims of deportation and mass murder and in the process to strengthen democracy, peace, and stability in Europe.[69] Members of the European Parliament (MEPs) backed the proposal in a resolution on "European Conscience and Totalitarianism" adopted by a majority in April 2009. The resolution refers to "all victims of totalitarian and undemocratic regimes in Europe," states the need to remember "Europe's tragic past," and asserts that a "common view of history," the acknowledgment of Nazism, Stalinism, and Fascism as a "common legacy," and a "comprehensive reassessment of European history" are prerequisites for European integration. While stressing the unique nature of the Holocaust, the resolution emphasizes the need to understand the legacy of the "double past" in Eastern Europe. One of its aims is to establish a "Platform of European Memory and Conscience" to bring together experts working on totalitarian history, as well as a pan-European documentation center or memorial for all victims of totalitarianism.[70]

The aim of achieving unity in Europe through a common view of the past is not new. However, while the Holocaust has formed the core of such an approach up till now, the 2009 resolution integrates East European experiences of dictatorship, thereby responding to the need for a unified European historical narrative after the Cold War. This approach could strengthen the focus on the Communist past in Germany. The resolution links remembrance with the commitment to uphold human rights, democracy, and freedom in Europe. To return to the speech mentioned at the beginning of this article, Merkel similarly linked the Nazi and GDR pasts by referring to freedom and democracy; elsewhere she has said that emphasizing these values is one way of creating a unified narrative on German history.[71] Nonetheless, the equationist formulation of the EP resolution is problematic. It mirrors the tendency to regard the crimes of the twentieth century as human transgressions rather than linking them to a specific nation.[72] This in turn runs the risk of abstraction, whereby responsibility for crimes is downplayed amid universal claims of victimhood. The resolution asserts, "from the perspective of the victims it is immaterial which regime deprived them of their liberty or tortured or murdered them for whatever reason."

Such a universalizing narrative on a "century of dictatorships" could provide an outlet for revisionist views. To this extent Morsch expressed concern that the German historians and intellectuals behind the initiative — "Das Jahr 1989 feiern, heißt auch, sich an 1939 zu erinnern!" — lent their support to the resolution.[73] However, it is too early to speak of a paradigm shift in either Germany or Europe. The debate on the EP's resolution indeed raised political tensions mirroring those in the debate on the "double past" in Germany. The resolution was drafted by members of the center-right EP-EDD party from Estonia, the Czech Republic, and Hungary and passed under the Czech Presidency of the EU, the president of this country having declared the crimes of Hitler and Stalin to bear essentially similar traits.[74] Most Socialist MEPs, however, rejected it for its equation of the two regimes.[75]

It is unlikely that the European resolution will transform the debate on the "double past" in Germany or that a European narrative will usurp any national narrative. Thomas Lutz perceives an increased internationalization of memorial sites, which makes comparisons between regimes increasingly likely.[76] Nonetheless, each site retains its own national significance. In Germany the national significance of memorial sites with a "double past" is still not underpinned by a unified understanding of history. Despite the best of intentions the "Faulenbach formula" is nearly impossible to implement in practice. Faulenbach himself concedes that the Nazi and GDR pasts are "weighted" differently: the unique and international nature of the Holocaust leads to its prioritization.[77] This view is perpetuated by the fact that many western Germans do not readily identify with the GDR past because it is not considered to impact on German identity to the same extent as the Nazi legacy. Yet as we have seen, there is also evidence of the tendency to focus on the Holocaust in eastern Germany. Faulenbach maintains that the GDR has not entered the German culture of remembrance to the extent that the Nazi past did in West Germany after 1968.[78] However, the debate on the GDR past is still young and may well intensify in the future.

Since unification, memorialization strategies on the "double past" in Germany have been instrumental in allowing the commemoration of victims of both Nazism and Communism, improving awareness of the two regimes and stimulating debate. What they cannot do is dictate preconceptions of and reactions to the memorial sites concerned. As we have seen, these are influenced by a range of factors such as differing historical interpretations and political affiliations (east-west, left-wing/right-wing), age, biographical experience, and of course education and the media. Victims' groups appear to favor a "segregated" approach to commemoration, which is understandable in view of their personal experience of suffering. However, memorial sites also have the task of providing an "inclusive" approach that remembers all levels of their history. In terms of the pedagogical role of these sites, an inclusive approach is important in enabling younger visitors in particular to draw links between past and present and to appreciate the challenges faced under both regimes. Rather than seeking to establish a unified narrative and to strike an impossible balance between memorialization of the Nazi and GDR regimes, it is perhaps best to accept that remembrance is asymmetric in this case and to aim instead for a "principle of contextualization," where both pasts are treated not as equals but on their own terms, and as equally important for an understanding of twentieth-century Germany.

Notes

[1] "Rede von Bundeskanzlerin Dr. Angela Merkel im Rahmen des 'Fests der Freiheit' am 9. November 2009 in Berlin," accessed 24 May 2010, http://www.freiheit-und-einheit.de/SharedDocs/Reden/FuE/BK_9Nov09Fest_der_Freiheit.html?nn=729004. All websites listed in this article were accessed on the same date.

[2] Berthold Kohler, "Der Tag der Deutschen," *Frankfurter Allgemeine Zeitung*, 9 November 2009.

[3] *Kein Vergessen*, "9. November 2009 — 71. Jahrestag der Pogromnacht," http://buendniskeinvergessen.blogsport.de/2009/10/19/9november-2009-71jahrestag-der-pogromnacht-kein-vergessen-kein-vergeben/.

[4] See http://www.23august1939.de/. Names included the historian Heinrich August Winkler, the writer Peter Schneider, and Marianne Birthler, the then Federal Commissioner for the Stasi Records.

[5] See "Platzecks SS-Vergleich löst Empörung aus," *Der Spiegel*, 2 November 2009.

[6] Andrew Beattie, "The Fight in the Prison Car Park. Memorializing Germany's 'Double Past' in Torgau since 1990," in *Memorialization in Germany since 1945*, ed. Bill Niven and Chloe Paver (Basingstoke: Palgrave Macmillan, 2009), 328–38, here 334. Also see Jürgen Habermas, "Zur Auseinandersetzung mit den beiden

Diktaturen in Deutschland in Vergangenheit und Gegenwart," in *Materialien der Enquete-Kommission 'Aufarbeitung von Geschichte und Folgen der SED-Diktatur in Deutschland* (Frankfurt am Main: Nomos Verlagsgesellschaft, 1995), 9:686–94.

[7] See Bill Niven, *Facing the Nazi Past: United Germany and the Legacy of the Third Reich* (London: Routledge, 2002), 43–44.

[8] See Beattie, "The Fight in the Prison Car Park," 334.

[9] Niven, *Facing the Nazi Past*, 46–50.

[10] Beattie, "The Fight in the Prison Car Park," 329.

[11] On the development of the Sachsenhausen memorial site see Günter Morsch, ed., *Von der Erinnerung zum Monument: Die Entstehungsgeschichte der Nationalen Mahn- und Gedenkstätte Sachsenhausen* (Berlin: Edition Hentrich Druck, 1996).

[12] Thomas Lutz, cited in Norbert Reichling, "Erinnerungsorte der SBZ- und DDR-Geschichte: Eine Expertentagung in Schwerin" (13–15 June 2002), http://www.hu-bildungswerk.de/onlinearchiv_ddr-erinnerungsorte.php.

[13] See Norbert Haase, "Zwischen Konsens und Konkurrenz: Deutsche Erinnerungskulturen im politischen Spannungsfeld," in *Historisches Erinnern und Gedenken im Übergang vom 20. zum 21. Jahrhundert*, ed. Thomas Schaarschmidt (Frankfurt am Main: Peter Lang, 2008), 27–44, here 38.

[14] Stefanie Endlich et al., eds., *Gedenkstätten für die Opfer des Nationalsozialismus. Eine Dokumentation* (Bonn: Bundeszentrale für politische Bildung, 1999), 2:23.

[15] Endlich, *Gedenkstätten*, 23.

[16] Schlußbericht der Enquete-Kommission "Überwindung der Folgen der SED-Diktatur im Prozeß der deutschen Einheit," Deutscher Bundestag, Referat Öffentlichkeitsarbeit, Drucksache 13/11 000, 13. Wahlperiode (10 June 1998), 303–4 (hereafter cited in text as *SB*).

[17] Other sites included the Topography of Terror, German Resistance Memorial Center, House of the Wannsee Conference, and Hohenschönhausen memorial site, all in Berlin, and the Museum of the History of German Division in Mödlareuth.

[18] See "Konzeption der zukünftigen Gedenkstättenförderung des Bundes," Deutscher Bundestag, 14. Wahlperiode, Drucksache 14/1569 (27 July 1999).

[19] See Niven, *Facing the Nazi Past*, 46–52.

[20] See Andrew Beattie, "The Victims of Totalitarianism and the Centrality of Nazi Genocide: Continuity and Change in German Commemorative Politics," in *Germans as Victims: Remembering the Past in Contemporary Germany*, ed. Bill Niven (Basingstoke: Palgrave, 2006), 147–63, here 157–60.

[21] Bernd Faulenbach, "Probleme des Umgangs mit der Vergangenheit im vereinten Deutschland: Zur Gegenwartsbedeutung der jüngsten Geschichte," in *Deutschland: Eine Nation — doppelte Geschichte; Materialien zum deutschen Selbstverständnis*, ed. Werner Weidenfeld (Cologne: Verlag Wissenschaft und Politik, 1993), 190.

[22] "Gesetz zur Errichtung der Stiftung Sächsische Gedenkstätten zur Erinnerung an die Opfer politischer Gewaltherrschaft" (Sächsiches Gedenkstättenstiftungsgesetz — SachsGedenkStG), 22 April 2003, http://www.stsg.de/cms/sites/default/files/u9/errichtungsgesetz.pdf.

[23] See Zentralrat der Juden in Deutschland, "Zentralrat legt Mitarbeit in der 'Stiftung Sächsische Gedenkstätten' nieder," Pressemitteilung, 21 January 2004, http://www.zentralratdjuden.de/down/PM_Saechsische_Gedenkstaetten.pdf. On the controversy see Martin Jander, "Waagschalen-Mentalität: Kontroverse Positionen zum Gedenkstättenstreit in Sachsen und zu einem vorläufig zurückgezogenen Antrag der CDU/CSU im Bundestag," http://d-a-s-h.org/dossier/11/06_waagschale.html.

[24] "Erklärung, VVN-BdA Sachsen" (January 2004), cited in Jander, "Waagschalen-Mentalität."

[25] On the history of Torgau and the struggle over commemoration see Endlich, *Gedenkstätten*, 754–57; Beattie, "The Fight in the Prison Car Park"; and Dokumentations- und Informationszentrum (DIZ) Torgau, http://www.stsg.de/cms/torgau/startseite.

[26] Beattie, "The Fight in the Prison Car Park," 330.

[27] Beattie, "The Fight in the Prison Car Park," 332.

[28] See Hendrik Lasch, "Eine Gedenkstätte mit vielen Jahren Verspätung," *Neues Deutschland*, 13 April 2010.

[29] See Uwe Gutzeit, "Opfer des Stalinismus ehrten Nazi," *Torgauer Zeitung*, 29 May 2010; and Christoph Dieckmann, "Mein Gedenken! Wehrmacht-Deserteure und Stalinismus-Opfer streiten in Torgau um die Erinnerung an ihr Leid," *Die Zeit*, 12 May 2010.

[30] On the dispute see Rolf Surmann, "Ausstellung 'Spuren des Unrechts' in Torgau und die Zurücksetzung der Opfergruppe der NS-Militärjustizverfolgten," *Gedenkstättenrundbrief* 154 (2010): 13–21.

[31] See Ariane Brenssell, "Torgau streitet um das richtige Gedenken," *die tageszeitung*, 11 May 2004.

[32] See Oliver Reinhard, "Fast ein Wunder," *Die Zeit*, 27 May 2010.

[33] Reinhard, "Fast ein Wunder."

[34] Deutscher Bundestag, "Förderung von Gedenkstätten zur Diktaturgeschichte in Deutschland: Gesamtkonzept für ein würdiges Gedenken aller Opfer der beiden deutschen Diktaturen," Drucksache 15/1874 (4 November 2003).

[35] See for example Volkhard Knigge, "Stellungnahme der Arbeitsgemeinschaft der KZ-Gedenkstätten in der Bundesrepublik Deutschland," 26 January 2004, http://www.asf-ev.de/aktuell/040616.shtml.

[36] See Aktion Sühnezeichen Friedensdienste, "Keine Gleichsetzung von NS- und SED-Unrecht! Aktion Sühnezeichen Friedensdienste unterstützt die Forderungen der NS-Verfolgten im Konflikt mit der sächsischen Gedenkstättenführung," Pressemitteilung 30 January 2004, http://www.asf-ev.de/aktuell/040131.shtml.

[37] Deutscher Bundestag, "Förderung von Gedenkstätten zur Diktaturgeschichte in Deutschland: Gesamtkonzept für ein würdiges Gedenken aller Opfer der beiden deutschen Diktaturen," Drucksache 15/3048 (4 May 2004).

[38] Deutscher Bundestag, 15. Wahlperiode, Ausschuss für Kultur und Medien, "Öffentliche Anhörung von Sachverständigen zum Antrag der CDU/CSU-

Fraktion 'Förderung von Gedenkstätten zur Diktaturgeschichte in Deutschland,'"
16 February 2005.
[39] Werner von Bebber, "'Schönbohm will der Mörder gedenken,'" *Der Tagesspiegel*,
9 May 2006.
[40] "Gemeinsam für Deutschland: Mit Mut und Menschlichkeit — Koalitionsvertrag
zwischen CDU, CSU und SPD," 10 October 2005, http://www.cducsu.de/
upload/koavertrag0509.pdf.
[41] "Kulturstaatsminister Neumann übergibt Diskussionsentwurf zum neuen
Gedenkstättenkonzept," Presse- und Informationsamt der Bundesregierung,
Pressemitteilung No. 260 (4 July 2007).
[42] See Salomon Korn, "Stellungnahme," *Gedenkstättenrundbrief* 140 (December
2007): 46–49, here 46.
[43] "Fortschreibung der Gedenkstättenkonzeption des Bundes: Verantwortung
wahrnehmen, Aufarbeitung verstärken, Gedenken vertiefen," Deutscher Bundestag,
16. Wahlperiode, Drucksache 16/9875 (19 June 2008) (hereafter cited in text as
G).
[44] Wolfgang Börnsen and Reinhard Grindel, "Gedenkstättenkonzept stärkt die
Erinnerungskultur," 13 November 2008, http://www.cducsu.de/Titel__
pressemitteilung_gedenkstaettenkonzept_staerkt_die_erinnerungskultur/
TabID__6/SubTabID__7/InhaltTypID__1/InhaltID__11265/Inhalte.aspx.
[45] See "NS-Gedenkstätten laut Zentralrat vernachlässigt," *Die Welt*, 14 November
2007.
[46] Volkhard Knigge, "Stellungnahme," *Gedenkstättenrundbrief* 140 (December
2007): 36–45. Also see "Kein Fortschritt in der Fortschreibung," 25 June 2008,
http://www.openpr.de/news/222057/Kein-Fortschritt-in-der-Fortschreibung.
html.
[47] Regina Mönch, "Strategie für das Gedenken," *Das Parlament*, 22 February
2010.
[48] "Empfehlungen der Expertenkommission zur Schaffung eines
Geschichtsverbundes 'Aufarbeitung der SED-Diktatur,'" 15 May 2006, http://
www.stiftung-aufarbeitung.de/downloads/pdf/sabrow-bericht.pdf.
[49] See Horst Möller, "Geteilte Erinnerung," *Die Welt*, 16 May 2006; and Stephan
Reinecke, "Die neue Vernünftigkeit," *die tageszeitung*, 8 June 2006.
[50] "Öffentliche Stellungnahme von Prof. Dr. Martin Sabrow zum Entwurf einer
neuen Gedenkstättenkonzeption des Bundes durch den BKM am 22. Juni 2007,"
http://hsozkult.geschichte.hu-berlin.de/index.asp?id=910&pn=texte.
[51] "Kritisch erinnern: Grüne Positionen zur Aufarbeitung der Vergangenheit.
Positionspapier," 11 December 2007, http://www.gruene-bundestag.de/cms/
archiv/dokbin/210/210458.fraktionsbeschluss_kritisch_erinnern.pdf.
[52] Cited in Mariam Lau, "Aus Sicht der Opfer — Erinnerung an die SED-
Diktatur," *Die Welt*, 8 June 2006.
[53] "Staatsminister Bernd Neumann: 'Konsequente und differenzierte Aufarbeitung
der SED-Diktatur ist und bleibt ein zentrales Anliegen der Bundesregierung,'"

Presse- und Informationsamt der Bundsregierung, Pressemitteilung No. 138 (12 May 2006).

[54] For details of the proposal see "Erinnerungskultur 'Geschichte vor Ort,'" http://www.mwfk.brandenburg.de/cms/detail.php?id=bb1.c.142083.de; and Landtag Brandenburg, 4. Wahlperiode, Plenarprotokoll 4/86 (14 May 2009), http://www.mwfk.brandenburg.de/media/lbm1.a.1492.de/Parlamentsdebatte. pdf. Criticism of the plans is outlined in Peter Nowak, "Kritik am Gedenkstättenkonzept," *Neues Deutschland*, 30 May 2009.

[55] Landtag Brandenburg, "Gesetzentwurf der Fraktion der SPD, der Fraktion der CDU (Neudruck): Gesetz über den Beauftragten des Landes Brandenburg zur Aufarbeitung der Unterlagen des Staatssicherheitsdienstes der ehemaligen DDR und von Folgen diktatorischer Herrschaften," Drucksache 4/7518 (13 May 2009). Subsequent quotations in this paragraph are from this document.

[56] Wolfgang Wippermann at the public hearing on the law in the Brandenburg Parliament, 18 June 2009. Unless otherwise stated, this and other references to the hearing can be found in the transcript at http://www.landtag.brandenburg.de/ sixcms/media.php/5701/Protokoll_der_48._Sitzung_am_18.pdf, or in the compilation of written statements: Landtag Brandenburg, Hauptausschuss, "Stellungnahmen zum Gesetz über den Beauftragten des Landes Brandenburg zur Aufarbeitung der Unterlagen des Staatssicherheitsdienstes der ehemaligen DDR und von Folgen diktatorischer Herrschaften," 17 June 2009.

[57] "Gesetz über den Beauftragten des Landes Brandenburg zur Aufarbeitung der Folgen der kommunistischen Diktatur" (Brandenburgisches Aufarbeitungs-beauftragtengesetz- BbgAufarbBG), 7 July 2009.

[58] See Axel Flemming, "Wie weit ist die Stasi-Aufarbeitung? . . . in Brandenburg," *Deutschlandradio Kultur*, 8 July 2009, http://www.dradio.de/dkultur/sendungen/laenderreport/991291.

[59] See "Stadtverordnete streiten über Parkplatzneubau in Ravensbrück," *Märkische Allgemeine*, 2 May 2009.

[60] Interview with Günter Morsch, January 2001.

[61] See Horst Seferens and Thomas Lutz, "Realisierungswettbewerb Neubau sowjetische Speziallagermuseum Nr. 7/ Nr. 1 (1945–50), Gedenkstätte und Museum Sachsenhausen," *Gedenkstättenrundbrief* 89 (June 1999): 41–43; Sylvie Legrand, "Die Verwaltung der Gedenkstätten in den neuen Bundesländern seit der Vereinigung," *Gedenkstättenrundbrief* 114 (August 2003): 3–13, here 7–8; and Niven, *Facing the Nazi Past*, 47.

[62] For evidence taken from visits to the Buchenwald memorial site see Annette Leo and Peter Reif-Spirek, "'Es darf sich dort entsprechend der vorhandenen Hinweissschilder frei bewegt werden': Eine Analyse von Berichten Thüringer LehrerInnen über Klassenfahrten zur Gedenkstätte Buchenwald," *Gedenkstättenrundbrief* 87 (February 1999): 12–20.

[63] See Haase, "Zwischen Konsens und Konkurrenz," 42.

[64] Reichling, "Erinnerungsorte der SBZ- und DDR-Geschichte."

[65] Daniel Gaede, "In der Gedenkstätte Buchenwald ist mehr möglich, als viele warhnehmen," *Gedenkstättenrundbrief* 87 (February 1999): 21–24.

[66] Leo and Reif-Spirek, "Es darf sich dort entsprechend der vorhandenen Hinweissschilder frei bewegt werden," 19.

[67] See "Stadt Oranienburg: Oranienburger Toleranzpreis," http://www.oranienburg.de/texte/seite.php?id=22868.

[68] Günter Morsch, "Geschichte als Waffe: Erinnerungskultur in Europa und die Aufgabe der Gedenkstätten," *Blätter für deutsche und internationale Politik* 5 (June 2010): 109–21, http://www.blaetter.de/archiv/jahrgaenge/2010/mai/geschichte-als-waffe.

[69] "Declaration of the European Parliament on the Proclamation of 23 August as European Day of Remembrance for Victims of Stalinism and Nazism," 23 September 2008, http://www.europarl.europa.eu/sides/getDoc.do?pubRef=-//EP//TEXT+TA+P6-TA-2008-0439+0+DOC+XML+V0//EN.

[70] "European Parliament resolution of 2 April 2009 on European Conscience and Totalitarianism," 2 April 2009, http://www.europarl.europa.eu/sides/getDoc.do?pubRef=-//EP//TEXT+TA+P6-TA-2009-0213+0+DOC+XML+V0//EN. http://www.europarl.europa.eu/sides/getDoc.do?pubRef=-//EP//TEXT+TA+P6-TA-2009-0213+0+DOC+XML+V0//EN

[71] "Rede von Bundeskanzlerin Dr. Angela Merkel zur Eröffnung der ständigen Ausstellung zur deutschen Geschichte im Deutschen Historischen Museum am 2. Juni 2006 in Berlin," Presse- und Informationsamt der Bundesregierung, 2 June 2006.

[72] See Inse Eschebach, "Nationale und postnationale Sprachen des Gedenkens: Theologisierung und Anthropologiesierung nach der deutschen Einheit," *Gedenkstättenrundbrief* 95 (June 2000): 3–10.

[73] Morsch, "Geschichte als Waffe."

[74] See Tunne Kelam MEP, "Europe Needs an Integrated Perception of Its Common History," 26 March 2009, http://www.eppgroup.eu/Press/showpr.asp?PRControlDocTypeID=1&PRControlID=8462&PRContentID=14680&PRContentLG=en.

[75] See "Political Divide Remains over Molotov-Ribbentrop Pact," 15 October 2009, http://www.euractiv.com/en/enlargement/political-divide-remains-molotov-ribbentrop-pact/article-186424.

[76] Thomas Lutz, "Stellungnahme zur Öffentlichen Anhörung zum Gedenkstättenantrag der CDU/CSU Fraktion am 16. Februar 2005 im Kulturausschuss des Deutschen Bundestags," 7 February 2005.

[77] Bernd Faulenbach, "Öffentliche Anhörung von Sachverständigen zum Antrag der CDU/CSU-Fraktion 'Förderung von Gedenkstätten zur Diktaturgeschichte in Deutschland' (16 February 2005)," Bundesdrucksache 15/3048.

[78] Faulenbach, "Öffentliche Anhörung."

Part 3: *Ostalgie*, Historiography, and Generational Memory

10: Living through the GDR: History, Life Stories, and Generations in East Germany

Mary Fulbrook

T HE EVENTS OF 9 NOVEMBER 1989 were initially greeted with what appeared to be virtually universal acclamation. Over the summer of 1989 the "Iron Curtain" that had divided Cold War Europe began to develop gaps and holes through which people were able to escape to the West. In the course of the early autumn, across East German towns and cities hundreds of thousands of people came out on the streets to demonstrate their disaffection with the regime. On the occasion of the GDR's fortieth anniversary celebrations, on 7 October 1989, the Soviet Union under Gorbachev's leadership had indicated its unwillingness to step in and shore up by force an unpopular Communist regime. On 9 October 1989, despite intense preparation and the real possibility of a bloodbath on the lines of the earlier Tiananmen Square massacre in China, the ruling East German Socialist Unity Party (SED) and its State Security Service, the Stasi, renounced the use of force and allowed a mass demonstration in Leipzig to proceed peacefully. In the face of widespread popular opposition and lacking in reliable support even among its own ranks, in the following weeks the SED itself began the process of unraveling its own grip on power. Long-time SED leader Erich Honecker was replaced by the ever-smiling Egon Krenz and, following a brief trip to Moscow from which Krenz returned apparently converted to the cause of reform, sweeping political changes were introduced. It was even an official spokesperson for the SED, Günther Schabowski, who on 9 November 1989 conveyed the momentous Politburo decision about new travel regulations, which effectively meant, as Western journalists and East Germans alike rapidly realized, that the wall would no longer serve its previous function — exercised for some twenty-seven years — of keeping East Germans inside the GDR against their will. The unification of Germany, which took place less than a year later, on 3 October 1990, was neither intended at this time, nor was it a direct outcome of this moment, yet the opening of the Berlin Wall removed the crucial precondition for the existence of an independent second German state, which could not continue to exist in face of a more

affluent democracy in the west. The capitulation of the SED regime on 9
November 1989 in the face of popular challenges and the loss of Soviet
support by force did, then, inaugurate the end of the GDR and the end of
the Cold War that had divided Europe since the defeat of Hitler. It was a
historic moment in the fullest sense of the term.

It was also a moment of apparently universal happiness — unlike previous moments of historical rupture in twentieth-century Europe following world wars and bloody revolutions. All sides seemed to agree. Germans
on both sides of the inner-German border — a border that was at the
same time the Cold War frontier of Europe, dividing East from West,
capitalism from Communism, the USA from the USSR — joined in
rejoicing; Berliners jumped on the wall and drank champagne, while the
world's television cameras recorded the baffled faces of GDR border
guards as streams of East Germans took the now legitimate, officially permitted opportunity to visit the previously forbidden territory of the formerly maligned and abominated West. The fall of the Berlin Wall was
indeed a moment that has rightly come to symbolize a major historical
turning point, experienced across Eastern Europe in slightly different patterns and with different timings, but with common ultimate significance:
the "end" of the Cold War and with this also the "end" of the "short
twentieth century."[1]

However, following the initial euphoria longer-term reflections and
"memories" have begun to cast the East German past in a rather different
light, more bitterly contested and more variously appropriated than one
might have thought possible on 9 November 1989. On the one hand
condemnation of the SED regime continued. During the 1990s, through
lengthy parliamentary commissions of inquiry (Bundestags Enquete-
Kommissionen), politicians focused on assessing the character and on
"overcoming" the consequences of the SED-dictatorship.[2] In the media
the role of the Stasi was a major focus of attention, with bitter controversies and quite tragic individual tales.[3] The roles of the churches came in for
sometimes devastating critique. The historiography of the GDR, with the
opening of the East German archives in the early 1990s, initially focused
heavily on repression and coercion, exploring the apparatus of power and
the ways in which people had allegedly become accomplices in a "second
German dictatorship" largely populated, in some accounts, by heroes, victims, and villains. On this version both western German conservative
political historians and former East German dissident historians came to
agree, as evidenced in the widespread reappropriation of the concept of
totalitarianism and the thesis that it was primarily repression and fear that
explained the long-term stability of the GDR over forty years.[4] Contested
landscapes of commemoration provoked heated debates over who and
what should be remembered, where and how, and at what cost to other
sites of memory. Even if some of these debates moved on with greater

sensitivity and differentiation in historical approaches over the course of time, for example, and with calls for the "professionalization" of commemorative sites and practices and greater involvement of "experts," there was nevertheless a continuing degree of political coloration of historical interpretations well into the twenty-first century.[5]

Of course condemnation of the GDR provoked angry responses from expected quarters; successor parties to the SED (the PDS and beyond) and others on the far left fiercely disputed the views of those whom they saw as continuing "Cold Warriors."[6] More surprising, however, was the registration of a growing sense among large numbers of eastern Germans that their past was being in some way misrepresented. While they had themselves played a major role in bringing down the old regime, among many of them there appeared to be a quite contrasting sense of longing for aspects of the lost GDR past. In part this yearning focused on material objects, food and consumer items, the "furniture" and "taste" of the past, in the much-discussed waves of *Ostalgie* (nostalgia for the East) that capitalism was of course rapidly able to exploit. In part, too, such *Ostalgie* was both reflected and encouraged by new forms of popular cultural representations of the GDR, including films such as Thomas Brussig and Leander Haußmann's *Sonnenallee* (1999) and Wolfgang Becker's *Good Bye, Lenin!* (2003) — the latter in particular unleashing a run on *Spreewaldgurken* (a popular East German brand of sour gherkins, pickled cucumbers, from the Spreewald area). These of course unleashed responses: Anna Funder's book on *Stasiland* (2004) and Florian Henckel von Donnersmarck's film *Das Leben der Anderen* (2006), a major box-office success focusing on the Stasi, variously recast the "second German dictatorship" not so much as farce but as tragedy (to paraphrase Marx on history repeating itself), even if as tragedy with a somewhat unlikely human face in the case of the latter work.

These cultural phenomena are well known and widely discussed. I would like here to consider in more detail a less familiar aspect, however, namely the ways in which both experiences and memories of the GDR were patterned by the ages at which people lived through the "same" periods of history; how "social generations" were variously formed and transformed by the historical ruptures, systems, and events through which people of different ages lived; and how their experiences and memories help to reflect and explain this most recent and contemporary period of German history. What follows is based on the approach and findings of a far larger project using a wide range of "ego-documents" (letters, diaries, memoirs) to analyze the formation and transformation of generational groupings across the twentieth century, starting well before the First World War; but the material deployed below in some detail is primarily drawn from an intensive analysis of some forty oral-history interviews and over 270 questionnaires carried out in and after 2005, providing an intriguing sample of eastern German views on their past from the perspective of more than a decade and a half after the fall of the wall.

Interestingly, at this time a majority of respondents saw their childhoods (in some cases going back to the 1920s and 1930s) and periods of young adulthood as among the "best times" of their lives and/or saw "the GDR" in one undifferentiated fashion as the "best time" of their lives. Similarly, a significant majority saw "the present" or "the period since unification" as among the "worst times" of their lives — to which older respondents often added the period immediately after the end of the Second World War, namely the later 1940s, which were characterized by a combination of hunger, bereavement, physical and psychological upheaval, and uncertainty about the future. The most striking general finding is the way in which, in retrospect, so many eastern Germans seemed to be yearning for what they later fondly re-construed as the apparently ordered and secure lives they had led in the formerly hated GDR. But such comments are generalizations: once explored in terms of the different experiences and perceptions of succeeding generations, the findings are far more differentiated and help to shed an intriguing light on the ways in which the East German dictatorship was variously sustained, undermined, and later remembered.

Generations in the GDR

Modes of transition across the historical rupture of 1945 are crucial for understanding the latter half of the twentieth century. In contrast to the widespread conception among Germans in both east and west of 1945 as a "Year Zero" ("Stunde Null"), the development of the East German dictatorship was in fact rooted in bitter political controversies that had been raging since the Weimar years and before. And even if it does not explain the foundation or development of a Communist state on the soil of the Soviet Zone of Occupation of defeated post-Hitler Germany, a generational approach is key to understanding some of the peculiarities of the ways in which the GDR was stabilized and "carried." It did not — as some accounts would have it — rest solely on force, repression, and the threat of Soviet tanks.

The "founding fathers" of the GDR were individuals who had already long been involved in political struggles in the preceding decades of ideological warfare between Fascism and Communism. Not only people from the so-called front generation (a long and actually highly diverse set of cohorts, the notion of "front generation" being more a product of political myth-making on the right in the 1920s than of any genuine commonality of experience) but also members of the "war youth generation" (born ca. 1900–1912 and too young to fight in the First World War) had played key roles in the Third Reich. Indeed, it was from the latter, the "war youth generation," that many of the major functionaries were drawn, putting into effect Hitler's murderous policies in the provinces and in the incorporated and occupied territories of the Greater German Reich. Yet a further fact is often overlooked: it was also from these generations that those who had been bitterly opposed to and persecuted by the Nazis, and who subsequently took up key political roles in the Communist cause after 1945, were drawn. The implicit "civil war" of the GDR, often viewed purely in Cold War terms, can only be fully comprehended in light of this longer-term political struggle. Moreover, in the self-proclaimed "anti-Fascist state" of the GDR, orientations during the Nazi period took precedence over the legacies of the First World War; "generational constellations" reformed, as earlier generational differences were now overridden by this overwhelming recent history of persecution and repression. In my view it is more appropriate to speak of a highly internally-divided "KZ generation" after 1945 in order to indicate, by referring symbolically to the concentration camps (*Konzentrationslager*, KZ) of the Nazi regime — which many Germans had sustained and under which others had suffered — quite what it was that continued to divide those who had been adults during the Third Reich. It was thus politics, rather than any alleged "key formative experiences," that determined which strands became dominant in the GDR after 1949. While the Right had gained ascendancy under the repressive power structures of the Third Reich, the left-wing minority that had survived persecution, imprisonment, and exile and remained in or returned to Germany after 1945, was finally able to try to shape the future with the help of Soviet backing after 1945. A generational approach is unlikely to get us very far if we seek in it an explanation of the founding and structure of this state.

But there is one cohort that stands out consistently in the historical record in quite remarkable ways and whose history is closely bound up with that of the GDR: what was effectively a second "war youth generation" whom I call the "1929ers," those born from the mid-1920s through to the early 1930s (ca. 1926–32). They turn out to be the most homogeneous cohort of the century. They were socialized entirely within the Nazi framework of Hitler's Third Reich, yet in the GDR they became the most committed Communists — and not merely among those who made contributions sufficient to warrant an entry in the GDR's *Who's Who* (retroactively produced as *Wer war Wer in der DDR*) but also more broadly.[7] As curious as it seems the 1929ers — these younger members of what is often seen in an unduly undifferentiated fashion as one long "Hitler Youth generation" — became both the backbone of the East German functionary system and also, among the wider population, generally the most supportive of the GDR regime, a comment true for women as well as men. They were far more likely to be members of the Communist SED or the bloc parties and to hold functionary positions or senior posts in the mass organizations, the "people's own factories" and industrial conglomerates, the media, and scientific and cultural institutions, as well as the Stasi than those just a few years older or younger. They were not only the most politically supportive cohort in the GDR, but also the least religious; and, on the evidence of oral history interviews and questionnaire research, they remained the most nostalgic for the GDR after its collapse in 1989.[8]

Slightly younger cohorts born during the Third Reich not only played a minor role in the GDR but also generally had the least positive attitudes toward it. They tended to be involved in "expressive" activities such as art and music, and to remain religious, rather than being practically involved in the Communist system. And those "born into the GDR," particularly the cohorts born in the early 1950s, were divided between a small minority of dissidents at one end of the spectrum, a small minority of outstanding sportspeople and regime supporters at the other end, and a grumbling, disaffected, but largely conformist majority — who, unlike the war youth generation and the 1929ers, were never seriously mobilized for a utopian cause and whose horizons were increasingly restricted to "making do" in the limited present rather than seeking to build a better future.

How can the disproportionate role of the 1929ers in the GDR be explained? Several factors are significant. Differences in participation compared to those a few years older can be "structurally" explained by a combination of demography and politics: there were very low birth rates during the First World War and differentially high death rates during the Second World War for older cohorts in contrast to the 1929ers; and those who did survive tended to be more tainted by activities during the Nazi period than were the youngsters who only reached adulthood with the foundation of the GDR in 1949. But it is less easy to explain the differences between the 1929ers and those born shortly afterwards, in the baby-boom years of the Third Reich, and here "cultural availability for mobilization" becomes significant.

The 1929ers' experiences of violence in the Second World War were far deeper and of a more directly personal nature than the experiences of the war youth generation, for whom violence remained far away at the front and could still to some extent be glorified. Hence, unlike the war youth generation the 1929ers turned away from, rather than embracing, violence. Whether or not they were male and old enough to be called up in the last, most bloody, phase of the war, the 1929ers experienced at first hand the violence of air raids on German cities, the violence of "treks" escaping in front of the approaching Red Army, or being expelled from their homelands in Eastern Europe after the war; they lost close relatives and friends in far greater numbers than did older cohorts in the First World War; their lives were more deeply disrupted physically and geographically, as well as emotionally. Analysis of letters to and from the front and life stories after the war suggests that these cohorts experienced the violence unleashed by Nazism in quite distinctive ways. They felt a sense of betrayal after the war and they searched for new ideologies and causes to which they could commit themselves, utterly renouncing the previous regime and searching, at an impressionable age, for another cause to which they could commit their energies. Why the 1929ers came to play a major role in the GDR is not explained by this alone, however.

Rejection of Nazism and the search for new solutions was common among members of this age group in both East and West Germany, but in the GDR, further factors now came into play. Given relatively stringent denazification and the high turnover of personnel in the East German state, many 1929ers rapidly rose to positions of responsibility in which Communist party discipline imposed further constraints (an "iron cage," to adapt Max Weber). They certainly had to accept the authority of the local representatives of the "anti-Fascist founding fathers" in the workplace, while those who had gone along with the Nazi regime too closely lost positions of power and responsibility in key areas of the state and economy — although the negotiation of authority between young and old in schools, offices, and factories was a complex matter. Christa Wolf, who was born in 1929, claimed to speak on behalf of her generation when she claimed that the 1929ers also suffered from a diffuse sense of at least partially shared guilt. As Wolf put it, very eloquently:

> Als wir fünfzehn, sechzehn waren, mussten wir uns unter dem niederschmetternden Eindruck der ganzen Wahrheit über den deutschen Faschismus von denen abstoßen, die in diesen zwölf Jahren nach unserer Meinung durch Dabeisein, Mitmachen, Schweigen schuldig geworden waren. Wir mussten diejenigen entdecken, die Opfer geworden waren, diejenigen, die Widerstand geleistet hatten. Wir mussten es lernen, uns in sie einzufühlen. Identifizieren konnten wir uns natürlich auch mit ihnen nicht, dazu hatten wir kein Recht. Das heißt, als wir sechzehn waren, konnten wir uns mit niemandem identifizieren. Dies ist eine wesentliche Aussage für meine Generation . . .
>
> Uns wurde dann ein verlockendes Angebot gemacht: Ihr könnt, hieß es, eure mögliche, noch nicht verwirklichte Teilhabe an dieser nationalen Schuld loswerden oder abtragen, indem ihr aktiv am Aufbau der neuen Gesellschaft teilnehmt, die das genaue Gegenteil, die einzig radikale Alternative zum verbrecherischen System des Nationalsozialismus darstellt.[9]

Whether a majority of 1929ers would have agreed with Christa Wolf is another matter. My interviews reveal only one (highly educated and professional) woman who echoed these sentiments, and indeed explicitly referred to Christa Wolf in doing so, suggesting perhaps that her reading of Wolf had influenced her own conceptions of the past. For other 1929ers across the social spectrum such considerations seem to have played a far less significant role, if indeed they featured at all.

More important here perhaps is quite another factor. The 1929ers' "construction of new lives" as young adults in the 1950s coincided with the "building up" (*Aufbau*) of the new state. What were retrospectively perceived as the "best times" in the 1929ers' private lives coincided with the most idealistic, creative phase of Walter Ulbricht's GDR, creating stronger emotional attachments to a state that appeared to be giving them "new life chances." The contrast between the "worst times" in the 1929ers' lives — the later 1940s — and the "best times" — either childhood (often right up through most of the war period) and/or the 1950s — is found again and again in the life stories collected in the course of research into this area.[10] A woman born in 1930, for example, listed as the best years of her life 1947 to 1957, giving as reasons "Berufsausbildung; Aufbauarbeit und Jugend-Freizeit-Leben."[11] Another woman, born in 1931, experienced the end of the war in East Prussia "mit allen Schrecken des 2. Weltkrieges." She recounts her autobiography through the next few years in a staccato, subject-less voice: "Vertreibung im Jahre 1947 aus der Heimat. Übersiedlung mit schwer kranker Mutter in die ehemalige DDR. Vater verstarb nach Verschleppung im April 1945 nach Siberien. Dann 17jährig alleinstehend u. mittellos schwere Zeit durchlebt." But then she continues, finally entering her own story as subject: "Nach Eheschließung 1951 u. Geburt des Sohnes begann ein neues Leben. Wir waren glücklich u. auch zufrieden mit unserem Leben."[12] Similarly, a woman born in 1930 listed as her best times her pre-school age and the period of childhood up to the outbreak of war; and then again "1951 — Ehe. 1953 — als wir unsere erste Wohnung bekamen und gleich danach als unser Kind geboren wurde."[13] A male, born in 1928, described his "worst times" as "Vor und nach 1945: Krieg, Zerstörung, Leid und Hunger." His "best times" included "ab 1948: vertrauensvolle, familiäre Bindung," as well as the periods 1950 to 1960 and 1970 to 1989: he believed that the GDR had given him "new chances" through "Aus- und Weiterbildung, Möglichkeit guter beruflicher und individ. Entfaltung, Förder. der Familie."[14] Another male, born 1929, listed as his "worst times" his immediate postwar period of imprisonment from 1945 to 1948 in a Soviet internment camp, but his "best times" followed on very soon, from 1950 to 1960: "Familiengründung, Berufsausbildung."[15] None of these individuals had entirely rosy views of the GDR more generally; qualifications and recognition of complexities are present in all retrospective accounts, as we shall see. But it is striking just how frequently the 1929ers mention the GDR as having given them particularly good new life-chances through education and fostering of their working lives as well as supportive family policies, and how their happiest times were those when they were young, in love, or starting new families after the horrendous destruction, devastation, and hunger of the later war and early postwar years. In general the chance to combine satisfaction in working life with a family and fulfilling leisure time was what the vast majority alleged had made them happy.

Moreover, those 1929ers of the "wrong" social backgrounds and political outlooks — that is, not from modest social origins or prepared to lean to the left — and who disliked the situation in the 1950s were old enough to make their own decisions and to flee for the West before the building of the Berlin Wall. Of the approximately three million who fled westwards before 13 August 1961, disproportionate numbers were young and skilled. Those 1929ers remaining were thus in a sense further "selected" as willing — for whatever reasons (often not from political commitment but, for example, out of family considerations or a sense of *Heimat*) — to make their lives within the GDR. And it was only one or two individuals who really ran into trouble with the regime, as in the case of one man who in 1963 was imprisoned for four years for having tried to help someone escape to the West. Curiously, up until that point he had been a virtually classic 1929er: the happiest times in his life were first his childhood and then the years 1946 to 1961.[16]

Over time, older issues began to fade as new challenges took priority for East Germans. Violence was largely concentrated at the physical and metaphorical borders of the walled-in state, in the frozen peace of the Cold War. Although military and security issues remained central, they were to some extent routinized after early years of forcible repression. "Re-settlers" from lost eastern territories became "GDR citizens"; social and economic changes brought new classes to dominance; and the SED version of history emphasizing "liberation" by the Red Army and exonerating "workers and peasants" from involvement in Nazism was a convenient, if somewhat dissonant, myth. In the later 1960s and early 1970s the GDR entered a period of relative stability, with international recognition and social transformation. "Coming to terms with the present" in the drab constraints of a society behind the wall was more important for most than either "overcoming the past" (a theme ever more insistently reiterated in the post-1968 West) or ideologically driven "mobilization for the future" (the refrain of the early period of postwar reconstruction in the East).

Younger cohorts, who had no choice about whether to stay or flee, experienced the GDR rather differently from the 1929ers, but none of them were as strikingly regime-supportive as the latter in their overall profile. There were some other, subtler, variations according to age. Members of those cohorts who might be termed "Children of the Third Reich," or "war children," who more or less consciously experienced the foundation of the GDR and certainly the building of the Berlin Wall, were somewhat different in outlook and attitudes from the varying younger cohorts who were "born into the GDR" and knew nothing else. The "Children of the Third Reich" remained, for example, more religious than either their younger or their older compatriots. They also had by far the most miserable lives overall: they seem to have been born at a time when they had the worst of all worlds. One third of those surveyed who gave answers with precise dates listed periods within the GDR as among their "worst times," unlike the other cohorts, where this was a rare exception. Arguably this was in part because they faced, as young adults, key experiences from which they could not escape: in the early 1960s the building of the wall and the introduction of military conscription, for example; from the mid-1960s the closing down of Ulbricht's experiments in cultural liberalization and the partial blocking of opportunities for educational and occupational advancement. But it is arguably also because they never fully trusted or committed themselves to any ideology and did not face the shock of violence or seem to experience the need for alternative ideological solutions that was so characteristic of at least the more articulate 1929ers.

There were also of course differences according to social and political backgrounds, cultural milieu, and personal choices that people were forced to make at various ages. Those born after the war were faced with choices, for example, between religious confirmation in church or secular state "coming of age" ceremonies as a young teenager; between military conscription or alternative service as a young adult male, with the latter condemning individuals to spending the rest of their lives on the fringes. As adults they had to make choices between retaining relationships with "Western contacts" as emotionally close relatives, or seeing them as "merely" a source of much-coveted Western goods and currency — or even, by contrast, a source of embarrassment hindering a conformist career in the GDR state service. And yet despite the continued growth of the Stasi, for younger cohorts the GDR increasingly appeared "perfectly normal," with predictable life courses for those who "followed the rules of the game." This was a matter not only of socialization but also, given the known sanctions for non-conformity, having to act in light of the expectations of the regime and to adapt aspirations and attitudes accordingly.

Even just a couple of years after the building of the Berlin Wall, visitors from the West observed changes in behavior and outlook among their East German counterparts. As one young West Berliner (born 1944) put it, following a visit to East Berlin in 1964 when she was particularly shocked by the attitudes of one state-supporting friend:

> Es war erschütternd für mich zu erleben, wie kleinmütig und furchtsam die Menschen drüben geworden sind . . . An Kühlschrank, Fernsehen, Auto ist natürlich nicht zu denken. Die Kinder werden im Fabrik-Kindergarten im Sinne des "Arbeiter- und Bauernstaates" erzogen, und er findet das in Ordnung, tritt demonstrativ für diesen Staat ein. Ist es Verblendung, locken billige Vorteile, oder ist es der Versuch, die Vergangenheit zu vergessen? Ich habe mich für ihn geschämt. Nicht die Mauer ist mürbe und bröckelt. Die Menschen

bröckeln auseinander . . . Wie kann man sich in 2½ Jahren so
verändern? . . . Und plötzlich sah ich mitten im Zimmer die Mauer
zwischen mir und diesem Abtrünnigen, der etwa 5 Meter entfernt
allein auf dem Sofa saß.[17]

For some young people, there were continuing conflicts with the state,
particularly over its anti-Western policies with respect to popular culture,
lifestyles, and music. Following brief periods of restrained official liberalization within limits (as in the period before the Eleventh Plenum of the
SED of 1965) there were repeatedly moments of clampdown and repression. But for others, as for example those from modest social backgrounds
who were able to realize major personal successes in the area of international competitive sports, the GDR offered opportunities that they could
never have dreamed of under any other system and for which many
remained grateful to the state — despite the horror stories of doping that
have emerged since unification.

Yet over time the regime's own emphasis on consumerism (in rivalry
with but also making concessions to the West) focused attention on material goods, while the growth of radio and television ownership increasingly
exposed people to global mass culture and a "here-and-now," individual-
istic attitude. The vast majority of those born into the GDR found, one
way or another, a means of making their way through a combination of
conformity and grumbling, deploying a variety of strategies — from reliance on networks of friends and contacts to supply scarce goods and services to handing in "Eingaben" or petitions and complaints to official
bodies — in order to achieve personal ends. The collective goals and aims
that had been espoused by the 1929ers — building the "better Germany,"
the transformation of society from exploitation to equality — dissipated
into the sands for most of those born into the already existing state. And
despite a rise in positive attitudes toward the GDR among young people
in the early and mid-1970s, a very marked collapse in support was evident
among a younger cohort some ten years later, from the mid-1980s.[18]
Neither grumbling adaptation nor a greater degree of disaffection leading
a few to retreat into alternative lifestyles and subcultures was, however, a
serious threat to regime stability.

There was one splinter of a generational group that deserves some
further attention, however, since it came to the fore in the next major
historical rupture, that of 1989. Many among the small groups of dissidents who in the later 1970s and 1980s played leading roles in the destabilization of the GDR were born in the late 1940s or early 1950s.
Individuals such as Vera Lengsfeld (Wollenberger), Ulrike Poppe, and
Bärbel Bohley provide examples both of the generational bias of opposi-
tional movements and of the gender shifts in a state that had fostered
female participation in the workplace and organizational life. Socialized
in Ulbricht's GDR, many had grown up believing in high ideals; and they

212 ♦ MARY FULBROOK

had come to maturity with the crushing of the Czech reformist "Prague Spring" by Warsaw Pact troops in 1968, which often provoked the first critical engagement with the shortcomings of Communism in practice. As parents of young children by the 1980s, members of this cohort were increasingly concerned by the renewed arms race and the introduction of military education in GDR schools, not to mention the economic decline and visible, palpable environmental deterioration in the context of the oil crises and Honecker's unsustainable economic and social policies. Increasingly frustrated by the unwillingness of the SED gerontocracy even to concede the existence of problems, let alone deal with them, small groups under the partial protection of the Protestant churches tried to provoke dialogue and change. In 1989 they were among the first to be demonstrating on the streets.

But these remained a tiny minority. Far more typical for this cohort was the response of attempted flight: nightly, through watching Western television; in the 1980s, by making applications for exit visas; in summer 1989, across the border between Hungary and Austria, or through West German embassies in Prague and elsewhere; and finally, after 9 November 1989, across the newly opened Berlin Wall.

How then did these succeeding cohorts differentially experience the impact of unification and reflect on their former lives in the GDR?

Life Stories and Views of the GDR after Unification

The fall of the Berlin Wall and unification with the West in 1989–90 was a major rupture in the lives of East Germans, with a different impact on both experience and narrated life stories depending on age at the time. The 1929ers, in their late 50s or early 60s in 1989, were frequently able to go into early retirement. Their problems were not so much economic as existential: they were forced, in a sense, to re-evaluate the whole of their lives. In light of "history" their own "life stories," which had been so closely and directly connected with the history of the GDR, might now in some sense be seen as having been in vain, yet many retained future-oriented aspirations (world peace, environmental concerns) echoing earlier profiles. Their retrospective evaluations of the GDR in comparison with the capitalist, democratic, united Federal Republic were nuanced but had a sense of wider ideals, as in the comments of one of the women already quoted:

> Gut war Arbeit, kostenlose Bildung, soziale Sicherheit,
> Kinderbetreuung, Gesundheitswesen.
> Keine Konsumgüter-Schwemme und kein Medienrummel mit vielen

öffentlichen Beleidigungen und Rufmord gegen Persönlichkeiten.
Jetzt mehr Informationen — aber welcher Nutzen für Bevölkerung!
Jetzt mehr Demokratie möglich — aber 5 Mio Arbeitslose mit
Folgen für Familien.
Und wie geht es weiter? Bleibt Frieden? Welche Perspektive haben
junge Leute? Was die Reichen "brauchen" u. was wird aus der
Umwelt?[19]

Another had spoken among her "worst times" of

Nach dem Krieg:
— jahrelanges, unerfülltes Hoffen auf die Heimkehr des vermissten
Vaters
— das Erschrecken, was mein Land anderen zugefügt hat; die Schuld
am Krieg, das Erfahren von KZ-Verbrechen
— die Fortsetzung des schon im Krieg begonnenen Hungerns.

But then she spoke of pride in the fact "daß es bei uns noch keinen Krieg
wieder gab (aber Trauer, daß es in der Welt noch so viele gibt)."[20]
Thus, although after 1989 they personally had little or nothing to lose
(the two exceptions in my sample being individuals who had suffered
from political repression in the GDR), 1929ers generally remained most
stubbornly defensive of the ideals and achievements of the state with
which their lives had been so closely bound. Some even came out with
statements defending the much-critiqued Stasi, as in the comment that
the MfS represented the "Schutz des von uns geleisteten Aufbaus," or "es
gibt den Dienst in allen Ländern."[21] They were also concerned about the
future in which their children and grandchildren would live, as in comments such as "nicht nur eigene Unsicherheit sondern auch die der
Kinder und Enkel."[22]

The "Children of the Third Reich" (born 1933–45) and the "first
Freie Deutsche Jugend generation" (FDJ1, born in the later 1940s and
early 1950s) experienced the transition of 1989–90 very differently from
those who were old enough to retire at the time of unification. Many of
the FDJ1 in particular had been at the forefront of the movements leading
to the fall of the wall or had undermined the claims to legitimacy of
Honecker's regime by their mass flight to the West, literally and meta-
phorically. They had played a disproportionate role in the destabilization
and demise of the GDR. But these cohorts were also subsequently the
greatest "losers" with regard to the ways in which unification actually
took place. The vast majority were of working age, and many found it
difficult either to retrain or to retain their old positions; women were
particularly adversely affected by disproportionate unemployment rates;
and there was a loss of cheap, subsidized childcare, which affected all
working parents. Having achieved what had for so many of this generation been a long-term aim of "arrival in the West," they now found it held

little by way of future prospects; accordingly they radically revised their views of the East German past, retrospectively seeing aspects of it in a far more positive light.

Somewhat more than one in five East Germans (over 20%) of working age were unemployed at the time of my research. The sense of sheer desperation about future prospects comes through very strongly in the responses of those born in the 1950s, even when they were not currently unemployed themselves. So many use phrases such as "Existenzängste," "nicht gebraucht werden," "keine berufliche Perspektive," "nicht zu wissen, wie es weitergehen sollte," "Unsicherheit im Job," and "allmählicher sozialer Abstieg in die Langzeitarbeitslosigkeit" that it would be impossible to quote individuals separately. Hardly surprisingly, the "best times," in retrospect, for the overwhelming majority of those from this "first FDJ generation" are seen, in undifferentiated fashion, as the period before 1989 in general, not only because of professed happy memories of actual experiences, but because at that time "die Zukunft war rosiger," one had a "gesicherte Zukunft."[23] Again and again they mention in justification of their retrospective preference for East German society notions such as "soziale Sicherheit," "gesicherte Existenz," "soz. Geborgenheit." Life in the GDR is characterized as having been "in Ordnung," an ordered, regular, even peaceful existence, "ruhigeres Leben," "ruhiger und sozial abgesicherter," "ruhiger gelebt," "nicht so stressig." Frequently the comment is made in contrast to contemporary united Germany, as in the following selection:

> "Bis 1990: Das Leben war in geregelten Bahnen mit normalen Höhen und Tiefen, ohne Ängste."[24]

> "Ich war neutral, aber der Mensch war im Gegensatz zu jetzt noch was wert.
> Man brauchte keine Zukunftsängste haben."[25]

> "Wenn man nicht mehr gebraucht wird, wird man zertreten."[26]

Or, at somewhat more length, to stand for many similar sets of comments:

> Keine Existenzängste (wie heute). Der Zusammenhalt der Menschen war damals sehr eng. Heute Ellenbogengesellschaft sogar in den Familien. Jeder denkt nur noch an sich selbst.
> In der ehemaligen DDR war man sozial abgesichert. Es gab keine Existenzängste wie heute. Heute ist der Mensch nur noch eine Nr. Heute leben wir in einem Bürokratenstaat.[27]

Interestingly, given their previous critiques of lack of political democracy in the GDR, as indicated in the last quotation many felt that political impotence was even worse in the new Germany. One woman, who had been born and grown up in the then Socialist new town of Stalinstadt, later renamed Eisenhüttenstadt, put it as follows:

> In der DDR konnte der Lebensunterhalt durch Arbeit finanziert wer-
> den. Man hatte Arbeit. Betreuung für die Kinder um arbeiten zu
> gehen. Der Lebensunterhalt in BRD (jetzt) ist nicht mehr mit
> eigenen Mitteln aufrecht zu erhalten. (Hartz IV.) Man hat kein
> eigenes Leben mehr. Es wird alles vorbestimmt vom Staat.[28]

People of this generation even registered a sense that previously — despite all the constraints about which they had complained and against which they had eventually come out to demonstrate — the possibility of some form of personal authenticity or self-realization was greater before than after unification: "Es war ein viel sichereres ruhigeres Leben und man hatte mehr Zeit man selbst zu sein."[29] They also frequently commented on the way in which it was previously possible to combine time for family and a full working life.

The groups whom one might more loosely call the 1989ers — those born roughly from the later 1960s onwards and in early adulthood at the time of unification — had again quite contrasting experiences of the periods before and after 1989.[30] They had generally "happy memories" of their childhoods in the GDR: many recalled the activities of the Young Pioneers and Free German Youth as fun, sociable experiences, and they had less exposure to the Stasi than did those who were adults during the GDR. Even where they did have Stasi experiences, these were often treated as less than serious; as one put it: "Ich empfand es als eher belustigend hin und wieder beobachtet und von der Polizei kontrolliert zu werden (wahr-scheinlich aus jugendlichem Leichtsinn?!). Habe aber auch nicht wirklich negative Folgen aushalten müssen — ab und zu Vorladungen oder Befragungen bei der Polizei ließen sich locker aushalten."[31] This particular individual was on the cusp of generations and involved in the various environmental and peace groups around her church, as well as the "unofficial scene" in the 1980s, yet she strongly agreed that it was possible to "lead a perfectly normal life" ("ein ganz normales Leben") — adding, however, "aber was ist schon normal?"

These later cohorts, the 1989ers, were already relatively cosmopolitan or international in outlook, growing up in a period of mass exposure to international media and particularly global youth culture. After unification "Honecker's children" were best placed to take advantage of new opportunities. They had "benefited" — as many saw it — from GDR childcare provision, youth organizations, education, and training programs. They were now able to study and work wherever they wanted, provided their skills and experiences matched economic needs. After unification they mingled with relative ease across cultural and geographical borders. Unlike previous youth cohorts aiming for utopian transformation following moments of historical rupture, the 1989ers were content to make their lives in the present. "Mobilization for a transformative future" was no longer on the historical agenda.

For all the concerns of a changing present, the pre-1945 past would nevertheless not go away. Interpreted and presented differently in East and West, in the 1990s the war years returned to haunt Germans with major controversies over sensitive topics ranging from memorials for victims (as in the case of the Berlin Memorial to the Murdered Jews of Europe) to the involvement of ordinary soldiers as perpetrators (as in the case of the controversial Wehrmacht exhibition) or more general German involvement in the Holocaust (as in the debates unleashed by the publication of Daniel Jonah Goldhagen's controversial analysis *Hitler's Willing Executioners*). Moreover, postunification attempts at "overcoming" the two German dictatorships were linked in complex ways, affecting patterns of self-representation. A perceived degree of western German triumphalism and superiority was undoubtedly rooted in claims of having successfully "overcome" a dictatorship already, while eastern Germans were arguably unduly defensive in their characterizations of life in the GDR and unduly concerned to paint it as "not all bad" in view of both their assumptions about western attitudes (whether justified or not) and their own (fully justified) sense that it was wholly inappropriate to suggest that the GDR was a dictatorship that was broadly similar to the Third Reich. Many eastern Germans may have felt after 1990 that they no longer had any kind of future; others were simply no longer concerned about the future. But the past, it seemed, would always be present.

Conclusions

At the start of her magisterial novel *Kindheitsmuster* Christa Wolf once tellingly remarked: "Das Vergangene ist nicht tot; es ist nicht einmal vergangen. Wir trennen es von uns ab und stellen uns fremd."[32] This is certainly very widely the case for those who lived through the Third Reich and made the transition from Nazism to the two postwar German states. Yet in the case of former GDR citizens, very often a somewhat different kind of relationship between the self and the recent past may be observed. Rather than a distancing ("stellen uns fremd") there was after 1989–90 more often a heightened sense of connection with or yearning for hidden, newly valued aspects of the former East German society that had been fostered within the repressive system of the GDR state, in part because of and in part in spite of it. Increasingly the eastern German "self" after 1989 was even in large measure defined precisely in terms of a remembered pre-1989 social world — a social world that had in complex ways been predicated on the repressive state so many had opposed and for which many people now retrospectively yearned.

In exploring generationally distinct ways in which eastern Germans engaged with the new present of the post-1989 world and reflected on the past they had lost, certain features are notable. First, actual experiences of transition and subsequent readjustment certainly did have an effect on the ways in which people reconceived their lives, but they did not fully determine such reconceptualizations. Previous patterns of engagement with the world — rooted in different periods of socialization, degrees of enthusiasm for one or another cause, personal investments of time and emotion — continued to affect modes of response to the new. At the same time heightened perceptions of the shortcomings of the new world threw into sharp relief some of the previously less consciously grasped aspects of the old, and this across generations. Very large numbers of eastern Germans, irrespective of age, now claimed that there had been better "relationships between people" ("zwischenmenschliche Beziehungen") and more "togetherness" ("Miteinander," "Füreinander," "Zusammensein," "Zusammengehörigkeit") in the GDR; that their society had been in some way kinder than that of the capitalist West; that they had been able to lead more peaceful and "ordered" lives — and all this despite the very obvious physical constraints and the breaches of human rights committed by the SED regime and the Stasi.

In the process of this last, final rupture of the "short twentieth century" in Germany — a rupture without war, which brought to an end the Cold War, and a rupture without the emergence of an entirely new regime or the active mobilization of new carriers of a future-oriented ideology — generations re-formed. But interestingly, unlike after the rupture of 1945, surprisingly large numbers of East Germans after 1989–90 did not reject their past and define themselves against it. The contrast is instructive: in 1945 the Nazi regime was brought down only through defeat in total war and not by Germans themselves, many of whom continued to support Hitler and the Nazi fatherland to the bitter end, whereas the GDR was brought down more or less by mutual consent. Yet within a couple of decades after 1945 the vast majority of Germans rejected what they had previously supported, while in the first two decades after 1990, many eastern Germans, by contrast, positively revalued what they had so recently rejected.

This is a not a political point about which of the two regimes was more or less deserving of later rejection on the part of its former citizens; it is simply a point about the ways in which Germans, across these transitions, redefined their own selves in light of previous regimes to which they had earlier enjoyed (if that is not an inappropriate word in this context) a quite different sort of relationship. Nor, after 1990, did eastern Germans fully embrace all aspects of the new "ideology" of the west — an ideology that was in any event committed to improvements in the present rather than the building of a better future. For the post-Wall youth generations, the future was now, the past a matter of rosy memories rather than real nostalgia. But among older generations there was a remarkable yearning for the past, and this yearning is not to be confused with one of its capitalist forms of expression, namely an *Ostalgie* often expressed for objects and products that capitalists and the tourist trade were only too eager to cash in on. There was a deeper way in which perceptions and representations of the past were intimately bound up with a sense of social relations, and hence a sense of an "east German self." If the SED had never succeeded in its unrealistic aim of creating uniform "socialist personalities," diverse experiences of the GDR had certainly left their mark on succeeding generations of its citizens in ways that they only began to grasp after the demise of the state through which they had lived and that so many had helped to bring down. And whether or not the life stories recounted by eastern Germans stand as adequate histories of this regime, historians cannot fully understand the GDR without taking these subjective experiences, perceptions, and representations of their lives into account.

Notes

I am very grateful to both the Leverhulme Trust and the Arts and Humanities Research Council of the UK for their very generous support of the research on which this paper is based. A fuller version of the general arguments and parts of the text may be found in my book *Dissonant Lives: Generations and Violence through the German Dictatorships* (Oxford: Oxford UP, 2011); a highly condensed summary of some aspects will also be appearing in Italian translation.

[1] But not the "end of history," as Francis Fukuyama sought to argue in *The End of History and the Last Man* (New York: Free Press, 1992).

[2] First results in Deutscher Bundestag, ed., *Materialien der Enquetekommission "Aufarbeitung von Geschichte und Folgen der SED-Diktatur in Deutschland,"* 9 vols. (Frankfurt am Main: Nomos Verlagsgesellschaft, 1995). Also see Mary Fulbrook, "Jenseits der Totalitarismustheorie? Vorläufige Bemerkungen aus sozialgeschichtlicher Perspektive," in *The GDR and Its History: Rückblick und Revision — Die DDR im Spiegel der Enquete-Kommissionen,* ed. Peter Barker (Amsterdam: Rodopi, 2000), 35–53.

[3] The turnover of personnel in East German professional life as a result of "destasification" appeared in some quarters to be trying to make up for inadequate denazification after 1945.

[4] A relatively early articulation by two eastern German historians is Armin Mitter and Stefan Wolle, *Untergang auf Raten: Unbekannte Kapitel der DDR-Geschichte* (Munich: C. Bertelsmann, 1993); on the western German side see for example

Klaus Schroeder, *Der SED-Staat: Partei, Staat und Gesellschaft* (Munich: Hanser Verlag, 1998).

[5] See for example Martin Sabrow et al., *Wohin treibt die DDR-Erinnerung? Dokumentation einer Debatte* (Göttingen: Vandenhoeck and Ruprecht, 2007).

[6] The relevant literature is too vast for a footnote. For an overview see for example Rainer Eppelmann, Bernd Faulenbach, and Ulrich Mählert, eds., *Bilanz und Perspektiven der DDR-Forschung* (Paderborn: Schöningh, 2003). See also my initial suggestion of this approach in "Reckoning with the Past: Heroes, Victims, and Villains in the History of the German Democratic Republic," in *Rewriting the German Past*, ed. Reinhard Alter and Peter Monteath (Atlantic Highlands, NJ: Humanities Press, 1997), 175–96.

[7] For more detailed analysis, see Mary Fulbrook, "Generationen und Kohorten in der DDR. Protagonisten und Widersacher des DDR-Systems aus der Perspektive biographischer Daten," in *Die DDR aus generationengeschichtlicher Perspektive: Eine Inventur*, ed. Annegret Schüle, Thomas Ahbe, and Rainer Gries (Leipzig: Universitätsverlag Leipzig, 2005), 113–30.

[8] For a preliminary analysis of findings from my own research in this area, see "'Normalisation' in Retrospect: East German Perspectives on Their Own Lives," in *Power and Society in the GDR, 1961–1979: The "Normalisation of Rule"?*, ed. Mary Fulbrook (Oxford: Berghahn, 2009), chapter 13.

[9] Christa Wolf, "Unerledigte Widersprüche. Gespräch mit Therese Hörnigk (Juni 1987/Oktober 1988)," in Christa Wolf, *Im Dialog: Aktuelle Texte* (Munich: Deutscher Taschenbuch Verlag, 1994), 29; also reprinted in *DDR-Geschichte in Dokumenten*, ed. Matthias Judt (Berlin: Ch. Links, 1998), 59–60.

[10] The following quotations come from a collection of some 271 lengthy questionnaires (qualitative and quantitative) carried out in the period from 2005 to 2009. Further details and a more quantitative analysis of the results can be found in Fulbrook, "'Normalisation' in Retrospect." My comments are also based on analysis of some forty oral history interviews, which have with one exception not been deployed explicitly here (see discussion below).

[11] 62, F, 1930 (in this and all following such references the initial number is the questionnaire number, M or F denotes gender, and the date is the year of birth of the respondent).

[12] 43, F, 1931.

[13] 85, F, 1930.

[14] 86, M, 1928.

[15] 231, M, 1929.

[16] 151, M, 1928.

[17] Landesarchiv Berlin (LAB), B Rep 015, Nr. 591, "Mein Besuch in Ost-Berlin," First prize, Heidrun H., born 28.8.1944, 8.

[18] A generalization based on the surveys carried out by the Leipzig Central Institute for Youth Research (Zentralinstitut für Jugendforschung) under Professor Walter Friedrich.

[19] 62, F, 1930.

[20] 85, F, 1930.

[21] 52, M, 1925, born Breslau, and 61, M., 1930, from East Prussia — interestingly, both from former "re-settlers" and members of the SED.

[22] 52, M, 1925.

[23] 2, F, 1951.

[24] 56, F, 1949.

[25] 2, F, 1951.

[26] 7, M, 1955.

[27] 8, F, 1957.

[28] 100, F, 1958.

[29] 160, M, 1953.

[30] There are of course differences between cohorts within this period, which will not be addressed in this article.

[31] 152, F, 1960.

[32] Christa Wolf, *Kindheitsmuster* (1976; Darmstadt: Luchterhand, 1979), 9.

11: Competing Master Narratives: *Geschichtspolitik* and Identity Discourse in Three German Societies

Thomas Ahbe

Two Rival German States and Two Competing Master Narratives: *Geschichtspolitik* in the 1950s and 1960s

T HE QUESTION AS TO WHY, following the "peaceful revolution" in the GDR and its accession (*Beitritt*) to the Federal Republic, the issue of "inner unity" continues to be so passionately debated in Germany requires some understanding of the history as well as the deep-rooted ideological and mental positions of the two rival German postwar states.[1] After 1945 escalating conflict over political and economic development was played out in the rivalry between the two German states, and the founding principles of East Germany and West Germany created two opposing political blocs. The master narratives that informed the societies of the two new states had the same goal, namely to try and make sense of the catastrophic National Socialist period and the Second World War and the trauma of German division, but also to exonerate a large percentage of their populations and integrate them into the new system. Both postwar states claimed to have drawn the correct conclusions from the historical catastrophe, and each accused the other of continuities with National Socialism.

The master narratives of both German states sought to establish legitimacy through a distorted image of their Western/Eastern counterpart as is exemplified in the interpretations of the uprising of 17 June 1953. The GDR always regarded this as an attempted putsch orchestrated by Fascist provocateurs sent by the West in which workers, misinformed by Western propaganda, became involved. In West Germany the East German uprising was to become one of the foundation stones of national identity, and until unification this date was the only public holiday in the FRG. Almost every Western commentator characterized the uprising as anti-totalitarian and as a late attempt to make up for the absence of any mass revolt during the Third Reich.[2] On 16 June 1954 the federal government's press and information service duly announced that the uprising that had taken place the year before was conclusive proof that the Germans *did* have the inner strength to withstand dictatorships and tyranny. In 1956 the SPD politician Carlo Schmid stated, "[der 17. Juni] hat viele Flecken hinweggewaschen, mit denen das ruchlose Regime des Nationalsozialismus unseren Namen beschmutzt hat. Dies gibt uns Deutschen wieder das Recht, auch in der Mitte von Völkern, die ihren Kampf um die Freiheit schon längst gewonnen haben, das Haupt hoch zu tragen."[3]

The comparison of the "brown" and "red" dictatorships and talk of totalitarian systems held ideological currency in West Germany until the mid-1960s.[4] Until then the West German attitude to the "Eastern Zone" was mainly informed by propaganda organizations, including, for example, the People's Union for Peace and Freedom, financed by the federal government and the American defense department, the campaigns of the nonpartisan Committee for an Indivisible Germany, and those US-subsidized publishers who offered left-wing criticism of the Communist dictatorship in the East.[5] The GDR, on the other hand, sought to provoke by stressing the Federal Republic's strong personal ties with the Third Reich. But it was not only through the myth of anti-Fascism that the GDR sought legitimacy. One of the central tenets of its legitimization discourse was the rhetoric concerning the Fascist and revanchist powers that were allegedly dominant in the FRG.[6] In 1965 the GDR state publishing house issued the so-called Brown Book in three editions, documenting the National Socialist past of some twelve hundred members of the elite who were now active in every professional sector in the FRG. The book allowed the GDR to kill two birds with one stone: on the one hand the normally isolated East German state was able to generate international interest; on the other it could put pressure on its Western competitor.

Once the (German) Basic Treaty of 1972 had eased the relationship between the two states, mutual perceptions began to change, especially the West Germans' view of the East Germans. This was largely a result of the personal impressions gained through visits to relatives, business trips, and, later, school excursions to the GDR, as well as the observations of West German journalists, who were newly established and accredited in the GDR.[7] As well as offering a critique of those in power, the latter were concerned with the problems of daily life in the GDR and considered these in the context of the state's ideals and official self-representation, which also served the East German population as a useful point of comparison. For most West Germans, especially young adults, the GDR was no longer "evil" or the totalitarian Communist enemy, but rather a country of unfamiliar Germans who were simply different from "us" in many ways.

In the 1970s and 1980s West German research into the GDR in the fields of contemporary history and the social sciences was influenced by modernization theory, conflict theory, elite theory, and systems theory and thus followed trends in mainstream international research. After 1990 it was totalitarianism theory that enjoyed an unexpected renaissance.[8] The historical treatment of the GDR began to prioritize certain themes — political structures and the apparatus of coercion, crimes and terror, and the victims. The extent to which the conformity or identification of large groups of the GDR population with the regime had stabilized East German society was of less interest.

The dominance of totalitarianism theory was reflected in the work of a number of academic institutions. Soon after it was established the government of the new federal state of Saxony decided to establish the Hannah Arendt Institute for Research on Totalitarianism, which began its work in 1993. Through research, conferences, and the funding of doctoral studies the institute focuses on research into the Communist and National Socialist regimes and publishes the results in various journals including the institute's own. Beyond academic debates among contemporary historians and social scientists, the totalitarianism concept became paradigmatic in politics, the media, and political education. This discourse led to polarizations within unified German society as exemplified by political debates on recent history and broader debates on the development of memorial sites.

Middle-Class and Working-Class Society

The main tendencies in the *Geschichtspolitik* (politics of history) of East and West Germany as summarized above influenced subsequent generations and especially people working in politics, culture, education, academia, and the media. People from all walks of life underwent different kinds of socialization in East and West Germany. In the 1950s attempts were made to alter the self-perception of the working class in the FRG and to encourage a middle-class consciousness. Dirk Schindelbeck und Volker Ilgen describe a campaign conducted in 1956 in their 1999 study *"Haste was, biste was!" Werbung für die Soziale Marktwirtschaft*. An advertisement from the end of that year reads,

> Der Klassenkampf ist zu Ende. Den Begriff des Proletariers gibt es nicht mehr. Im freien Deutschland vollzieht sich eine geschichtliche Wandlung: der ehemals klassenbewusste Arbeiter wird zum selbstbewussten, freien Bürger. Ein Mann, der auf lange Sicht plant, der für seine Kinder eine gründliche Schulung verlangt, der durch Eigentum die Freiheit seiner Familie zu sichern sucht, das ist der Arbeiter von heute.[9]

In the East, too, propaganda talked of a "geschichtliche Wandlung" (historical turn). On the centenary of the 1848 revolution a huge banner hanging in the center of war-damaged Leipzig declared the end of the bourgeois epoch: "Das Bürgertum hat 1948 und in der Folgezeit versagt. Die Führung im Kampf und Einheit, Demokratie und Frieden ist der Arbeiterklasse zugefallen."[10]

In the East denazification was part of an effort to end the class system. The middle class, the Junkers, and most of the landed gentry no longer played a role in the economy, hence lost their influence on society and everyday life. Some of them left for the West, as did many of those people who did not want to be part of the new society or who had to flee. The social profile of the East German elite thus changed: between 1945 and 1955 for example, one hundred fifty thousand former production workers took on leading roles in the state and economy.[11] A working-class society thus developed. The farmers, doctors, engineers, professors, and school directors may have stayed as they were and non-working-class social milieus still existed, but these had a working-class accent. The sociologist Wolfgang Engler describes the normative and dominant influence of the working class thus:

> Die Ostdeutschen lebten in einer Gesellschaft, in der die Arbeiterschaft sozial und kulturell dominierte und die anderen Teilgruppen mehr oder weniger "verarbeiterlichten". Es wäre eine Absurdität zu behaupten, die ostdeutschen Arbeiter hätten die politische Herrschaft ausgeübt. Aber das soziale Zepter hielten sie in der Hand. Anschauungen, Meinungen, Konventionen, Kleidungs- und Konsumgewohnheiten und nicht zuletzt die Alltagssitten richteten sich nach den Normen und Idealen der arbeitenden Klassen.[12]

The focus of everyday life in East Germany was therefore quite different from that in the bourgeois West. Over generations the East German mentality began to change, though the GDR's ideological program played only a minor role in this. Representatives of the working class did not need to be advocates of state ideology, and the bourgeois milieu was easily reconciled with pro-Socialist sentiments.

The oft-cited "social warmth" that existed in the GDR, the feeling of social equity, also undoubtedly had a suffocating and destructive side. According to Engler:

> Die Feindseligkeit, die konsequenten Außenseitern in der DDR entgegenschlug und zur inneren Kapitulation drängte, wurzelte in demselben Egalitarismus, der in anderen Zusammenhängen Solidarität verbürgte. In einer arbeiterlichen Gesellschaft soll sich niemand über die anderen erheben, aber auch niemand untergehen. Wer nicht nur ungewöhnlich lebte, sondern überdies Rat und Hilfe der anderen verschmähte, selber Auskunft wußte, provozierte die Normalitätserwartungen der Umwelt gleich doppelt. Ihm war nicht beizukommen und auch nicht zu helfen. Das zurückgewiesene

Beistandsangebot verband sich mit dem enttäuschten
Konformitätsverlangen und pervertierte. Wer notorisch auf seiner
Arroganz bestand, der durfte nicht nur, der sollte scheitern und die
Überlegenheit der kollektiven Vernunft möglichst schmerzlich
erfahren.[13]

For those who had internalized middle-class conventions and patterns of
behavior, this proletarianization of East German society meant the loss of
these traditionally held and normative functions. This is the perspective
from which the author Irene Böhme comments on the process:

> Sittenzerfall — Der ganze bürgerliche Plunder, über Bord mit ihm.
> Knicks und Verbeugung der Kinder: ein Zeichen der Verkrüppelung.
> Aufstehen vor Älteren, Vorgesetzten: ein Überrest des
> Untertanengeistes. Wir alle sind "per Du", denn wir sind alle in der
> Gewerkschaft. Bei Tisch benehmen wir uns, wie es in einer
> Proletarierküche üblich ist. Mit Schürze und Hausschuhen auf die
> Straße, mit dem Blaumann ins Gasthaus, die Arbeitskleidung ist ein
> Ehrenkleid. Bunte Perlonschürzen überfluten Fabriken, Läden,
> Ambulatorien und Kontore. Bald bemerkt niemand mehr, wie häßlich
> sie sind. Sie sind praktisch. . . . Zur neuen Art des Zusammenlebens
> gehört, daß man anders miteinander redet als früher. Man spricht
> deftig, grob und geradezu, nennt das offen und ehrlich.[14]

Though exaggerated, this reference to the aesthetic and formal dimensions of the workers' society does underline its difference from bourgeois
society.

Studies into people's perception of their class have shown to what
extent the psychological and ideological paradigms of the working and
middle classes have left their mark. These studies present people's subjective views; objective sociological criteria are not considered. It is interesting to see how the two now unified populations continue to define
themselves according to subjective class distinctions. In 1992–93, 61% of
those from the former GDR, descendents of the workers' society, identified themselves as working or lower class and only 37% as middle class. It
was almost exactly the opposite in the west, where only 29% saw themselves as working or lower class and 57% saw themselves as members of the
middle class.

In both societies, then, a significant number of people identify with a
particular class to which, according to objective, sociological criteria, they
do not actually belong. The class with which they identify is that which
represented the respectable pillar of society in the narratives of the two
German states. In the East this was the working class; in the West it was
the middle class. One might have expected these differences to level off
gradually once the GDR and its conditions of socialization had vanished,
but studies in 2000 and 2001 showed that the situation had barely

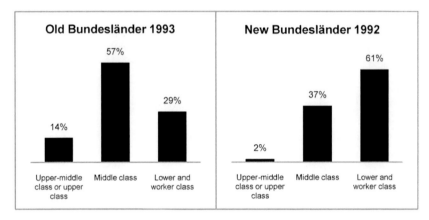

Fig. 11.1. Subjective class identification in west and east Germany in 1992 and 1993. Data taken from Thomas Gensicke, Die neuen Bundesbürger. Eine Transformation ohne Integration (Opladen: Westdeutscher Verlag, 1998), 148.

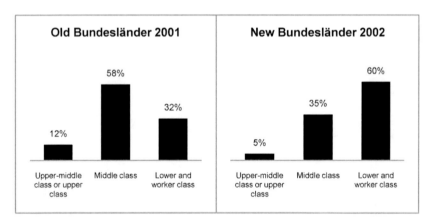

Fig. 11.2. Subjective class identification in west and east Germany in 2001 and 2002. Data from Gunnar Winkler, ed., Sozialreport 2002: Daten und Fakten zur sozialen Lage in den neuen Bundesländern (Berlin: Trafo Verlag, 2002), 48.

changed. Such identification with a particular class appears to be deeply ingrained in the mentalities of both eastern and western Germans.

The Socio-Psychological Aspects of Unification

Competing notions of normality that evolved from socialization processes in East and West Germany and had not previously been given much thought suddenly collided in the years after unification. This process has been addressed in a large number of memoirs and academic studies and through wide media coverage. Studies by the political scientist and therapist Wolf Wagner have proved especially instructive here. Wagner moved from Berlin to teach at a continuing-education college in Erfurt in the former GDR and describes the tensions that emerged in the patterns of communication between eastern Germans and western Germans in the 1990s. He adopts the "culture shock" model, according to which successful communication depends on spontaneous communication patterns and established negotiation practices, the significance and appropriateness of which are repeatedly reaffirmed within a specific cultural context.[15] When people from different cultural backgrounds come together and behave according to their usual patterns, they are often not understood as they would expect to be, resulting in a breakdown in communication. Wagner offers simple examples to encapsulate just how conflict-laden the differences between eastern and western German socialization were in the 1990s. In the eastern German context, for example, it is usual to shake hands with colleagues at the beginning and at the end of the day, something that happens less often in the west. An adherence to habitual modes of behavior can lead to undesired consequences and frustrations in the daily intercultural interaction between east and west Germans. The eastern Germans may be convinced that the western Germans are refusing to shake their hand, that they are arrogant, aloof, and rude. The western Germans, on the other hand, may think of the eastern Germans, who seemingly never stop trying to shake hands, as overly familiar, old-fashioned, and provincial. Similar mutual misunderstandings emerge when it comes to the conventions of small talk. Whereas eastern Germans are prone to talking about shortcomings, grievances, and even personal problems, western Germans prefer simple and trivial topics. In their respective cultures this works perfectly well: the style of communication in the east engenders closeness, a sense of belonging, empathy, or even solidarity; likewise, the established western German conduct produces a comfortable, positive situation in which the agents can be as witty or discrete as is necessary. It is only when eastern and western Germans come together and behave as is "proper" according to their respective conventions that friction occurs. The eastern Germans regard the talkative western Germans as superficial and standoffish, and the latter in turn believe the former to be carping, maudlin, and impossible to please.

Similar differences in western and eastern German socialization are apparent in the ways in which conflicts between groups are handled. While eastern Germans have a tendency to agree tacitly, to compromise, but also to ignore conflict, western Germans are generally more competitive and independent, and challenging another individual is regarded as normal rather than disruptive. When these two communication styles come into contact, the eastern Germans regard the western Germans as aggressive, domineering, and egocentric and consider themselves to be supportive, ready to compromise, and able to see the whole picture. Western Germans, by contrast, see the eastern Germans as cowardly, conformist, and inhibited, whereas they think of themselves as open-minded, unafraid, and honest. Accordingly, those socialized in West Germany see themselves as being in competition with those around them and strive harder for individuality and self-fulfillment. According to Wagner, for those socialized in the GDR, community takes precedence over individuality, and the cohesion and attunement of the collective is held in higher regard.

The differences between eastern and western German socialization are perhaps best illustrated by the impressions of a West German journalist who lived in the GDR in the 1970s and an eastern German journalist's experiences in the 1990s. They offer two reflections of the so-called spur of ambition (*Stachel des Ehrgeizes*), or different forms of self-presentation. During the course of her research into the GDR the West German journalist often visited private parties and noticed that West German women often made the best first impression since they were more glamorous. Apart from a little eyeshadow, the East German women avoided make-up altogether. During the course of the evening, however, the East German women would begin to catch up: they had, she noted, "eine unnachahmliche Art, zu beobachten, leise zu lächeln und dann plötzlich aus dem Stand heraus sehr direkt zu sein." Moreover,

> Dahinter stecke ein Selbstbewusstsein, das nicht von äußeren Dingen abhänge. Andererseits brächte die Gleichheit einen Typ Mensch hervor, dem der Stachel des Ehrgeizes fehle, der gehorsam, obrigkeitsgläubig und angepasst sei. Biederkeit allüberall. Die Salzstangen, die Sofakissen mit Kerbe, die Parteinelken in Zellophan, die verstaubten Blattpflanzen unter Neonlicht, die Aktentaschen und Wattejacken, die geblümten Einkaufsbeutel und die Nylonblusen überm Rock, außerdem werde zuviel Torte gegessen. Alles wahr, alles unwahr.[16]

The journalist from the GDR takes this as a cue for her own observations:

> Der Knick im Sofakissen kommt in den besten Familien vor, auch im Westen. Biederkeit zeigt sich so oder anders. Provinzialität, Mittelmaß und Opportunismus existieren in vielerlei Spielart. Auch Karrierismus kann spießig sein. Kurz nach Mauerfall bin ich auf einem wichtigen Empfang eines wichtigen Verlagshauses. Man plaudert, macht einander Komplimente, ist nett, wo es sich lohnt. Da erscheint der Boss. Ich kenne ihn, weil sein Konzern die Zeitung, bei der ich arbeite, aufgekauft hat und er öfter in die Redaktion kommt, um Auflagensteigerung anzumahnen. Der Boss steht an einer Art Tresen, ich daneben, in diesem Moment bin ich der Macht zufällig nahe. Und

dann, erst ungläubig, dann irritiert, nehme ich eine unterirdische Bewegung wahr. Männer im Smoking drängeln mich Schritt für Schritt weg vom Tresen, weg von dem Mann, der die Macht verkörpert. Unaufhaltsam wie eine Naturgewalt schiebt sich die schwarze Herde näher und näher zum Mächtigen. Als gehorche sie einer Vorbestimmung. In der Herde ist auch der nette Kollege aus Hamburg, mit dem ich mich eben noch prima unterhalten hatte. Ein physisch spürbarer Verdrängungsvorgang spielte sich da ab, unbewusst und instinktiv, sozusagen genetisch, der Stärkere überlebt. Nach zehn Minuten bin ich Weg vom Fenster, der "Stachel des Ehrgeizes" war mir noch nicht gewachsen.[17]

The differences of opinion described by Wagner — conformist/authentic East Germans and egocentric/individualistic West Germans — are typical of the conflict between the middle classes from the former East and West Germany. After unification the gulf was at its greatest in the communication practices and self-presentation of employees, qualified personnel, and academics. Other east-west conflicts arose in the world of the eastern German industrial worker, where it was less a question of behavior and conduct and more an issue of eastern German industrial workers having lost their power to negotiate, the "passive strength" that they had had in the GDR, as well as their symbolic status as the most important, indeed, the "vanguard" class. The industrial sociologist Werner Schmidt identifies not just the usual conflict of interests between workers and managers but the clash between those socialized in middle-class and working-class societies. In his study of the transformation process in the metalworking industry, he found a so-called ideology of productive work among industrial workers from the former GDR. Related to this, according to Schmidt, is "die schwer korrigierbare Überzeugung, daß die eigene Gruppe die einzig wirklich produktive, . . . und damit wichtigste sei, auf die niemand verzichten könne."[18] The same ideology was used to identify those groups that did not actually do any (meaningful) work. Workers distinguished themselves from those "below" them — the "lazy," the "anti-social" and "work-shy" — and from those "above" (in higher positions) — the "big heads" and the "useless lot up there."[19] After 1990 this working-class consciousness and "ideology of productive work" clashed with new procedures and hierarchies. The eastern German manager of a ball-bearing works described the asymmetrical privileges that had been introduced between 1992 and 1994 and the simultaneous dwindling respect of the worker thus: "Wir haben also, wir haben immer gelernt: ein Mensch ist ein Mensch! Egal, ob der nun Werkleiter ist oder ein Kumpel an der Maschine, du hast die alle gleich behandelt. So. Und das ist hier [im nun westlich gemanagten Wälzlagerwerk] nicht so."[20] Both of these examples from the 1990s serve to highlight how different the results of being socialized in the workers' society are from being socialized in bourgeois society.

The cultural phenomenon of the working class is also sustained by the economic and social factors that were behind the transformation process in the east.[21] The economy of the former GDR is dependent on and dominated by that in the west. The new *Bundesländer* thus constitute "eine Region mit kapitalistischer Marktwirtschaft ohne einheimisches Kapital und einheimische Eliten."[22] In the two decades of transformation the new *Länder* have not, for the most part, been able to emulate the West German model of middle-class society or to establish the middle class required for this purpose.[23] Instead, 25% of the population in the new *Länder* are now part of the "abgehängte Prekariat" ("neglected underclass").[24] Only 4% of western Germans belong to this same group. The members of this "underclass" comprise skilled workers on the minimum wage, the unemployed, people attempting to be self-employed, and those on welfare benefits. Another significant group is the unemployed, half of whom are caught in the spiral of poverty and hopelessness generated by the Hartz IV reforms to the welfare state. Of those people of working age, it is these individuals who have the least job security (if they have a job at all) and who face the greatest financial uncertainty. They see themselves on the losers' side and without any opportunity of getting back on track.

East-west differences continue to exist in everyday life. There are differences in fertility rates, in attitudes toward justice and freedom, and in combining motherhood with a career. In 2004 eastern German mothers were having their first child on average about a year earlier than those in the west,[25] and eastern German mothers between the ages of twenty-five and forty-five are four times more likely to agree with the idea of combining career and motherhood than their western counterparts.[26] More western Germans prefer the idea of having no children and of staying single, and when western German women do have children, they tend to marry. Eastern Germans, by contrast, are more interested in having children but consider parenthood and marriage much less a matter of course. For this reason the eastern German pattern is described as a "Kombination von Familialismus und Deinstitutionalisierung," which is to say that there is less faith in (new) institutions than there is in the family (as authority).[27] Accordingly, while parents and children are emotionally closer in the east than in the west, there is a greater distance between them and social institutions. This applies also to the institution of marriage: at 58%, the number of children born out of wedlock is almost three times higher in the east than the 22% in the west.[28]

Eastern and western German identities also vary in terms of social values. Eastern Germans are generally as committed to the state as they are to issues of freedom and equal opportunity,[29] hence they also perceive considerable tension between the values that they believe should be a priority for society and those that actually are its priority. They believe that social justice should be the most important value but find that in fact "freedom" is.[30] They believe that the value of freedom is not sufficiently emphasized in connection with other key values such as social justice and responsibility, and that it is therefore played down. This is reflected in the varying interpretations of the value of freedom and justice between eastern and western Germans. While most educated western Germans understand freedom as "freedom of action," eastern Germans define it as freedom from need.[31] Social justice, meanwhile, is understood by the majority of eastern Germans to mean a society in which "everyone has the same opportunities" and not, as is often suggested, a society in which "everyone has the same standard of living."[32]

East German Discourses since 1990

Once the smaller GDR had decided to accede to the larger (old) FRG, which involved taking on all of its institutions and norms, the old East German elite and its skilled and managerial staff were ousted as a result of legal rulings and the dismantling and restructuring of businesses and institutions. They were partly replaced by western Germans and also by those members of the eastern German sub-elite whose professional advancement had been hindered by the GDR authorities. In general, eastern Germans remain underrepresented in elite positions and managerial roles. Sociologists in Germany routinely conduct detailed surveys of elites, and the last such pre-unification study was carried out in 1981. By the time of the next study, in 1995, it was clear that the representation of eastern Germans in various elite sectors in Germany needed to be researched. In 1995, 20% of the population were from the former GDR, but the percentage of eastern Germans in elite positions was an altogether different matter. To give some examples, in the judiciary and military the percentage of eastern Germans in elite positions was zero, in the economy it was 0.4%, and in academia 7.3%. At 12% and 13% the underrepresentation of eastern Germans was slightly less dramatic in the media and culture industries. The one area where they were not underrepresented was in politics.[33] Overall, the supervision and management of the authorities, the economy, academia, media, and culture in the new *Länder* was in the hands of the so-called *Wessis*, and these personnel and ideological hierarchies have proved to be self-perpetuating; in 2004 the numbers of western Germans in leading managerial positions in the economy and in the public sector had increased further.[34] By the end of the 1990s, however, the first generation of eastern German journalists, social scientists, and historians had qualified and trained under the guidance of western German mentors and begun to exert some influence on eastern discourse, and now the issue of eastern or western German provenance has begun to lose meaning; of future significance will be the question of identification — in other words, the guiding values and master narratives of the new members of the "media and political classes."[35]

These personnel developments and the related mindset form the parameters for the discourse on eastern German identity since 1990. In united Germany the media approached this new development in the way that all media does in a modern critical culture: it surveyed, investigated, interpreted the "other," and compared it to western German norms. Discussing eastern Germans — the stranger, the other — meant talking about one's own identity. Since 1989 ongoing "Ost-Diskurse" have determined the presentation of the eastern Germans and their culture.[36]

Three factors have governed the way the "Ost-Diskurse" have been shaped and articulated in the media. First, national broadcasters and broadsheets were able to take over the small market in the former GDR without any major editorial changes. Second, the management of the newly implemented broadcasters and most of those working for the newly restructured regional newspapers in the new federal states were from the west.[37] And third, the eastern Germans failed to provide an adequate professional counter-discourse. Eastern German spokespeople were used only so long as they conformed to the established direction of the "Ost-Diskurse."

The westernization of the eastern German media landscape meant that the eastern Germans saw themselves, their GDR past, and their culture — including their success or failure in the process of rebuilding the East ("Aufbau Ost") — described and evaluated mainly from a western German perspective and thus missed a forum through which their views could be presented, be it the eastern German experience of the transformation process or their newly-won insights into the GDR and the recently unified Germany. The national papers, that is the western German print media, mostly wrote about the eastern Germans from a western perspective and were therefore ignored by eastern German readers.[38]

Ostalgie as Reaction

One of the consequences of this absence was the development of various forms of *Ostalgie*, five of which will be outlined below.

1. *Ostalgie* in Advertising

The advertising campaign for a cola brand originating in the GDR is paradigmatic for the commercially motivated use of this discourse. In 1992 Club Cola identified itself as eastern German; its slogan — "Hurrah, I'm still alive!" ("Hurra, ich lebe noch!") — declared its allegiance and portrayed it as a survivor of the transition process. The

Fig. 11.3. Advertisement from 1992. Kultur- und Werbegeschichtliches Archiv Freiburg.

remainder of the advertising text — "it may be laughed off by some, but it won't be killed off" ("Von einigen belächelt, ist sie doch nicht tot-zukriegen") — echoed the discussions about identity being conducted in eastern German canteens and living rooms, essentially: We made it and we won't let them get us down. The advertisement continues: "Club Cola — The Berlin cola. Naturally refreshing. Not as sweet, but plenty of taste. . . ." ("Club-Cola — die Cola aus Berlin. Natürlich frisch. Weniger süß. Aber mit viel Geschmack . . ."). It thus takes on some of the eastern German stereotypes of the western Germans, namely that the "other" Germans are perfumed and thus artificial, fake — that is, the opposite of "naturally refreshing, not as sweet."[39] The eastern German electronics brand RFT provides another example of the use of *Ostalgie* in advertising in trying to attract customers by inverting previously existing assumptions in the slogan "east German and therefore good" ("ostdeutsch, daher gut").

Fig. 11.4. Advertisement from 1992. From Horizont: Zeitung für Marketing und Medien 45.6 (November 1992): 40.

2. *Ostalgie* as a Layman's Practice

Ostalgie has frequently been identified as GDR nostalgia. Some define it as an increasing trivialization of the GDR accompanied by a defensive position regarding the challenges of transformation, or even as a provocative polemic that relativizes the crimes of the GDR state. Such forms did exist, but *Ostalgie* in the 1990s was more complex. It was an informal way of

working through profound changes. These included the "peaceful revolution" and the sudden dissolution of the GDR — which had always emphasized its power and longevity — the sudden replacement of its omnipresent
and uniform range of products, and the subsequent introduction of the
federal German system in East Germany. By attending or organizing
"*Ostalgie* parties," members of certain eastern German milieus were finally
able to bid farewell to the GDR and take a degree of self-assurance with
them into the new present.

Ostalgie parties were like historical carnivals: the costumes were typical
GDR outfits or uniforms, the rooms were decorated with flags, portraits
of politicians, and banners sporting ironic propaganda slogans. Just as
carnivals have a stage repertoire, so, too, did *Ostalgie* parties: Honecker
and Ulbricht look-alikes presented the grotesque pathos and convoluted
jargon of the GDR's self-identity, hit songs and pop songs were played,
parodies of Socialist hymns and "workers' songs and battle songs," and
people sometimes danced to modified Young Pioneer songs. Those who
attended these parties may have been wistful, but they were also celebrat-
ing this restaged GDR's loss of power.

3. *Ostalgie* as Business

In both the former East and West Germany, industry has capitalized on
East German memories repackaged as books, audio-recordings, games,
and cult and designer products. But *Ostalgie* products also serve new fashions, for symbols and signs from the GDR period are now welcomed by
young people looking for a style that distinguishes them from others.

4. *Ostalgie* in Films and TV Shows Made after 1990

These films and programs are a composite of the third and fifth examples
since they are just as much about business as they are messages about self-
understanding and the defense of an eastern German identity. Trivial comedies such as *Go Trabi Go* (1991) and *Sonnenallee* (1999), which offered a
slapstick treatment of the GDR past, were particularly successful. The
tragi-comedy *Good Bye, Lenin!* (2003) offered a more thoughtful perspective and duly won awards at home and abroad. It did not just try to make
sense of the GDR past or thematize the post-1990 problems between east
and west, but also managed to address the mourning of the disappearance
of the GDR, the project with which the protagonist's mother and a not
insignificant number of eastern German viewers had been engaged for a
considerable part of their life, as well as a non-judgmental belief in a
Socialist vision. It was notable that when the then minister of culture
Christina Weiss invited members of the Bundestag to a special screening of
the film on 2 April 2003, only a third of them attended. In the summer of
the same year, various TV stations began broadcasting "*Ostalgie* Shows."[40]
The Trabis, mopeds, wall-to-wall cupboards and domestic products,

DDR-Box
Die Grundausstattung
Blechdose, 23 x 23 x 7 cm
14,95 €, 26,90 SFr*
ISBN 3-359-01470-7

Das dicke DDR-Buch
224 S. mit vielen, durch-
gängig farbigen
Abbildungen, geb.
mit SU
19,90 €, 34,90 SFr
ISBN 3-359-01445-6

Das Rekordbuch
224 S. mit vielen, durch-
gängig farbigen
Abbildungen, geb.
mit SU
19,90 €, 34,90 SFr
ISBN 3-359-01461-8

Fig. 11.5. "DDR Box" and GDR books published by Eulenspiegel-Verlag Berlin, from Eulenspiegel's Autumn 2004 catalogue.

fashion and pop music of the GDR were reproduced on stage while artists, athletes, and TV stars from the former GDR, as well as western GDR correspondents, chatted about East Germany amid these props. Criticism concerning the programs' aesthetic was uniform, and the political assessment of the *Ostalgie* shows provoked heated debates and even the conclusion, "They minimize the dangers that represent an ideological threat to democracy and ridicule the victims."[41]

5. *Ostalgie* as Marginalized Counter-Discourse

The *Ostalgie* parties are over. What remains is a multitude of amateurish GDR museums, a few of which are now beginning to achieve professional standards. It seems as though the people who established "alternative" GDR museums did so in order to present a counter to the "official" and professional GDR museums, where the emphasis is on representing repression and indoctrination as well as the poverty and ugliness of daily life in the GDR.

The various small-circulation newspapers, internet platforms, underfinanced journals, and small publishing houses are an important aspect of this counter-discourse. They provide many professionals with a forum not available to them in the better-established institutions and media. Contributing to this discourse are former GDR academics and professionals who lost their positions after 1990. On the one hand, GDR history is now written from a Socialist perspective that is no longer restricted by party discipline, censorship, and the once off-limits archives. In other words this is a version of GDR history that was not possible under the specific conditions governing academic research in East Germany. On the other hand it is a reaction to the dominant discourse on confrontation with the GDR past. The questions posed within this discourse are addressed and discussed from a personal perspective, and the results of official research into the GDR are added to or amended. Sometimes the contributors to this discourse seek to emphasize that they were right at the time, defending their opinions just as polemically and tendentiously as those defending the opposite view.

These aspects of *Ostalgie* do not by themselves constitute an eastern German identity. Through their representation in the media they also define western German identity, presenting it as a counter-identity to that in the east. The specific character of the western Germans' discourse on the former GDR, which in the 1990s led to the aforementioned gaps in the discourse and the emergence of *Ostalgie*, does not appear much changed today, as several recent articles analyzing recent media discourses have shown.[42] These conclude that the media image of eastern Germans, which sometimes relies on a highly selective use of facts, continues to support western German identities.[43] What this means for eastern Germans is that they operate in a (media) world in which the media's prevailing view of them is as an unknown, "foreign" group. This view stems from a western German position that, as the Germanist Kersten Sven Roth has convincingly argued, functions as the "Normal Null."[44] "Eastern German discourses" determine the rhetoric and the ways of thinking about the former GDR. They comprise a "wirklichkeitserzeugender Modus" (method that shapes reality), a socio-institutional matrix of understanding, interpretation, and presentation.[45] All of this means that the competing identities rooted in German division do not diminish but in fact are reasserted.[46]

The specific eastern German identity depicted through these discourses is often seen as romanticizing or suppressing the GDR, or even as constituting a direct threat to democracy. Surveys, however, do not substantiate these fears. Only a small percentage of eastern Germans (10% in 2002[47] and 2006,[48] and 9% in 2010[49]) want to "have the GDR back at all costs." Surveys conducted in 2010 offer a more differentiated picture. A significant number of eastern Germans confirmed that life is better for them now compared to life in the GDR: 19% agreed that life had mostly improved in the years since 1990, and 23% agreed that the years have "improved rather than worsened." This contrasts with the 27% of eastern Germans who believe that life during this period "has improved as much as it has worsened" and the 18% for whom life after unification has "worsened rather than improved."[50] In total then, only 42% of eastern Germans see themselves as on the winning side. This is partly due to the fact that East German workers, who in 1990 constituted 63% of the GDR population, count as "unification's biggest losers."[51] Half of them have been forced into early retirement, into job-creation schemes, into low-capital start-up businesses, and into unemployment, while many women have had to give up their careers altogether. A quarter of the eastern German population is living in unfavorable economic circumstances ("abgehängte Prekariat") and the majority of this group comprises members of the former working class of the GDR.[52]

A rather different picture emerges when eastern Germans compare their current lives not with their lives in the GDR, but with those of contemporary western Germans. Although 42% of eastern Germans identify improvements in their personal lives, they still feel themselves to be members of the eastern German community and as such feel they are second-class citizens. In 1995, 72%[53] of eastern Germans believed this; in 2002 the figure was 57%,[54] and it was 64%[55] in 2008. One of the possible reasons for this is that as a "dependent economy," a region with a capitalist economy but with "no local capital or indigenous elite," eastern Germany makes the west wealthier — while the west poses obstacles to development in the east.[56] The east lacks the local elites that might exert independent influence, articulate the eastern German experience, opinions, and wishes, and utilize economic, social, and cultural resources to facilitate a more independent eastern German society and help overcome the differences between east and west.

The discrepancies between eastern Germany and western Germany are in part attributable to the significant differences in eastern and western Germans' savings and salaries, which have hardly changed in the twenty years since unification. In 1996 eastern German employees earned 75% of what those in western Germany earned, and this figure had risen to only 79.6% in 2009.[57] The differences in average financial assets in east and west are even more pronounced. West Germans aged seventy or over have on average savings and assets of 62,400 euros compared with the 23,700 euros of their contemporaries in the east; for those aged between sixty and sixty-nine the ratio is 52,200 euros in the west to 20,500 in the east; for those aged between fifty and fifty-nine the ratio is 38,100 euros in the west to 17,700 euros in the east. It is only among younger generations that the differences are less marked.[58]

The feeling of being second-class citizens, still widespread among eastern Germans, is based as much on the tangible sense of being materially worse off as it is on the feeling that the specific memories, interpretations, and values of most of the former GDR's population are not integrated into "eastern German discourses" in the media, education, and politics, but simply ignored or even stigmatized. This is particularly evident in the remembrance culture and the politics of history.

Opposing Memories in Two Decades of German Unity

Political scientists, historians, sociologists, and cultural historians have carried out detailed research into the GDR in the two decades since its collapse.[59] Both the nature of inquiry and the interpretation of results, however, tend to be from a western German perspective. Furthermore, the political and media discourses present a one-sided account of the current research in history and the social sciences: the history of the SED regime and its crimes still resonates more profoundly than does the GDR's social, cultural, and everyday history, something that was especially apparent in the anniversary year of 2009.[60]

These discourses have led to a fragmentation of collective memory of the GDR, of which the historian Martin Sabrow has identified three forms:[61]

(1) the state's preferred memory of the dictatorship, which is predominant in public memory and focuses principally on the apparatus of power and repression and on the duality between perpetrators and victims. This type of memory attaches greater importance to the fundamental difference between political freedom and subjugation than to socio-economic benefits and thus regards the Stasi rather than "the feeling of security within society" as the key to understanding and evaluating the GDR.

(2) the memory of having adapted oneself to the regime to "get by," which is predominant throughout the society of the former GDR and centers on the conflicts, solutions, and successes in a predominantly heteronomous society. These memories are concerned with the relationship between the power of the state and everyday normality. It is thus a narrative of "the right life in the wrong one" and of self-assertion in politically and materially challenged circumstances — in other words the sentiment that "we will not allow our biographies to be taken from us; not everything was bad."

(3) the memory of progress that clings to the Socialist or post-capitalist project ideology, which is much less present in public memory and is maintained by former members of the GDR elite and by younger left-wing activists. In addition to the process of sanitizing and justifying the GDR past, the central issue concerns the moral and political comparison of the two German states. Major contemporary problems such as the global financial crisis and the consequences of German military deployment are thus always bound up with the question of the GDR's legitimacy. This form of memory can be summarized using an old GDR phrase coined in the sixteenth-century Peasant's War: "our grandchildren will fight it out better."

There is now a clear difference between the western German idea of the GDR, which is largely shaped by contemporary history, and that of most eastern Germans, and this is evident in the surveys that consider the GDR's historical legitimacy. Most eastern Germans surveyed do not believe that the GDR was a reprehensible regime that was doomed to fail from the start. When asked whether "it was an attempt to build a fairer society that ultimately failed," eastern Germans answered as follows:[62]

	Yes	To some extent	No
1990	63.4	19.3	12.2
1995	74.8	14.9	6.6
1999	72.9	17.3	7.1

Eastern responses to the question of whether the GDR was an *Unrechtstaat* (state not governed by the rule of law) make for interesting reading. In 1994, not long after the GDR's demise, 33% answered "true," 17% were unsure and 50% said "untrue." Western Germans saw things quite differently:[63]

If someone says: "The SED state was an *Unrechtsstaat*," would you say it is true or untrue? (Figures in percent)

June 1994	Western German	Eastern German
True	73	33
Untrue	15	50
Undecided	12	17
Total	100	100

The situation in 2009 was different due to the new generations surveyed. That eastern German opinion had changed was evident from a survey conducted by the Institute for Market Research in Leipzig for the magazine *Super Illu*, which published the results in March 2009:[64]

"Was the GDR an *Unrechtsstaat*?" (Figures in percent)

March 2009	Total East Germans	18–29 year olds	30–49 year olds	50 years and over
yes	28	32	29	25
to some extent	25	18	23	29
no	41	37	43	41

It is noticeable that the number of those unsure as to whether the GDR was an *Unrechtsstaat* ("to some extent") had risen to 25%, and there had been a larger decrease in the numbers of those who saw the GDR as an *Unrechtsstaat* than in those who denied this. What is particularly striking about the 2009 survey is the difference between age groups: on the one hand it shows that the younger generation, which only knew the GDR from the media, judged it more harshly than those who experienced the state as young people and adults: 32% of 18–29-year-olds agreed that the GDR was an *Unrechtsstaat* as opposed to 29% of 30–49-year-olds; and only 25% of those aged 50 and over agreed. The statistics are similar for those for whom the GDR was not an *Unrechtsstaat*: 37% of 18–29-year-olds agreed compared to 43% of 30–49-year-olds and 41% of those aged 50 and over.

The second noticeable development in terms of age is apparent in the variance in those responding "to some extent." Only 18% of 18–29-year-olds believed that the GDR was partly an *Unrechtsstaat* and partly a *Rechtsstaat* (state based on the rule of law); by contrast, the older generation sided more firmly with this point of view (23% of 30–49-year-olds and 39% of those 50 and over). It is apparent, then, that the three possible options (yes, to some extent, no) are more evenly distributed among the older generations than among 18–29-year-olds, where there is a sharper divide.

In their assessment of the GDR, young people are less willing or able to acknowledge any nuances or grey areas than are older generations. They tend toward an unequivocal view of the GDR as either an *Unrechtsstaat* or a *Rechtsstaat*. Less than a fifth of them chose the option "to some extent." This black-and-white view is a reflection of the tendency for young people not just to make undifferentiated assessments but also to identify strongly with or distance themselves from certain issues. It also points to the tensions between the various memory narratives that young eastern Germans must draw upon to construct an image of the GDR — either the informal, relatively marginalized memory discourses within families and in alterna-

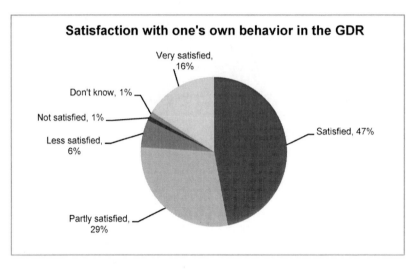

Fig. 11.6. Level of satisfaction with one's own conduct in the GDR (2007).
Data from Jenaer Zentrum für empirische Sozial- & Kulturforschung, ed.,
Zur sozialen Lage der Opfer des SED-Regimes in Thüringen: Forschungsbericht
im Auftrag des Thüringer Ministeriums für Soziales, Familie und
Gesundheit *(Erfurt, 2008), 52.*

tive contemporary history, which range from a romanticized, simplified approach to a self-critical view of the GDR, or the critical or even demonizing discourse shaping the image of the GDR in schools, politics, political education, and the media.

The respondents assessed their own behavior during the GDR more positively than they did the conditions in which they lived. Most eastern Germans claimed that, despite difficult circumstances, they behaved decently or worked to improve things. At the same time, they are confronted with images and accounts of the GDR and of eastern Germans in the media, politics, and education that may reinforce western Germans' sense of identity but that remain unacceptable to most eastern Germans.[65] These discourses imply that eastern Germans did not sufficiently distance themselves from the dictatorship and thus underline their apparent guilt and involvement. On the other hand, these debates also point to the constant repression and the state's shortcomings and thus establish the majority of eastern Germans as victims, though the latter pride themselves on having coped with life in the GDR. These views invariably prompt the indignant reply that the GDR cannot be understood if you did not experience it first-hand. A study conducted in Thüringen in 2007 is representative of how eastern Germans regard their own conduct in the GDR. The majority (63%) stated that they were either "very satisfied" or "satisfied" with their own conduct; only 7% were less satisfied or dissatisfied.[66]

Geschichtspolitik since 1990: The Return of a "New" Master Narrative?

In unified Germany, discourses on identity, history, and politics are informed by the master narrative of the "two German dictatorships." This narrative is bound up with totalitarian theory, according to which the unified Federal Republic is positioned equidistant from the Third Reich and the GDR. Talk of the "two German dictatorships" narrows the gap between the crimes of National Socialism, with its racist and imperialistic ideology and social Darwinism, and the crimes of the GDR, with its anti-capitalist and collectivist class-war ideology. In so doing, it legitimizes history as well as contemporary politics in the Federal Republic; however, this may give western Germans a sense of identity, but the majority of eastern Germans are unable to connect with such a narrative.

Totalitarian theories are particularly evident in the policies and debates regarding history and memorialization. The law concerning the establishment of the Saxony Memorial Site Foundation, which was passed by the government of Saxony in 2003, is a perfect example. It does not distinguish between the Third Reich and the GDR, but rather aims to commemorate "politische Gewaltverbrechen von überregionaler Tragweite, von besonderer historischer Bedeutung, an politische Verfolgung, an Staatsterror und staatlich organisierte Morde . . ., die Opfer politischer Gewaltherrschaft und den Widerstand gegen *die Diktaturen*"[67] (italics added). The current conflicts surrounding the official inauguration of the memorial site at Fort Zinna in Torgau and the memorial's inscription also exemplify the difficulties facing the Saxony Memorial Site Foundation in highlighting the differences and historical causalities between the Nazi and GDR regimes (for details of this controversy, see the chapter by Caroline Pearce in this volume).

Unified Germany's master narrative, which is based on totalitarian theory, not only influences perceptions of contemporary history, in narratives on identity and in political education it focuses on the importance of parliamentary structures and political freedom, while other issues that are just as important for a democracy receive inadequate attention. This implies that the social deficits that do not explicitly affect the political right of freedom — issues such as equal opportunities or social justice, freedoms compromised by economic factors, the state's weakness in relation to the private economy — have a latent potential to threaten democracy. For most of the western German population, whose ideology and socialization is shaped by middle-class society, this narrative has an integrative impact and helps to shape identity, but it will hardly resonate with the population of the former GDR, whose ideology and socialization were shaped by a working-class ethos.

This politics of history has implications for public understanding and for identity formation. It supports the unified FRG's master narrative, which is weighted in favor of political freedoms and parliamentary democracy, and routinely ignores other issues such as the social foundation of democracy and the material and cultural resources that facilitate wider social participation throughout the population. Any indignation in response to the social problems mentioned above, which only indirectly affect the political right of freedom, is repeatedly denounced as an attack on democracy.

For most of the western German population, whose ideology and socialization are shaped by middle-class society, this narrative helps to shape a common identity, but it will hardly resonate with the majority of the population of the former GDR, whose ideology and socialization were shaped by a working-class ethos. This master narrative would seem only to serve the current elite, for the enduring one-sided and negative portrayal of the GDR curtails ideas about political alternatives and reform, and simply validates the current federal German political system.

Translated from the German by Nick Hodgin,
with assistance from Caroline Pearce

Notes

[1] The process known as unification or reunification is termed "accession" in the "Decision by the People's Chamber Concerning the Accession of the German Democratic Republic to the Federal Republic of Germany's Basic Law of 23 August 1990" and in the Unification Treaty ("Upon the accession of the German Democratic Republic to the Federal Republic of Germany in accordance with Article 23 of the Basic Law . . ."). The term "accession" will be used here to refer to this process.

[2] Edgar Wolfrum, *Geschichtspolitik in der Bundesrepublik Deutschland. Der Weg zur bundesrepublikanischen Erinnerung 1948–1990* (Darmstadt: Wissenschaftliche Buchgesellschaft, 1999), 78.

[3] Wolfrum, *Geschichtspolitik in der Bundesrepublik Deutschland*, 385.

[4] Up to the 1960s scholarly debates on the GDR tended to center on totalitarianism theories, although these did little to change attitudes in either state. After this period a more differentiated approach emerged with the introduction of new theories on the GDR. See Jens Hüttmann, "'De-De-Errologie' im Kreuzfeuer der Kritik. Die Kontroverse um die 'alte' bundesdeutsche Forschung vor und nach 1989," *Deutschland Archiv* 40, no. 4 (2007): 671–81.

5 See Klaus Körner, *"Die Rote Gefahr": Antikommunistische Propaganda in der Bundesrepublik 1950–2000* (Hamburg: Konkret Literatur Verlag, 2003); Stefan Creuzberger, *Kampf für die Einheit: Das gesamtdeutsche Ministerium und die politische Kultur des Kalten Krieges 1949–1969* (Düsseldorf: Droste, 2008); and Stefan Creuzberger, "Das BMG in der frühen Bonner Republik," *Aus Politik und Zeitgeschichte* 1/2 (2009): 27–33, http://www.bpb.de/ publikationen/11SG4B,0,Das_BMG_in_der_fr%FChen_Bonner_Republik.html.

6 Monika Gibas, "'Bonner Ultras', 'Kriegstreiber' und 'Schlotbarone'. Die Bundesrepublik als Feindbild der DDR in den fünfziger Jahren," in *Unsere Feinde: Konstruktion des Anderen im Sozialismus*, ed. Silke Satjukow and Rainer Gries (Leipzig: Leipziger Universitätsverlag, 2005), 75–106.

7 See especially Jutta Voigt, *Westbesuch: Vom Leben in den Zeiten der Sehnsucht* (Berlin: Aufbau-Verlag, 2009).

8 See Hüttmann, "'De-De-Errologie' im Kreuzfeuer der Kritik," 676.

9 Dirk Schindelbeck and Volker Ilgen, *"Haste was, biste was!": Werbung für die Soziale Marktwirtschaft* (Darmstadt: Wissenschaftliche Buchgesellschaft, 1999), 147.

10 The image comes from Karl-Detlef Mai's archive and was published in Monika Gibas, *Propaganda in der DDR* (Erfurt: Landeszentrale für politische Bildung, 2000), 16.

11 Rainer Geißler, *Die Sozialstruktur Deutschlands: Zur gesellschaftlichen Entwicklung mit einer Zwischenbilanz zur Vereinigung*, 2nd ed. (Opladen: Westdeutscher Verlag, 1996), 240.

12 Wolfgang Engler, *Die Ostdeutschen: Kunde von einem verlorenen Land* (Berlin: Aufbau-Verlag, 1999), 200.

13 Engler, *Die Ostdeutschen*, 300.

14 Irene Böhme, "Jugendbande oder der missbrauchte Idealismus," in *In Sachen Erich Honecker: Kursbuch 111*, ed. Klaus Markus Michael and Tilman Spengler (Berlin: Rowohlt, 1993), 13–23, here 18.

15 Wolf Wagner, *Kulturschock Deutschland: Der zweite Blick* (Hamburg: Rotbuch, 1999), 127–46.

16 Voigt, *Westbesuch*, 125. Voigt is citing the following publication by her West German colleagues Eva Windmöller and Thomas Höpker, *Leben in der DDR* (Hamburg: Gruner und Jahr, 1976).

17 Voigt, *Westbesuch*, 125–26.

18 Werner Schmidt and Klaus Schönberger, *"Jeder hat jetzt mit sich selbst zu tun": Arbeit, Freizeit und politische Orientierungen in Ostdeutschland* (Konstanz: Universitätsverlag Konstanz, 1999), 62.

19 Schmidt and Schönberger, *"Jeder hat jetzt mit sich selbst zu tun,"* 59.

20 Werner Schmidt, *Betriebliche Sozialordnung und ostdeutsches Arbeitnehmerbewusstsein im Prozess der Transformation* (Munich: Hampp, 1996), 79.

21 See Gunnar Winkler, ed., *Sozialreport 2004. Daten und Fakten zur sozialen Lage in den neuen Bundesländern* (Berlin: Trafo-Verlag, 2004), 68.

[22] Winkler, *Sozialreport 2004*, 72.

[23] Michael Hofmann, "Schwierige Suche nach gesicherten Verhältnissen: Von einer erwerbstätigen sozialen Mitte kann kaum gesprochen werden — Was die Region prägt, ist eine neue Armut," *Das Parlament* 38 (2009): 6.

[24] Friedrich Ebert Stiftung, "'Gesellschaft im Reformprozess': Die Friedrich-Ebert-Stiftung untersucht Reformbereitschaft der Deutschen" (2006), http://www.fes.de/inhalt/Dokumente/061016_Gesellschaft_im_Reformprozess.pdf, 83, accessed 20 June 2010.

[25] Evelyn Grünheid, "Überblick über die demographische Entwicklung in West- und Ostdeutschland von 1990–2004," in *Die Bevölkerung in Ost- und Westdeutschland: Demographische und gesellschaftliche Entwicklungen seit der Wende*, ed. Insa Cassens, Marc Luy, and Rembrandt Scholz (Wiesbaden: VS Verlag für Sozialwissenschaften, 2009), 12–47, here 24.

[26] Jürgen Dorbritz and Kerstin Ruckdeschel, "Die langsame Annäherung — Demografisch relevante Einstellungsunterschiede und der Wandel in den Lebensformen in West- und Ostdeutschland," in Cassens, Luy, and Scholz, *Die Bevölkerung in Ost- und Westdeutschland*, 261–94, here 279.

[27] Dorbritz and Ruckdeschel, "Die langsame Annäherung," 287.

[28] Grünheid, "Überblick über die demographische Entwicklung in West- und Ostdeutschland von 1990–2004," 24.

[29] Thomas Bulmahn, "Das vereinte Deutschland — Eine lebenswerte Gesellschaft?" *Kölner Zeitschrift für Soziologie und Sozialpsychologie* 52, no. 3 (2000): 405–27.

[30] Erik Gurgsdies, "Demokratie ohne Gerechtigkeit — Wasser auf die Mühlen rechtsextremistischer Parteien: Anmerkungen anlässlich der Landtagswahl in Mecklenburg-Vorpommern im Lichte neuer empirischer Untersuchungen," *Deutschland Archiv* 40, no. 2 (2007): 215–22, here 216. See also Michael Edinger and Andreas Hallermann, *Politische Kultur in Ostdeutschland: Die Unterstützung des politischen Systems in Thüringen* (Frankfurt am Main: Peter Lang, 2004).

[31] Gunnar Hinck, "Ostdeutsche Marginalisierung," *Deutschland Archiv* 40, no. 5 (2007): 808–14, here 811.

[32] "Social justice" was translated as "equal opportunities" by 81% and as equal living standards by 17%. See Gurgsdies, "Demokratie ohne Gerechtigkeitü," 216.

[33] Jörg Machatzke, "Die Potsdamer Elitestudie — Positionsauswahl und Ausschöpfung," in *Eliten in Deutschland: Rekrutierung und Integration*, ed. Wilhelm Bürklin and Hilke Rebenstorf (Opladen: Leske + Budrich, 1997), 35–69.

[34] Winkler, *Sozialreport 2004*, 72.

[35] Siegfried Jäger, *Kritische Diskursanalyse: Eine Einführung*, 2nd ed. (Duisburg: DISS, 1999), 143.

[36] See also Thomas Ahbe, "Ost-Diskurse. Das Bild von den Ostdeutschen in den Diskursen von vier überregional erscheinenden Presseorganen 1989/1990 und 1995," in *Diskursmauern: Aktuelle Aspekte der sprachlichen Verhältnisse zwischen Ost und West*, ed. Kersten Sven Roth and Markus Wienen (Bremen: Hempen, 2008), 21–53; and Thomas Ahbe, Rainer Gries, and Wolfgang Schmale, eds., *Die*

Ostdeutschen in den Medien: Das Bild von den Anderen nach 1990 (Leipzig: Leipziger Universitätsverlag, 2009).

[37] See also the study conducted by the Mitteldeutscher Rundfunk (MDR) and the 2004 edition of *Umschau* cited in Peer Pasternak, "Wissenschaftsumbau: Der Austausch der Deutungseliten," in *Am Ziel vorbei: Die deutsche Einheit — Eine Zwischenbilanz*, ed. Hannes Bahrmann and Christoph Links (Berlin: Ch. Links Verlag, 2005), 221–36, here 224–25.

[38] For further details see "15 Jahre nach dem Fall der Mauer: Die Entwicklung der Zeitschriftennutzung in den neuen Ländern," Institut für Demoskopie Allensbach 2004: 21; for a summary see http://www.ifd-allensbach.de/main.php?selection=73&rubrik=0.

[39] The advertisement is pictured in Thomas Ahbe, "Deutschland — vereintes, geteiltes Land: Zum Wandel sozialer Strukturen und Meta-Erzählungen," in *Fremde Brüder: Der schwierige Weg zur deutschen Einheit*, ed. Niels Beckenbach (Berlin: Duncker & Humblot, 2008), 55–97, here 76.

[40] ZDF began with its "Ostalgie-Show" on Saturday, 17 August 2003; on Friday, 22 August, MDR started its weekly "Ein Kessel DDR" (six episodes); a day later SAT-1 began its Saturday show "Meyer und Schulz — die ultimative Ost-Show" (broadcast on 23 und 30 August); and on 3 September the weekly "Die DDR-Show" began on RTL (four episodes). The wave of *Ostalgie* finished with two trashy "GDR Specials" as part of Pro Sieben's "Kalkofes Mattscheibe" series on 6 and 13 October.

[41] See Ahbe, "Deutschland — vereintes, geteiltes Land," 922.

[42] For more on this see Julia Belke, "Das Bild der Ostdeutschen im öffentlich-rechtlichen Fernsehen: Eine Diskursanalyse des ARD-Politmagazins KONTRASTE in der Zeit von 1987 bis 2005," in Ahbe, Gries, and Schmale, *Die Ostdeutschen in den Medien*, 135–80. In the same volume see also Juliette Wedl, "Ein Ossi ist ein Ossi ist ein Ossi . . . Regeln der medialen Berichterstattung über 'Ossis' und 'Wessis' in der Wochenzeitung *Die Zeit* seit Mitte der 1990er Jahre," 113–34.

[43] Bettina Radeiski and Gerd Antos, "'Markierter Osten': Zur medialen Inszenierung der Vogelgrippe auf Rügen und am Bodensee," in Roth and Wienen, *Diskursmauern*, 55–67.

[44] Kersten Sven Roth, "Der Westen als 'Normal Null': Zur Diskurssemantik von 'ostdeutsch' und 'westdeutsch,'" in Roth and Wienen, *Diskursmauern*, 69–89.

[45] Sabine Hark, "Feministische Theorie — Diskurs — Dekonkstruktion: Produktive Verknüpfungen," in *Handbuch Sozialwissenschaftliche Diskursanalyse*, ed. Reiner Keller, Andreas Hirseland, Werner Schneider, and Willy Viehöver (Opladen: Leske + Budrich, 2001), 1:353–71, here 362.

[46] Thomas Ahbe, "Du problème de 'l'unité intérieure' dans l'Allemagne unifiée," in *L'Allemagne unifiée 20 ans après la chute du Mur*, ed. Hans Stark and Michèle Weinachter (Lille: Editions Septentrion, 2009), 71–89. See also Ahbe, "Ost-Diskurse."

[47] Gunnar Winkler, ed., *Sozialreport 2002: Daten und Fakten zur sozialen Lage in den neuen Bundesländern* (Berlin: Trafo-Verlag 2002), 54.

48 Klaus Schroeder, *Die veränderte Republik: Deutschland nach der Wiedervereinigung* (Stamsried: Vögel-Verlag 2006), 725.

49 Sozialwissenschaftliches Forschungszentrum Berlin-Brandenburg e.V. (SFZ), "Sozialreport 2010: Daten und Fakten zur sozialen Lage 20 Jahre nach der Vereinigung — 1990 bis 2010 — Positionen der Bürgerinnen und Bürger" (Berlin: SFZ, 2010), 28, http://sfz-ev.de/.

50 SFZ, "Sozialreport 2010," 22.

51 Michael Vester et al., *Soziale Milieus im gesellschaftlichen Strukturwandel: Zwischen Integration und Ausgrenzung* (Frankfurt am Main: Suhrkamp, 2001), 533.

52 See Vester et al., *Soziale Milieus im gesellschaftlichen Strukturwandel,* and Friedrich-Ebert-Stiftung & TNS Infratest Sozialforschung, *Gesellschaft im Reformprozess.*

53 "Stolz aufs eigene Leben: SPIEGEL-Umfrage — Viele Ostdeutsche trauern der alten Zeit nach," *Der Spiegel,* 3 July 1995: 40–42, here 49.

54 Elisabeth Noelle-Neumann and Renate Köcher, eds., *Allensbacher Jahrbuch der Demoskopie: 1998–2002* (Munich: K. G. Saur, 2002), 11:521.

55 Institut für Interdisziplinäre Konflikt- und Gewaltforschung der Universität Bielefeld: Presseinformation GMF-Survey (2008), http://www.uni-bielefeld.de/ikg/download/Pressemappe2008.doc.

56 Winkler, *Sozialreport 2004,* 69, 72.

57 SFZ, "Sozialreport 2010," 73.

58 Western Germans aged between forty and forty-nine had savings of 29,900 euros compared with savings of just over 18,700 euros among eastern Germans; for those under forty the ratio was 13,200 euros to 10,700 euros. See SFZ, "Sozialreport 2010," 77.

59 Rainer Eppelmann, Bernd Faulenbach, and Ulrich Mählert, eds., *Bilanzen und Perspektiven der DDR-Forschung* (Paderborn: Verlag Ferdinand Schöningh, 2003). Four years later Jens Hüttmann mentioned 1,800 completed research projects about the GDR. See Hüttmann, "De-De-Errologie' im Kreuzfeuer der Kritik," 671.

60 The Bonn-based media institute Media Tenor was clearly relieved to observe that "the commemorations and reviews of the fall of the wall and GDR history brought the negative image of the GDR to the fore. In recent years television news reports have been less concerned with the Stasi and the border regime." According to this institute, the contemporary historiography of the GDR is directly analogous to its trivialization: "The less the news reports mention the GDR's shadowy sides, the more the nostalgic retrospection of well-connected ex-functionaries and memory propagandists such as Gysi and Thierse will penetrate." See Media Tenor, "Gedenktage dämpfen die Ostalgie," 29 September 2009, http://www.media-tenor.de/newsletters.php?id_news=668.

61 Martin Sabrow, "Die DDR erinnern," in *Erinnerungsorte der DDR,* ed. Martin Sabrow (Munich: C. H. Beck, 2009), 11–27.

[62] Jürgen Hofmann, "Identifikation und Distanz," in *Deutsche Fragen von der Teilung bis zur Einheit*, ed. Heiner Timmermann (Berlin: Duncker & Humblot, 2001), 431–49, here 435 (note: not everyone surveyed responded, hence the discrepancy from 100% here).

[63] These statistics are from Noelle-Neumann and Köcher, *Allensbacher Jahrbuch der Demoskopie: 1993–1997*, 10:584.

[64] *SUPER Illu*, March 2009, no. 13: 23 (note: not everyone surveyed responded, hence the discrepancy from 100% here).

[65] Thomas Ahbe, "Die Ost-Diskurse als Strukturen der Nobilitierung und Marginalisierung von Wissen: Eine Diskursanalyse zur Konstruktion der Ostdeutschen in den westdeutschen Medien-Diskursen 1989/90 und 1995," in Ahbe, Gries, and Schmale, *Die Ostdeutschen in den Medien*, 59–112.

[66] Heinrich Best and Michael Hofmann, eds., *Zur sozialen Lage der Opfer des SED-Regimes in Thüringen: Forschungsbericht im Auftrag des Thüringer Ministeriums für Soziales, Familie und Gesundheit* (Erfurt: Thüringer Ministerium für Soziales, Familie und Gesundheit, 2008), 52.

[67] "Gesetz zur Errichtung der Stiftung Sächsische Gedenkstätten zur Erinnerung an die Opfer politischer Gewaltherrschaft" (Sächsisches Gedenkstättenstiftgesetz — SächsGedenkStG), 22 April 2003, §2, http://www.stsg.de/cms/sites/default/files/u9/errichtungsgesetz.pdf.

12: "Worin noch niemand war": The GDR as Retrospectively Imagined Community

Peter Thompson

This essay is dedicated to Jan Robert Bloch, who died in May 2010.

A Vision

The future was a beautiful place, once.
Remember the full-blown balsa-wood town
on public display in the Civic Hall?
The ring-bound sketches, artists' impressions,

blueprints of smoked glass and tubular steel,
board-game suburbs, modes of transportation
like fairground rides or executive toys.
Cities like *dreams,* cantilevered by light.

And people like us at the bottle bank
next to the cycle path, or dog-walking
over tended strips of fuzzy-felt grass,
or model drivers, motoring home in

electric cars. Or after the late show —
strolling the boulevard. They were the plans,
all underwritten in the neat left-hand
of architects — a true, legible script.

I pulled that future out of the north wind
at the landfill site, stamped with today's date,
riding the air with other such futures,
all unlived in and now fully extinct.

The future was a beautiful place, once.

— Simon Armitage[1]

SIMON ARMITAGE'S POEM on the beauty of the lost future points to a fundamental truth about *Ostalgie* that I would like to address here — namely that it has only marginally to do with the GDR as it was constituted and probably even less to do with real nostalgia for that state. The set of events and attitudes we have observed in the twenty years since the fall of the Berlin Wall and the unification of Germany could be transposed to many different places and can be said to have its roots in the nature of what it is to be born or, in Heidegger's terms, thrown into this world at any specific time and place. What I wish to do here is to use the fall of the Berlin Wall, the collapse of the GDR, and the twenty years since the unification of Germany to conduct a wider philosophical investigation into the place of memory and politics within a significant turning point in human history. Of course the contingency of the event has a wider universal context and — in true Hegelian fashion — that wider context is also the product of contingent events, but my emphasis here will be on what the period since 1989 can tell us about the relationship between what was, what is, and what might be.

The poet is the one figure whose whole raison d'être is to attempt a link between the ontological and the ontic, to use Heidegger's version of the universal and the contingent for a moment — between the nature of our existence and the ways in which our existence is played out. The historian, the political scientist, and the philosopher can only do their best to limp along behind, picking up and reassembling the pieces. The point I shall be making here is that *Ostalgie* represents a common sense of loss attached to an object of desire that is actually about the desire rather than the object. The psychological defense mechanism this sets up could be interpreted as one of the basic motivations behind nostalgia, and recognition of this takes us directly to the heart of the matter of memories of the GDR twenty years after its disappearance.

Twenty years after 1989 we are confronted with a situation in which, according to the most recent survey data, 57% of eastern Germans believe that the GDR had more good than bad sides and 49% believe that there were a few problems but that it was possible to live a good life there. As many as 8% were of the opinion that life in the GDR was better than it is today, and 11% said that they wanted the old GDR back. Commenting on this survey, the historian Stefan Wolle said: "Es ist eine neue Form der *Ostalgie* entstanden. Die Sehnsucht nach der heilen Welt der Diktatur geht weit über die ehemaligen Funkionäre hinaus."[2] However, the point of this essay will be to point out that the phrase "Heimweh nach der Diktatur" represents a fundamental misunderstanding of the nature of the *Heimweh* felt by eastern Germans and that it is these mistaken attitudes that are at the root of the continuing dislocation of Germany.

In order to discuss the apparent problem of *Heimweh* it will first be necessary, however, to discuss the concept of *Heimat* in both its theoretical and political senses. In doing so I shall argue that, far from longing for dictatorship, the current nostalgic identification with the GDR on the part of former East Germans represents instead a sublimated desire for a freedom beyond that on offer under present circumstances, and that the nostalgia inherent in the term *Ostalgie* is actually a longing for a future that went missing in the past rather than for a past that never had a Socialist or Communist future. As Ernst Bloch points out in the introduction to *Das Prinzip Hoffnung*, the past is not something finished and behind us, but merely the breeding ground for the future.[3] A past that refuses to pass does so not out of stubbornness or caprice or in an arbitrary fashion, but because it contains within it elements of the future that have not yet fully played themselves out. It is not just a sense of a "Vergangenheit, die nicht vergehen will" here, as Nolte would have it,[4] but of one that cannot pass because it has not yet found its final resting place, which can only be the future. *Ostalgie*, therefore, is not some interesting and incomprehensible foible, but could be said to be the expression of a living hope for the future, no matter how unlikely it may seem.

The reason for choosing to look at this question in the context of Ernst Bloch's work is that his philosophy is centrally concerned with issues of hope, desire, utopia, belief, impulse — all part of a forward-looking dynamic. *Das Prinzip Hoffnung* was originally to be called "Dreams of a Better Life," and it is dedicated to cataloguing and interpreting all human behavior in the context of how it illuminates a sense of hope. However, this is not some naive and abstract optimism but a *principle* of hope — that is, the hope is something that desires to transcend the present but also knows it has to be rooted in present conditions. Further, present conditions are those that have emerged out of the past, and it is that past that continues to condition what is possible in future. This dialectic of the subjective and objective conditions for future development means that at all points in history, past, present, and future exist coterminously in the form of what Bloch calls *Ungleichzeitigkeit*, or non-synchronicity. In his *Erbschaft dieser Zeit*, written in 1934 and dealing with the ways in which Fascism managed to mobilize the past for the future, he posited that there was a constant and ineluctable intermingling of past, present, and future in any given historical situation. Thus the future is always present in the past, and in turn the future will always contain an element of return to the past. I would like to examine here the way Bloch's concept of *Ungleichzeitigkeit* can be applied to the GDR both before and after the fall of the Berlin Wall and to see whether there is within what appears to be an entirely anamnetic and backward-looking sense of *Ostalgie* the pre-illumination of a forward-looking yet fundamentally misunderstood dynamic. Just as Bloch maintained that the dynamic nature of Fascism had been misunderstood because of the way it had been able to mobilize dreams of a supposedly better past, so I shall argue here that the non-synchronous nature of *Ostalgie* has also been fundamentally misunderstood.

Dreams of a better life, no matter what ideological form they take, are also always predicated on the notion of a *Heimat* and a sense of coming home. This can take a reactionary, exclusivist, and racist form as in the case of Fascism and yet, as Bloch pointed out, Communism, too, appeals to the idea of a future utopian *Heimat*, despite its scientific pretensions. *Ostalgie* as a phenomenon is in this sense both the desire to come home and the sense of an irreparable loss of home with the loss of the GDR. For this reason in addition to Bloch I shall also call in evidence Slavoj Žižek, a contemporary philosopher and psychoanalyst whose concern with our nature as a species obsessed with the fetishization of the "objet petit a" as an unconscious recognition of the impossibility of gaining access to the "objet grand A" becomes immediately relevant to our understanding of the way in which the GDR stood in for — rather than represented — a Socialist home that was always unobtainable.[5] A combination of Bloch's theory of *Ungleichzeitigkeit* and Žižek's fetishization theories will give us a means of understanding what *Ostalgie* is as well as charting its likely future, given both the current socio-economic situation and its politico-cultural context.

Underpinning as well as linking these temporal and psychological/philosophical aspects is the widespread sense among citizens of the former GDR that they have become foreigners in their own land. The sense of historical disjuncture is compounded by a geographical one related to notions of community and *Heimat*. As we shall see below, I refer here not only to *Heimat* as the identifiable place where one once or has always felt at home, but in the Blochian sense of somewhere that we all unconsciously know we once had — but in which we have never yet — set foot. Bloch's *Heimat* is a non-existent home, cut loose from the past and projected into the future but never actually existing in the present. *Heimat* here, there-fore, has an expressly utopian, even romantic, dimension, and in much of the literature of the past twenty years dealing with German (dis)unity there is the palpable feeling that without going anywhere people have had to change countries. In that sense they have become exiled from what they were without ever having arrived somewhere they might feel at home. The GDR may have offered a roof over their heads and the united Federal Republic a more comfortable roof, but not yet the sense of *Heimat*. The dislocation that this entails has left a vacuum of unfixed identification and uncertainty. Regina Bittner demonstrates this conundrum convincingly in her essay "Kulturtechniken der Transformation," in which she points out that in 1990 the East Germans experienced what is called in the literature on migrant communities a "culture shock" that is overcome in various ways and stages.[6]

First there comes a period of self-ethnicization in which the process of assimilation is more or less consciously resisted; then comes dissatisfaction with the living conditions of the guest country. This is followed by a sense of having lost any self-determination and finally of being treated like sec-ond-class citizens. It is only with the arrival in a foreign country that, as

Toralf Staud points out, immigrants start to define their own ethnicity.[7] While this is undoubtedly the case and, indeed, that self-ethnicization seems to deepen rather than lessen with the third generation, if not the second, the problem in the case of the ex-GDR is that it is not ever possible to arrive in a foreign country when it is already your own, and yet it is also not possible to ethnicize oneself when one is indigenous to the country in which one has not yet arrived.

It is this sense of comprehensive temporal, psychological, social, geographical, and political dislocation and loss that characterizes the debate about *Ostalgie*. However, it would be a mistake to think that this sense of dislocation is peculiar to eastern Germany. It is merely a sharpened example of a general *Unbehagen in der Moderne* (to paraphrase both Freud and Lyotard) that afflicts us as a species that finds itself on the way from settled community to flexible society without, in many cases, having to venture past one's own front door.

In Simon Armitage's poem we see that the plans for the future had been "underwritten in the neat left-hand / of architects — a true, legible script." Transferred to the history of Socialism we might see this as a description of the utopian dream of a Communist future as it had been written down by its own architects, Marx and Engels, with their "true," legible theories. The deformed GDR that emerged out of the exigencies of the Cold War was damaged in time by its further degeneration into a mere conduit for the power interests of its Soviet architects. Never able to cut the red umbilical cord to the East that kept it alive, the architects' script became ever more illegible as well as unintelligible.

This degeneration and deformation of Socialism during the Honecker years represented a system in which the socio-economic stability of the "Unity of Economic and Social Policy" replaced culture as the fetishized "objet petit a" of an unattained Socialism. During the two short decades of Honecker's rule (1971–89) any abstract intellectual or cultural appeal to the greater good or the future made sense to neither the Party nor the working class, who had lived in the symbiotic self-delusion of "you pretend to work and we'll pretend to pay you." In the 1970s and 1980s, as the SED's reduction of politics to the formulaic defense of the Soviet Union and the mere fact of the social ownership of the means of production replaced any cultural or political understanding of the GDR, the tension between its promise and reality left many intellectuals high and dry, paradoxically forced to defend something they did not support for fear of destroying something they did. As Volker Braun recognized already in his 1990 poem "Das Eigentum," the GDR was a state that was at one and the same time both the perversion and the fulfillment of the old dream of a Socialism on German soil, the very land of the architects, and therefore one whose disappearance was also at one and the same time both a good and a bad thing:

Da bin ich noch: mein Land geht in den Westen.
KRIEG DEN HÜTTEN FRIEDE DEN PALÄSTEN.
Ich selber habe ihm den Tritt versetzt.
Es wirft sich weg und seine magre Zierde.
Dem Winter folgt der Sommer der Begierde.
Und ich kann *bleiben wo der Pfeffer* wächst.
Und unverständlich wird mein ganzer Text.
Was ich niemals besaß wird mir entrissen.
Was ich nicht lebte, werd ich ewig missen.
Die Hoffnung lag im Weg wie eine Falle.
Mein Eigentum, jetzt habt ihrs auf der Kralle.
Wann sag ich wieder *mein* und meine alle.[8]

This sense of continuity within change, which at the same time recognizes that a complete inversion of the usual coordinates has taken place, is a central aspect of life in the ex-GDR. As we see here in Braun's poem, those who were critically supportive of the GDR unleashed a process that quickly developed a dynamic that led ineluctably to the demise of the state itself. Just as Gorbachev had not wanted to destroy the Soviet Union via the policies of perestroika and glasnost, so Braun and the other dissidents did not seek the end of the GDR and the unification of Germany. And yet they helped to bring it about. The reference to the falsity of the socialized means of production is clear, and yet that which he did not possess has been torn from him. Equally, the Socialism he never lived had come to an end. This constant reference to the absence of something that was never present is a recurrent theme in much of the literature and political comment of the past two decades and thus represents the sense that although the world has shifted on its political axis and changed beyond all recognition, the people of the ex-GDR have somehow neither shifted nor, in André Brie's phrase, arrived in the Federal Republic.[9] But this is because rather than becoming refugees and expellees, the usual fallout of a failed state, the failed state itself had moved on, leaving the people with the sense that they were already refugees in their old country and were pitched into a double alienation in their new one. Volker Braun writes: "Da bin ich noch: mein Land geht in den Westen," yet East Germans were expected to jump on board with no idea about what the destination might be or with whom they were going to have to share their carriage. It should be no surprise, therefore, that the stability and stagnation of the Honecker years in the GDR should perform the role of retrospectively imagined *Heimat*.

In another poem in a volume from 2005, Braun relates being stuck motionless in a traffic jam on the A9 near Coswig — a road that leads from Berlin to Nuremburg but on which he is going nowhere. Ernst Bloch's son, Jan Robert (to whom *Das Prinzip Hoffnung* is dedicated) is with him in the car as they look out of the window:

Wie nun. Ich bin gefahren. Aber
Ich habe mich nicht fortbewegt. Darum
Werden wir erst fahren müssen.

These lines paraphrase Bloch's oft-repeated contention that what characterizes us as a species as well as the history in which we live and which we have created is that none of it is yet complete: "Wie nun? Ich bin. Aber ich habe mich noch nicht. Darum werden wir erst," said Ernst Bloch in the epigraph to *Spuren*, a book dedicated to tracing the lines of development in human society and history, emphasizing that what we take to be facts are mere snapshots of a process that is unfolding in a way that frightens us into a fetishization of the snapshots.[10] As Žižek maintains, "the fetish is the embodiment of the Lie which enables us to sustain the unbearable truth."[11] If the unbearable truth is that the ground of what we are has been cut away from underneath us, especially if we were complicit in that undercutting — "Ich selber habe ihm den Tritt versetzt," as Braun puts it above — then the fetishization of the lie becomes everything. Memories of the GDR are thus a fetishization of an uncanny or unheimliche *Heimat* in which the *Unheimlichkeit* rests in the fact that it existed only as an imaginary reflection of a non-existent reality.[12] As Bernhard Schlink says: "Heimat ist ein Ort nicht als der, der er ist, sondern als der, der er nicht ist."[13]

The dialectical aspect of this dynamic, however, is that in the case of the GDR specifically, and of Socialism in general, the fetishization is of a past that itself contained within it a teleological fetishization of the future. As Bloch put it when trying to analyze the emergence of a backward-looking Fascism within a modernist context: "Consciousness does not directly flow from being, especially not for the employees and middle strata of the modern city who seek salvation in the past, but also not for the proletarianized peasantry for whom much older ideas have been reawakened and remythologized. Subjectively these express a 'pent-up anger,' objectively a romantic anti-capitalism that seeks its future in a better image of the past."[14]

It could be argued, therefore, that the GDR under Honecker was a system not only of symbiotic self-delusion but also of an infinite suspension of the dialectic of change within a reified reality. The very idea of "real existing Socialism" embodies the transformation of a lie into a fetish that served to cover up the reality of a non-existing Socialism. This dialectical *Ungleichzeitigkeit* in which the dreams of the future are to be found only in the dreams of the past complicates people's relationship to the present, transforming it from a mere reified moment within an ongoing process into an ultimately deferred gratification in which it becomes pleasurable to bear a grudge about an unrealized past-future, regardless of — indeed, precisely because of — the apparent benefits of a better present. In the case of the GDR the loss of the state can therefore accurately be described as the loss of a loss.[15]

Nietzsche called this *Ressentiment* in which the pain that accompanies one's own sense of inferiority is projected onto an external "objet petit a" a fetishized Other[16] — in this case clearly the western Germans. What has happened in eastern Germany is that this sense of *Ressentiment* — as with everything else in capitalist modernity that has the potential to threaten it — has been functionalized and incorporated into the systemic imperative to "Enjoy Your Symptom!" as Žižek would put it.[17] The psychological role of this form of resentment, however, is a paradox in that it is actually a precondition for the acceptance of the given. In the gap between desire and drive, the fetishized object of desire — namely the GDR — produces in the "Ostalgist" a shift from the loss of that object to loss as an object in its own right.[18] The absence of the fetishized object consequently produces an "enjoyment" of the very absence of the object. *Ostalgie* is in this sense a good example of what Lacan and Žižek mean when they speak of *jouissance*, a reveling in the perverse pleasure of being unhappy. *Ostalgie* thus becomes an essential means of "traversing the fantasy" in which an engagement with a GDR that never was is actually a precondition for living in a state that denies the possibility of there ever being a "real" GDR of the kind that never was. The utopian dream becomes the means by which an accommodation is found with the fact that there can be no utopia and that the desire for a utopia is in itself considered totalitarian within the prevailing ideology (*D*, 287).

However, it could also be seen as a sublimated recognition that, rather than the reality of Communism being something that "went wrong" at some point, failure was always built into its very emergence. This supposition is based on two factors, the first a universal truth and the second a specific varietal truth:

(1) The universal truth of social change is that all systems and all forms of social organization emerge only out of a process of failure and negativity. No social system emerges fully formed and perfect, but is born out of pain, blood, exploitation, violence, revolution, and war. There is no past or existing social system that has avoided this reality, nor will there be one in the future. Even the emergence of a new form of ecological capitalism — if that is to be the best future we can anticipate — is predicated on the driving of our species and others to the brink of extinction in the name of the valorization of capital.

(2) The particular truth of Communism is that it emerged out of what was only an apparent breakdown of capitalism in a country that had not yet even started to become capitalist, and its survival could only be guaranteed through a ruthless defense of its Communist utopian premise — which was in any case predicated on the desire to put an end to pain, blood, exploitation, violence, revolution, and war. In that sense, rather

than argue that Stalinism was somehow a perversion of the original
Communist dream, one must admit that it was actually inherent within not
only the implementation of the dream, but within the dream itself.

This means that one is faced with a binary choice in attitudes toward
the utopian *Heimat* of some future beautiful society. Either the traditional
liberal Popperian view is taken that the very process of constructing it will
automatically lead to authoritarian rule and that it should therefore be
rejected at all costs in favor of liberal pragmatism, or the position can be
taken that, yes, it will almost inevitably lead to authoritarian rule but this
is the only way for Communism to become a reality — by wading through
the excrement and blood that is the precondition of its ultimate triumph.
That is a truth that Marx and Lenin saw with their concept of the dictatorship of the proletariat and that Stalin saw through with his regime of the
dictatorship of the Party. This was also the reason Bloch, despite being a
humanist, Hegelian, unorthodox, and in many ways philosophically liberal
Marxist, also unconditionally defended Stalin's Soviet Union up to and
including the purges and trials of 1936–37.

Bloch's point, even in his later work *Naturrecht und menschliche
Würde*, is that, tempting and comfortable though it is to be a liberal prag-
matist, this is only possible if one is prepared to disavow the vanishing
mediator of the violence out of which liberalism emerged and on which it
still bases its power.[19] Liberal democratic Western capitalism, he maintains,
emerged out of several centuries of valorization for which many millions
paid with their hard labor. It relied on the enslavement, transportation,
and brutal exploitation of millions of slaves, and it continued to enslave
many millions of people outside the metropolitan centers. Any liberal face
it possessed was also the result not of a gift from above, but of the struggle
of the subaltern on the one hand and the very real threat of Socialism/
Communism on the other, without which democratic concessions would
never have been made.

One might add to this that Bloch in his time, like Marx before him
and Žižek today, was fully aware of the overwhelming success of the capitalist paradigm. All of them have recognized that this paradigm has
depended on an absolute mastery over the whole of nature and society in
a way that threatens its very existence but is also the only precondition for
the achievement of Socialism. One of his favorite quotations from Marx,
for example, is that Communism will represent the "Vermenschlichung der
Natur und die Naturalisierung der Menschen."[20] Both Bloch and Žižek
maintain that capitalism's success in all areas is the thing that now means
it has to disappear for the sake of both mankind and nature whereas, paradoxically, the failure of Communism is the very thing that makes clear that
in the long run it can be the only alternative.

The corollary to this is that they are forced to admit the fundamental
flaw in Communism and that therefore to support it meant and means

having to defend the indefensible, precisely because its failure was pre-
programmed. If one does wish to defend it, one also has to admit that
under the historical conditions in which it emerged there was never any
alternative to the wrong road. We might therefore say that both Bloch and
Žižek maintain that Communism is constantly doomed to fail in all its
forms until it is ultimately successful, at which point history can finally
commence because at that point there will be no alternative to the right
road. This insight brings us back to Bloch and the title of this essay, "Worin
noch niemand war," which is taken from Bloch's most famous quotation,
namely the final paragraph of *Das Prinzip Hoffnung*:

> Der Mensch lebt noch überall in der Vorgeschichte, ja alles und jedes
> steht noch vor Erschaffung der Welt, als einer rechten. Die wirkliche
> Genesis ist nicht am Anfang, sondern am Ende, und sie beginnt erst
> anzufangen, wenn Gesellschaft und Dasein radikal werden, das heißt
> sich an der Wurzel fassen. Die Wurzel der Geschichte aber ist der
> arbeitende, schaffende, die Gegebenheiten umbildende und über-
> holende Mensch. Hat er sich erfaßt und das Seine ohne Entäußerung
> und Entfremdung in realer Demokratie begründet, so entsteht in der
> Welt etwas, das allen in die Kindheit scheint und worin noch niemand
> war: *Heimat*. (*PH*, 1628)

This paragraph contains within it all of the elements discussed above. Non-
synchronicity is its central motif in that the reference back to our childhood — a constant trope in the literature on *Ostalgie* and represented most
clearly by the movie *Good Bye, Lenin!* (2003) — is a constant attempt to
find the future within the past. However, as it is impossible to achieve
reconciliation with the past, it is necessary to seek it with the future. That
in turn, however, cannot be achieved simply by wishing it so. Bloch is careful to point out that Aristotle's *dynámei on* — the abstract possibility based
on a Dionysian drive and the desire to live differently — is not sufficient
to make it happen. The *dynámei on* has to be predicated on a *kata to dyna-
ton* — that which is possible, specifically real, material, objective conditions. Bloch calls this a true realism, representing "die *Einheit von
Hoffnung und Prozeßkenntnis*" (*PH*, 727; italics in original).

This means that what might be possible in the future is based on a
latent possibility in history that can be brought out only by human action.
When the two work together — Bloch's laboring, creative human beings
— then it will be possible to transcend the given. This will only happen,
Bloch says, when all other possibilities have exhausted themselves. The
main purpose of the committed, engaged political movement in the mean-
time — in history — is therefore to seek out glimpses of the utopian dream
in both past and present, the *Vorscheine*, or pre-illuminations as he calls
them, while at the same time creating the basis for a realization of the
utopian dream through concrete work on the ground. It is only then that

history proper will begin with true genesis not at the beginning, but at the end of history. Like Žižek's attack on the desire for partial enjoyment through the reduction of the role "objet petit a" to that of fantasy, Bloch's defense of a concrete utopia was not a fetishization of an abstract demand for a certain type of society, but a recognition of the forms that a *Vorschein* such as *Ostalgie* might take. It is not merely a pre-illumination of a fantasy *qua* fantasy, but of a potential reality as a partial object of the not-yet-become. In both Bloch and Žižek, therefore, fantasy carries not only a reductive and obscurantist dimension, nor yet the inescapable circularity of eternal recurrence, but also contains within it the unconscious preconditions for liberation (*D*, 323–27). Within an anamnetic *Ostalgie* there is a hidden proleptic element in that an uncritical reflection of the GDR carries both a critical distance from the present and an openness to an as yet unknown future.

This in turn brings us to Bloch's other great insight into this future *concrete* utopia: that it is not something programmatic, a set of blueprints for a real future, but that it is both emergent out of its own reality and always already present in what we unconsciously know. In other words the future will represent the outcome of the concrete process of arriving there, including its mistakes and dead-ends, rather than following some previously conceived plan — the traditional approach to utopia from Thomas More onwards. This understanding of the apparent oxymoron of a concrete process is taken directly from Hegel, who used the term in its original sense of *con crescere* — that is, a growing-together of all the objective and subjective tendencies at work in history. It is concrete only in the abstraction of its potentiality and, as Verena Kirchner points out, using this model of non-synchronous human history means that all that we live and have lived becomes a "prozessuales Noch-Nicht."[21] Through this process the utopian and "ostalgic" *Heimat* of the GDR, as a state that stands in for and is a fetishization of an as yet unobtainable reality, takes on the role of a flawed emblem of a possible future.

Utopia is therefore concrete because (a) it has always been present in human society, (b) it already exists in our everyday lives and hopes, and also precisely because (c) it does not exist and will only be the concrete product of an as yet unfinished process rather than a teleologically predetermined end point. *Ostalgie* is merely an attempt by those who cannot see a way forward to the *Not Yet* to fix an image of a period in which they thought they had already arrived. It is for that reason that *Good Bye, Lenin!*, for example, starts with soundless images of an idyllic 1970s life in the *Niche* provided by the country *Dacha*, a refuge not only from the grimy reality of East Berlin life but also from the grim reality of a stalled and frozen history.

Given this paradox, *Ostalgie* is a Janus-headed monster, a sigh of despair at bearable circumstances but — in addition to the very real sense of welfare stability the GDR represented for many — also the faint echo of the old idea of what the GDR might one day have possibly become but never did. It is a desire for the promise and not the reality of the GDR. As Žižek points out, the main device within *Ostalgie* is thus the sense of a "lack of a lack," and the desire for liberation and progress is also desire for return to something that was in any case only ever partially present.[22] Equally, as Bloch maintains, the future is a completion of the multiple possibilities that continue to exist in history. All history becomes counterfactual because many of the strains it contains can be revived and incorporated into future possibilities, something Bloch called *"Zukunft in der Vergangenheit"* (*PH*, 8). This can perhaps be reversed in the case of *Ostalgie*, which exists as a form of *Vergangenheit in der Zukunft*. It is nostalgia not for the GDR that was, but the GDR that was not, so that — to paraphrase Benedict Anderson's idea — the GDR is not only a retrospectively imagined community but, more importantly, is arguably actually a retrospective imagination of a future imagined community.[23] In this sense it maintains a hope in the future of which Simon Armitage gives us only a resigned glimpse.

Both Bloch and Žižek have emphasized in their work the need to understand the nature of hope, people's deep need to belong, and the desire to find a place where one can just be without thought and consciousness. Žižek is fond of quoting Lacan's twist on Descartes's "cogito ergo sum" in which he says, "I think where I am not, therefore I am where I do not think."[24] This means that there is an eternal split between being and consciousness with the latter seen as something that gets in the way of the former. Bloch, too, said something similar when he maintained that that which simply is ("das Seiende" in Heidegger's terms) is always just a dress rehearsal for Being ("das Sein"), but that *Heimat* represents a "beginnende[s] Sein wie Utopie" (*PH*, 728). Of course the impossibility of Being, as opposed to just being, is the ultimate human drive: the desire for desire that leads us to settle for the simulacrum of desire in the form of a fetishized object such as the GDR as a reality or Communism as a concept — or Christ as object, God as concept for that matter. It is this desire to belong that is behind *Ostalgie*, not just a desire to belong to the retrospectively imagined community of the GDR, and the recognition of the impossibility of either going back or going forward is a traumatic experience.

This is why Žižek maintains that films like *Good Bye, Lenin!*, *Das Leben der Anderen* (2006), and *Helden wie wir* (1999) are part of a traumatic "detraumatization," the enactment of parting from the GDR and acquiring distance from it (*D*, 64). In acquiring that distance, however, what *Good Bye, Lenin!* in particular does is allow people to move closer toward a model of the GDR not as it really was, but rather as those who founded, fought for, believed in, opposed, resisted, and ultimately destroyed it wished it had been. *Ostalgie* thus becomes nostalgia for the place in which being and consciousness are reunited. As Žižek says, the past "contains hidden, non-realized potentials, and the authentic future is the repetition/ retrieval of *this* past, not of the past as it was, but of those elements in the past which the past itself, in its reality, betrayed" (*D*, 141). In fact *Good Bye, Lenin!* is actually about the very absence of a true GDR before its disappearance and a concrete recognition that it was bound to disappear. In that sense and in contrast to the usual interpretation given to it, it could be seen as a far more realistic portrayal of the reality of the GDR than *Das Leben der Anderen*.

As Žižek points out and as Bloch was constantly aware, "the 'eternity' of dialectics means that the de-legitimization is always retroactive. What disappears 'in itself' always deserves to disappear."[25] The only GDR that can exist as *Heimat* in the sense in which it is presented in the fiction within a fiction in *Good Bye, Lenin!* is therefore the non-existent one, whereas the SED's description of the GDR in the 1970s as a system of real existing Socialism is actually a very clear admission of the non-existence — and therefore ultimate disposability — of what they thought of as concrete and pragmatic Socialism. Real, existing Socialism was thus actually a perverted reflection of a non-existing Socialism beneath which a generally intact desire for a real real-existing Socialism in the form of a not yet-existing Socialism played its utopian role.

As is so often the case, issues and ideas that philosophers, sociologists, and political scientists struggle endlessly to bring under control are rendered clear and succinct by the poet's simple line. If we return to Simon Armitage's poem, we can see that the comma that separates the past from the future in the line "The future was a beautiful place, once" by locating the latter in the former, renders a perfect example of the Blochian idea of the non-contemporaneity of peoples' lives and of an as yet unattainable *Heimat* to be found in the future as a memory of a dream. This is married to Žižek's sense that *Ostalgie* is a memory of a society dreamed of, unlived in, and yet remembered.

Maybe the utopia of this misremembered *Heimat* and retrospectively imagined community is always just beyond our reach, not just because it is always misremembered, but because it is also always transformed into a passive process of forgetting. Nietzsche called this the transformation of the "Nicht-wieder-los-werden-können" into an active process of "Nicht-wieder-los-werden-wollen."[26] We do this because in order to be able to countenance a possible future, we have to make ourselves believe that it is one that was always already possible in the past — that what we do and what we have done is not just a confluence of contingent and coincidental events, but represents a historical necessity that has to be defended and fought for, both retrospectively and proleptically. As Wolfgang Emmerich points out,[27] Nietzsche calls this a "Gedächtnis des Willens,"[28] in which the process requires one to decide on the link between necessity and contingency. The question remains whether an experiment like Socialism in its Soviet and GDR forms was merely a mistake produced by an extraordinary historical conjuncture by a group of deluded and dangerous people, or does it actually occupy a place within a logical and necessary historical process of human liberation? If the former, then it has no point to it, and if the latter, then what does its failure say about the possibility and future of human liberation itself?

Nietzsche's point (and with him Bloch and Žižek) is that even though history tends to be a series of contingent events, the pattern that emerges lends it a semblance of necessity. The dialectical interaction between contingency and necessity is what produces history, and in turn it is history that produces the future. More importantly, those who have been active in trying to shape both the past and the future in a non-pragmatic way have to believe that they were doing so as part of the fulfillment of a greater plan, be that political or religious. The hardest human challenge is to view the past as something that has passed and may as well never have happened or have happened entirely differently, and to think that everything one has done was not only unnecessary but directly harmful and counter-productive. As Nietzsche says when discussing the tendency to justify past behavior on a collective and individual basis, the common response is: "Das habe ich getan, sagt mein Gedächtnis. Das kann ich nicht getan haben, sagt mein Stolz und bleibt unerbittlich. Endlich — gibt das Gedächtnis nach."[29]

Nietzsche, of course, sees this as a regrettable thing, as something that leads to self-delusion, weakness, and *Ressentiment*, and this is also the common (Western) view of much of what we call *Ostalgie*. However, where *Ostalgie* is not just a marketing tool for selling more T-shirts with the *Ampelmännchen* on them, properly understood it actually contains a serious political and philosophical message — namely that in the retrospectively imagined utopian *Heimat* of the GDR, what is too often seen as a nostalgic harking back can also be seen as an optimistic though unconscious harking forward to a return to the better state that has not yet become:

"The future was a beautiful place, once."

Notes

[1] Simon Armitage, "A Vision," *Tyrannosaurus Rex Versus the Corduroy Kid* (London: Faber and Faber, 2006), 12.

[2] Julia Bonstein, "Heimweh nach der Diktatur," *Der Spiegel*, 29 June 2009, http://www.spiegel.de/spiegel/0,1518,633180,00.html.

[3] Ernst Bloch, *Das Prinzip Hoffnung* (1959; Frankfurt am Main: Suhrkamp, 1985), 8 (hereafter cited in text as *PH*).

[4] Ernst Nolte, "Vergangenheit, die nicht vergehen will: Eine Rede, die geschrieben, aber nicht gehalten werden konnte," *Frankfurter Allgemeine Zeitung*, 6 June 1986.

[5] Slavoj Žižek, *The Parallax View* (Cambridge, MA: MIT, 2006), 252.

[6] Regina Bittner "Kulturtechniken der Transformation," *Aus Politik und Zeitgeschichte* 28, "Deutschland seit 1990," 6 July 2009, http://www.bpb.de/pu blikationen/4Q5LFV,0,0,Deutschland_seit_1990.html.

[7] Toralf Staud, "Die ostdeutschen Immigranten," in *Das Neue Deutschland. Zukunft als Chance*, ed. Tanja Busse and Tobia Dürr (Berlin: Aufbau, 2003), 266–81.

[8] Volker Braun, "Die Zickzackbrücke," *Ein Abrißkalender* (Halle: Mitteldeutscher Verlag, 1992), 84.

[9] Brigitte Fehrle, "Mißverständnisse mit Brie," *Berliner Zeitung*, 27 August 1996.

[10] Ernst Bloch, *Spuren* (1930; Frankfurt am Main: Suhrkamp, 1969), n.p.

[11] Slavoj Žižek, *On Belief* (London: Routledge, 2001), 13.

[12] See Peter Thompson, "*Die unheimliche Heimat*: The GDR and the Dialectics of Home," in *From Stasiland to Ostalgie*, ed. Karen Leeder (Oxford: Oxford German Studies, 2009), 278–87. Some of the arguments in this text are developments of ideas first broached in the earlier essay.

[13] Bernhard Schlink, *Heimat als Utopie* (Frankfurt am Main: Suhrkamp, 2000), 33.

[14] Ernst Bloch, "Sokrates und die Propaganda," *Die neue Weltbühne* 47, 19 November 1936, in Ernst Bloch, *Vom Hasard zur Katastrophe, Politische Aufsätze 1934–1939* (Frankfurt am Main: Suhrkamp, 1972), 107; cited in Anson Rabinbach, "Unclaimed Heritage: Ernst Bloch's Heritage of Our Times and the Theory of Fascism," *New German Critique* 11 (Spring 1977): 5–21.

[15] Slavoj Žižek, *Interrogating the Real* (London: Continuum, 2006), 46.

[16] Friedrich Nietzsche, "Erste Abhandlung: 'Gut und Böse', 'Gut und Schlecht,'" in *Zur Genealogie der Moral: Eine Streitschrift* (1887; Stuttgart: Reclam, 1997), 43.

[17] Slavoj Žižek, *Enjoy Your Symptom* (London: Routledge, 2008).

[18] Slavoj Žižek, *In Defence of Lost Causes* (London: Verso, 2008), 328 (hereafter cited in text as *D*).

[19] Ernst Bloch, *Naturrecht und menschliche Würde* (1961; Frankfurt am Main: Suhrkamp, 1999).

[20] Karl Marx, "Ökonomisch-philosophische Manuskripte," in Karl Marx and Friedrich Engels, *Historisch-kritische Gesamtausgabe* (Berlin: Marx-Engels Verlag, 1932), 3:114–16.

[21] Verena Kirchner, "*Das Nichtgelebte* oder Der Wille zur Utopie: Ernst Blochs Hoffnungs-Philosophie und die Demonstration vom 4. November 1989 — Zu einer Erzählung von Volker Braun," in *Wendezeichen? Neue Sichtweisen auf die*

Literatur der DDR, ed. Roswitha Skare and Rainer B. Hoppe (Amsterdam: Rodopi, 1999), 229–50.

[22] Slavoj Žižek, *For They Know Not What They Do* (London: Verso, 2008), lxxxii.

[23] Benedict Anderson, *Imagined Communities: Reflections on the Origin and Spread of Nationalism* (London: Verso, 1991).

[24] Jacques Lacan, *Écrits: A Selection*, trans. Alan Sheridan (London: Tavistock, 1977), 157.

[25] Slavoj Žižek, *Living in the End Times* (London: Verso, 2010), 27.

[26] Nietzsche, "Erste Abhandlung: 'Gut und Böse', 'Gut und Schlecht,'" 47.

[27] Wolfgang Emmerich, "Cultural Memory East v. West: Is What Belongs Together Really Growing Together?," in Leeder, *From Stasiland to Ostalgie*, 243–53, here 243.

[28] Nietzsche, "Erste Abhandlung: 'Gut und Böse', 'Gut und Schlecht,'" 47.

[29] Friedrich Nietzsche, *Jenseits von Gut und Böse* (Stuttgart: Reclam, 1993), 72.

13: GDR Historiography after the End of the GDR: Debates, Renewals, and the Question of What Remains

Stefan Berger

WITH THE END OF THEIR STATE the future of GDR historians also became questionable. Like many other GDR elites, historians found themselves under attack in the newly unified Germany. In the 1980s many West German and Western historians had been very willing to concede an increasing professionalization of GDR historiography; they had identified areas where GDR historians were working in innovative ways, and they were keen to develop a dialogue with their GDR counterparts. In the late 1980s Alexander Fischer and Günther Heydemann epitomized the general mood among West German historians when they wrote that GDR historiography had successfully managed the "transition from a selective representation of German history to an integrated one."[1] Its legitimating function, they argued, "cannot be the sole criterion for its assessment." In various fields, they continued, the GDR had achieved "international recognition," and in view of the "considerable historiographical achievements" of GDR historians, their counterparts in the FRG were taken to task for "their failure to engage in a critical dialogue with Marxist-Leninist historiography in the GDR." After the fall of the Berlin Wall many Western historians changed their tune. Supported by East German dissidents or those who wished to appear as dissidents, Western historians now argued that GDR historians had produced nothing of enduring value, that they had always been in the pay of Communist ideologues and produced propaganda, not history.

GDR historians were charged with not conforming to the high professional standards that allegedly ruled in West Germany and the "free West" more generally. Hans Ulrich Wehler's harsh judgment on GDR historiography came as a surprise to many, as he had always taken the view before 1989 that it was important to engage with GDR historians. Now he wrote: "One can forget tons of East German literature. . . . Almost everything . . . that has been written on the German labor movement can be thrown away."[2] Others described GDR historians as "mediocre SED henchmen" or "plebeians of the mind."[3] Commissions dominated by West Germans were set up to judge the academic credentials of each individual historian at the Academy of Sciences in East Berlin, which was dissolved altogether as it did not fit into the West German landscape of research and higher education that was simply exported wholesale to the former East Germany.[4] With this the western Germans not only missed an opportunity to reform their own (in many respects) antiquated system of higher education, they also created havoc in the former East German system.

While many Academy historians had been favorably evaluated and the evaluation commission recommended integrating many of them into the new all-German system of higher education, there were simply not enough jobs for former Academy historians. What is more, the jobs that did exist were often taken by highly qualified West Germans, whom the West German system had been overproducing for many years. At the universities commissions (again largely staffed by West Germans) assessed East German historiography, but often in a far less open way. No clear criteria for their assessments were published, and sometimes secret references served as the basis for decisions on the continued employment of East German historians. Those who had not been found wanting in academic terms were still often dismissed as they were found guilty of collaborating with the Stasi. Few questions were asked about what such collaboration consisted of, despite the fact that everyone who had traveled to the "capitalist West" from the GDR had had to have some contact with the security service. Not all of them had betrayed colleagues or students, and it remains highly debatable whether academics should have been sacked for having Stasi contacts. Of course if their actions had resulted in harm done to colleagues or students, then there was indeed a moral issue that would have made it difficult to retain those historians, but where no such harm was done and where historians had simply written meaningless reports for the Stasi, was sacking them really justified?

In any case the net result of all these evaluations was that only a handful of GDR historians survived in the all-German system of higher education. Many of the younger generation of GDR historians soon gave up looking for a place in the system and chose different career paths. The GDR historical profession as it had developed since 1949 was completely destroyed. Many West German historians perceived a Communist East German historiography as an inglorious episode in a proud historiographical tradition associated with historicism and social scientific approaches associated with the West German Bielefeld School. It is worth pointing out that this fate has not been shared by historiography elsewhere in post-Communist Eastern Europe.[5] Communist regimes fell there as well, but the institutions and structures of historiography continued. Historians no doubt toned down their commitment to Marxism-Leninism, but they remained in their posts — and often saw the change as liberation from the fetters of Marxist-Leninist dogmas. By contrast, most of the historians in the GDR did not have the chance to reinvent themselves in a post-Communist world.

The few former East German historians who did survive the first half of the 1990s often faced bitter accusations. For example those who were working at the Research Center for Contemporary History in Potsdam (ZZF) were publicly castigated for being allegedly second-rate and for having been apologists for a Communist dictatorship.[6] In light of the lasting legacy of these debates and the near-silencing of East German voices in today's unified German historiography, it is worthwhile in a volume dedicated to the history of the afterlife of the GDR to review the balance sheet of East German historiography and ask whether perceptions of failure and mediocrity, which have been very much to the fore in unified Germany, are indeed justified.

It is easy to forget today that the division of Germany into four zones of occupation after 1945 and two German states after 1949 did not result in the immediate division of the German Historical Association (Verband der Historiker Deutschlands). In West Germany a conservative-national(ist) historiography continued to hold sway and most of those who were willing to renounce or, better still, deny their sympathies for National Socialism could continue their careers relatively unhindered. The historical profession in West Germany never issued an apology to those who had been exiled after 1933 and certainly never invited them back as a group. Few historians in the West attempted to explain the success of National Socialism with reference to specifically German developments. Those who did, including the octogenarian Friedrich Meinecke, were often called "Nestbeschmutzer" (literally, those willing to foul their own nest), despite the fact that they, like Meinecke, were hardly radical in their critique. In the more mainstream German historiography, attempts abounded to salvage German national history from the ruins of the Third Reich and declare a major gulf between bad Nazi racism and good German nationalism. The latter was represented above all by the national-conservative resistance to National Socialism, especially those military leaders who spearheaded the military coup of 20 July 1944.[7]

It is against this background in West Germany that the reform of the historical profession in the Soviet zone of occupation must be judged. During the initial phase of Soviet rule, few university historians were dismissed from their positions. This was in line with the official policy of the Soviet authorities and their Communist German allies to build broad anti-Fascist alliances and remove only those who had sided too strongly with the National Socialist regime. However, the more the division of Germany looked to be irreversible and the more the GDR established itself on the map of Europe, the more the government in East Berlin attempted to build a historical profession that was ideologically more conformist to the ruling Communist Party. "Bourgeois" historians were now either sacked or viciously attacked for their lack of commitment to the new state. Many of them fled to the West, where they were greeted with open arms as direct evidence of the ruthlessness and brutality of East German Communism. Those who attempted to come to an arrangement with the Communist state in the hope of building bridges between West and East Germany found themselves increasingly unable to hold together a deeply divided historical profession.

Karl Griewank is a good example of such a non-Marxist, "bourgeois" professor who played a major role in reestablishing historical studies in post-1945 East Germany while at the same time retaining respect among his West German colleagues. He had made his early career under the Nazis but had maintained his distance, never joining the Nazi Party and instead becoming a member of the Confessional Church (Bekennende Kirche). At the University of Jena, where he moved in 1947 (from Berlin), he even became dean of the humanities faculty. After having been elected to the Committee of the German Historical Association, the official all-German historical body, which was dominated by West Germans, he tried hard to mediate between West and East German historians, refusing to accept the division of Germany and of German historians. He pleaded with his West German colleagues to accept Marxist interpretations of history as one possible view among others while he promoted a liberal and deeply Christian view of history among his own students in East Germany. However, he was helpless to prevent the persecution of some of his star students by the state authorities in East Germany, and he also deeply resented the strong conservatism of Gerhard Ritter, one of the doyens of West German postwar historiography. Griewank's suicide in 1953 probably had more to do with a long history of depression than with the political situation at the East German universities, but it still seemed a powerful symbol of the futility of attempts to mediate between East and West German historiography during the hot phase of the Cold War.[8]

From the Communist GDR's perspective, an enforced transformation of the historical institutions of the country was part and parcel of its attempt to build its own loyal elite and went hand in hand with a reform of the university system. Between 1953 and 1958 higher education in the GDR expanded tremendously; at the same time the Socialist Unity Party (SED) insisted more and more that the GDR's leading academics should also be committed Marxists and, ideally, Party members. Although the transformation of the GDR's higher education into a training ground for Communist cadres was a long-drawn-out process that encountered much opposition, it was eventually far more successful in the GDR than in other East European Communist states. In some professions, notably medicine and engineering, "milieu persistence" and continuity of personnel remained strong throughout almost the entire existence of the GDR, but in other subject areas, including history, the Communist state was more successful in grooming its new elite. By 1961, 90 percent of all university historians were members of the SED. "Workers' and Peasants' Faculties," which were supposed to act as a springboard for a new proletarian elite, did not operate well everywhere, but in the humanities and social sciences some of the up-and-coming university professors took this route.[9] They saw themselves as the intellectual and professional elite of a new Communist Germany that claimed to have broken decisively with German national traditions.[10]

Compared with the initial decades in West Germany, the postwar years in the Soviet zone and later the GDR were indeed characterized by attempts to come to terms with the National Socialist past, even if there was a functionalist element to such attempts — namely to create an "anti-Fascist consensus" in East-German society — and even if there remained many areas where this "coming to terms" remained deficient. The Third Reich was explained by reference to the dominance of capitalist interests in the state, but many early commentators went far beyond this and portrayed the whole of German national history from the medieval period onward as a catastrophic path culminating in National Socialism. Alexander Abusch's writings are perhaps the most famous expression of this entirely negative view of German national history.[11] Those in charge of constructing a new Communist Germany, however, soon came to think that it would be difficult to build a new state on the basis of an entirely negative German identity, hence they quickly condemned "theories of misery" and instead promoted the idea of two distinct paths in German history. One represented the reactionary negative tradition from feudalism, Luther, absolutism, Frederick II, Bismarck, and Prussian militarism to Hindenburg and Hitler and was seen to culminate in the present-day Federal Republic of Germany. The second path went from the peasants' war, Thomas Müntzer, the early labor movements, Wilhelm Liebknecht and August Bebel, and the left wing of the SPD in Imperial Germany to the KPD in the Weimar Republic and the Communist resistance against National Socialism. The GDR portrayed itself as heir to this positive tradition in German history.[12]

Undoubtedly the greater willingness of GDR historians to explore the German roots of National Socialism also had to do with the considerable input of those who had been persecuted by the Nazis and had either been exiled or joined the Communist resistance. Many leading names of the first generation of GDR historians had impeccable anti-Fascist credentials.[13] They included the SED members Alexander Abusch, Alfred Meusel, Jürgen Kuczynski, Ernst Engelberg, Leo Stern, Walter Markov, Heinz Kamnitzer, Hermann Duncker, Albert Schreiner, and many more who, as Communists and trained historians, came to dominate the profession in the GDR in the 1950s. As Walter Markov recalled, the Communist cadres at the University of Leipzig were aware that it would take them years to build up a cohort of Marxist historians, which is why they deliberately sought to recruit among those anti-Fascists who had been forced into exile by the National Socialists.[14]

Exiles from National Socialism thus came to play an influential role in building the GDR's historical institutions, notably the Institute of History at the Academy of Sciences, the German History Museum, and the Institute for Economic History, all in East Berlin. They also dominated and led the history faculties at the GDR universities, where they trained the first generation of homegrown Marxist-Leninist historians in East Germany. Precisely in order to control this training more effectively, the faculties of history at the Universities of Jena, Rostock, and Greifswald were closed and history as a subject was concentrated at the Universities of Berlin, Leipzig, and Halle, where Institutes for the History of the German People were founded. Among the GDR-trained historians were such household names of GDR historiography as Kurt Pätzold, Fritz Klein, Hartmut Harnisch, Willibald Gutsche, Siegfried Prokop, and Manfred Kossock. The discipline founded its own historical journals, organized its own conferences, and undertook its own publishing projects — some of which were explicitly commissioned by the SED, which also employed its own historians at the Institute of Marxism-Leninism (IML), which was founded in 1947 (as the Marx-Engels-Lenin Institute) and acted as the ideological watchdog of historical studies in the GDR. The Institute of Social Sciences, founded in 1951 and, like the IML, directly under the guidance of the SED, also had an important role in the shaping of the historical profession. Party historians could also be found at the SED's own Party University in East Berlin, the Pedagogical University in Potsdam, and the University of Economics in East Berlin.

While the outspoken anti-Fascism of GDR historiography contrasted positively with the apologias and the silence emanating from West German history departments, the legitimizing function of this anti-Fascism for the GDR cannot be ignored,[15] because the historians' willingness to deal more thoroughly with the German traditions feeding into National Socialism was rooted in the Communist state's desire to portray itself as the morally better Germany and to discredit the FRG.

Tensions between East and West German historians came to a head at the Historikertag (German Historians' Conference) in Trier in 1958.[16] The West German-dominated leadership of the Historical Association had strongly criticized the lack of academic freedom in the GDR and refused to let any of the members of the GDR delegation speak at Trier, so the GDR historians left the congress under protest. All of this was in marked contrast to the congress in Ulm two years earlier, where there had been several attempts to come to a productive dialogue between non-Marxist West German and Marxist East German historians. However, while many

272 ◆ STEFAN BERGER

GDR historians had attempted to move to an open competition with their West German counterparts, the SED changed tack late in 1956, which led to the confrontation in Trier two years later. The attempt to overthrow Hungarian Communism in 1956 had demonstrated to the SED the dangers of encouraging open dialogue with non-Marxists. In response the SED started various campaigns against "revisionist tendencies," which also had consequences for the historical profession.

The chief editors of the *Zeitschrift für Geschichtswissenschaft* (ZfG), Fritz Klein and Joachim Streisand, were fired. The director of the Museum for German History, Alfred Meusel, came under intense pressure for suggesting that Marxist GDR historians should join the all-German Historical Association. The SED now insisted that any idea of mutual coexistence between rival conceptions of history was mistaken and that it was the clear task of GDR historians to fight the historical conceptions of the "class enemy" in the FRG. GDR historians subsequently set up their own association, which confirmed the existence of a separate GDR historiography in a separate German state. None other than Walter Ulbricht defined the main task of GDR historiography as developing a national counter-concept to the history of the FRG, and discrediting their West German colleagues and the West German political system more generally remained one of the foremost tasks of East German historiography. This can be exemplified most clearly by reference to the publication in 1977 of a massive tome of essays documenting the support of many leading West German historians for the National Socialist regime.[17] This "Brown Book" alleged an unbroken continuity between Nazi and West German historiography, the message being that Fascism was still alive and well in the FRG. The book and its authors frequently overstated their criticism, and they were also not averse to making up evidence where none existed in the archives. While the book can be criticized on many accounts, the "brown roots" of parts of West German historiography were beyond doubt and were confirmed by a younger generation of West German historians from the 1980s onwards who dug into the past of foundational figures such as Werner Conze, Theodor Schieder, and Hans Rothefels. They rarely referred to the GDR's "Brown Book," however, which showed that its reception in the FRG was largely non-existent. In keeping with the spirit of the Cold War it had been very widely dismissed as the result of SED history propaganda and agitation.

Given that the legitimacy of the GDR as the morally better Germany was at the heart of the mission of the historical profession in the GDR, national history continued to take center stage. This in itself was not unusual; after all, national history had become the dominant form of history writing throughout Europe during the nineteenth century. In the Communist regimes of Eastern Europe it remained dominant after 1945 and merged with a Marxist-Leninist discourse on class.[18] In GDR historiography as elsewhere in Eastern Europe some exceptions only confirmed the rule. For example Walter Markov and later Manfred Kossock made the University of Leipzig internationally renowned with their research on the comparative history of revolutions.

Markov in particular must be viewed as one of the most interesting representatives of GDR historiography. Imprisoned for his Communist resistance to National Socialism, he was among those who shaped GDR historiography in the late 1940s until, falling foul of the Stalinist dogmatism of the SED, he was accused of Titoism in 1951 and excluded from the Party. Despite never rejoining he remained a life-long Communist. He was a specialist on the French Revolution and concentrated on the far left wing of the Jacobins, and his biography of the radical priest Jacques Roux became a major contribution to the field. It was reissued in 2009 by the Leipziger Universitätsverlag and certainly merits rereading today. Markov was well connected in particular among Communist French historians, and he turned his interest to the comparative history of revolutions in the 1960s. As founding director of the University of Nigeria in Nsukka in 1962–63, he helped build up history as a discipline and then taught at the University of Santiago de Chile in 1970–71. In the GDR he became the key mentor for the development of area studies, taking on the job of director of the new Institute for Africa and Near Eastern Studies at the University of Leipzig in 1968. He published several important works on world history, and his interest in the comparative history of revolutions was carried on at the University of Leipzig by his pupil Manfred Kossock. Markov was not the only historian of international standing in the GDR, but his short biography may serve here as an example of the merits of GDR historiography — merits that were all too easily forgotten after 1990.[19]

Markov's and Kossock's interest in non-German topics was unusual. The overwhelming resources of the historical profession in the GDR went into constructing a national history fit for the Communist German state. A new multi-volume German history begun in 1951 was supposed to present a Marxist master-narrative, and in 1955 the SED Politbüro adopted a so-called history resolution, calling on the GDR's historians to develop lessons from German history that would legitimize the GDR, delegitimize the FRG, and contribute to contemporary political struggles. A "basic national concept" (*nationale Grundkonzeption*) was developed that portrayed the SED and the revolutionary German labor movement as representative of the true national interests of the German people. The *Zeitschrift für Geschichtswissenschaft*, the historical journal in the GDR, founded in 1953, was dominated by German topics and was seen by leading historians and politicians as one of the most important means of nationalizing the GDR's historical consciousness along Marxist-Leninist lines. In the 1950s the *ZfG* was still relatively keen on developing international contacts and including foreign authors, but in subsequent decades the percentage of international authors and themes outside of national history declined, reaching an all-time low in the 1980s.[20] The growing nationalization of the *ZfG* coincided with an increasing desire to depict the FRG as hostile to the true national interests of the German people. As Albert Norden stressed in 1964, "The people find the nation only through socialism; only socialism merges the nation and people into one."[21] For GDR historiography the nation thus remained one of the basic structures of society. It was often portrayed as a given, an almost natural force. Essentialist notions of "the national" were by no means uncommon among GDR historians, and the link between history and national identity remained unchallenged in GDR historiography. Even some of the old Prussian nationalist myths were upheld.[22]

All of this can be seen in the one-volume *Kleine Enzyklopädie — Deutsche Geschichte*, published in Leipzig in 1965 and edited by Eckhard Müller-Mertens, Erich Paterna, and Max Steinmetz.[23] In the preface to this popular national history, the editors highlighted the need for "a strong national and socialist consciousness" (*EDG*, 18), which would help Socialism in the GDR to succeed. The book was meant as a specific contribution to developing such a consciousness among the broader population, and like their Prussian counterparts in the nineteenth century, GDR historians were not averse to projecting national identity back to the Middle Ages. Thus the Franconian Reich of the ninth century was seen as the origin of the "development of the German people and state," for the East Franconian people developed a "consciousness of community" that ultimately was channeled into the "formation of a German nationality" (28). Again in line with Prussianism, the *EDG* condemned a succession of medieval German monarchs for pursuing "utopian plans for power in Italy and the Mediterranean" (78), thereby neglecting the early unification of a more centralized German nation state. The absence of a strong national monarchy was subsequently described as the most important reason the German lands became the victim of the Thirty Years' War. Like August von Sybel and Heinrich von Treitschke, the *EDG* authors saw the "wars of liberation" against Napoleon as the most important germ for the nineteenth-century national movement. In their account the events of 1806 culminated logically in the unification of Germany in 1871: "The struggle against foreign rule became a historical necessity due to the vital interests of the German people" (206). The year 1848 was described as a national uprising in which the working class for the first time "proved itself . . . as a most decisive national force" (273). Here the *EDG* deviated from traditional Prussianism in that the collective hero of national history was no longer the Hohenzollern dynasty but the German working classes and those speaking on their behalf, namely revolutionary Social Democrats before 1914 and the Communist Party after 1919. Even the Franco-Prussian War served a "just aim: national unity" (295) Whereas revisionists and reformists in the pre-First World War SPD were described as "anti-national" traitors, the KPD was seen as working tirelessly for "the interests of the nation" in the Ruhr conflict, the economic depression, and the fight against National Socialism (337). The text culminated in a hymn to the SED leading the struggle for German unity against those in the FRG keen on permanently dividing the German fatherland.[24] As the example of the *EDG* underlines, GDR historians by no means abandoned the long tradition of using national history to boost national identity.

Their commitment to the Socialist nation of the GDR went hand in hand with their attachment to the idea of *Parteilichkeit* — partisanship, which became an important benchmark for GDR historians. Their commitment to Marxism-Leninism meant that they rejected the ideal of objectivity that had guided "bourgeois" historiography in the past. Instead, they argued, history had to take sides in the struggle to emancipate the working classes and aid the workers' avant-garde, that is, the Communist Party. They therefore consciously wrote history from the perspective of the working classes. The exact meaning of partisanship led to one of the major theoretical debates in GDR historiography in 1956. In the *ZfG* Jürgen Kuczynski had called for more scientificity (*Wissenschaftlichkeit*)[25] in the field and thus indirectly attacked the increasing political conformism. Upholding the idea of partisanship in Marxist-Leninist historiography, he argued that greater *Wissenschaftlichkeit* paradoxically led to more partisanship because the historical reality itself was partisan; in other words, because the historical reality showed the objective process of the rise of the working class and the decline of the bourgeoisie, the historical process was on the side of Marxism-Leninism. Renouncing the idea of "objectivity" as ideology, Kuczynski instead endorsed the partisan perspective in historical writing, arguing that the partisan perspective in Marxist-Leninist historiography should not be mistaken for Party-political conformism. Rather, such a perspective was in line with the progressive forces in history.

Kuczynski's intervention came at a time when the SED had decided to tighten the screws of political conformity, and the Party reacted with an intense campaign against him. No fewer than nine articles appeared in the *ZfG* opposing his views in 1957 and 1958, and he was accused of "unprincipled eclecticism" and "bourgeois objectivism."[26] While in the long run Kuczynski's "scientific partisanship" was more useful as a theoretical underpinning of a Marxist-Leninist historiography than the political conformity demanded by the SED, most GDR historians were neither willing nor able to follow him. They found it easier to pay lip-service to the ideological dogmas of Marxism-Leninism in the introductions and conclusions to their monographs, while continuing with the mainstream positivism that characterized so much of the historical production in Germany from the nineteenth century onwards. This was particularly true for many areas of historiography that were not too highly politicized.

Nevertheless, many West German historians took issue with their East German colleagues' partisanship. Upholding the principle of the objectivity of scientific historical endeavor, they argued that history had become the handmaiden of politics in the GDR and was therefore indistinguishable from propaganda. While scientific objectivity and source-based criticism were allegedly the benchmarks of Western historiography, East German historiography was described in terms of bending historical facts in order to legitimate the Communist dictatorship. In his thoughtful attempt to historize GDR historiography, Martin Sabrow avoided such condemnation by adopting the position of an anthropologist examining a field that followed different standards and rationales from that in the West.[27] He argued that GDR historians should not be judged against Western benchmarks and instead should be perceived against the background of their own rules and norms. This led to a very sensitive reading of GDR historiography that avoided evaluation and political denunciation and highlighted the differences between conditions of historical production in the divided Germany. However, one should also acknowledge the argument put forward by Ralf Possekehl, who criticized Sabrow's approach for orientalizing GDR historiography and making it into something odd, peculiar, and exotic.[28] In fact the anthropologist's perspective made GDR historiography into a deviant when measured against the anthropologist's own historiographical norms, which are invariably those of the alleged Western scientific objectivity. Sabrow's approach did at least avoid the widespread condemnation that dominated perceptions of GDR historiography in the first half of the 1990s. It therefore remains one of the most sophisticated attempts to discuss the shortcomings without ignoring the special qualities and characteristics of the historical profession in East Germany.

The argument that GDR historiography became more professional and, by implication, more like Western historiography, is confirmed by the greater freedom of GDR historians to write about subjects previously regarded as controversial and taboo. During the 1980s West and East German historians increasingly attended each other's conferences and recognized each other as colleagues producing work that did not have to be denounced but required critical engagement. Historians close to the West German Social Democratic Party and the East German Socialist Unity Party met in March 1987 to discuss ideological differences and possibilities for future cooperation, indicating that by the second half of the 1980s a climate of cooperation and relatively open discussion prevailed.[29] Georg Iggers, a US-based historian and one of the outspoken proponents of such a dialogue, published a book that assembled some of the most innovative work produced by GDR historians, seeming to confirm the idea of an increasing professionalism among them.[30] By the time of the GDR's collapse, its historians had become well-integrated and accepted members of the international "ecumenical community" of historians.[31] Then came the destruction of the GDR and of GDR historiography, which was largely completed in the first half of the 1990s. In the final part of this article I would like to consider where this left the field.

Among the older, more established generation of GDR historians the devaluation of their lifetime work produced much bitterness and resentment, which was ultimately channeled into an alternative historical culture that survives in the new *Bundesländer* to this very day.[32] A surprising number of those who had been purged from the system founded a variety of historical associations and societies in order to maintain scholarly networks of communication. Some of them are linked to the successor party of the SED, Die Linke (previously the Party of Democratic Socialism, or PDS), which has its own historical commission to organize conferences and issue statements on behalf of the party on key historical anniversaries such as the unification of the SPD and SED in 1946 and the building of the Berlin Wall in 1961. The Rosa Luxemburg Foundation, the party political foundation of Die Linke, also provides a forum for history debates at the national and regional (*Länder*) level. One of the most active foundations is Helle Panke — Rosa Luxemburg Stiftung Berlin, which has been publishing the *hefte zur ddr-geschichte* since 1992 with a circulation of around five hundred per issue. More recently the *hefte* have turned their attention from GDR history to the interconnectedness of East and West German history after 1945.[33]

A variety of organizations with no direct political links also continues to promote forms of historical culture that carry on GDR historiographical traditions, including among their members many former GDR historians who remain sympathetic to Die Linke, for example the Leibnitz-Societät (Leibnitz Society), which sees itself as the continuation of the dissolved Academy of Sciences; the Berliner Gesellschaft für Faschismus- und Weltkriegsforschung (Berlin Society for Research on Fascism and World War), founded in 1992 by Werner Röhr; and the Gesellschaftswissenschaftliche Forum e.V. (Forum for Social Sciences) in Berlin, also founded in 1992. These associations have been producing a vast amount of "grey literature," but they have also forged links with small eastern German publishing houses that sustain this alternative historical culture with a steady stream of publications.

Many of the historians active in this alternative historical culture are motivated by a desire to defend their own achievements as scholars and to counter a perceived silencing of GDR historiography. Sometimes they critically reassess their own former judgments, but often they write the history of the GDR and of divided Germany as an antidote to what they perceive as the dominant wholesale condemnation of the GDR and the glorification of the FRG in the mainstream historiography of unified Germany. It is striking to what extent this alternative historical culture has been engaged in examining and questioning GDR historiography, which can be seen as an exercise in "coming to terms" with their own past. Most historians, reflecting on their work in the GDR, are adamant that it was "scientific" (*wissenschaftlich*); they consider themselves seekers of "historical truth" who are committed to sober, rational analyses.[34] There is a great deal of disillusionment and bitterness in these reflections, as many former East German historians clearly see themselves as victims of a West German witch-hunt after 1990. They have the distinct feeling that they were out-maneuvered by their West German colleagues, who did not even shy away from dissolving internationally renowned research groups such as the one on the comparative history of revolutions led by Manfred Kossock and based in Leipzig and the one on the history of the Second World War led by Wolfgang Schumann and based in Berlin.[35] They have memories of West German colleagues hastily withdrawing from planned joint research projects with their East German counterparts and replacing purged East German historians with West Germans.

These historians portray GDR historiography as being firmly rooted in anti-Fascism, which they contrast with the implication of West German historians in National Socialism, something that did not harm their careers in the early Federal Republic.[36] They argue that whereas the early Federal Republic was all too willing to give post-Fascist historians a second chance, the doors have remained firmly shut to post-Communist historians in unified Germany. They insist on the innovative potential of early Marxist-Leninist historiography in the GDR, which they routinely juxtapose to the continuity of a stifling historicism in West Germany. Even if they admit that much of this potential remained unrealized in the GDR, there is an almost utopian element in these reflections in that they seek to defend the methodological and theoretical premises of Marxist-Leninist historiography. While they readily accept that they were too close to the Communist state and its leading party, they insist that their work contributed to the progress of historical knowledge. Most former GDR historians do not see themselves as "party workers at the historical front," but rather as "loyal dissidents" who regret that they were often too loyal.[37]

Although most GDR historians deplore their fate, they are also often self-critical regarding their inability to withstand and act more independently of the ideological leadership of the SED and its ideologues. As Mario Kessler has written, it was the eagerness with which many GDR historians anticipated and sought to preempt the latest ideological turns of the Party that ultimately led to a self-inflicted dependency on the Communist rulers.[38] Fritz Klein talks about his own "unworthy behavior" when faced with allegations against colleagues from his own institute, and his personal failure to stand up for those colleagues in front of the assembled might of the Party.[39]

Most historians were dedicated SED members and most also depict the SED as an instrument of oppression. Even doyens of GDR historiography such as Kuczynski escaped a trial and dismissal only by a hair's breadth in 1953, when the SED was keen to purge those who had been in exile in the West.[40] It is therefore perhaps hardly surprising that many GDR historians talk about their growing disillusionment with Socialism and describe the Party bureaucracy as an almighty apparatus against which any form of opposition would have been pointless. The typical narrative is one of early enthusiasm for Communism, repeated disappointments with Communism, "inner struggles" to find a position toward Communism and the parallel desire to remain true to one's early ideals, and the realization that their own (sometimes cowardly, but always all too human) actions led to the ultimate failure of this desire.[41]

A self-critical approach has also characterized the GDR historians' reflections on their work about the GDR itself. They have readily admitted mistakes and blind spots and combined questions about their own capacity as historians with searching analyses of the country to which they once belonged. Where did the GDR go wrong? What congenital defects did it have? It is no coincidence that many of these reflections focus on repeated attempts to reform Communism in the GDR; the years 1948, 1953, 1956, 1961, and 1968 figure prominently in these narratives. A particular concern with Stalinism has also emerged as a favored topic in post-Communist historical writing since 1990. This interrelationship between personal biography and historical reflection about the place of the GDR in a wider postwar history of Germany is especially marked in Günter Benser's *DDR —gedenkt ihrer mit Nachsicht* (2000). There is some nostalgia here, but it is not the historical equivalent of the movie *Good Bye, Lenin!* (2003). Overall it is a frank and critical engagement with the many shortcomings of the GDR, but it includes a desire to escape the complete condemnation of the GDR that echoed from many public statements of East German historians after 1990 and a very personal concern to bring one's own positive experiences in and with the GDR into congruence with an overall balance sheet for this failed state.[42]

A willingness to be self-critical is combined with a desire to keep one's head high against the tide of western German accusations and western German attempts to declare entire biographies worthless. Part and parcel of this self-assertive mood in the self-reflective literature of GDR historians is the emphasis on the reform potential inherent in the SED during the 1980s. Siegfried Prokop, for example, has emphasized the willingness of many ordinary SED members to use perestroika and glasnost to reform Communism from below.[43] In Ralf Possekehl's analysis of Socialist reform discourses inside the SED during the 1980s, the borders between GDR dissidents and SED become very fluid indeed.[44] And Stefan Bollinger also locates SED reformers and dissidents on the same side of the barricades in 1989 — both are described as the losers in a unification dictated by West Germany.[45]

To some extent the strong concern with German national history that was such a prominent feature of GDR historiography as discussed above is reflected in the many positive statements by GDR historians on German national unity. Deeply critical of the form that unification took after 1990, there is an often sentimental and emotional attachment to the idea of the German nation. Joachim Petzold, for example, has written about unification as the fulfilment of an "innermost desire."[46] Stefan Doernberg waxes lyrical about the "natural tendency for national unity" in the revolution of 1989 that reminds him of his own love for Germany when he returned to the country in Soviet uniform in 1945.[47] Sometimes the failure of the GDR has even been ascribed to a "national defect" in Socialist Germany,[48] and some GDR historians who had championed the "two nations theory" before 1989, such as Walter Schmidt, quickly changed their position and acknowledged the power of national sentiments.[49]

While the remnants of GDR historiography form an alternative historical culture that has been battling against the odds to gain some attention in public debates on German history, its long-term prospects are poor because it relies almost entirely on the support of people who are now well beyond retirement age. It is safe to predict that these remnants of a separate East German historiography are a generational phenomenon that will disappear in the next two decades.

By way of conclusion one might ask: What was lost with the destruction of GDR historiography? Some West German historians have by now admitted that this destruction was unnecessarily harsh and thorough,[50] but the damage has been done. It is difficult to say whether GDR historiography would have freed itself from its ideological shackles and developed a critical Marxist perspective in dialogue with Western Marxisms that have enriched Western historical writing since the days of Karl Marx, but in one (positive) scenario, a revamped Marxist GDR historiography would have contributed to a Marxist tradition within the German historical profession. In comparison to its East German counterparts, the West German historical profession was always characterized by its strong anti-Communism. Marxist historians were deliberately kept at the gates of the hallowed halls of academic history, and only a handful could be found at West German universities, unlike in France, Italy, Britain, and post-Franco Spain. In some respects, therefore, the integration of GDR historiography could have done away with this German anomaly.

Interestingly, some of the most innovative work now in other Eastern European historiographies (including work influenced by Western Marxist approaches) is being done by the younger generation of historians, trained and socialized in the post-Communist world. Perhaps it is difficult to teach old dogs new tricks. One should not overestimate the potential of GDR historiography to transform itself into something that would have been innovative and cutting-edge, but then again, how much Western —

including West German — historiography could be called that over the long decades of the Cold War? Some of the books produced by the representatives of GDR historiography will undoubtedly retain their value, and some of those historians will hopefully be remembered by future generations for the work they produced. As a whole, GDR historiography does not leave a legacy; there are no heirs and no futures. As Simone Lässig has written: "The East German historical profession left no trace on the academic culture of united Germany: not on the methodologies and theories historians employ, not on the topics they study, and certainly not on the way the historical profession and the study of history are organized."[51] Like GDR history overall, GDR historiography will eventually find its place in a wider story of German historical writing, but it is a place firmly confined to the past.

Notes

[1] This and the following quotations in this paragraph are taken from Alexander Fischer and Günther Heydemann, eds., *Geschichtswissenschaft in der DDR*, vol. 1, *Historische Entwicklung, Theoriediskussion und Geschichtsdidaktik* (Berlin: Duncker & Humblot, 1988), 3–30. Unless otherwise stated, the translations from German in this article are the author's own.

[2] Hans-Ulrich Wehler, "Hart widersprechen und mit dem Unfug stets konfrontieren," *Frankfurter Rundschau*, 24 September 1992.

[3] Karlheinz Blaschke, "Akademiker als Pförtner," *Frankfurter Allgemeine Zeitung*, 27 June 1990, and Herbert Gottwald, "Es gab nicht nur Anpassung und Stagnation: Plebejer des Geistes degradierten die Geschichtswissenschaft in der ehemaligen DDR," *Frankfurter Allgemeine Zeitung*, 10 December 1990.

[4] On the reform of the East German higher education system see Jochen Gläser, "Die Akademie der Wissenschaften nach der Wende: Erst reformiert, dann ignoriert und schliesslich aufgelöst," *Aus Politik und Zeitgeschichte*, 11 December 1992; Ulrich Schneckener, "Vertane Chance und die 'Dialektik der Abwicklung,'" *Frankfurter Rundschau*, 17 November 1994; Jürgen Kocka and Renate Mayntz, eds., *Wissenschaft und Wiedervereinigung. Disziplinen im Umbruch* (Berlin: Akademie Verlag, 1998); and Wolfgang Richter, ed., *Unfrieden in Deutschland, Weissbuch 2: Wissenschaft und Kultur im Beitrittsgebiet* (Berlin: GNN Verlag, 1993).

[5] On the post-Communist transformation in Eastern Europe see Sorin Antohi, Balázs Trencsényi, and Péter Apor, eds., *Narratives Unbound: Historical Studies in Post-Communist Eastern Europe* (Budapest: CEU Press, 2007).

[6] On the controversy surrounding the ZZF, see Mitchell G. Ash, "Geschichtswissenschaft, Geschichtskultur und der ostdeutsche Historikerstreit," *Geschichte und Gesellschaft* 24 (1998): 283–304.

[7] On the development of postwar West German historiography see Winfried Schulze, *Deutsche Geschichtswissenschaft nach 1945* (Munich: Oldenbourg, 1993).

[8] Tobias Kaiser, *Karl Griewank (1900–1953): Ein deutscher Historiker im "Zeitalter der Extreme"* (Stuttgart: Franz Steiner, 2007).

[9] Here workers who lacked the necessary educational qualifications to attend university were trained so that they could then transfer in.

[10] On the transformation of East German history departments in the context of the restructuring of the whole system of higher education see Martin Sabrow, *Das Diktat des Konsenses: Geschichtswissenschaft in der DDR (1949–1969)* (Munich: Oldenbourg, 2001); also Ilko-Sascha Kowalczuk, *Legitimation eines neuen Staates: Parteiarbeiter an der historischen Front — Geschichtswissenschaft in der SBZ/DDR 1945–1961* (Berlin: Ch. Links, 1997); and Ulrich Neuhäußer-Wespy, *Die SED und die Historie: Die Etablierung der marxistisch-leninistischen Wissenschaft in den fünfziger und sechziger Jahren* (Bonn: Bouvier, 1996). On the transformation of the East German higher education system more generally see Ralph Jessen, *Akademische Elite und kommunistische Diktatur* (Göttingen: Vandenhoeck & Ruprecht, 1999), and Ilko-Sascha Kowalczuk, *Geist im Dienste der Macht: Hochschulpolitik in der SBZ/DDR 1945–1961* (Berlin: Ch. Links, 2003). For comparative perspectives see John Connelly, *Captive University: The Sovietisation of East German, Czech, and Polish Higher Education, 1945–1956* (Chapel Hill: U of North Carolina P, 2000).

[11] Alexander Abusch, *Der Irrweg einer Nation: Ein Beitrag zum Verständnis deutscher Geschichte* (Berlin: Aufbau, 1946).

[12] Joachim Streisand, "Progressive Ideen der deutschen Vergangenheit und ihre Verwirklichung in der DDR," *Zeitschrift für Geschichtswissenschaft* 12 (1964): 1335–40.

[13] Mario Kessler, *Exilerfahrung in Wissenschaft und Politik: Remigrierte Historiker in der frühen DDR* (Cologne: Böhlau, 2001).

[14] Walter Markov, *Zwiesprache mit dem Jahrhundert: Dokumentiert von Thomas Grimm* (Berlin: Aufbau, 1989), 180.

[15] Kurt Finker, *Zwischen Integration und Legitimation: Der antifaschistische Widerstandskampf im Geschichtsbild und Geschichtsschreibung der DDR* (Leipzig: Leipziger Universitätsverlag, 1999).

[16] Martin Sabrow, "Ökumene als Bedrohung: Die Haltung der DDR-Historiographie gegenüber den deutschen Historikertagen von 1949 bis 1962," in *Historikertage im Vergleich*, ed. Gerald Diesener and Matthias Middell (Leipzig: Leipziger Universitätsverlag, 1996), 178–202.

[17] Gerhard Lozek, ed., *Unbewältigte Vergangenheit: Kritik der bürgerlichen Geschichtsschreibung in der BRD* (Berlin: Akademie Verlag, 1977).

[18] Gita Deneckere and Thomas Welskopp, "The 'Nation' and 'Class': European National Master-Narratives and Their Social 'Other,'" in *The Contested Nation: Ethnicity, Class, Religion, and Gender in National Histories*, ed. Stefan Berger and Chris Lorenz (Basingstoke: Palgrave Macmillan, 2008), 135–70.

[19] Walter Markov, *Wie viele Leben lebt der Mensch? Eine Autobiographie aus dem Nachlass* (Leipzig: Faber & Faber, 2009).

[20] Matthias Middell, "Autoren und Inhalte: *Die Zeitschrift für Geschichtswissenschaft* 1953–1989," in *Historische Zeitschriften im internationalen Vergleich*, ed. Matthias Middell (Leipzig: Akademie-Verlag, 1999), 235–96.

[21] Albert Norden, "Die Nation und wir," in *Zeitschrift für Geschichtswissenschaft* 12 (1964): 1116.

[22] Stefan Berger, "National Paradigm and Legitimacy: Uses of Academic History Writing in the 1960s," in *The Workers' and Peasants' State: Communism and Society in East Germany under Ulbricht 1945–1971*, ed. Patrick Major and Jonathan Osmond (Manchester: Manchester UP, 2002), 244–61.

[23] *Kleine Enzyklopädie — Deutsche Geschichte*, ed. Eckhard Müller-Mertens, Erich Paterna, and Max Steinmetz (Berlin: Aufbau, 1965) (hereafter cited in text as *EDG*).

[24] A detailed analysis of the more academic, multi-volume *German History* is provided by Martin Sabrow in "Planprojekt Meistererzählung: Die Entstehungsgeschichte des 'Lehrbuchs für deutsche Geschichte,'" in *Geschichte als Herrschaftsdiskurs: Der Umgang mit der Vergangenheit in der DDR*, ed. Martin Sabrow (Cologne: Böhlau, 2000), 227–86.

[25] The term "scientificity" is unusual in English and is used here to denote the commitment to scientific rigor and method.

[26] Heiko Feldner, "History in the Academy: Objectivity and Partisanship in the Marxist Historiography of the German Democratic Republic," in Major and Osmond, *The Workers' and Peasants' State*, 262–77.

[27] Sabrow, *Das Diktat des Konsenses*. In this article I use the term "historize" rather than the more usual term "historicize" to indicate a difference between "historism" as the idea of the historical evolution of all human development (*Historismus*) and the teleological belief that history is moving in a particular direction (Karl Popper's *Historizismus*). While these concepts are related, they ultimately express two very different ideas about the relationship of the present to the past and should therefore be kept analytically apart. By using only one term for both concepts, the English language muddies the waters here, which is why I think a neologism such as "historization" can be usefully introduced.

[28] Ralf Possekehl, "Kuriositätenkabinett oder Wissenschaftsgeschichte? Zur Historisierung der DDR-Geschichtswissenschaft," *Geschichte und Gesellschaft* 24 (1998): 446–62.

[29] The discussions are documented in Susanne Miller and Malte Ristau, eds., *Erben deutscher Geschichte: DDR-BRD — Protokolle einer historischen Begegnung* (Reinbek: rororo, 1988).

[30] Georg Iggers, ed., *Ein anderer historischer Blick: Beispiele ostdeutscher Sozialgeschichte* (Frankfurt am Main: Fischer, 1991).

[31] On the idea of historiography as an "ecumenical community" see Karl Dietrich Erdmann, *Toward a Global Community of Historians: The International Historical Congresses and the International Committee of Historical Sciences 1898–2000* (Oxford: Berghahn, 2005).

[32] Stefan Berger, "Former GDR Historians in the Reunified Germany: An Alternative Historical Culture and Its Attempts to Come to Terms with the GDR Past," *Journal of Contemporary History* 38 (2003): 63–84.

[33] See http://www.helle-panke.de, accessed 11 June 2010.

[34] For some of the many examples see Fritz Klein, *Drinnen und Draussen: Ein Historiker in der DDR* (Frankfurt am Main: Fischer, 2001), 128; Kurt Pätzold, "Leben, Studium und gemeinsame Anfänge wissenschaftlicher Forschungen in Jena (1950–1961)," in *Geschichtsschreibung in der DDR zum Zweiten Weltkrieg: Biographische und historische Beobachtungen*, ed. Thüringer Forum für Bildung und Wissenschaft e.V. (Jena: Rosa-Luxemburg-Stiftung Thüringen, 2001), 27; and Wolfgang Küttler, "Vorwort," in *Zur Geschichte der Historiographie nach 1945*, ed. Alfred Loesdau and Helmut Meyer (Berlin: Verlag, 2001), 7.

[35] Personal interviews with Manfred Weißbecker (5 December 2001), Werner Röhr (28 November 2001), and Siegfried Prokop (23 November 2001).

[36] Paradigmatic in this respect is Werner Berthold, "Postfaschistische Historiker der Alt-BRD und antifaschistische Historiker der Ex-DDR in totalitaristisch-egalisierender Sicht," in Thüringer Forum, *Geschichtsschreibung*, 225–46.

[37] Some examples include Wolfgang Küttler, "Theoretisch-methodische Grundlagen der DDR-Geschichtswissenschaft zum 19. und 20. Jahrhundert," in Thüringer Forum, *Geschichtsschreibung*, 9–22; and Günter Benser, "Denkanstösse für den Umgang mit DDR-Geschichte," in *Das lange kurze Leben der DDR*, ed. Jenaer Forum für Bildung und Wissenschaft e.V. (Jena: Rosa-Luxemburg-Stiftung Thüringen, 2000), 12. "Party workers at the historical front" is a term coined by Kowalczuk in *Legitimation eines neuen Staats*. Jürgen Kuczynski famously called himself a "loyal dissident" in *"Ein linientreuer Dissident": Memoiren 1945–1989* (Berlin: Aufbau, 1992).

[38] Kessler, *Exilerfahrung*, 312.

[39] Klein, *Drinnen und Draussen*, 296.

[40] Matthew Stibbe, "Jürgen Kuczynski and the Search for a (Non-Existent) Western Spy Ring in the East German Communist Party in 1953," *Contemporary European History* 20:1 (2011): 61–79.

[41] A good example of such a narrative structure is Eckart Mehls, *Unzumutbar: Ein Leben in der DDR* (Berlin: Trafo-Verlag, 1999).

[42] Günter Benser, *DDR — gedenkt ihrer mit Nachsicht* (Berlin: GNN, 2000).

[43] Siegfried Prokop, ed., *Die kurze Zeit der Utopie: Die "zweite" DDR im vergessenen Jahr 1989/90* (Berlin: SBV, 1994).

[44] Ralf Possekehl, "Sozialismusreformdiskurse in der SED seit 1985," in *Die PDS — Herkunft und Selbstverständnis: Eine politisch-historische Debatte*, ed. Lothar Bisky et al. (Berlin: PDS, 1996), 142–47.

[45] Stefan Bollinger, *1989 — eine abgebrochene Revolution: Verbaute Wege nicht nur zu einer besseren DDR?* (Berlin: Trafo-Verlag, 1999).

[46] Joachim Petzold, *Parteinahme wofür? DDR Historiker im Spannungsfeld von Politik und Wissenschaft* (Potsdam: ZZF, 2000), 367.

[47] Stefan Doernberg, *Ein Deutscher auf dem Weg nach Deutschland: Bericht eines Zeitzeugen über das Jahr 1945* (Berlin: Helle Panke, 2000), 7.

[48] Gerhard Lozek, *Stalinismus — Ideologie, Gesellschaftskonzept oder was?* (Berlin: Klartext, 1993), 23.

[49] Walter Schmidt, *Das Zwei Nationen Konzept der SED und sein Scheitern* (Berlin: Helle Panke, 1996).

[50] Interview with Jürgen Kocka, *Sozialismus* 9 (1999): 17–20.

[51] Simone Lässig, "Between Two Scholarly Cultures: Reflections on the Reorganisation of the East German Historical Profession after 1990," *Central European History* 40 (2007): 499–522, here 501.

Contributors

THOMAS AHBE is a Leipzig-based social scientist, writer, and commentator whose articles and essays have appeared in a wide number of newspapers and journals. He has written and edited numerous books on eastern German affairs including *Geschichte der Generationen in der DDR und in Ostdeutschland: Ein Panorama* (with Rainer Gries, 3rd ed., 2011), *Die Ostdeutschen in den Medien: Das Bild von den Anderen seit 1990* (ed. with Rainer Gries and Wolfgang Schmale, 2009), *Identitätskonstruktionen: Das Patchwork der Identitäten in der Spätmoderne* (ed. with Heiner Keupp, Wolfgang Gmür, et al., 4th ed., 2008), and *Ostalgie: Zum Umgang mit der DDR-Vergangenheit in den 1990er Jahren* (2005).

PERTTI AHONEN is senior lecturer in history in the School of History, Classics, and Archaeology at the University of Edinburgh. He is the author of *After the Expulsion: West Germany and Eastern Europe 1945–1990* (2003) and *Death at the Berlin Wall* (2011), and coauthor of *People on the Move: Forced Population Movements in Europe in the Second World War and Its Aftermath* (2008).

SILKE ARNOLD-DE SIMINE is lecturer in German in the Department of European Cultures and Languages at Birkbeck, University of London. Her research interests lie in nineteenth- and twentieth-century German literature and early film, gender studies, cultural memory, and museum studies. She is editor of *Memory Traces: 1989 and the Question of German Cultural Identity* (2005).

STEFAN BERGER is professor of Social History at the University of Bochum, where he also is Director of the Institute of Social Movements and the House for the History of the Ruhr. He has published widely on comparative labor history, the history of historiography in Europe, and on nationalism and national identity. His most recent publications are *Friendly Enemies: Britain and the GDR, 1949–1990* (with Norman LaPorte, 2010), *Nationalizing the Past: Historians as Nation Builders in Modern Europe* (ed. with Chris Lorenz, 2010), and *Kaliningrad in Europa: Nachbarschaftliche Perspektiven nach dem Ende des Kalten Krieges* (2010).

LAURA BRADLEY is senior lecturer in German at the University of Edinburgh. She is the author of *Cooperation and Conflict: GDR Theatre*

Censorship, 1961–1989 (2010) and *Brecht and Political Theatre: "The Mother" on Stage* (2006), and she is currently coediting a collection of essays called *Brecht and the GDR: Politics, Culture, Posterity* with Karen Leeder.

MARY FULBROOK, FBA, is professor of German history at University College London. Her most recent work is *Dissonant Lives: Generations and Violence through the German Dictatorships* (2011) and *Ordinary Nazis: Reflections on Memory, Terror and a Small Town in Poland* (2012), and she is currently directing the AHRC-funded project "Reverberations of War in Germany and Europe." She has written widely on the GDR, including *Anatomy of a Dictatorship: Inside the GDR* (1995) and *The People's State: East German Society from Hitler to Honecker* (2005). Her other books include *A Concise History of Germany* (2004); *A History of Germany, 1918–2008: The Divided Nation* (2008); *German National Identity after the Holocaust* (1999); *Historical Theory* (2002), and a number of other works on German and European history. She has also made a documentary film on the GDR.

NICK HODGIN is lecturer in German and Film Studies at the University of Lancaster. He has published widely on German film and is the author of *Screening the East: Heimat, Memory and Nostalgia in German Film since 1989* (Berghahn, 2011). His current research projects include an edited volume on subversion in the GDR, East German cinema (DEFA) and visual culture, and international film.

ANNA O'DRISCOLL studied and worked at universities in Maynooth, Tübingen, and Vienna. She received her PhD in 2010 from University College Dublin, facilitated by a Humanities Institute of Ireland scholarship and an IRCHSS scholarship. She has since contributed an article on Angela Krauß to *Transitions: Emerging Women Writers in German Language Literature* (ed. Valerie Heffernan and Gillian Pye, forthcoming), as well as an article on Dagmar Leupold's *Nach den Kriegen* to *German Life and Letters*. She is currently working as a freelance translator.

STUART PARKES is emeritus professor from the University of Sunderland (UK). His publications include *Writers and Politics in West Germany* (1986), *Understanding Contemporary Germany* (1997), and *Writers and Politics in Germany 1945–2008* (2009). He is also the coeditor of several volumes on contemporary German literature, including *Seelenarbeit an Deutschland: Martin Walser in Perspektive* (ed. with Fritz Wefelmeyer, 2004) and *German-Language Literature Today: International and Popular?* (ed. with Arthur Williams, 2000).

CAROLINE PEARCE is lecturer in German at the University of Sheffield. Her research interests are in the history and culture of post-1945

Germany, with a particular focus on the process of remembering and confronting the National Socialist past. Her current research examines the role and development of monuments and memorial sites in the former East and West Germany. She is the author of *Contemporary Germany and the Nazi Legacy: Remembrance, Politics and the Dialectic of Normality* (2007).

GÜNTER SCHLUSCHE studied architecture in Berlin and completed a master's degree in Urban Planning at the London School of Economics and a PhD in Urban Development at the Technical University Berlin. He has worked in urban planning, architecture, and environmental projects for more than thirty-five years. From 1981 to 1987 he was project manager for the International Building Exhibition (IBA 1987) in West Berlin. After managing the unique urban restructuring process of Berlin for the Stadtforum Berlin after the fall of the Wall, he was chief planner on the project to construct the Memorial to the Murdered Jews of Europe, designed by Peter Eisenman, in central Berlin from 1996 until 2005. He is now responsible for the Berlin Wall Memorial.

PETER THOMPSON is senior lecturer in German as well as the director of the Centre for Ernst Bloch Studies at the University of Sheffield. He has published widely on German politics, history, literature, and philosophy and is at present engaged on a three-year British Academy-funded project on "Ernst Bloch and the Return of Religion." He is coeditor with Slavoj Žižek of a forthcoming edition of essays, *Ernst Bloch and the Privatisation of Hope*. In addition to his academic work, he is a regular contributor to *The Guardian* on religion and secularism, and is a program maker for BBC Radio.

ANDREAS WAGNER studied history and Marxism-Leninism in the GDR. His doctoral thesis (published in 1997) analyzed changes in working life at the Rostock brewery from 1878 to 1955. He is a member of Politische Memoriale e. V., an association that coordinates and supports the work of memorials in the German federal state of Mecklenburg-Vorpommern. He also sits on the editorial board of the journal *Zeitgeschichte regional. Mitteilungen aus Mecklenburg-Vorpommern* and has written numerous articles on historical sites in Mecklenburg-Vorpommern and their pedagogical role.

Index